T0298704

# Law in the Pursuit of Development

*Law in the Pursuit of Development* critically explores the relationships between contemporary principles and practice in law and development. Including papers by internationally renowned, as well as emerging, scholars and practitioners, the book is organised around the three liberal principles which underlie current efforts to direct law towards the pursuit of development. First, that the private sector has an important role to play in promoting the public interest; second, that widespread participation and accountability are essential to any large-scale enterprise; and third, that the rule of law is a fundamental building block of development.

This insightful and provocative collection, in which contributors critique both the principles and efforts to implement them in practice, will be of considerable interest to students, academics and practitioners with an interest in the fields of law and development, international economic law, and law and globalisation.

**Amanda Perry-Kessaris** is Reader in Law and Director of the International Economic Law Justice and Development Programme at Birkbeck College.

# Law, development and globalization
Series Editor: Julio Faundez
*University of Warwick*

During the past decades, a substantial transformation of law and legal institutions in developing countries has taken place. Whether prompted by market-based policies or the international human rights movement, by the relentless advance of the process of globalization or the successive waves of democratization, no area of law has been left untouched. The aim of this series is to promote cross-disciplinary dialogue and cooperation among scholars and development practitioners interested in understanding the theoretical and practical implications of the momentous legal changes taking place in developing countries.

Other titles in the series:

**State Violence and Human Rights: State Officials in the South**
*Andrew M. Jefferson and Steffen Jensen (eds)*

**The Political Economy of Government Auditing: Financial Governance and the Rule of Law in Latin America and Beyond**
*Carlos Santiso*

**Global Perspectives on the Rule of Law**
*James J. Heckman, Robert L. Nelson and Lee Cabatingan (eds)*

Forthcoming titles in the series:

**Marginalized Communities and Access to Justice**
*Yash Ghai and Jill Cottrell (2009)*

**Social Movements, Law and the Politics of Land Reform**
*George Meszaros (2010)*

**Governance Through Development: Poverty Reduction Strategies and the Disciplining of Third World States**
*Celine Tan (2010)*

# Law in the Pursuit of Development

## Principles into Practice?

Edited by
Amanda Perry-Kessaris

 Routledge
Taylor & Francis Group

LONDON AND NEW YORK

First published 2010 by Routledge
2 Park Square, Milton Park, Abingdon, Oxon, OX14 4RN

Simultaneously published in the USA and Canada
by Routledge
711 Third Avenue, New York, NY 10017, USA

A GlassHouse book

*Routledge is an imprint of the Taylor & Francis Group, an informa business*

© 2010 editorial matter and selection Edited by Amanda Perry-Kessaris,
individual chapters the contributors

Typeset in Baskerville by Taylor & Francis Books

*British Library Cataloguing in Publication Data*
A catalogue record for this book is available from the British Library

*Library of Congress Cataloguing in Publication Data*
Law in the pursuit of development : principles into practice? / edited by
Amanda Perry Kessaris.
p. cm.
Includes bibliographical references and index.
1. Law and economic development. I. Perry-Kessaris, Amanda.
K3820.L445 2009
343'.074–dc22
2009023875

ISBN10: 0-415-48589-4 (hbk)
ISBN13: 978-0-415-48589–0 (hbk)

ISBN10: 0-203-86352-6 (ebk)
ISBN13: 978-0-203-86352-7 (ebk)

For Belinda and Chris Perry, my editors for life.

# Contents

# List of tables and figures

# List of abbreviations

| | |
|---|---|
| ABS | Access and Benefit Sharing |
| ADB | Asian Development Bank |
| ADR | Alternative Dispute Resolution |
| AFA | Arbitration Fairness Act |
| AfDB | African Development Bank |
| AIDS | Acquired Immune Deficiency Syndrome |
| AOA | Agreement on Agriculture |
| ARTF | Afghanistan Reconstruction Trust Fund |
| Berne Convention | Berne Convention for the Protection of Literary and Artistic Works (1869) |
| BMC | Biodiversity Management Committees |
| BTC | Baku-Tbilisi-Ceyhan |
| BVRM | The Bourse Régionale des Valeurs Mobilières |
| CAFTA-DR | Central America-Dominican Republic United States Free Trade Agreement |
| CALE | Center for Asian Legal Exchange (Japan) |
| CAO | Compliance Advisor/Ombudsman Office |
| CAS | Country Assistance Strategy |
| CBD | Convention on Biodiversity |
| CDF | Comprehensive Development Framework |
| CEDAW | Convention on the Elimination of All Forms of Discrimination Against Women |
| CEPEJ | European Commission for the Efficiency of Justice |
| CERDP | Community Empowerment for Rural Development Project |
| CLEP | UN Commission on Legal Empowerment of the Poor |
| CMAC | Capital Market Advisory Council (Rwanda) |
| CMAU | Capital Markets Authority of Uganda |
| CPIA | Country Policy and Institutional Assessment |
| CRP | Compliance Review Panel |
| CRZ | Coastal Regulation Zone |
| DFID | Department for International Development |
| DLP | Draft Land Policy |

| DSE | Dar es Salaam Stock Exchange |
|---|---|
| EAC | East African Community |
| EASEA | East African Securities Exchange Association |
| EBRD | European Bank for Reconstruction and Development |
| EIA | Environmental Impact Assessment |
| EMG | Emerging Markets Group |
| EPA | Economic Partnership Agreements |
| EPA | Environmental Protection Agency |
| ESRC | Economic and Science Research Council |
| ETI | Ethical Trading Initiative |
| EU | European Union |
| FFV | Flowers and fresh fruit and vegetables |
| FOS | Financial Ombudsman Service (UK) |
| G8 | Group of Eight (Canada, France, Germany, Italy, Japan, Russia, UK, USA) |
| GAC | Governance and Anti-Corruption |
| GATT | General Agreement on Tariffs and Trade |
| GATS | General Agreement on Trade in Services |
| GDP | Gross Domestic Product |
| GNI | Gross National Income |
| GSP | Generalized System of Preferences |
| HABITAT | United Nations Human Settlement Programme |
| IBRD | International Bank for Reconstruction and Development |
| ICA | International Court of Arbitration |
| ICC | International Chamber of Commerce |
| ICCLC | International Civil and Commercial Law Centre (Japan) |
| ICCPR | International Covenant on Civil and Political Rights |
| ICESCR | International Covenant on Economic Social and Cultural Rights |
| ICRs | Implementation Completion Reports |
| ICRG | International Country Risk Guide |
| ICT | Information and Communication Technologies |
| ICZMP | Integrated Coastal Zone Management Plan |
| IDA | International Development Association |
| IDB | Inter-American Development Bank |
| IDF | Institutional Development Fund |
| IDLO | International Development Law Organization |
| IFC | International Finance Corporation |
| IFI | International Financial Institutions |
| ILO | International Labour Organization |
| IMF | International Monetary Fund |
| IP | Intellectual Property |
| IPRs | Intellectual Property Rights |
| J4P | Justice for the Poor programme |
| JBIC | Japan Bank for International Cooperation |

| | |
|---|---|
| JETRO | Japan External Trade Organization |
| JICA | Japan International Cooperation Agency |
| JSDF | Japanese Social Development Fund |
| LICUS | Low-income countries under stress |
| LMI | Legal Modernization Initiative |
| LSE | London Stock Exchange |
| MCC | Millennium Challenge Corporation |
| MDB | Multilateral Development Banks |
| MDTFs | Multi-Donor Trust Funds |
| METI | Ministry of Economy, Technology and Industry (Japan) |
| MFN | Most Favoured Nation |
| MIGA | Multilateral Investment Guarantee Agency |
| MoEF | Ministry of Environment and Forests (India) |
| MOFA | Ministry of Foreign Affairs |
| MSRDC | Maharashtra State Road Development Corporation |
| NAFTA | North American Free Trade Agreement |
| NBA | National Biodiversity Authority |
| NGO | Non-Governmental Organization |
| NHPC | National Hydro Power Corporation |
| NIE | New Institutional Economics |
| NSE | Nairobi Stock Exchange |
| NYSE | New York Stock Exchange |
| ODA | Official Development Assistance (Japan) |
| OECD | Organisation for Economic Cooperation and Development |
| OPIC | Overseas Private Investment Corporation (USA) |
| PBA | Performance-Based Allocation |
| PCF | Post-Conflict Fund |
| PDR | People's Democratic Republic |
| ROL | Rule of law |
| ROTCM | Rwanda Over-The-Counter Market |
| SEC | Securities and Exchange Commission (USA) |
| SEZs | Special Economic Zones |
| SIFMA | Securities Industry and Financial Markets Association |
| SPF | State and Peace-Building Fund |
| SPF | Special Project Facilitator (Asian Development Bank) |
| SPLM | Sudan Peoples' Liberation Movement |
| SSCP | Sethusamudram Ship Channel Project |
| StAR | Stolen Asset Recovery |
| STDP | Southern Transport Development Project (Sri Lanka) |
| TRIPs | Agreement on Trade-Related Intellectual Property Rights |
| UDHR | Universal Declaration of Human Rights |
| UN | United Nations |
| UNAMA | United Nations Assistance Mission to Afghanistan |

| | |
|---|---|
| UNCESCR | United Nations Committee on Economic Social and Cultural Rights |
| UNDP | United Nations Development Programme |
| UNDPKO | United Nations Department for Peacekeeping Operations |
| UNESCO | United Nations Educational, Scientific and Cultural Organization |
| UNESCO Convention | Convention on the Protection and Promotion of the Diversity of Cultural Expressions (2005) |
| UNEP | United Nations Environment Programme |
| UNESCO Declaration | Universal Declaration on Cultural Diversity (2001) |
| UNODC | United Nations Office on Drugs and Crime |
| USAID | United States Agency for International Development |
| USE | Uganda Securities Exchange |
| WAEMU | West African Economic and Monetary Union |
| WCD | World Commission on Dams |
| WFE | World Federation of Stock Exchanges |
| WTO | World Trade Organization |

# Notes on contributors

**Klaus Decker** is a French- and German-trained lawyer working at the World Bank on justice reform in Africa, Asia, Europe and Latin America since 2002. His portfolio includes project work, knowledge management and partnership with international justice expert bodies.

**Julio Faundez** is Professor of Law and currently the Head of Warwick Law School. He holds degrees from Universidad Católica de Chile and Harvard University and has written extensively on law and democratization in Latin America (*Marxism and Democracy in Chile* (1989) and *Democratization, Development and Legality: Chile 1831–1973* (2007)); and on legal reform and governance (*Good Government and Law* (1997) and *On the State of Democracy* (2007)). He is co-editor in chief of the *Hague Journal on the Rule of Law*.

**Linn Hammergren** is an independent consultant specializing in judicial reform, anti-corruption and governance issues. She has a PhD in Political Science and between 1986 and 1998 managed judicial reform projects and did related research for the World Bank and USAID.

**Kanchi Kohli** is a researcher and activist with Kalpavriksh Environmental Action Group, based in Delhi. Over the last eleven years, her work there has related to action research, campaigns and advocacy on various environment and biodiversity issues, which has included support to grass-roots groups and networks. She has put together joint publications related to key environment-related regulations and their impacts. Kanchi also writes widely for the print and web based media. Outside of Kalpavriksh she co-coordinates an Information Dissemination Service for Forest and Wildlife Cases in the Supreme Court of India.

**Andreas Kotsakis** is undertaking research on critical environmental law at the Law Department, London School of Economics. He has taught environmental law at the University of Westminster and legal method at SOAS. His research interests lie in the areas of law and geography, critical legal theory and law and ethics.

**Fiona Macmillan** is Corporation of London Professor of Law at Birkbeck College, University of London. Her published research has focused on the areas of corporate regulation and intellectual property law. She has a particular interest in the ways in which business enterprises use intellectual property rights as a basis for entrenching power. Recently, her work has addressed the legitimacy and use of corporate power internationally through a consideration of the role and functions of the World Trade Organization.

**Patrick McAuslan** is Professor of Law in the School of Law at Birkbeck College, University of London. He has been active in the areas of land, law and development as a teacher, author and consultant since he was a founder member of the Faculty of Law at the University of Dar es Salaam in Tanzania in 1961. He has worked for UN and donor agencies as a consultant on land policy, land management and natural resource management in Africa, Asia, the Caribbean and Europe; for the UN (HABITAT) in Nairobi as Land Management Adviser (1990–93) and co-ordinator (1992–93) of the Urban Management Programme; and as Senior Technical Adviser (1999–2000) to a DFID project in Uganda to assist the Government of Uganda to implement the innovative Land Act, 1998 which he helped draft.

**June McLaughlin** is a doctoral student at Queen Mary, University of London. She is an arbitrator for FINRA and an instructor and content expert for the University of California at Irvine Paralegal Extension Program. Previously, she worked on the floor of the NYSE.

**Manju Menon** is a member of Kalpavriksh Environmental Action Group. She has been involved in several environmental research projects and in advocacy. She is currently pursuing a PhD at the Centre for Studies in Science Policy, Jawaharlal Nehru University, New Delhi.

**Bronwen Morgan** is Professor of Socio-Legal Studies at the University of Bristol and an Associate Fellow of the Centre for Socio-Legal Studies, University of Oxford. She has a PhD in Jurisprudence and Social Policy from the University of California at Berkeley and her research focuses on the political economy of regulatory reform and global governance.

**Suresh Nanwani** is a lawyer working in the Asian Development Bank (ADB) and a visiting lecturer in the School of Law, Birkbeck College, University of London. He was formerly associate secretary of the ADB Compliance Review Panel and co-authored the ADB Accountability Mechanism policy paper. He has lectured and published extensively on international financial institutions, law and policy reform, accountability mechanisms and institutional governance and responsibility.

**Amanda Perry-Kessaris** is Reader in Law and Director of the International Economic Law Justice and Development Programme at Birkbeck College, and author of *The Legal System as a Determinant of FDI* (2001), *Law and Development in the 21st Century* (with John Hatchard, 2003) and *Global Business, Local*

*Law* (2008). She is currently working on the principles, effects and defects of the economic approach to law and development.

**Dzenan Sahovic**, PhD, is a political scientist and a guest lecturer in Peace and Conflict Studies at Umea University, Sweden. His main research interest is the role of culture in peace-building processes and he is currently conducting research on reconstruction of material culture in post-war Bosnia Herzegovina. This research is a part of the Cambridge University-led European CRIC project: <http://www.cric.arch.cam.ac.uk>.

**Ann Stewart** is Reader and Associate Professor at the School of Law, University of Warwick. She teaches and researches in the field of gender and the law with a focus on international development, particularly issues relating to South Asia and Africa.

**Veronica L. Taylor** is the Dan Fenno Henderson Professor of Asian Law and Director of the Asian Law Center at the University of Washington. Her work focuses on law and society in Asia, Japanese commercial law, applied regulatory theory, and rule of law and development.

**Valentina S. Vadi** is a PhD candidate at the European University Institute, Florence and is a member of the Board of Editors of the European Journal of Legal Studies. She holds degrees in international law and political science from the University of Siena, both *summa cum laude*, and a Magister Juris (LLM) from the University of Oxford in European and Comparative Law. She has published several articles concerning investment law, cultural heritage and intellectual property. She has worked as a research assistant at the Academy of European Law, the European University Institute and the University of Oxford.

**Sally Wheeler** is Professor of Law, Business and Society at Queen's University Belfast. She is interested in political consumerism, business ethics, corporate governance, corporate social responsibility and the gaps in between them.

# Acknowledgements

In addition to producing excellent work, the contributors to this volume have been upbeat and timely, making this project infinitely more enjoyable than it might otherwise have been. Bronwen Morgan has been an enthusiastic force behind this volume, beginning with her role as co-organiser of the conference that lies at its heart. I am grateful to Sally Wheeler and the Socio-Legal Studies Association Executive Committee for wholeheartedly supporting that conference. Thanks to Valerie Kelly at Birkbeck for once again leaping to my aid.

I cannot thank Maria Pope enough for the talent and warm spirit that she brings to her work. Like all self-respecting children, mine help and hinder my professional progress in equal measure. Long may they continue on their merry and enchanting way. To Nicos, an exceptionally generous team-mate, I will forever be trying to return your favours.

A. P. K.
London, June 2009.

# Foreword

*Bronwen Morgan*

The relationship between law and development, in the context of an integrated global economy, has moved from a niche area of study to an increasingly central location in scholarly enquiry over the past several decades. This shift is simultaneously reconstructing the core questions and approaches in what might once have been called 'law and development' but is increasingly seen as part of global governance or the transnationalisation of legal orders. Professional socio-legal studies meetings illuminate this. In July 2007, over 2,000 scholars from 72 countries gathered in Berlin for an international meeting of socio-legal scholars. Seventy out of the roughly 600 papers presented were devoted to transnational issues: almost a sixth of the conference proceedings.

Many of these papers appeared in one of two 'collaborative research networks' that organized a series of linked papers and attracted large audiences. One network focused on 'transnational legal orders'; the other titled itself 'rule of law, state-building and transition', explicitly citing the changed nature of the political economy of global law and development as a reason for rejecting the label of 'law and development'. These two research networks often provided complementary perspectives on similar issues of legal change linked to economic and social development. What seemed to be emerging was an increasing interest in cross-border legal norm-creation and implementation from the perspective of the 'developed' world, coinciding with an enduring interest from the perspective of 'developing' countries in the ways in which their domestic trajectories are shaped by such processes. At the same time, the coherence of a distinction between 'developed' and 'developing' countries was increasingly muddied.

The intensified overlap between the concerns of these two strands could be seen as a natural outgrowth of the increasingly juridified nature of inter-dependence between the 'developed' and 'developing' worlds, coupled with the absence of any structural alternative to the capitalist model for economic development. Whereas prior to the post-colonial era, the legal dimensions of cross-border interdependence were embedded within intra-imperial political relations, since the acquisition of national sovereignty for ex-colonies, such inter-dependence (or dependency, depending on one's political assessment) has become much more explicitly premised on legal regimes. Thus the early attention of studies on transnational legal orders was focused on transatlantic economic competition and cooperation, particularly the World Trade Organization and the GATT legal regime. By contrast, 'law and development' scholars focused more on international financial institutions and the effect of conditionally-structured aid on domestic policy trajectories.

As the scope of transnational legal regimes widens well beyond trade, competition and intellectual property, issues such as public health and cultural heritage have become increasingly juridified, and both financial conditionality and legality increasingly encompass these kinds of non-market issues. Just as the original vision of the European Union as a trading compact has expanded well beyond market integration, so too, albeit in uneven and patchy ways, have cross-border relations in other regions and globally. And as legal regimes aimed at establishing market access and integration extend their reach, state-building efforts and transitions from colonialism or communism are drawn inexorably into the same transnational juridified space that first attracted the attention of 'transnational legal orders'. Thus the two strands of scholarship increasingly overlap, and can benefit from mutual dialogue.

With these developments comes a fertile opportunity for a newly configured field that entices both more traditional international lawyers, and those who carry out empirical work, to contribute their perspectives to the relationship between law reform and economic and social development in a globalizing world. Just such an opportunity was the hope of the conference from which many of the chapters in this volume originate, which was held in London in December 2007, sponsored by the Socio-Legal Studies Association (UK).[1] Additional perspectives from people working more directly in the field have expanded the collection of perspectives offered in these pages. We hope that the combination will go some way towards supporting a network of scholars whose efforts can help to craft new solutions linking principles and practice in ways that facilitate law's ongoing pursuit of development.

## Note

1 The aims of the Socio-Legal Studies Association are to 'advance education and learning and in particular to advance research, teaching and the dissemination of knowledge in the field of socio-legal studies.' For audio recordings and presentations of proceedings of the conference Justice, Power and Law: In pursuit of development, organised at Birkbeck College, London by Bronwen Morgan and Amanda Perry-Kessaris on December 10, 2007, see <http://www.kent.ac.uk/nslsa/content/view/166/139/#justice>.

# Chapter 1

# Introduction

## Amanda Perry-Kessaris[*]

In the fifties, sixties and seventies it was called the Law and Development Movement; in the eighties it continued without a name; in the nineties and through the turn of the century it morphed from 'good governance programs' to 'the rule of law and development.'

(Tamanaha 2009:1)

## The present volume

This volume explores relationships between contemporary principles and practice in law and development. It is organised around three liberal principles which underlie many current efforts to direct law towards the pursuit of development: first, that the private sector has an important role to play in promoting the public interest; second, that widespread participation and accountability are essential to any large-scale enterprise; and third, that the rule of law is a fundamental building block of development. Contributors were selected not only because of their ability to address the key themes at the centre of the volume, but also with a view to creating a lively and balanced mix of practitioners, early-career and established academics, and geographical specialisations.[1] They critique both the principles underpinning contemporary law and development programming and efforts to implement them in practice.

In editing this collection I have sought to ensure that specialist subjects are accessible to law and development generalists. I have also tried to include as many online resources as possible, in order to open up the field to those who may not have easy access to materials. Unless otherwise stated, all weblinks have been checked in June 2009.

### Private sector, public interest

The first part of the volume presents a series of pieces that consider the increasingly muddy, sometimes artificial, yet eternally significant, interactions between 'public' and 'private' interests. We begin with the idea that economic liberalisation has in many ways decentralised decisions as to where the proper balance between public and private interests lies. Sally Wheeler (Chapter 2) asks under what circumstances the private decisions of individual consumers can be regarded as 'political consumption', capable of contributing to the public objective of achieving social justice. Ann Stewart (Chapter 3) continues the theme using, among other tools, global value chain analysis to explore one sphere in which consumer decisions may impact on social justice: agribusiness in Kenya. Valentina Vadi (Chapter 4) then shifts our attention to how public international law relating to investment and intellectual property rights leaves regulatory gaps through which the private interests of pharmaceutical companies are able to control public access to medicines. Fiona Macmillan (Chapter 5) continues the interrogation of privately held intellectual property rights, asking if they act as further barriers to public well-being that may threaten nascent rights to cultural self-determination. Finally, Kanchi Kohli and Manju Menon (Chapter 6) use the example of environmental legislation in India to demonstrate how liberalisation programmes may cause public interests to become subservient to private interests.

### Participation and accountability

In the second part of the volume, contributors consider the principles of participation and accountability, and their implementation in practice. Suresh Nanwani (Chapter 7) initiates the debate by critically assessing the internal accountability mechanisms of multilateral development banks which, in an effort to improve participation, are open to project-affected persons. Remaining at the international level, Andreas Kotsakis (Chapter 8) traces the aggrandisement of local participation in a more specific field: the protection of biodiversity under international conventions. He asks how, in practice, can local communities participate in a system of such top-down origins and orientation? Finally, June McLaughlin (Chapter 9) reminds us that participation is important to private as well as public enterprises. She explains that the systems of dispute resolution currently developing in many African stock exchanges are in danger of becoming just as exclusive, and potentially partial to certain users, as the Western systems upon which they are based.

### Instituting the rule of law

In this final part, contributions focus on efforts to institute the rule of law as both a means to, and an objective of, development. Veronica Taylor (Chapter 10) opens the debate with a reminder and several questions. Asian nations, in particular Japan, are increasingly active practitioners of law and development. To what extent are their approaches distinctive? Is there such a thing as *the* rule of law? Next Julio Faundez (Chapter 11) relates how those involved in legal and judicial reform at the World Bank first warmly greeted, and then quietly dropped, the broader vision of development espoused in the Comprehensive Development Framework and its soul mate, Nobel laureate Amartya Sen. Linn

Hammergren (Chapter 12) follows, casting a critical eye over the efforts of the World Bank to promote the rule of law in Latin America, concluding that they have not infrequently been ineffective and unpopular. Nor does she expect this tendency to change. However, she also cautions us to stop erroneously crediting – or saddling – the World Bank with the tag of market leader in the law and development sphere. Klaus Decker (Chapter 13) pursues the topic of World Bank efforts on the rule of law, specifically its successes and failures in post-conflict situations. The arena of post-conflict situations is further illuminated by Dzenan Sahovic (Chapter 14). Echoing the cultural keys played by Taylor and MacMillan, he uses Grid-Group Cultural Theory to demonstrate how rule-of-law programmes differ and why they may fail. Finally, Patrick McAuslan (Chapter 15) draws our attention to what he regards as one of the most important front lines in all conflicts: access to land. Using the example of Afghanistan, he shows how struggles for land arise before, during and after the headline hostilities are completed; and suggests that official responses are sometimes too divorced from reality to offer practical solutions.

## Mapping law and development

This is the second time in recent years that I have found myself introducing a collection of pieces that address the intersections between law and development.[2] Once again, I have enjoyed the rich variety of topics, locations and perspectives. But once again I have been struck by the absence of a shared analytical framework, a set of reference points, for this field of ours. As Brian Tamanaha recently put it, ours:

> ... is a poorly constructed category that lacks internal coherence. Every legal system ... undergoes development (or regression) so there is nothing special about this; meanwhile, the multitude of countries that have been targeted for law and development projects differ radically from one another. Hence there is no uniquely unifying basis upon which to construct a 'field.' Law and development work is better seen, instead, as an agglomeration of projects perpetuated by motivated actors supported by funding. This is not meant as a cynical characterization but an accurate description that puts law and development activities in a more adequate frame.
>
> (Tamanaha 2009: 6)

This is all true. But what to do? One possible way forward may lie in a story I heard recently. An economist was chatting with a surgeon. 'In an emergency, how do you know where to begin?' asked the economist. 'We always have our checklist: Airways, Breathing, Circulation, Disability, Exposure and environment' replied the surgeon. The economist pondered his more than three decades in water resources management in developing countries, and wondered 'What is my ABC?' Soon he had set out a framework encapsulating all the elements of water management systems: Assessment, Bargaining, Codification, Delegation, Engineering and Feedback (Perry 2008, Perry forthcoming).[3] The framework was adopted by the Middle East and North Africa Region of the World Bank as a basis for categorising, and thereby better understanding, its activities in the field of water management (Jagannathan et al. 2009).

Members of the world's second oldest profession we may be, but do we – practitioners and academics at the intersection of law and development – have an ABC, an index or a map for our field? If we do, it has not yet, to my knowledge, been articulated.

We address the same well-trodden paths, circling around issues such as the rule of law, poverty, inequality, conflict, sustainable development, intellectual property rights, access to justice; and actors such as multinational enterprises, children, multilateral development banks, judges, civil society, women, bureaucrats and indigenous peoples. But we do not have a systematic way of classifying our discussions.[4] As a result, we do not always notice how our work fits together; we do not allow ourselves to build upon each others' work as effectively as we might; we unconsciously block those who concentrate their efforts in other fields from drawing on and contributing to our work, and we spend not insignificant amounts of time reinventing various wheels.[5] The nature of the concerns at the heart of our field – poverty, drought, humiliation, desolation, violence, injustice, death – demand that we do the best we can. Might we not be more effective if we were better organised?

Before I go on to outline my proposed map, a note of caution. I have been inspired by the ABCs of medicine and water management but these are not functionally equivalent to my proposed map for law and development. The medical ABC arose from, and is intended to be of use in, situations of acute emergency.[6] It identifies a strict hierarchy of priorities to be followed in order to diagnose and treat any patient in crisis anywhere. Cover the ABCs and you will not miss anything. If conditions change, you start the ABC again. By contrast, the water ABC is intended to categorise past, present and future responses to chronic water crisis. It is essentially positive, not normative. It does not offer a strict hierarchy of action: although engineering should definitely wait for assessment, it is not essential that engineering wait for codification. Similarly, my proposed law and development map is intended for circumstances generally less dramatic than the medical:[7] to ensure that when theorists and practitioners act – in speech, writing or otherwise – at the intersections between law and development, they know, and can explain, where those acts fit into the bigger picture.

In the remainder of this section I will map five aspects or categories of law and development work that may be handily, or reductively, summarised as ABCDE. It is important to note that a given act of law and development might fall into a number of categories. Also, let me emphasise that this is no recipe for law and development, no hierarchical, chronological or otherwise normative template. It is simply a map.

## Assessment

The first aspect or category of law and development to be mapped is the assessment of existing rights and duties (substantive and procedural) both in principle ('on the books') and in practice ('in action'). For example, in this volume Ann Stewart outlines the complex political, economic and legal context in which Kenyan women engage in the agribusiness activities; and Linn Hammergren assesses the World Bank's influence on the donor community and concludes that it has been overstated. Some forms of assessment, such as the increasing use by multilateral and national actors of legal 'indicators' to assess legal systems, may be more contentious than others.[8] But law and development acts, whether theoretical or practical, usually begin with some form of assessment. Separately, and on a normative note, they surely ought to.

## Building

Second, the work of law and development involves building capacity in the forms of new infrastructure, rules and personnel – for example, creating secure courts; computer systems; well-qualified lawyers, bureaucrats and judges; judicial benchbooks; well-drafted laws; well-maintained law reports and so on. Such components are a common feature of law and development activity in many multilateral development banks and aid agencies. For example, a key task of a World Bank Legal and Judicial Reform project in Sri Lanka, mentioned by Klaus Decker in this volume, was to improve insecure, hot, decaying courthouses (see Perry 2001).[9] Also in this volume, June McLaughlin highlights the importance of physical and information technology infrastructure in the operation of stock exchanges in East Africa. Other would include legislative drafting, legal transplants, and judicial acts, such as the introduction by an activist judiciary of public interest litigation to India (see, for example, Perry-Kessaris 2008: 110–12 and 133–38).

## Contestation

The third, most complex, overtly and covertly controversial, law and development act is the contestation of existing and future rights and duties (substantive and procedural). Here actors are making a normative bid, explicit or implicit, to privilege or to render subservient certain values or interests. Law and development acts tend to revolve around the need for change, from which new winners and losers are likely to result, so acts of contestation are prevalent in law and development work. For example, in this volume the terms of consumer trade (Wheeler; Stewart), culture (Macmillan; Sahovic; Taylor), property (Vadi; McAuslan) and environment (Kotsakis; Kohli and Menon) are each contested. Contestation may occur both within an individual law and development act, such as a chapter in this book, and between multiple law and development acts.

For example, Fiona Macmillan's contribution to this volume can be read as documenting the actual and potential international contests between, on the one hand, international intellectual property rights, and on the other hand, cultural rights; and as concluding that intellectual property rights have retained the upper hand. In addition, her contribution can be read as itself engaging in a second level of contestation between multiple concepts of 'development'.

## Delegation

The fourth category of law and development acts is the delegation to individuals and institutions of responsibilities and arrangements for implementation. Some examples of this category are the posting by donors of practitioners to client states to offer technical legal assistance; and the establishment by a state of an anti-corruption task force. Also included in this category would be creation and implementation of the rules of operation under which the delegated activities took place such as, for example, the guidance developed by the United Nations in relation to its 'rule of law' activities (McInerney 2009), or the operating procedures of the Asian Development Bank Accountability Mechanism (Nanwani, in this volume). Major questions surrounding such acts include the suitability of those personnel and rules. For example, preliminary findings from a survey by Cynthia Alkon (2009) of technical legal assistance providers working in Afghanistan suggest that many respondents were entirely unprepared for, and unenthusiastic about the impact of, their activities; while in this volume Dzenan Sahovic warns of the likely existence, and consequences, of cultural mismatch between peacekeepers and their host states. Also in this volume, Veronica Taylor identifies the limited supply of eligible Japanese lawyers as a determinant of the nature of future Japanese engagement in technical legal assistance.

## Evaluation

Finally, there is the evaluation of activities that fall into each category of the framework and the feeding back of lessons learned. For example, in this volume Julio Faundez feeds back qualified applause to the World Bank for its decision, albeit temporary, to place Amartya Sen's work at the centre of its legal reform agenda. Elsewhere in this volume, Patrick McAuslan delivers a devastating evaluation of international technical assistance on land law and policy in Afghanistan. 'Evaluation' includes evaluation of evaluation – for example, efforts to improve the evaluation processes used by various actors. In this sense Nanwani's contribution to this volume can be read as an evaluation of key evaluative mechanisms of two multilateral development banks: the Asian Development Bank Accountability Mechanism and the World Bank Inspection Panel.

## Conclusion

An enormous amount of practice and scholarship resides at the intersections of law and development, and there is every reason to expect that body of work to grow. If the benefits of that work are to be maximised (and the detriments minimised), we need a map by which to navigate the field.

Doubtless some will be horrified by the very idea of attempting to pin down such a rich and diverse field; shy away from the simple terminology that I have chosen; hear normative undertones in what I am presenting as an essentially positive tool. Of course it is impossible ever to be entirely neutral. In drafting a map we necessarily have to summarise: focus on some things, ignore others, often not even knowing that we have done so until someone else points it out. I look forward to the discussion. In the meantime it is my great pleasure to introduce in more detail the law and development acts that form this volume which touch on each aspect of the ABCDE map.

This volume addresses the principles and practice of law and development. In the terms of the ABCDE map which I am proposing, contributors are engaging in acts of assessment, building, delegation and evaluation. Perhaps most importantly, they are contesting values and interests about which difficult, explicit choices must be made when law is directed towards the pursuit of development.

## Notes

\* Thanks to Cynthia Alkon, Elin Cohen, Kevin Davis, Julio Faundez, Linn Hammergren, Nicos Kessaris, Suresh Nanwani, Chris Perry, Veronica Taylor and Valentina Vadi for their very helpful comments.

1 Decker, Hammergren, Kohli, Menon and Nanwani are primarily practitioners, while Macmillan, McLaughlin, Kotsakis, Sahovic, Stewart, Vadi, Wheeler and I act predominantly in the realms of principle (although in so doing we may pay a good deal of attention to practice). Faundez, McAuslan and Taylor straddle the principle-practice divide.

2 See Hatchard and Perry-Kessaris (2003).

3 The basic ideas are set out in Perry (2003). The elements in detail are: assessment of water availability; bargaining over principles for water sharing; codification of rules governing the day-to-day distribution of water; delegation of responsibilities and arrangements for implementation; engineering of necessary infrastructure; feedback of lessons and best practice. 'Feedback' was added during discussions of the ABCDE framework at a meeting of the Arab Water Council in Abu Dhabi (March 2008).

4 For examples of the issues collected under the umbrella term 'law and development' see the websites listed at the end of this chapter.

5 Benjamin van Rooij provides a useful example of this last point in his critique of the recent popularity of 'bottom-up' legal development:

> The sudden popularity of these new approaches shows how much legal development cooperation is a field of trends, where doubts about effectiveness force legal reformers to regularly shift from one paradigm to the next, enthusiastically applauding the seemingly new, while sacrificing the caricaturized old.
>
> (van Rooij 2009: 1)

6 The framework was developed by Dr Jim Styner, who crashed his plane in rural Nebraska in 1976:

> [He] sustained serious injuries, three of his children sustained critical injuries, and one child sustained minor injuries. His wife was killed instantly. The care that he and his family received was less than adequate; it was evident that the small rural hospital and its staff had little or no preparation for a situation of this magnitude. There was an obvious lack of training for proper triage and injury treatment. The surgeon, recognizing how inadequate his treatment was stated, 'when I can provide better care in the field with limited resources that what my children and I received at the primary care facility, there is something wrong with the system and the system has to be changed' (ATLS website).

The framework has been formalised as the Advanced Trauma Life Support (ATLS) Program.
7 Although those acts may sometimes occur in the context of an emergency, such as war-torn Afghanistan.
8 See, for example, Davis and Kruse (2007); Perry-Kessaris (2003) and (2008); Rodri-quez-Garavito (2009).
9 See also Nanwani and Ayus (2007) for a recent example of a legal education and judicial training project in the Maldives.

# References

Alkon, C. (2009) 'Be careful who you fire: A survey of rule of law development assistance providers in Afghanistan'. Paper presented at the Law and Society Association Annual Meeting, Denver, 28 May 2009.

Davis, K. E. and Kruse, M. (2007) 'Taking the measure of law: the case of the Doing Business project', *Law and Social Inquiry* 32:1095.

Hatchard, J. and Perry-Kessaris, A. J. (eds) (2003) *Law and Development: facing complexity in the 21st century*, London: Cavendish.

Jagannathan, N. V., Mohammed, A. S. and Kremer, A. (eds) (2009) *Water in the Arab World: Management Perspectives and Innovations*, Washington D.C.: World Bank.

McInerney, T. (2009) 'An unnoticed upheaval: recent United Nations efforts to build an international normative framework for rule of law'. Paper presented at the Law and Society Association Annual Meeting, Denver, 28 May 2009.

Nanwani, S. and Ayus, M. A. (2007) 'Strengthening legal education and judicial training in the Maldives: a case study', *International Islamic University Malaysia Law Journal* 15 (2):171.

Perry, A. J. (2001) *Legal Systems as a Determinant of FDI: lessons from Sri Lanka*, London: Kluwer.

Perry, C. J. (2003) 'Non-state actors and water resources development: An economic perspective', *Non-State Actors and International Law* 3:103.

——(2008) 'The ABCDE of water management'. Draft guidance note contribution to the draft paper for the Arab Water Academy courses.

——(Forthcoming) 'River Basin Agreements as facilitators of development' in L. P. Onn (ed) *Water Issues in Southeast Asia: present trends and future directions*, Singapore: Institute of Southeast Asian Studies.

Perry-Kessaris, A. (2003) 'Finding and facing facts about legal systems and FDI in South Asia', *Legal Studies* 23(4):649.

——(2008) 'Recycle, reduce, and reflect: information overload and knowledge deficit in the field of foreign investment and the law', *Journal of Law and Society* 35(s1):67.

Tamanaha, B. Z. 'The Primacy of Society and the Failure of Law and Development' (May 19, 2009). St. John's Legal Studies Research Paper No. 09–0172. Online: <http://ssrn.com/abstract=1406999>

van Rooij, B. (2009) 'Bringing justice to the poor: bottom-up legal development cooperation', Working Paper. Online: <http://ssrn.com/abstract=1368185>

## Useful websites

(ATLS) Advanced Trauma Life Support
  <http://www.facs.org/trauma/atls/about.html>
Foundation for International Environmental Law and Development
  <http://www.field.org>
(IDLO) International Development Law Organization
  <http://www.idlo.org>
International Economic Law Justice and Development (Birkbeck)
  <http://www.bbk.ac.uk/law/prospective/taughtmastersdegrees/ieljd>
Law and Development (World Bank)
  <http://www.worldbank.org/legal>
Law and Development Blog
  <http://lawprofessors.typepad.com/lawdevelopment>
Rule of Law and Development (World Bank)
  <http://go.worldbank.org/9OTC3P5070>
The Law and Development Review (Berkeley Electronic Press)
  <http://www.bepress.com/ldr>
Democracy and Governance (USAID)
  <http://www.usaid.gov/our_work/democracy_and_governance/technical_areas/rule_of_law>

# Chapter 2

# Political consumption: possibilities and challenges

*Sally Wheeler*

Anne Stewart, in her contribution to this collection (Chapter 3), makes the point that actors involved in Southern agricultural production are linked to Northern consumers through value chains. The social labelling of products as ethical or fair-trade gives consumers an opportunity to think behind the product label *simplex*. The focus of my contribution is on the nature of doing just that – thinking and then acting on that additional information as an intentional political statement. The chapter examines what it might mean to be a political consumer and how acts of political consumption can be identified. The paper concludes by considering whether political consumerism has the potential to mount sustained pressure for redistribution or whether its fragmentary and informal nature makes it merely a distraction from more traditional modes of political engagement.

There is evidence that consumers are increasingly making product choices based on their assessment of the ethical footprint of products. I am using the label 'ethical' here in a very generic sense to include fair-trade, organic, energy-efficient, and employment-code-compliant products; unlike my use of 'political' in this paper, which I use to describe a very particular act in relation to consumption. The Ethical Consumerism Report (formerly the Ethical Purchasing Index) points to the growth of the ethical purchase market in the UK over successive years. It counts as ethical purchases the goods and services that I list above and it produces figures for each category. The Report for 2007 claims that the ethical purchase market is now worth £32.3 Billion out of a total consumer market of over £600 billion (The Cooperative Bank 2007). On one level this is unremarkable; it is a relatively small figure in the face of total consumer spend and we have no idea of the robustness of the ethical market in the face of the recession in the global North (Auger et al. 2003). However on another level the speed of growth of the ethical market figure is something to take note of – between 2006 and 2007 the market increased by nine per cent and one in four consumers involved in the ethical market asserted that they had 'campaigned' on an environmental or social justice issue in 2007. This presents a much more positive picture than that painted by Vogel (2005: 47–49), who relies on evidence from earlier in the decade to suggest that there is a large gap between the rhetoric of ethical purchase and the actuality of ethical purchase.

I am concerned with the nature of the act of political consumption – how can consumption or non-consumption for this reason be distinguished from choices based upon lifestyle issues or the desire to eat food perceived to be healthier or safer, for example (Sassatelli 2006)? Politically-based consumption allows individuals a direct connection with the strategies of multi-national corporations, the structure of agricultural practice in geographically faraway states and an opportunity for engagement with the globalized market. Both 'buycotts' and boycotts fall with the boundary of political consumption. It blurs the distinction between the usually private, inward-looking act of consumption and the self-interested persona of the consumer and the outward-looking and public nature of citizenship activity within a democratic polity (cf Hilton 2001, Cohen 2001). I consider whether the coming together of these previously separate identities and the opportunities for political activity that are created can be a sustainable force for change and democratic engagement.

## Traditional political participation and political consumerism

### Changing nature of political participation

Traditional methods of political engagement through electoral participation do not create these opportunities in the same immediate way. A dedicated political consumer may wish to alter their relationship with the democratic state in order to pursue these goals. The harnessing of consumption strategies in relation to food in particular has a long history (Trentmann 2007), by governments – the 'buy British' campaign of the 1970s; by NGOs – the Nestle Food Supplement Campaign of the 1980s; and by unions. What is new about political consumerism is that it is a movement begun and energized from below by individuals working alone. As Beck and Gernsheim (2001: 44) point out 'citizens [can] discover the act of shopping as one in which they can always cast their ballot – on a world scale ... '. It is not surprising that promoters of the importance of political consumerism view the steady decline in political participation through the medium of nationally based elections as being linked to the rise of activist politics on a collective or individual basis (Hertz 2001, Stolle et al. 2005). Ironically the empirical evidence for this is taken from a survey of which roughly a third of the respondents were Swedish, a state where, as I comment below, traditional political participation is not showing the same decline as elsewhere. Political consumers see the market and not states as responsible for inequalities in distribution, global justice and social development. Consequently they interact with the market and not with traditional political structures that they view as ineffective in reflecting or securing their choices (Stolle and Hooghe 2004: 273, Shaw et al. 2006). On one level the market is being used to achieve non-market goals that traditionally would be thought of as the province of the state or state-sponsored supra-national bodies. But on another level these developments emphasize the perceived dominance of transnational corporations in the global market and the move from a production society to a service-centred consumer society.

Voter participation in the UK in national elections has, with the occasional blip, been declining steadily since 1950. Participation in local elections has also dropped to a figure below 40 per cent of the electorate (Rallings and Thrasher 2003). In the same time frame membership of political parties has also declined. There is considerable, if not universal, agreement that the pattern evident in the UK is reflected across Western Europe, Japan and North America (Dalton 2004, Pharr and Putnam 2001) while in the rest of the world the decline is most marked in the 1990s. Theorists of voting patterns posit a connection between first-time eligibility to vote, participation and non-participation; a voter who votes on the first occasion that they are eligible to do so is likely to continue participating, conversely non-participation at this stage is likely to signal a life-time of disaffection with electoral politics. In the UK there appears to be significant non-participation among the cohort most recently eligible to vote (Franklin 2004). This would suggest that electoral participation is unlikely to rise in the near future (O'Toole at al. 2003). Pateman (1970: 43) opined that participation is key to the existence of a democratic polity. It is the touchstone of legitimacy for democratic governance and also an indicator of the degree of connection and responsibility individuals feel towards their political representation. While there are those who would assert that voting is not as important as we may think it is in terms of individuals expressing their preferences (Morison 1998, Morison and Newman 2001: 177), it is the case that a failure to take part in the most accessible form of participation available expresses disenchantment with all the choices available and a rejection of ownership of, and responsibility for, policies pursued. It is an expression of frustration with the notion of taking traditional collective action to determine the solution to collective problems.

### Explanations for change

According to Bennett (2003) the late modern period of the 1970s onwards has seen the onset of economic globalization and communication systems. This has introduced citizens to 'the identity project' and the rise of the individual self. Society is an advanced market society. Lifestyle diversity is publicly celebrated and there has been a decline in the acceptance of binding institutions. Bennett presents this as being illustrated by a menu of effects, all or some of which can be observed in most post-industrial democracies. These effects can be illustrated by looking at how they play through into the positions taken by a number of key explanations offered for social and political change. The first focuses on the decline of social capital. This is the 'bowling alone' thesis put forward by Putnam (1993, 2000). In simple terms Putnam sees a breakdown of traditional ideas of civic engagement. Social bonds have disintegrated and along with them any sense of community giving rise to essentially selfish citizens who fail to recognize the importance of collective action through political participation.

Citizens are in this position because they have chosen to move away from the collective pastimes and community values of their forbears. Solitary habits such as television-watching are considered preferable pursuits compared with the more companionable ten-pin bowling. Political consumerism can be seen as the act of an individual whose trust in political institutions is low and whose lifestyle is characterized by an atomized existence. Putnam's work has generated an intense debate around whether in fact there is a loosening of associational relationships in older democracies (Norris 1996, Hall 1999, Pattie et al. 2003) and at a more macro level whether his thesis is not creating a sense of loss for a community spirit that was only so warm, welcoming and supportive in remembrance (Delanty 1998, Sennett 1998: 143). Of more lasting interest to the argument that I advance in the text that follows is Putnam's later refinement of his thesis that forms of association are narrower in focus than before, rather than simply not existing at all, and that social capital is not evenly distributed across society (Putnam 2004). New forms of association around gender, single-issue politics and minority religion leave behind those who were previously part of vibrant local churches and trade unions and those left behind are the citizens most in need of social capital.[1]

In contrast to the bleakness of Putnam's thesis there is the more optimistic notion of the 'critical citizen' advanced by Norris (1999). In common with Putnam, Norris' critical citizens have also chosen their destiny. They are better educated and more knowledgeable than previous generations of citizens and the form of representational democracy on offer is not sufficiently attractive to engage them. These citizens are economically secure and certain of their position in the world and as a consequence of this they defer less to authority and strong leaders, and see more value in self-expression (Inglehart and Abramson 1994). They care less about wages and pensions, more about less personal values such as global hunger and poverty, environmentalism and human rights (Inglehart 1997). This points to a diverse range of primarily non-economic values being brought into politically motivated consumption, not least a care and concern for others (Barnett et al. 2005). To support this, many NGOs report a rise in membership and the ESRC-funded Citizen Audit findings demonstrate an increasing commitment on behalf of individuals to engage in informal and extra-parliamentary political behaviour around a banner of commodities and consumption practices (Pattie and Syed 2003). To me this is classical political consumerism; for Norris it is *cause-orientated* activity, to be distinguished from traditional political activism which is described as *citizen-orientated* activity (Norris 2007: 639); for Micheletti (2003: 25) it is *individualized collective action.*

A variation on the theme of critical citizens is that citizens are now more empowered as consumers of goods than as workers. Economic globalization, about which I say more below, has seen mass employment, and so the possibility of workplace activism, move away from developed countries to the global South. The retreat of the state that has occurred in the UK and other EU countries and the rise of new public management in its wake have resulted in the provision of core services through a variety of agencies and not-for-profit bodies which are not perceived as being directly accountable through electoral mechanisms. The individual citizen now has a more meaningful relationship with a variety of private and quasi-public actors than it does with the state (Rose 1999: 166) and consequently needs recourse to a politics that is relevant to this position. Schudson's description (1998) of the trajectory of the relationship of citizens to the democratic state tells a similar story. Citizens have moved from a deferential position enjoyed in the eighteenth century, to a partisan citizenship prior to the First Wold War, to an informed citizenship enjoyed in the era when diverse sources of media enabled criticisms of policy, to a monitorial citizenship. Complexities of globalization and stripped-down states only allow/encourage citizens to monitor what is important to them and others in a general sense. Consequently they need a politics that allows them to do this. The difficulty with the idea of critical citizens or monitorial citizens is that there are arguably many more citizens finding themselves in a position of insecurity as a result of socio-economic factors, such as flexible work practices and the globalization of commodity production, and unable to identify what they need to monitor in order to secure their position.

## Optimists

The elision of geographical space and virtual space that is globalization is taken up by Giddens (1998, 1999, 2000). Access to information through the Internet and greater opportunities for travel have assisted in the breakdown of identity based on geographical location and tradition. In a globalized market events far from an individual's actual physical location can have an effect on their economic and social existence. In the Giddensian theory of modernity the structural changes to social and economic life that have followed on from post-Fordism have thrust the individual into the spotlight in a way that is different from the market individualism of the New Right. As Giddens describes it, these changes go to the root of the

> ... constitution of personal identities. The self becomes a reflexive project ... Individuals cannot rest content with an identity that is simply handed down, inherited, or built on a traditional status. A person's identity has in large part to be discovered, constructed, and actively sustained.
>
> (Giddens 1994: 82)

Empowerment strategies produced by government, such as civil and human rights legislation, have produced more active and reflexive citizens than before who seek an individual identity and reject top-down systems of power and ideas of collective identity. The world (for which read Western world; other societies have retreated into stronger formations of local identity under the same pressures) has gone through an age of de-traditionalisation, societies have become more ethnically diverse and as a result individuals are selecting different moral choices from a menu of alternatives (Bentley and Halpern 2003: 82). It can no longer be assumed, as the traditional political party structures assume, that a particular attitude to private health care, for example, also signals a particular predictable attitude to free trade or crime and justice issues.

As part of this individuation thesis the individual has become, through personal choice, a consumer of services and commodities empowered to embark upon political activities and strategies of their own. Thus Giddens pushes the position of the individual into that of citizen-consumer. The idea of the empowered individual as a citizen-consumer has been seized upon by the reformers of public services. Successive Labour administrations have built on the Thatcherite idea of active consumers emboldened by the Citizen's Charter, contrasted with passive citizens, to create the idea of individual consumers choosing public-service provision to suit their particular needs rather than being bound by collective provision (Clarke et al. 2007). Bauman offers a devastating critique of this idea of citizen-consumer which is based not only on the decline of state sovereignty in terms of the state deciding on questions of distribution (Bauman 2007: 65–66) but also on the rise of the rule of the commodity market. In this, individuals themselves are relegated to being commodities. They are not emancipated from the idea of 'no choice' or 'limited choice' but instead conquered and colonized by the commodity market (Bauman 2007: 61–62).

Giddens offers an optimistic reading of the situation that individuals find themselves in. They are empowered to be responsible for themselves and their world. Life politics is about individuals operating outside the formal political system and free from those hierarchies at a local level (Giddens 1994: 14). In the context of political consumerism this is similar to the model of political responsibility offered by the late Iris Marion Young (2004, 2006). Influenced by Hannah Arendt, Young's conception of the political is one that exceeds government and statehood and becomes the act of reorganising or reordering, as an individual, some aspect of collective life and of persuading others to do the same. Responsibility is grounded not in fault, blame or liability, nor based upon some clarion call to care in a moral sense about people less well off than ourselves in a faraway country, but on the act of social connection; by using products that are produced in a way that involves environmental degradation or sweated labour, for example, we are connected to but not responsible for those activities. She uses the anti-sweatshop movement in the US as the exemplar of her model. Political consumers have engaged in 'episodic campaigning' by focusing on specific products and publicly ascribing responsibility for the conditions in which they are produced to specific actors such as universities, which bulk-buy clothing made in this way and put their own branding on it, even though the institutions are directly to blame for them (Micheletti and Stolle 2007). Political responsibility is forward-looking in that it leaves blame and fault in the past and centres instead on a recognition that injustice is not acceptable.

Young's model is outcome-centred; it asks that outcomes be sought which try to address and alter injustice. To take up responsibility for injustice an individual needs to reflect on, and persuade others to reflect on, structural inequalities and the causes of those inequalities and then be prepared to think through how means can be designed to change those inequalities. Young acknowledges that responsibility may be discharged through engagement with the state but is more in favour of the promulgation of a public discourse at the level of individuals. For her, political responsibility translates into a model of political action based on the parameters of connection, power and privilege. Connection involves working to remove the anonymity of inequality by asking questions of importers and retailers, for example, about the sourcing and manufacture of their products. The power to challenge inequality varies depending on one's location in the process but even end-of-chain consumers have the power to make corporations change their practices if they choose to use it. The notion of privilege in Young's model is more difficult as those who benefit from cheap products may not be in a position to afford others available at a higher price. This of course supposes that higher-price goods are more likely to be 'clean', which is not necessarily the most accurate of assumptions.

### Pessimists

Both Bauman and Beck take the same elision of geographical space and virtual space as Giddens. They see economic globalization as characterized by the same factors as Giddens and they also see an individualized world removed from traditional political engagement. There the similarity ends. Beck's concern is with the migration of responsibility for political decisions from elected representatives and related governance structures into the domain of unelected 'experts' (Beck 1997). Rapid scientific change has left governments in reaction-only mode while scientists, technology experts and lawyers, in thrall to multinational capital (Beck 2000: 89), drive forward an agenda in which they decide on the acceptability and management of risk. An example of this is issues of food safety. As Beck's thesis stands it is not the concern of this paper, hence my rather succinct summary of what is a much richer position; however, Beck's response to his *risk society* thesis is of major concern to this paper. What he advocates is a 'sub-politics' in which citizens, through direct action, challenge the unelected and unaccountable experts and reinvigorate democracy (Beck 1999).

Bauman offers an account of the depoliticizing effect that the move from a production-based society to a consumer-based society has had (Bauman 1998: 90). Those who had been outside the enfranchising effect of the work ethic had previously been connected to society through welfarist policies (Bauman 2007: 126). A move from a production-led society to a consumer society leaves those individuals outside traditional political structures. Welfare-state institutions that provide opportunities for greater social citizenship produce parliamentary democracies with greater voter turnout. This might explain why democracies such as Sweden have not suffered the decline in voter participation that the UK has, for example. Greater social citizenship through welfare produces a more positive experience of government (Lister 2007). Individuals are haunted by the demands of membership of the consumer society. It is not an issue of individual choice as to whether to participate or not but an issue of fate. As Bauman expresses it 'individualization is a fate, not a choice … to refuse to participate in the individualizing game is emphatically *not* on the agenda' (Bauman 2001: 46–47, 2007: 60). Bauman looks at the creation of global marketplaces and sees market pressures replacing political legislation. Power has been separated from politics and capital has been separated from geographical location (Bauman 1999: 72–78, 122–23). This last point is, of course, not dissimilar to the one made by Giddens. The difference is that Bauman explicitly recognizes that globalization has both winners and losers. The power of individual states has no purchase in the world that Bauman and Beck see and this decline is represented by political apathy and a rejection of traditional opportunities for political participation (Bauman 2004: 51–52). Citizens are abandoned by those structures that validated them as consumers of politics. For Bauman an individual can now see their life as a succession of self-contained and self-sustained units.

## An act of consciousness?

Whether an individual is a critical citizen, a citizen taking responsibility or a citizen abandoned by traditional securities, what makes them into political consumers 'wandering round the shops. … actualizing a philosophy of life'? (Douglas 1996: 86). By this I mean whether it is possible to distinguish political consumers from the general body of consumers. What motivations do political consumers have that other consumers do not and can this be pulled into a general descriptor of the process that consumers go through in order to make the decision to use their purchasing power to further particular social justice goals? The empirical evidence available to answer this question comes from the small number of studies that have been carried out in relation to consumer boycotts of particular goods. While not an exact parallel – participation in consumer boycotts raises an issue of collective action and individuals' perception of how the collective-action problem can be overcome or accommodated (John and Klein 2003) – the questions are close enough to offer an insight into consumer decisions. The study by Kozinets and Handelman (1998) points to individual participation in these activities being linked to ideas of individuality and moral self-realization. Sen et al. (2001) offer a similar explanation in that they term it as a desire to help – self-interest is subordinated to the desire to help others. These empirical psychological explanations map quite neatly onto the ideas examined above as to why individuals might reject traditional political participation or look to make an additional political statement.

Young's model of political action aims to move relationships from the unconscious to the conscious using her idea of connection, and to then shape those relationships so that individuals recognize their responsibility. The work of Paulo Freire provides a three-stage description of the process of conscientization or the awakening of critical consciousness (Freire 1973: 19). In his terms

conscientization means 'learning to perceive social, political and economic contradictions and to take action against the oppressive elements of reality'. Freire's
work is of course grounded in radical pedagogy and, although his work is widely
applied in many other disciplines, this influences the way in which he describes
the stages (Rossatto 2005: 13). More importantly Freire has inspired those
engaged in critical literacy studies to see the success of neoliberal regimes as
grounded in depoliticized consumer culture, passive consumerism and hostility
to any challenges to economic interest (McLaren and Farahmandpur 2005). It
seems apt therefore to use his ideas of creating engagement in this context.
Freire did apply the political thought that underlay his pedagogy more widely
towards the end of his life. He connected critical consciousness to the need to
create solidarity to oppose the 'neoliberal discourse spreading through the world'
and to counteract the fatalism that accompanied explanations of problems such
as hunger and unemployment at the end of the twentieth century.

Much of Freire's work is expressed in terms of how knowledge is transferred
and acquired and is written in opposition to what would be, for most of us, the
traditional model of education through knowledge banking.[2] The first stage
involves a very limited understanding of reality. In the context of Freire's work
this might mean that an individual knows what is required for them to survive.
The perception is that the world is static and cannot be changed. The second
stage involves grasping that the world is a more complex place and that there
are many other issues beyond mere survival but there is no understanding of
causal relations. There is a need to overcome feelings of powerlessness in relation to the size of the task of change and recognize that individuals can play a
role. Educators would view this second stage as the place where transformative
learning takes place; a space in which the individual undertakes critical appraisal
of previous unquestioned assumptions (Mezirow 1981). In the third stage the
individual has a much deeper knowledge of reality which requires an understanding of issues, their causes and effects and a willingness to revise knowledge.
At the third stage the individual has achieved critical conscientization: the ability
to analyze, problematize (pose questions) and affect the sociopolitical, economic
and cultural realities that shape their life. In the context of political consumption
this will involve questioning privilege and entitlement. It requires extensive self-
reflexivity to understand how one's identity has been shaped by hitherto dominant discourses around ideas of product choice governed by cheapness at end
production point or by design label (Sakamoto and Pitner 2005).

Conscientization is part of a dialogical process that Freire considers can only
take place in 'authentically democratic regimes' (Mackie 1980). Causal reality
has been grasped and individuals as a result are in a position to transform
situations rather than simply recognize and adapt to them (Kenway and Modra
1992). As McLaren puts it:

> Freirean pedagogy is ... about the struggle for critical consciousness read
> against the powerful dialectical contradictions of capitalism that exist

between productive labor and capital and between production and exchange and their historical linkage and development.

(McLaren 2001: 127)

The thrust of conscientization is that it goes beyond the language of critique and explanation and moves into the dynamics of achieving change (Torres 1994). It is only through active engagement that individuals can re-engage with politics. Individual action is a way of re-politicising society through consumption. As engaged consumers, individuals can become reunited with politics rather than being mere passive consumers of politics. The natural consequence of this Freiran-inspired process is that individuals will have to choose between products, to evaluate claims made by corporations and ultimately to take responsibility for the fate of others when they make choices. An interrogation of so-called 'codes of conduct' presented by individual industries, individual corporations or global actors such as the UN is also required. To ignore the chance for interrogation and to engage instead in unthinking and uncritical endorsement of 'green', 'clean' and 'fair' product claims and marketing strategies is to ignore the opportunity to achieve social change.

The interrogation I suggest may well result in difficult choices for the individual between equally deserving causes, but to be in a position to make this choice is to be an engaged political consumer. The availability of global information, the ease of global communications and the decline in the importance of physical place and presence have made identifying the menu of choices much easier. However choosing between such often contradictory positions remains difficult: locally sourced food with no air miles or fair-trade food; environmental concerns versus the need for industrial and infrastructure development in the South; clothes produced in a sweatshop or the loss of a job for someone who will starve as a result; organic food but from a country known to have a poor human rights record, for example. Inevitably some issues and some products will be accorded a higher priority than others – electrical products and mobile phones, for example, tend to be judged according to environmental concerns rather than concerns about the conditions in which their component parts were assembled. Additionally judgments about issues of social justice are likely to be made from the standpoint of the expectations of Western society with solutions devised by Western society (Basu 2001). This is a fault that political consumers are likely to share with some members of the development movement and is not an argument for discouraging their activism. There are conflicting stories from science with no fixed expert view as to the 'right' thing to do. The point here is that the decision to become a political consumer is a voyage of self-discovery. Narratives for action abound but there are no grand narratives (Cherrier 2007). The message from political consumerism will be similar to that from the anti-globalization alliances – confused with multiple and conflicting outpourings but underscored by clear and obvious commitment from the participants.

## Limitations of political consumerism?

The notion of resistance through political consumerism has attracted a high degree of celebration among anti-neoliberal commentators but there is now an emerging critique from this quarter that sees political consumption as maintaining the status quo by being within the market, and so perpetuating its existence, rather than outside it. For each product or practice that is subject to condemnation the market provides the ultimate solution by producing either a substitute product or an entire new philosophy of consumption in the form of the 'green' product range (Rojeck 2004: 305). From those rooted in the political tradition of participation through voting there is the objection that this type of individual action is anti-democratic and exclusionary (Young 2001). Both these general perspectives break down into a series of points on a spectrum of scale and scope but taken together they are powerful contrary arguments. Critics within these two schools of thought would be united in condemning political consumerism as a politics of resistance and not reconfiguration; it is oppositional only. For the first school it is simply not ambitious enough to achieve structural change without the enlistment of others and for the second it is the absence of any conventionally recognizable ideology. The absence of recognizable ideology is of course deliberate. Political consumerism is about selecting which battles to fight based on actual choices rather than abstract ideology (Bang 2007: 195–96).

Littler (2005) asks the questions 'Who is the I?' and 'Who is included?' The first of these questions goes to the heart of the anti-neoliberal critique that political consumers have effectively mainstreamed their activities into already privileged lives and can fit campaigning for social and political change into their High Street-centred Starbuckscopia lives (Low and Davenport 2007, Macdonald 2007). The second question addresses the idea that political consumerism is a way of bypassing state-level politics characterized by full franchises, safeguards for minorities to be represented and consultation systems ensuring policy development and the aggregation of citizens' views, and replacing it with a politics of individual commitment that, no matter how meritorious the individuals, privileges those with the financial resources to make product choices and the education to make informed choices. There is an idealization of traditional political structures here in that there is still an issue about who is consulted and how consultation evidence is dealt with but at least there are structures set up to achieve ostensible democratic consent. The politics of commitment are likely to have only a short-term life and short-term incremental success, if any, without larger structures to support them and offer continuity. The idea of political consumerism snuggling nicely into larger structures begins to sound very much like the creation of collective-action structures and NGOs. These bring with them the problems of capture, passivism and the free-rider problem (Eden 2004). Political consumers have no mandate to dictate by the results of their actions what product choices are available to others or perhaps more importantly to indicate to corporate actors which of their behaviours are or are not acceptable to the polity. NGOs do not have this mandate either. However it would be unfortunate if participants in political consumerism were conceived of as being in opposition to or undermining collective structures such as NGOs or unions. It is possible that they may be members of either or both, or that they are simply invigorated by individual action in a way which they are not by the idea of collective membership and action.

The attraction of political consumerism is that it offers a strategy for politicization from below. Its very essence is captured by the idea of bypassing the political institutions that characterize traditional political structures. As such it has the potential to include those, for example women, who, for a variety of reasons, are under-represented and often feel marginalized and excluded from traditional political activism (Micheletti 2004). Beck, in the context of his work on risk, posits the idea of conventional political engagement being replaced with what he terms 'subpolitics' – a politics from below. In practical terms subpolitics has much in common with political consumerism and both of them can be subjected to the same general critique (Mythen 2004: 170–75). In addition to arguments around democratic engagement and inclusion there are issues around the construction of power that are hinted at by both. Political power is seen almost as a zero-sum game in the sense that it is either possessed or not. The reality is much more nuanced than this and this is demonstrated by the potential for state capture and adoption of the groups engaged in subpolitics and individuals engaged in political consumerism. This might, of course, answer the charge that political consumerism can only achieve a short-term incremental intervention but it imposes a political organizational structure on those who have expressly disavowed one.

Political consumers do not appear to be as strong as states when it comes to a confrontation with the capitalist global economy and there is an argument that efforts at a politics of reconfiguration and redistribution should be the domain of states and that extra-state activities serve only to weaken and undermine states. However states it seems have required no encouragement to float off the activities of regulation of corporate activity or at least, to the extent to which they are in a position to use regulatory intervention, they have consistently declined to do so. Instead they have encouraged consumers and corporations to act in a responsible and engaged manner by selling and choosing products that reflect good practice. This masks the absence of regulation and still allows the collection of taxation revenue from corporate profits (Hay 2007: 85). States have encouraged corporations to engage in corporate social responsibility and philanthropic activities. There is the possibility of a democratic deficit here as corporations have no mandate to decide on the delivery of services and benefits if these would otherwise be provided by the state. The answer is that the decline of welfare regimes in general means that in the absence of corporate intervention directly or in support of third-sector activities these services and benefits would not be provided. This strengthens the position of the corporate sector as it becomes a mechanism for them to control public spending and ensure minimal government interference (Himmelstein 1997). Political consumerism might result in the development of defensive corporate social responsibility activities rather than pro-active and thus more expansive and innovative activities, but this underscores the issue of what drives globalization and the global economy rather than presenting a problem for consumer political activity.

## Conclusion

Political consumerism as a form of activism is to be encouraged. It offers a route into political engagement for those who are outside more traditional political structures through choice or because they feel that they do not offer a direct enough focus on areas of concern to them. Individuals who are currently disenchanted with the political process have the opportunity to rediscover a sense of political commitment. Political consumerism does create tensions with conventional political expression in the area of democratic voice and inclusion but these tensions are not so serious that the two cannot coexist.

Confused messages, short-term successes and oppositionary discourses might characterize political consumerism but its potential as a tool for foregrounding issues and thus achieving change should be valued and celebrated.

## Notes

1 See, for example, Gray and Caul (2000), who view the decline of trade unions, which traditionally mobilized political engagement, as the key to falling voter turnout.
2 The most comprehensive guide to Freire's work is Taylor (1993).

## References

Auger, P., Burke, P., Devinney, T. M. and Louviere. J. J. (2003) 'What will consumers pay for social product features', *Journal of Business Ethics*, 43: 281–304.
Bang, H. (2007) 'Critical theory in a swing: political consumerism between politics and policy', in M. Bevir and F. Trentmann (eds) *Governance, Consumers and Citizens*, Basingstoke: Palgrave Macmillan, 191–230.
Barnett, C., Clarke, N. Cloke, P. and Malpass, A. (2005) 'The political ethics of consumerism', *Consumer Policy Review*, 15: 45–51.
Basu, K. (2001) 'The view from the tropics', in A. Fung, C. F. Sabel and D. O'Rourke (eds) *Can We Put An End To Sweatshops?* Boston: Beacon Press, 59–64.
Bauman, Z. (1998) *Work, Consumerism and the New Poor*, Buckingham: Open University Press.
——(1999) *In Search of Politics*, Cambridge: Polity.
——(2001) *The Individualised Society*, Cambridge: Polity.
——(2004) *Wasted Lives*, Cambridge: Polity.
——(2007) *Consuming Life*, Cambridge: Polity.
Beck, U. (1997) *The Reinvention of Politics*, Cambridge: Polity.
——(1999) *World Risk Society*, Cambridge: Polity.
——(2000) *Brave New World of Work*, Cambridge: Polity.

Beck, U. and Gernsheim, E. (2001) *Individualization*, London: Sage.

Bennett, W. L. (2003) 'Lifestyle politics and citizen-consumers', in J. Corner and D. Pels (eds) *Media and the Restyling of Politics*, London: Sage, 137–50.

Bentley, T. and Halpern, D. (2003) '21st century citizenship', in A. Giddens (ed) *The Progressive Manifesto*, Cambridge: Polity, 73–96.

Cherrier, H. (2007) 'Ethical consumption practices: co-production of self-expression and social recognition', *Journal of Consumer Behavior*, 6:321–55.

Clarke, J., Newman, J. Smith, N., Vidler, E. and Westmarland, L. (2007) *Creating Citizen Consumers*, London: Sage.

Cohen, L. (2001) 'Citizen consumers in the United States in the century of mass consumption', in M. Daunton and M. Hilton (eds) *The Politics of Consumption*, Oxford: Berg, 203–22.

Dalton, R. (2004) *Democratic Challenges, Democratic Choices: the erosion of political support in advanced industrial democracies*, Oxford: Oxford University Press.

Delanty, G. (1998) 'Reinventing community and citizenship in the global era: a critique of the communitarian concept of community', in E. Christodoulidis (ed) *Communitarianism and Citizenship*, Aldershot: Ashgate, 33–52.

Douglas, M. (1996) *Thought Styles*, London: Sage.

Eden, S. (2004) 'Greenpeace', *New Political Economy*, 9: 595–610.

Franklin, M. (2004) *Voter Turnout and the Dynamics of Electoral Competition in Established Democracies since 1945*, Cambridge: CUP.

Freire, P. (1973) *Education for Critical Consciousness*, New York: Seabury.

Giddens, A. (1994) *Beyond Right and Left*, Cambridge: Polity.

——(1998) *The Third Way*, Cambridge: Polity.

——(1999) *The Runaway World*, London: Profile Books.

——(2000) *The Third Way and its Critics*, Cambridge: Polity.

Gray, M. and Caul, M. (2000) 'Declining voter turnout in advanced industrial democracies, 1950–97', *Comparative Political Studies*, 33: 1091.

Hall, P. (1999) 'Social capital in Britain', *British Journal of Political Science*, 29: 417–61.

Hay, C. (2007) *Why We Hate Politics*, Cambridge: Polity Press.

Hertz, N. (2001) 'Better to shop than vote?' *Business Ethics: A European Review* 10(3): 190–93.

Hilton, M. (2001) 'Consumer politics in post-war Britain', in M. Daunton and M. Hilton (eds) *The Politics of Consumption*, Oxford: Berg, 241–60.

Himmelstein, J. (1997) *Looking Good and Doing Good: corporate philanthropy and corporate power*, Bloomington: Indiana University Press.

Inglehart, R. (1997) *Modernization and Postmodernization: cultural, economic and political change in 43 societies*, Princeton: Princeton University Press.

Inglehart, R. and Abramson, P. (1994) 'Economic security and value change', *American Political Science Review*, 88: 336–54.

John, A. and Klein, J. (2003) 'The consumer boycott: consumer motivations for purchase sacrifice', *Management*, 49: 1196–1209.

Kenway, J. and Modra, H. (1992) 'Feminist pedagogy and emancipatory possibilities', in C. Luke and J. Gore (eds) *Feminisms and Critical Pedagogy*, New York: Routledge, 138–66.

Kozinets, R. and Handelman, J. (1998) 'Ensouling consumption: a netnographic explanation of boycotting behavior', *Advances in consumer research*, 25: 475–80.

Lister, M. (2007) 'Institutions, inequality and social norms: explaining variations in participation', *BJPIR*, 9 20–35.

Littler, J. (2005) 'Beyond the boycott', *Cultural Studies*, 19: 227–52.

Low, W. and Davenport, E. (2007) 'To boldly go ... exploring ethical spaces to re-politicise ethical consumption and fair trade', *Journal of Consumer Behavior*, 6: 336–48.

Macdonald, K. (2007) 'Globalising justice within coffee supply chains? Fair Trade, Starbucks and the transformation of supply chain governance', *Third World Quarterly*, 28: 793–812.

Mackie, R. (1980) 'Contributions to the thought of Paulo Freire', in R. Mackie (ed) *Literacy and Revolution*, London: Pluto, 93–108.

McLaren, P. (2001) 'Che Guevara, Paulo Freire, and the politics of hope: reclaiming critical pedagogy', *Cultural Studies* < = > *Critical Methodologies*, 1: 108–31.

McLaren, P. and Farahmandpur, R. (2005) *Teaching Against Global Capitalism and the New Imperialism*, Maryland: Rowman and Littlefield.

Mezirow, J. (1981) 'A critical theory of adult learning and education', *Adult Education*, 32: 3–24.

Micheletti, M. (2004) 'Why more women? Issues of gender and political consumerism', in M. Micheletti, A. Follesdal and D. Stolle (eds) *Politics, Products and Markets*, New Brunswick: Transaction, 245–64.

Micheletti, M. and Stolle, D. (2007) 'Mobilizing consumers to take responsibility for global social justice', *Annals AAPSS*, 611: 157–75.

Morison, J. (1998) 'The case against constitutional reform', *JLS*, 25: 510–35.

Morison, J. and Newman, D. (2001) 'On-line citizenship: consultation and participation in New Labour's Britain and beyond', *International Review of Law, Computers and Technology*, 15: 171–94.

Mythen, G. (2004) *Ulrich Beck*, London: Pluto Press.

Norris, P. (1996) 'Did television erode social capital? A reply to Putnam', *Political Science and Politics*, XXIX: 474–80.

——(1999) *Critical Citizens: global support for democratic government*, Oxford: Oxford University Press.

——(2007) 'Political activism: new challenges, new opportunities', in C. Boix and S. Stokes (eds) *The Oxford Handbook of Comparative Politics*, Oxford: Oxford University Press, 628–49.

O'Toole, T., Marsh, D. and Jones, S. (2003) 'Political literacy cuts both ways: the politics of non-participation among young people', *The Political Quarterly*, 74: 349–60.

Pateman, C. (1970) *Participation and Democratic Theory*, Cambridge: Cambridge University Press.

Pattie, C. and Syed, P. (2003) 'Citizenship and civic engagement: attitudes and behaviour in Britain', *Political Studies*, 51: 443–68.

Pattie, C., Syed, P. and Whiteley, P. (2003) 'Civic attitudes and engagement in modern Britain', *Parliamentary Affairs*, 56: 616–33.

Pharr, S. and Putnam, R. (2001) *Disaffected Democracies: what's troubling the trilateral countries?* Princeton: Princeton University Press.

Putnam, R. (1993) *Making Democracy Work: civic traditions in modern Italy*, Princeton: Princeton University Press.

——(2000) *Bowling Alone: the collapse and renewal of American community*, New York: Simon and Schuster.

——(ed.) (2004) *Democracies in Flux*, Oxford: Oxford University Press.

Rallings, C. and Thrasher, M. (2003) 'Local electoral participation in Britain', *Parliamentary Affairs*, 56: 700–715.

Rojeck, C. (2004) 'The consumerist syndrome in contemporary society: an interview with Zygmunt Bauman', *Journal of Consumer Culture*, 4: 291–312.

Rose, N. (1999) *Powers of Freedom*, Cambridge: Cambridge University Press.

Rossatto, C. A. (2005) *Engaging Paulo Freire's pedagogy of possibility*, Maryland: Rowman and Littlefield.

Sakamoto, I. and Pitner, R. (2005) 'Use of critical consciousness in anti-oppressive social work practice: disentangling power dynamics at personal and structural levels', *British Journal of Social Work*, 35: 435–52.

Sassatelli, R. (2006) 'Virtue, responsibility and consumer choice', in J. Brewer and F. Trentmann (eds) *Consuming Cultures, Global Perspectives*, Oxford: Berg, 219–50.

Schudson, M. (1998) *The Good Citizen: a history of American civic life*, New York: Free Press.

Sen, S., Gürhan-Canli, Z. and Morwitz, V. (2001) 'Withholding consumption: a social dilemma perspective on consumer boycotts', *Journal of Consumer*, 28: 399–417.

Sennett, R. (1998) *The Corrosion of Character*, New York: Norton.

Shaw, D., Newholm, T. and Dickinson, R. (2006) 'Consumption as voting: an exploration of consumer empowerment', *European Journal of Marketing*, 40: 1049–67.

Stolle, D. and Hooghe, M. (2004) 'Consumers as political participants? Shifts in political action repertoires in western societies', in M. Micheletti, A. Follesdal and D. Stolle (eds) *Politics, Products and Markets*, New Brunswick: Transaction, 265–88.

Stolle, D., Hooghe, M. and Micheletti, M. (2005) 'Politics in the supermarket: political consumerism as a form of political participation', *International Political Science Review*, 26: 245–69.

Taylor, P. (1993) *The Texts of Paulo Freire*, Buckingham: Open University Press.

The Cooperative Bank (2007) *The Ethical Consumerism Report 2007*, Manchester: The Cooperative Bank. Online: <http://www.co-operativebank.co.uk/images/pdf/ethical_consumer_report_2007.pdf >.

Torres, C. (1994) 'Education and the archaeology of consciousness: Freire and Hegel', *Educational Theory*, 44: 429–45.

Trentmann, F. (2007) 'Before 'Fair Trade': empire, free trade, and the moral economies of food in the modern world', *Environment and Planning D: Society and Space*, 25: 1079–1102.

Vogel, D. (2005) *The Market for Virtue*, Washington DC: Brookings.

Young, I. (2001) 'Activist challenges to democracy', *Political Theory*, 29: 670–90.

——(2004) 'Responsibility and global labor justice'. *Journal of Political Philosophy*, 12: 365–88.

——(2006) 'Responsibility and global justice: a social connection model', *Social Philosophy and Policy*, 23: 102–30.

## Useful websites

Good With Money (The Cooperative Bank)
    <http://www.goodwithmoney.co.uk/report-download>

# Chapter 3

# Engendering responsibility in global markets: valuing the women of Kenya's agricultural sector

*Ann Stewart**

## Introduction

For the last quarter of a century, development policies have been geared towards integrating African agriculture into the world market. The structural adjustment policies of the World Bank and International Monetary Fund have sought to provide the economic and fiscal infrastructure for the development of the open, integrated, global markets envisaged in the multilateral trading framework of the World Trade Organization Agreement on Agriculture and various regional trading initiatives. In Africa, the development of global markets has been underpinned by a range of land reform policies. These are in part aimed at improving efficiency in the smallholding farming sector by creating 'asset' value in land which has traditionally been held primarily for its 'use' value.[1] A side effect of these policies has been the development of an African agribusiness sector based primarily on horticulture, which relies on a plentiful supply of relatively cheap, 'flexible' labour.

This chapter considers how these developments have impacted upon women's position in Kenya, an agriculture-based economy with a significant agribusiness sector. The chapter constructs two archetypes: women smallholder farmers and women who work in the agribusiness sector. It argues that if we do not recognise women's social reproductive roles and the gendered assumptions implied in these responsibilities, they face deep injustices, both as farmers and as workers. The chapter then widens the discussion to consider the ways in which feminist concepts such as those based upon ethics of care and responsibility may be used in the governance of global markets, and to suggest the need for a wider and more redistributional understanding of gendered justice.

## Kenyan agriculture in global context

Agriculture is a significant part of Kenyan life, comprising about 30 per cent of Gross Domestic Product (GDP). Of the 30.4 million population, 78 per cent live in rural areas, with about 75 per cent in the area designated as medium to high agricultural potential (20 per cent of land area) (Central Bureau of Statistics

2002).[2] This section first explores some of the key international regulatory forces affecting Kenyan agriculture generally. It then considers the position of Kenyan farmers and factory workers in the global value chain for a particular sector of agribusiness: horticulture.

## Key international regulatory forces

Agricultural production in the developing world has been subjected to the rigours of structural adjustment programmes of the World Bank and the International Monetary Fund (IMF) since the 1980s. These programmes 'impose[d] a neo liberal agenda of fiscal restraint, open trade and capital accounts, and privatisation on indebted developing countries' (Razavi 2003: 2). Since the World Bank and IMF-led structural adjustment policies of the 1990s, Kenya has cut tariff rates by half and decreased spending on agriculture by 50 per cent.

Since the 1994 adoption of the Agreement on Agriculture (AOA) as part of the Agreement Establishing the World Trade Organization, agriculture has also been the subject of international trade rules. These rules are directed towards reducing and eliminating 'traditional pillars of agricultural protection' such as import quotas and government subsidies, thereby exposing individual farmers more directly to global market forces. Particular attention has been paid to input-intensive commercial agriculture including agribusiness organisations (Williams 2003: 48).[3]

In principle, such a liberalisation regime should 'increase growth and income in each country and result in a wide range of assorted benefits' such as 'increased employment, lower food prices and enhanced access to technology' (Williams 2003: 48). Women might access the benefits of non-traditional agricultural exports either by transforming their farming activities through commercialisation and diversification or by commanding a higher income from working as employees in an expanding agribusiness sector, and purchasing, rather than producing, cheaper food including imports.

It is widely acknowledged that the above liberalisation strategies have not been successful in generating general economic growth. The failure is particularly stark in Africa, which has seen policy interventions of unparalleled range and depth over the past two decades, but where both export and food crop sectors have performed poorly. Indeed, there has been a steady decline in sub-Saharan Africa's agricultural exports as a share of global trade in agriculture (Razavi 2003: 14. See also World Bank 2008). One problem is that the mere 'reduc[tion of] trade barriers has not been sufficient to generate new demand for developing country exports' (Williams 2003: 49). Another is that local, especially small-scale, producers have frequently been unable to compete with cheap agricultural imports entering newly liberalised African markets.

Kenyan agriculture has found some protection from the rigours of international trade law as a consequence of its colonial past. On its independence from British colonial rule, Kenya's position within the Commonwealth ensured that it maintained its trading relations with the UK and, as an African state within the Lomé Conventions (1975–95), its exports were granted some preferential treatment by the then European Community.[4] The Lomé system was replaced by the Cotonou Agreement (2000) following a 1996 ruling by the World Trade Organization's dispute settlement body (on petition from the USA) that, as a non-reciprocal, preferential trade arrangement between ACP countries and the European Union, it violated WTO rules.

The Cotonou Agreement introduces Economic Partnership Agreements (EPA) which seek to ensure reciprocal access to markets and the phased removal of all trade preferences and trade barriers between all partners.[5] EPAs were to be negotiated and introduced by the end of 2007 when the WTO waiver ran out, but when this proved to be wholly unrealistic, a number of Interim EPAs were negotiated, including one with the East African Community of which Kenya is a member (EU 2007 and 2008). As a result, Kenya is presently able to maintain WTO-compatible access to EU markets but, with its fragile economy and an unstable political context, it remains highly vulnerable to shifts in European agricultural trade policies and to the wider power structures of the world trading system.[6]

### Global value chains and Kenyan horticulture

The Kenyan horticultural sector has grown substantially over the last 15 years so that exports of flowers and fresh fruit and vegetables (FFV) now constitute a major foreign exchange earner. In 2003 these exports were worth approximately US$ 460 million and accounted for roughly a quarter of all Kenyan exports (EPZA 2005). So, it is clear that some Kenyan farmers specialising in horticulture, including floriculture, have successfully integrated themselves into the global trade in agriculture.

Overall, 85 per cent of all horticultural exports and 99 per cent of all cut flowers are supplied to the EU. The UK (34 per cent) and the Netherlands (31 per cent) import the majority of Kenya's horticultural exports to the EU; the UK and France are the biggest importers of Kenya's fresh vegetable exports to the EU; and the UK imports 25 per cent of cut Kenyan flowers exported to the EU (EPZA 2005. See also *The Guardian* 2006).

Using global value chain analysis, it is possible to reveal how 'global production and consumption systems are integrated' (Gereffi et al. 2005: 79) and how globalisation has changed trading and production strategies both within the private realm of firms, and the public realm of state economic policies (Gereffi and Korzeniewicz 1994, Kaplinsky 2000, Gereffi et al. 2005).[7] The term 'value added chain' refers to 'the process by which technology is combined with material and labour inputs, and then processed inputs are assembled, marketed and distributed' (Gereffi et al. quoting Kogut 2005:79). Of particular relevance to this chapter are 'buyer-driven' commodity chains. These are found in those industries in which large retailers and brand companies organise decentralised production networks in a variety of exporting countries, often located in the global South. So, the production of a Nike sports shirt or a Zara dress will involve a complex network of contractors producing in a variety of settings from homework to large-scale factories different elements (for example, zips in country/context A, cutting and stitching in country/context B, pressing and packing in country/context C) of the garments. Specifications for the products are supplied by the retailer or the company that designs and/or markets the branded products but does not make them. Although they do not own the factories, they exert substantial control over how, when and where the manufacturing takes place and largely determine how much profit accrues at each stage in the chain.

The UK market, which imports a quarter of cut Kenyan flowers in the EU, is dominated by large supermarkets which control over three quarters of all UK FFV sales and between 70 and 90 per cent of sales of fresh produce from Africa (Dolan et al. 1999: 9).[8] This dominance is a consequence of both Kenya's close ties with the UK, and the supermarkets' position in global value chains and dominance of UK retail markets generally. Supermarkets aim to provide a wide range of low-priced goods to consumers in a hugely competitive market, thereby producing high returns for their shareholders. To do this they establish global value chains which ensure that Kenyan farmers and their workers are responsive to, and dependent upon, the desires of European consumers.

Kenyan agribusiness chains are relatively simple. The retailer will develop the product, such as a bouquet of flowers specifically targeted at St Valentine's Day or a tray of washed and prepared baby vegetables in a plastic pack. It will monitor sales through tills at the end of a particular day and email an order the following midday for delivery overnight to a supplier in Kenya. There is no written contract, and the orders will vary according to daily demand, but there are very detailed product specifications, such as the precise length, diameter and straightness of a green bean or the size of a podded pea. There will also be quality and food-safety standards to be met, such as the need for no pesticide residues. Let us assume that the supplier is also a large commercial farmer who either grows crops or obtains them from smallholders who have been provided with the seeds and the specifications. The smallholders will bring their crops to a local collective sorting house where they will be graded. The crop will be accepted if it meets the specification and if there is demand that day. FFV products are often unsuitable for sale in a local market, or even for use as animal fodder, so those that are rejected for export are wasted. The crop is brought from the farms to a packing house near the airport where it will be cut, prepared and packaged. The packs will, if necessary, be refrigerated and flown out overnight.

Value chain analysis allows us to do more than simply chart the now complex passage of a product from design to production to marketing. It aims to establish how and where value is added to the product during its journey, with the wider objective of tracking and improving the global distribution of income (Kaplinsky 2000: 9). Substantial chunks of value tend to be added at a few key stages, such as the transformation of a pineapple into 'perfectly ripe and naturally sweet segments' held in a plastic container with an integrated collapsible fork. Similarly, high quality chain management and coordination add value by ensuring that there is a steady supply of products of exactly the same quality throughout the year. The important question for the purposes of this chapter is whether Kenyans, especially Kenyan women, are appropriately rewarded for the value that they create.

### Rewarded for value-added?

By placing a premium on product development, value chain coordination and marketing, the system delivers the bulk of the gain to those involved in marketing and retailing, rather than those growing crops. Only those producers and exporters who can meet phytosanitary standards and provide large-scale sorting, packaging and refrigeration services benefit from significant opportunities to secure an additional slice of the value added. Smallholder farmers, particularly women, find it almost impossible to undertake the investment required for such post-harvest activities. So, while in 1992 almost 75 per cent of FFV for export were grown by smallholders (Dolan et al. 1999: 23), by the end of the 1990s, the market was dominated by 'the ten leading exporters', which were responsible for '70 per cent of Kenya's FFV exports'. Moreover, of those exporters, 'the four largest bought less than 20 per cent of their supplies from small farms' (Kaplinsky 2000: 23).[9]

Prices obtained by farmers are heavily influenced by the imperatives of low and/or competitive shelf prices[10] and the relative bargaining positions of the parties throughout the supply chain. Farmers usually receive only a small proportion of the final price paid by consumers in European supermarkets. In Kenya the figure is about 14.1 per cent while smallholder producers probably receive an even lower proportion. Supermarkets retain by far the largest share (46 per cent), although this includes 13.5 per cent for losses from unsold stock.[11] Thus much of the added value is distributed primarily in the global North, while much of the risk is pushed down the chain to the most vulnerable: the 'flexible' workers and smallholder farmers.

FFV products are labour intensive to grow, sort and pack. In order to minimise the costs associated with fluctuating orders, and thereby secure a profit, the farmer must have access to a pool of cheap, relatively unskilled, 'flexible' labour.

Women are usually incorporated into agribusiness supply chains to keep costs down (Smith et al. 2004). They tend to be concentrated in the value-added stages of picking, packing and processing. Companies see women 'as more productive, with nimble fingers and a capacity to perform the delicate and tedious work to fulfil the quality imperatives of overseas buyers' (Barrientos et al. 2003: 1514). Paradoxically, the tasks that they perform attract lower pay rates, perhaps because their income is perceived to be merely supplemental to their household budgets. In fact, the majority of women are the main or sole earner (Barrientos et al. 2001: 8). Rates of pay are above the ungenerous statutory minimum,[12] but many workers report that their wages do not cover their basic needs, and that they are not always paid properly – or even at all – for overtime.[13] Because women tend to lack an assured income, they are extremely vulnerable to abuse in their workplaces.

The exigencies of buyer-driven commodity value chains place huge pressures on producers to meet time deadlines. Orders vary and employees are required to work overtime at little or no notice. Although there is a legal limit of 48 hours work a week, women in pack-houses can be required to work up to eight hours per day overtime. This causes huge problems for women with childcare responsibilities, who may have to leave young children in the care of older siblings (with the knock-on effect on their schooling) or unsupervised and unfed for long periods.[14]

UK supermarkets have the economic power to define market relations. However, as the following sections will show, the extent to which women are rewarded for the value they have created is substantially affected by the interaction between three factors: their position in Kenyan society, the pressures of international economic law, and the failures of Kenyan labour and land law.

## Women of the Kenyan agricultural sector

Markets are commonly regarded as value-neutral, unshaped by social or gender norms. But people engage with markets – whether as producers, consumers or workers – not as abstract factors of production but as embodied social beings. Women's wider social reproductive and gender roles deeply affect their engagement with markets, often leaving them relatively vulnerable and disadvantaged.

First, while public life, including work, is organised through legal relationships, family life tends to be conducted predominately through relationships of care and trust (Tronto 1993). Much of the agricultural work undertaken by women is 'informal', unregulated by contracts of employment or labour laws, because women often labour as family members, rather than owners, on farms. Like all activities which take place within families and local communities, such agricultural labour is guided by wider community norms which embody assumptions about gender roles.

Second, activities undertaken in formal markets are more valued, both economically and socially, than unpaid activities undertaken within the family, predominately by women (Tronto 1993, Lewis and Guillani 2005, Hassim and Razavi 2006).[15] For example, trading in food is valued more highly than the provision of food security through subsistence. So those who sustain themselves outside the market, or at its margins, are often overlooked in policymaking. Yet even women's unpaid labour has been shown to support the development of global trading relations (Hoskyns and Rai 2007, Barrientos et al. 2001 and 2003).

Third, when women do undertake employment in the 'public' (formal or informal) sphere, they often continue to carry out their 'private', 'social reproductive' responsibilities.[16] Not only are their individual burdens increased by entering the formal sector, there is also a risk that general social capital will suffer if the time and effort spent on their unpaid work is not adequately replaced. A woman's ability to replace herself in the home – retaining a child-carer, buying rather than growing food – is dependant not only on adequate and consistent sources of income, but also on the availability of sources of support, and on her ability to access them.

In this section we explore the position of Kenyan women as smallholder farmers and as workers in the agribusiness sector. In the process, we see that women tend to be disadvantaged by both national and international laws, not least because they fail to recognise and protect women's socially reproductive roles. These responsibilities have become evermore burdensome in recent years due to cutbacks in state-based social safety nets (Molyneux and Razavi 2002: 16–24; Hassim and Razavi 2006) and the effects of the AIDs pandemic, which has greatly intensified care responsibilities by orphaning millions of children and undermining the production of staple foods through the loss of working-age adults (World Bank 2008: 224–25).[17]

### Smallholding farmers

The vast majority of Kenyan women are associated with agriculture: roughly 70 per cent of the agricultural labour force is female; over 90 per cent of rural women work on family farms (Dwasi 1999, World Bank 2007). They constitute 64 per cent of subsistence farmers, and produce approximately 60 per cent of farm-derived income.[18]

### ... and international economic law

Women farmers in Kenya have generally failed to reap the much vaunted benefits of liberalisation.[19] Women often farm marginal land with simple or no tools and very little access to fertiliser or extension training. 92 per cent of Kenyan women farmers use only hand cultivation, as compared to 62 per cent of men (Williams 2003: 65). Many cannot afford the chemicals, fertilisers and other farm inputs necessary to produce cash crops or to access export markets.

Unable to benefit from market access, women small farmers are likely to be actively disadvantaged by liberalisation. First, the reduction of government support (such as credit, fertilisers and water) that is associated with the rolling back of the state hits small farmers, including women, hard. Second, tariff reductions reduce the tax base, forcing governments to reduce social welfare spending, which disproportionately affects women because of their social roles.

Third, liberalisation attracts cheap imports which undercut the domestic produce which rural women have been encouraged through diversification programmes to market. Until the early 1990s, most smallholding farmers were able to make a sufficient living in subsistence agriculture. Not any more. Cheap imports compete with the food they produce, threatening their income base. In order to increase family incomes at a time of growing insecurity, women across sub-Saharan Africa have taken on more responsibility for the family farm, including the production of cash crops and participation in food processing activities, as men have sought non-farm employment away from villages, often migrating to urban areas (Garcia 2004: 82). As the size of family landholdings has decreased, most now rely on a range of sources of income which may include informal trading or providing services. In Kenya, some rural women have joined micro and small enterprises in village markets where they trade farm products such as milk, maize, beans and vegetables (Williams 2003: 63, World Bank 2007: Chapter 2). Others have also been obliged to migrate to find seasonal work not necessarily in agriculture[20] and to seek casual work on other smallholding or commercial farms. As we shall see in the following section, women find a further set of complications when they become employees. But first we explore the land tenure system in Kenya which, once again, adds to the burden carried by women in the Kenyan agricultural sector.

## ... and Kenyan land law

At the height of neoliberal orthodoxy in the 1980s and early 1990s, multilateral development banks (MDBs) and many bilateral development agencies exerted considerable pressure on African states to liberalise land markets. This policy was based on a 'presumption that there was a direct causal link between formalisation of property rights and economic productivity', and that formal titling provides the certainty required for investment (Nyamu-Musembi 2006). A number of African states accordingly enacted new Land Acts (McAuslan 1998 and 2003) which tended to seek to establish individual ownership rights and an institutional framework for maintaining a titles register. Agricultural land tenure in Kenya is an extremely complex issue.[21] Land is subject not only to the state law system,[22] but also to the customary land tenure systems of its 42 ethnic communities.[23] Under the long-running Kenyan formalisation process, owners of customary titles are given a fee simple estate in the land,[24] which can then be used and disposed of with minimal restrictions.[25] The process is widely recognised to be inefficient, corrupt and incoherent. It has also been criticised for failing women.

Policymakers and many women's organisations expect the poor, and women in particular, to benefit from the formalisation of land rights. A range of 'gender cases' are made. The business (economic efficiency) case, promulgated by the World Bank during the 1990s, argues that because customarily women rarely own land outright, their access to land is conditional and uncertain. For instance, they cannot rely on their title to access formal credit. They are therefore unable to convert or upgrade their activities to engage in international trade. Nor is their contribution translated into potential property accumulation (World Bank 2003b, World Bank 2007).[26]

But the business case for formal titling of rural land[27] now appears overly simplistic (Nyamu-Musembi 2006, Hunt 2005). The main constraints faced by women farmers relate not to their lack of full formal title, but from their lack of capital, their inability to command labour and the difficulties they face in accessing markets. Furthermore, there is little evidence of efficiency gains from the introduction of individual, registered ownership. Rather, there have been some inefficient, anti-competitive abuses of dominant positions: wealthy, powerful men have registered individual titles at the expense of women and the poor.[28] In Kenya, the existing system of titling has not facilitated access to formal credit (the business case) for Kenyan small farmers generally (Nyamu-Musembi 2006).[29] In any case, it is estimated that only one per cent of registered private land owners are women, and another five to six per cent hold land in joint names (World Bank 2007).

A second constituency supports formalisation of land rights in order to strengthen women's general position in society. In the absence of formal rights, women's access to and control over land is mediated through customary marriage, divorce and inheritance norms which support inequalities and create conflicts (Ikdahl et al. 2005). The argument goes that formal, individual land rights can improve women's bargaining position within the family and community institutions.[30] In truth the overwhelming majority of women live their lives within customary systems often untouched by formal laws which merely provide a backdrop to transactions relating to land in registered areas. Local customary practices of adjudication provide the immediate framework (Nyamu-Musembi 2006) and customary understandings of multiple, coexisting uses for land still operate. But this does not stop formalisation processes from doing substantial damage at the margins. Formalisation often actually weakens a woman's capacity to mobilise social support for a claim to property within the family or kinship network. One problematic scenario relates to the fact that, under most customary systems, land is held by the clan and allocated by men for certain uses, some of which are performed by women. Under the formalisation exercise, men's allocative power is separated from, and privileged over, women's use rights, which are downgraded to become merely derivative (Ikdahl et al. 2003).[31] Customary rights of use are not recognised under the Registered Land Act, and so are not included as overriding interests.[32] Furthermore, once a husband registers himself as owner of land, a wife's interests under customary law cease to exist. On his death, she cannot rely on her customary law entitlements when faced with the competing registered claims of third parties.[33] A second problematic scenario arises from the fact that according to statutory law applicable in Kenya[34] spouses gain no propriety interests through marriage and, in the event of a dispute involving land, legal ownership is evidenced by title.[35] So, the interaction between formal titling and a separate property regime tends to reinforce women's exclusion from property and increase their insecurity.[36] Finally, formalisation reduces the possibilities for supervision by traditional social institutions, while at the same time not providing women with access to state-based regulatory frameworks.

Proponents of an 'evolutionary theory of land rights' have rejected formalisation, arguing that customary law systems are more favourable to women than state law (Whitehead and Tsikata 2003).[37] They seek to build land security from customary tenures and institutions (World Bank 2003a: 62–64). However, this approach fails to recognise that women often lack power to negotiate within local community-based institutions, particularly over scarce assets such as land. Attempts to address gender inequality that are based solely on either 'public' formal law reform or 'private' customary law evolution fail to capture relationships which straddle the two spheres. Partly as a result of successful women's activism, there is growing recognition of the need to combine these perspectives within both the work of the policy community (see World Bank 2003a: 57–60) and state law reform initiatives.[38]

It is also important to note that the Kenya Land Alliance has campaigned hard, and with some success, to include principles of gender equality in the land reform process (see Kenya Land Alliance 2004). The National Land Policy Formulation Process has been conducted by the Government of Kenya funded principally by the UK Department for International Development (see further the Ministry of Land Website). The resulting draft National Land Policy under consideration by the Cabinet in October 2008 includes 'gender and equity principles' (National Land Policy Secretariat 2007; see also Human Rights Watch 2003).

Finally, Kenya has recently been involved in a protracted and highly conflictual process of constitutional reform resulting in a draft constitution which embodied principles of democracy, accountability, people's participation, human rights and social justice (Ikdalh et al. 2003: 98). Chapter 7 of this draft constitution, which dealt with the development of a national land policy, included a commitment to gender equality in relation to access, ownership and control of benefits of land and other resources including those which are inherited. It would have offered a basis for protecting women's rights to agricultural and other land when they occupy without ownership rights (Ikdalh et al. 2003: 99). However, it was rejected in the 2005 referendum, in part because of its commitment to gender equality (UN General Assembly 2007). Another draft is presently under consideration.[39]

### Employees in the agribusiness sector

Official statistics are scarce, but research conducted in the late 1990s[40] estimated that between 40,000 and 70,000 workers were employed in the Kenyan flower industry, of which 75 per cent were women and 65 per cent were defined at that time as temporary or seasonal workers.[41] It was estimated in 2003 that another 70,000 workers, the majority of whom were women, were employed in related industries (EPZA 2005).

The majority of Kenyan women work for themselves as family farmers, but increasing numbers are moving into paid employment in sectors such as services and horticultural export. In so doing they are contributing to a growth in female employment worldwide (ILO 2007).[42] The International Labour Organization (ILO) sees increased employment 'as a major step forward in terms of freedom and self determination for many women – even though it does not always entail getting a decent job right away' (2007: 10).[43] To be sure, women are clustered in the more vulnerable and insecure areas of employment which have attracted fewer work-related benefits. They also suffer from a lack of recognition for their wider social reproductive role.

### ... and Kenyan labour law

Until recently, Kenyan labour laws offered limited protection to workers, especially women. A major constraint was the fact that employment rights and work-related benefits tended not to extend to casual and seasonal workers – the roles most commonly filled by women (Dwasi 1999). Much has changed following an ILO-sponsored project aimed, among other things, at harmonising labour laws in the East African Community. A new framework was introduced in late 2007 and represents a significant improvement for workers, especially women.[44]

A casual employee is defined as a person 'the terms of whose engagement provide for his payment at the end of each day and who is not engaged for a longer period than twenty-four hours at a time' (Section 2, Employment Act 2007). Section 37 now provides for the conversion of casual employment if continuous for one month or an aggregated period of three months into a contract of service for which the employee is entitled to 28 days period of notice of termination in writing (Section 35 (1) (c)). If, after conversion, the person is employed for two months he/she is entitled to the same rights as someone initially employed on a contract of service (Section 37 (3)).

Such an 'employee'[45] is now entitled to expect a number of minimum conditions of employment, including rights to pay, sick and annual leave, safe working environments and so on.[46] There is a new duty for the state, labour court and employers to promote equality of opportunities (including specifically for migrant workers) and for employers to strive to eliminate discrimination in employment policy and practice and to pay equal remuneration for work of equal value (Section 5 (1) (a) (b), (2) and (5) Employment Act 2007).[47] There is a specific requirement not to discriminate or harass employees or potential employees on grounds of sex, and sexual harassment is specifically recognised and defined (Sections 5 and 6). Women employees with a contract of service are entitled to three months' paid maternity leave and job security, and men to two weeks' paid paternity leave (Sections 5(3)(a) and 29).

If fully implemented, these new provisions could improve the formal rights of casual workers and offer improved work-related benefits to women workers covered by their provisions. However, gaps remain. Employers are entitled to dismiss an employee summarily for fundamental breach of obligations (Section 44)[48] and the Act offers considerable scope for interpretation based upon cultural considerations. Researchers found that many women fear pregnancy because they risk losing their jobs despite legal entitlement (Barrientos et al. 2001). No minimum wage is set in the new framework. Instead, the Kenyan

Minister for Labour continues to be authorised to set wage guidelines for employers, but does not fix standards for these guidelines.[49] Consequently the level is very low, often ignored.[50]

Furthermore, these reforms do not tackle the broader normative context, in which women hold the primary responsibility for family food provisioning and care, with minimal state welfare support, and in which they are denied equal access to training, to management roles, and to representation on workplace bodies and within trade unions (Barrientos et al. 2001). Women contribute up to 80 per cent of the labour involved in household and reproductive activities and agricultural production. They work longer hours than men. They have poorer health and nutritional status and high levels of maternal mortality. Although women are the main agricultural producers, they rarely participate in the decisions which affect production.

## Towards gender justice?

Markets separate productive and valued activity from the unvalued and reproductive, thereby marginalising many women both within the market and more widely in society. Those women who are able to access global markets do so from a position of weakness, located within higher risk and more vulnerable activities, either as workers or as marginal suppliers of goods. Those who continue to pursue a livelihood in local markets must contend with the shadows of global markets, often finding themselves disadvantaged by changes associated with market development.

How can women ensure that global trading no longer builds on, nor further builds, gender injustices? Much depends on the extent to which gender roles and responsibilities within the family and society are valued in the national and international regulation of markets. In this section we explore two very different governance contexts in which women's claims for recognition of their labour might be heard.

### Human rights discourse

Many regard human rights as empowering women to counter the liberal economic emphasis on flexibility of labour and productivity of land (see Ikdahl et al. 2005). At an international level, women's rights discourse has successfully worked within the international human rights framework and beyond to highlight some forms of gender-based injustices, particularly on matters concerning violence against women. However, it has yet to challenge the dominant discourse associated with the regulation of multilateral trade. How might this be done?

The discourses of human rights and of trade have developed in parallel. Attempts to draw them together have tended to be unsuccessful. For example, attempts to introduce a human rights discourse within the World Trade Organization framework have largely failed.[51] The inclusion of a 'social clause' requiring all members to enforce minimum labour standards was opposed by the majority of states, particularly in the developing world, and business lobbies (Braithwaite and Drahos 2000: 235).[52] An alternative would be to develop what Harrison (2007) describes as a 'compliance and co-operation' approach,[53] which calls for the introduction of a system for auditing the impact of the trading system on gender and human rights. Where negative effects were identified, states would have clear grounds on which to introduce redistributional policies to counter them. However, such an approach would require the development and acceptance, at both international and state levels, of a robust feminist development law analysis – one which remoulds present understandings of rights to ensure that they encompass issues relating to care. There are few signs of this as yet.

The first challenge is to develop a rights framework which fully incorporates social and economic issues. Martha Nussbaum has attempted to do this through her 'capabilities approach', which has met with considerable support within development studies. She proposes a list of human functional capabilities which she considers to be of central importance in human life[54] and asks whether a woman is capable of doing them, and what resources are necessary to enable her to do so (Nussbaum 1999: 233).[55] She distinguishes her approach from general human rights discourse on the grounds that she focuses not only on rights, but also on the need for resources to substantiate them.[56] The developing 'jurisprudence' associated with the Convention on the Elimination of All Forms of Discrimination Against Women (1979; hereinafter CEDAW) offers ways of ensuring that women's roles are factored into policy development and implementation that are in some respects similar to the capabilities approach. For example, recognising the interactions between productive and reproductive issues, it addresses concepts such as 'indirect discrimination' and 'substantive equality'. The CEDAW Committee of 2007 used these concepts to critique Kenya sharply for the lack of data on women's employment, the weaknesses of its (pre-reform) labour laws and inadequacies in family and land laws (CEDAW Committee, 2007).

### Purchasing social justice?

If public rights strategies have limitations, do consumer-based movements offer more? As we have seen, retailers profit

> from the system of social reproduction which organises both the daily reproduction of the labour force (i.e. the processes which ensure that workers replenish their labour power between the end of one working period (day) and the next), and the generational reproduction of the labour force (i.e. the ongoing production and nurturing of working people who over time grow and develop into workers who supply labour power to the corporation).
>
> (Pearson 2007: 745)

In other words, the value of poor women's unpaid and paid labour is redistributed to rich shareholders and consumers.[57] Marketing associated with agribusiness value chains ensures that some African women (and men) working in agriculture are now far more transparently linked with Northern consumers.[58] 'Social labelling' initiatives which link development-focused activism with consumer interests have revealed to consumers and shareholders the inequalities between retailers and producers which lead to economic injustices for both workers and small-scale farmers (see the websites of Oxfam Trade Justice and Women Working Worldwide). Two types of initiative have emerged which seek to encourage retailers and consumers to value the workers and suppliers of the developing world: fair trade, which tends to impact on women working as small farmers, and ethical trading, which relates primarily to women working as employees.[59]

## Ethical trading

Ethical-trading initiatives, as expressed through codes of conduct, have emerged in three forms. First, there are independent social codes, in particular the US-based SA 8000 and the UK-based Ethical Trading International Base Code, which resulted from harmonisation of individual codes (see SA8000 and UK ETI Base Code websites). Second, there are individual company codes (see EUREPGAP Website). Finally, there are sectoral codes (Barrientos et al. 2001).

Retailers have no direct employment relationship with the workers in Kenya and are not legally responsible for the implementation of the labour rights to which these workers may be entitled. Instead they require their chain partners to adopt codes of conduct. For example, leading UK retailers such as Tesco use codes based on the Ethical Trading Initiative (ETI) Base Code, which is based upon core labour standards set out in UN and ILO conventions.[60] Their codes are not focussed specifically on issues relating to gender and, like Kenyan state law, are weaker on those employment-related issues which are of particular interest to women.[61] They are also of limited use in tackling the broader socio-economic circumstances that affect women workers (social norms and practice, education, domestic responsibilities and gender relations), especially when, as in Kenya, the national legislation with which they interact has hitherto been weak (Barrientos et al. 2001, 2003 and 2007).

These initiatives are incorporated into the governance of mainstream value chains. They are not directed towards changing the wider trading and production relations which underpin the chains. Nor do they address the imperatives imposed by the hugely price-competitive UK food market, which lead retailers to adopt 'just in time' delivery procedures. So they fail to incentivise employers to adopt progressive labour relations.

The self-regulatory nature of ethical trading initiatives has been the subject of considerable criticism for being discretionary, unenforceable and specific rather than universal.[62] Codes may reflect rights discourse, but they create private rights, unenforceable through state law. However, it is important to recognise that the process by which some codes are developed triggers public debate about issues which specifically affect women, such as maternity rights and protection from abuse in the workplace. And where codes are fully implemented, they may ensure that some women (and men) have access to minimum international labour rights. But the codes do little to redistribute value towards women within these chains (see Luce 2005, Kabeer 2004).

It is also significant that these codes fail to reach those most in need. In economies with tiny formal sectors which offer few other opportunities for paid work, agribusiness is often the best sector for women to work in. This group of women workers have become visible to international activists and to some Northern consumers because they are clearly linked to the global market via the governance of supply chains. Women who eke out an existence in the informal unregulated sector, or struggle along as small farmers, are equally tied to the global market, but they are less visible. It is much less evident how private consumer-instigated 'rights' might be extended to them.

### Fair trade

Fair-trade schemes have a longer history than ethical trading. They are rooted in charitable and development movements, and seek to ensure better trading conditions for small producers of food products. As such they are more explicitly focused on changing the relations of production than on ensuring minimum employment rights.[63] Such schemes are based not on supply chains, but on the principle of trading partnerships 'based upon dialogue, transparency and respect'. They seek greater equity in international trade, particularly for marginalized producers and workers in the global South (Barrientos and Tallontire 2006: 6). They involve direct purchase from small producers; guaranteed minimum prices which are never below market price; price premiums for social investment; credit allowances; and long term relationships with producers.[64]

One possible way forward for those seeking to improve the position of women in international trade would be to use the concepts associated with the fair-trade movement to 're-regulate' global value chains. The aim would be to exert more control over supermarket retailers and to persuade them to redistribute value within the chain, thereby associating fairness with a very modest amount of economic redistribution.[65] Such an initiative may offer women small farmers greater opportunities to meet the exacting standards of the global market and receive slightly more of the value of their labour. If the farmers were able to negotiate a price premium for social investment then this could be distributed in a way which recognises the value of social reproduction, for instance through support for childcare, improved local healthcare and access to water. However, much would depend upon the extent to which such initiatives stimulated changes in prevailing social norms.

Much bolder measures on an international level are needed to achieve any degree of economic redistribution which would start to recognise the overall value of women's work. One such measure would be what Pearson has called a 'Maria' tax, which is based on Tobin's proposal to tax foreign-currency trading to pay for development activities (2003).[66] While Tobin's tax is not targeted, a Maria tax would be directed at the promotion of gender equality and could be a local hypothecated tax to provide services which complement the productive role of women – transport systems, childcare, education and training, and health services (Pearson 2007: 746). Kabeer (2004) argues in a similar vein for a universal citizen benefit, which would provide a floor for everyone funded by some redistribution (by citizens of the global North) of the value created by global trade.

In a global economy that is becoming increasingly interdependent and increasingly unequal, a struggle for some degree of redistribution from North to South, from rich to poor, from capital to labour, and from more to less privileged forms of labour, is the only basis on which claims to international solidarity on workers' rights can have any moral force. Such redistribution, moreover, has to be a matter of right rather than gift, welfare, charity or 'aid' (Kabeer 2004: 30).

## Conclusion

There is little evidence that agricultural liberalisation and global value chains have led to rising returns for local producers generally or for the wider economies in which they operate (Kaplinsky 2000: 4–6).[67] Increased access to global markets may provide opportunities for women in the developing world to gain access to greater resources. But the pressures of buyer-driven value chains, coupled with underlying social norms and inadequate national regulation, ensure that it often does little to tackle their fundamental inequality.

To tackle gender injustices we need to move from individual ethical actions and rights campaigns to tackling the trade value system. Robust human-rights-based gender audits of the impact of trade may start to reveal the true cost of global trade. Could these provide the basis for campaigns for a universal citizen's social benefit – a social rather than economic minimum wage – funded by our consumption?

## Notes

* I would like to thank Amanda Perry-Kessaris for her very helpful comments and editorial contribution to drafts of this chapter.
1 'Asset value' refers to the values obtained by renting and/or eventually selling the land. 'Use value' refers to the value of produce from the land.
2 Following figures extracted from Ministry of Lands and Housing 2005.
3 The 2008 World Development Report on Agriculture for Development argues for a greater emphasis on gearing up smallholder farming in Africa in particular (World Bank 2008).
4 The Lomé Conventions (I to IV) ensured that European countries maintained their supply of raw materials and privileged position with established markets in former British, Dutch, Belgian and French colonies, collectively known as the African,

Caribbean and Pacific Countries (ACP). Most agricultural and mineral exports were free of duty and there was preferential access to some products based upon a quota system. In addition the European Community (now European Union) offered aid and investment.

5 The Cotonou process is based on the principles of differentiation and regionalisation and removes any preference based upon the existing ACP grouping. Instead countries are encouraged to create and negotiate EPAs as regional trading blocs. Kenya is a member of the East African Community. The position is complicated by the exemption of ACP countries which are defined by the United Nations as Least Developed Countries, which have preferential trading relations with the EU.

6 For a critique of the Interim EPA and the impact of the recent political instability see Ong'wen (2008).

7 It 'describes the full range of activities which are required to bring a product or service from conception, through the intermediary phases of production (involving a combination of physical transformation and the input of various producer services), delivery to final consumers, and final disposal after use' (Kaplinsky 2000: 8).

8 Tesco, Sainsbury's, ASDA and Safeway account for nearly 75 per cent of all food sales in the UK including the sale of fresh vegetables. Marks and Spencer and Waitrose, which brand themselves based on the quality of their food, also purchase fresh fruit and vegetables and flowers from Kenya and Africa generally.

9 While Kenya has a large number of flower firms, about 5,000, just 24 large and medium-scale flower operations supply 75 per cent of total exports (Barrientos et al. 2001:7).

10 Some of these products are retailed at the top end of the price range where there is still fierce competition for customers between the retailers.

11 Exporters and importers will also include in their costs an element to cover losses in transit.

12 For an unskilled employee in Kenyan agriculture this was KSh1,642 per month or KSh68.90 per day, less than US$ 1 per day (1 May 2002 – 31 April 2003).

13 It is estimated that the women's workload increased from 60 hours a week in the 1960s and 1970s to 96 hours a week in 1980, and to 103 hours a week in 1993 (Dwasi 1999).

14 Other women have migrated from their villages and have left children behind to be cared for by grandparents because they could not afford to keep them with them.

15 Feminists have repeatedly demonstrated that this strict division between production, associated with the public sphere, and reproduction, associated with the private sphere, is damaging and ill-conceived (O'Donovan 1985; Barnett 1998: Chapter 6; Rittich 2002; Elson and Cagatay 2000). The public world of work is dependent on the provision of social reproduction, and a society must nurture its population if it is to function. So feminists have argued that, if further injustices are to be avoided, the labour involved in social reproduction must be counted as work, and be included in economic evaluations. See Hoskyns and Rai (2007) for a detailed discussion of this point. They argue that to value unpaid work, economists will need to develop new ways of measuring value because adding unpaid work on to existing categories would be inadequate.

16 The activities associated with sustaining life and social relationships – including family and social provisioning undertaken through subsistence farming, such as collecting water and cooking fuel, bearing children, caring for the young, old and sick and maintaining social rituals – are characterised in feminist analysis as 'social reproduction'.

17 See also World Bank (2003b and 2007) for more detail on women's economic position in Kenya.

18  This mirrors the picture across sub-Saharan Africa, where most small-scale farmers
are women, producing as much as 80 per cent of basic foods:

> ... food crops produced for household consumption or for the local market, such
> as vegetables and tubers, generally tend to be cultivated and marketed by
> women, while commercial or industrial crops, cultivated on a much larger scale
> either for direct export or for further processing (e.g. cotton and sugar), are more
> frequently the economic domain of men (Garcia 2004: 78)

19  For an excellent account of the effect of agricultural liberalisation policies on gender
relations in rural areas see UNRISD (2005: Chapter 6).
20  Informal economy is defined as: economic activity and enterprises that are not
registered, not regulated and do not pay taxes (UNRISD 2005: 76). Generally
informal employment comprises 72 per cent of non-agricultural employment in sub-
Saharan Africa, 84 per cent for women, 63 per cent for men. In Kenya, the figures
are women 83 per cent and men 48 per cent. 42 per cent of this informal working in
Kenya is self-employment in the non-agricultural sector; 58 per cent is wage
employment. Men constitute the majority (56 per cent) in the first, and women 67
per cent in the latter waged category (UNRISD 2005: 76–78). The number of
women working for wages outside the agricultural sector has risen significantly in
Kenya in particular in recent years to about 38 per cent of the total in 2002
(UNRISD 2005: 53).
21  There are at present approximately 75 legislative acts relating to land. See Benschop
(2002: Chapter 5) for detailed discussion of gender issues relating to land.
22  Government-owned land (in theory, due to colonialism, all land) is governed by the
Government Lands Act (1915), which grants powers to the President to make grants
or dispositions of any estates, interests or rights in or over un-alienated government
lands. Much government land has been converted to private ownership in recent
years. The Trust Lands Act (1939) recognises group rights in areas occupied in the
colonial period by native peoples. Such trust land, which is not registered under the
Registered Land Act (1963), makes up 63 per cent of the total land area. However,
this land is also increasingly being transferred into private or state ownership.
23  There are three distinct categories of land rights holding: government (public) land;
trust land which comprised the former native reserves; and private land derived from
grants to individuals of government land and by the process of adjudication and
consolidation in the native reserves (Ministry of Lands and Housing 2005).
24  The Registered Land Act (1963) applies to land formerly held under customary law
(native reserves and trust land) and the Transfer of Property Act (1882) applies to land
in settler-occupied and formerly settler-occupied areas.
25  Sale of agricultural land registered under the Act is regulated by the Land Control
Act (1967) and use is regulated by the Agriculture Act (1955). Any sale is subject to
the consent of the local land control board, which is supposed to prevent undue
fragmentation of land and to protect the interests of wives and mature children by
obtaining their consent. The boards however perform badly (Ikdahl 2005: 93).
26  In earlier versions, this case constructed land as very much part of the public domain
of production, but this position was later modified somewhat to take account of
women's role in producing the food which is crucial to the survival of the family
(Ikdahl et al. 2005, World Bank 2008).
27  Nyamu-Musembi (2006) offers a strong critique of its replacement for slum dwellers,
based on the work of De Soto (2000).
28  See Whitehead and Tsikata (2003) for a comprehensive discussion of these points in
relation to sub-Saharan Africa.

29  Although small farmers do make use of informal credit arrangements (see Nyumu-Musembi 2006).

30  This dichotomy between public and private has been reproduced in the tendency of state-based land tenure reform initiatives to treat separately those 'private' issues relating to marital property ownership and inheritance rights which involve customary laws and are constructed as family law. For an account of the land law reform process in Uganda where this dichotomy played a key part see Matembe (2002) and Tripp (2002).

31  It is possible to register joint ownership up to a maximum of five people. However the incidence of joint registration is very low, and tiny in the case of spouses. The Act does allow rights of occupation, derived from customary law, to be noted on the register but 'many families did not bother to do [this] for they saw no possibility of a piece of paper vesting any more rights in the family representative than he would have had at custom' (Ikdahl et al. 2003: 91).

32  Section 30 lists the rights which are capable of overriding the rights of an absolute proprietor. Customary rights are excluded. Such rights are not capable therefore of qualifying the absolute proprietor's rights unless they are recorded on the register against his/her name. The separation between customary and state law has been confirmed in case law in *Obiero v. Opiyo* (1972) and *Esiroyo v. Esiroyo* (1973), although there have also been some conflicting judgments. See *Muguthu v. Muguthu* (1968) and *Gatimu Kingara v. Muya Gathangari* (1976). However, the very recent case of *Kiarie v. Wanjku* (2007) suggests that the courts may be more willing to recognise customary interests in registered land. The High Court considered it would be unconscionable and contrary to fundamental rights to life to remove two daughters from registered land which had been transferred absolutely to a second wife. It held that the daughters had a legitimate expectation that as children they would have beneficial interests over family land.

33  The Kenyan Court of Appeal so ruled in 1988, upholding the interests of a financial institution holding a mortgage over the land in question: *Wangari Wanjohi v. Continental Credit Finance Ltd* (1989) at 42 (Nyamu-Musembi 2006: 21).

34  Marital property is regulated by the English Married Women's Property Act of 1882 in the absence of a Kenyan statute. The Act was extended in *Karanja v. Karanja* (1976) to cover parties married under customary law.

35  The courts have followed the common-law system of recognising beneficial interests and have considered and recognised non-monetary contributions by housewives to the acquisition of matrimonial property (Ikdahl 2003: 87–88).

36  In *Rono v Rono* (2002) the High Court used concepts of non-discrimination to award equal shares to daughters of a polygamous man who died intestate. These concepts fell within the Convention on the Elimination of All Forms of Discrimination Against Women (CEDAW) (1979), which Kenya has ratified but not incorporated in domestic legislation. However, the precise relationship between formal laws relating to marriage, family property and succession and customary laws in this area is uncertain (World Bank 2007: Chapter 3 and UN CEDAW 2006).

37  See Hunt (2005) for a succinct and insightful discussion of such an approach in relation to Kenya.

38  The discussion often revolves around the place of customary law within a 'modern' state: for instance, the extent to which customary laws are recognised and protected from commitments to equality in a bill of rights, as in South Africa. In Tanzania, custom-based land law systems must now take account of state-based commitments to gender equality. See Ikdahl et al. (2005) for discussion of the position in five sub-Saharan states.

39  The present Constitution (as revised in 2001) contains general provisions ensuring equality before the law and non-discrimination on grounds of sex (Articles 70 and 82

(2)) but Article 82 (4–6) exempts customary and personal law matters particularly relating to marriage, divorce and inheritance. Agricultural land is also exempted. Articles 90 and 91 discriminate directly: women cannot bequeath citizenship.

40 The following discussion relies on the research findings of Stephanie Barrientos, Catherine Dolan and Anne Tallontire, who undertook a one-year research project into gender and ethical trade in South Africa, Kenya and Zambia. It was funded by the UK Department of International Development (Barrientos et al. 2001 and 2003).

41 As we shall see, the regulation of casual and temporary work has recently changed. However, until 2008 casual and temporary workers were legally required to be promoted to permanent status after eight months, but they were often found returning year after year on renewed temporary contracts (Barrientos et al. 2001: 8).

42 The ILO categorises 'work' as: unpaid contributing family members (e.g. working on a family-owned farm); own-account working (e.g. cultivating a plot and selling the produce) and paid employment. In sub-Saharan Africa generally, four in 10 working women are contributing family workers, compared with two in 10 men. 'Female contributing family workers are not likely to be economically independent' (ILO 2007: 1–2). While own-account working can assist women to combine work and family responsibilities, it is associated with low incomes and poverty (World Bank 2008).

43 A move out of agricultural employment is also regarded as progress. The UN Millennium Development Goal 3, 'Promote gender equality and empower women', uses the share of women in wage employment in the non-agricultural sector as an indicator of progress (ILO 2007: 10).

44 The Employment Act (2007); Labour Relations Act (2007); Occupational Safety and Health Act (2007); Work Injury Benefits Act (2007); Labour Institutions Act (2007) replaced a range of outdated legislation.

45 A contract of service is an agreement, whether oral or in writing, and whether expressed or implied, to employ or to serve as an employee for a period of time (Section 2, Employment Act 2007).

46 The Employment Act 2007 provides that all workers with a contract of service of three months or more must have a written contract stating the particulars of employment (Section 9). Minimum conditions of employment include one day off in seven (Section 27), reasonable housing accommodation or a housing allowance (Section 31), access to drinking water (Section 32) and medicines (Section 33); after two months of employment, seven days' full-pay and seven days' half-pay sick leave per year (Section 30); after 12 months' service, 21 days of annual leave (Section 28). The worker is entitled to a healthy and safe working environment (Occupational Safety and Health Act 2007) and rights to form and belong to a trade union and to collective bargaining (Labour Relations Act 2007).

47 The employer bears the burden of proving that discrimination did not take place.

48 Section 44 provides a non-exhaustive list of acts which may constitute such conduct. Furthermore, the Pensions Act allows the government to dismiss its employees at any time and without compensation and section 8 permits dismissal 'in the public interest' (Sections 5 and 8, Pensions Act).

49 The Minister recommends guidelines for different salaries for different types of trade and geographical areas (Dwasi 1999: 365).

50 The Federation of Kenya Employers has expressed anxiety over the cost of the measures, particularly those relating to longer maternity leave, and consider they could be 'endangering employment opportunities for female employees' (Ikimani 2007).

51 There is a 'glimmer' of a social clause in the North American Free Trade Agreement 1992 (Braithwaite and Drahos 2000: 236). Furthermore, Section 301 of the United States Trade Act 1974 permits trade sanctions against states that fail to observe workers' rights. This was used rarely and selectively (Steiner and Alston 2000: 1360).

52 The US, France, Norway and the International Trade Union Movement wanted freedom of association and right to collective bargaining; elimination of forced labour; abolition of child labour and elimination of discrimination in the workplace.

53 See Harrison's detailed discussion (2007) of the way in which these two systems have developed and the ways in which human rights can be deployed within the World Trade Organization.

54 These would include (a) bodily health: being able to have good health, including reproductive health; to be adequately nourished; to have adequate shelter; (b) bodily integrity: being able to move freely from place to place; to be secure against violent assault, including sexual assault and domestic violence; and (c) control over one's environment: being able to hold property, having the right to seek employment on an equal basis with others (Nussbaum 1999: 235).

55 For discussion of the contribution of entitlements approaches see Nussbaum (2000, 2003), Stewart (2004) and Elson (2003), who applies the approach specifically to economic issues relating to women.

56 'Analysing economic and material rights in terms of capabilities thus enables us to set forth clearly a rationale we have for spending unequal amounts of money on the disadvantaged … to assist their transition to full capability' (Nussbaum 1999: 241).

57 See Fagan (2006) for a discussion of ethical shopping.

58 A picture of a named woman, smiling and looking healthy, appears above a rack of grapefruit (each with a sticker announcing it as 'foundation' fruit) in a leading UK supermarket. A supermarket which markets itself as part of the Ethical Trading Initiative sells a pack of prepared and packaged beans bearing a label which states that it is a product of Kenya. The beans or grapefruit might additionally or alternatively be labelled as 'fair-trade'.

59 There is a growing literature on issues of corporate social responsibility and its relationship to human rights discourse. See for instance Dine (2005) and Dine and Fagan (2006). For a more detailed discussion of ethical sourcing see Barrientos and Dolan (2006) which contains an excellent glossary of fair-trade and ethical-trade organisations with short descriptions of the content of specific codes and labelling initiatives.

60 The ETI Base Code has nine clauses primarily directed towards 'process' rights (no use of forced or child labour; no harsh or inhuman conditions; freedom of association and the right to collective bargaining; no discrimination) and 'outcome' rights (safe and hygienic working conditions; living wages; no excessive work hours; regular employment and written work contracts) (see ETI Base Code Website). For discussion by Tesco's Executive Director for Corporate and Legal Affairs on the ETI Base Code see Tesco (2007).

61 The codes do not cover maternity or paternity leave, protection for pregnant women or childcare.

62 See Arthurs (2002) and Muchlinski (2007) for a wider discussion of this from both labour and corporate law perspectives.

63 See Tallontire (2006) for more discussion of developments within the fair-trade movement.

64 Divine Chocolate offers an example of the development and achievements of a fair-trade initiative (see Divine Chocolate website), as does Oxfam's coffee campaign (see Campher 2006). For Fairtrade conditions of certification see Fairtrade website.

65 A recent example of this approach is provided by Traidcraft, one of the pioneers of the UK fair-trade movement, in its report on the sourcing of fresh vegetables from developing countries and from Kenya in particular. It argues inter alia for a shared allocation of risk, which is specified in contracts; shared market information and two-way communications; and loyalty to good suppliers and a recognition of the role of smallholder farmers (Traidcraft 2007).

66 'Such a tax, even if it were set as low as a fraction of one per cent, would raise between 50 and 100 billion dollars a year' and effectively double current aid budgets (Pearson 2003: 31).

67 'The process is described as *"immiserising growth"* where there is increasing economic activity (more output and more employment) but falling economic returns' (Kaplinksy 2000: 7; italics in original).

# References

(AOA) Agreement on Agriculture (1994) Annex 1A of the Agreement Establishing the World Trade Organization, Marrakesh, 15 April 1994. Online: <http://www.wto.org/english/docs_e/legal_e/14-ag.pdf>

Agriculture Act (1955) Chapter 318 of the Laws of Kenya. Online: <http://www.kenyalaw.org/kenyalaw/klr_home>

Arthurs, H. (2002) 'Private Ordering and Workers' Rights in the Global Economy: corporate codes of conduct as a regime of labour market regulation', in Conaghan, Fischl and Klare (eds) *Labour Law in an Era of Globalisation*, Oxford: Oxford University Press.

Barnett, H. (1998) *Introduction to Feminist Jurisprudence*, London: Cavendish Publishing.

Barrientos, S., Dolan, C. and Tallontire, A. (2001) 'Gender and Ethical Trade – A Mapping of the Issues in African Horticulture'. Online: <http://www.nri.org/NRET/genderet.pdf>

——(2003) 'A gendered value chain approach to codes of conduct in African horticulture', *World Development Report*, 13(9): 1511–26.

Barrientos, S. and Dolan, C. (eds) (2006) *Ethical Sourcing in the Global Food System*, London: Earthscan.

Barrientos, S. and Smith, S. (2007) 'Do workers benefit from ethical trade? Assessing codes of labour practices in global production systems', *Third World Quarterly*, 28(4): 713–29.

Braithwaite, J. and Drahos, P. (2000) *Global Business Regulation*, Cambridge: Cambridge University Press.

Campher, H. (2006) 'Oxfam's coffee campaign: an NGO perspective', Barrientos, S. and Dolan, C. (eds) (2006) *Ethical Sourcing in the Global Food System*, London: Earthscan.

(CEDAW Committee) United Nations Committee on the Elimination of All Forms of Discrimination Against Women (2006) *Consideration of Combined 5th and 6th Reports of States Parties Kenya* UN CEDAW/C/Ken/CO/6. Online: <http://www.un.org/womenwatch/daw/cedaw/reports.htm>

Central Bureau of Statistics (2002) *Population Census Report 1999*, Nairobi: Government of Kenya.

Convention on the Elimination of All Forms of Discrimination Against Women (CEDAW) (1979). Online: <http://www.un.org/womenwatch/daw/cedaw/text/econvention.htm>

Dine, J. (2005) *Companies, International Trade and Human Rights*, Cambridge: Cambridge University Press.

Dine, J. and Fagan, A. (eds) (2006) *Human Rights and Capitalism*, Cheltenham: Edward Elgar.

Dolan, C., Humphrey, J. and Harris-Pascal, C. (1999) *Horticulture Commodity Chains: the impact on the UK market of the African fresh vegetable industry*, IDS Working Papers 96, Sussex: Institute of Development Studies.

Dwasi, J. (1999) 'A study in international labor standards and their effect on working women in developing countries: the case for integration of enforcement issues in the World Bank's policies', *Wisconsin International Law Journal*, 17: 347.

Elson, D. (2003) 'Gender justice, human rights and neo liberal economic policies', in M. Molyneux and S. Razavi (eds) *Gender Justice, Development and Rights*, Oxford: Oxford University Press.

Elson, D. and Catagay, N. (2000) 'The Social Content of Macroeconomic Policies', *World Development*, 28: 7. Online: <http://ssrn.com/abstract=252984>

Employment Act (2007) Act 11 of 2007. Online: <http://www.kenyalaw.org/kenyalaw/klr_home>

*Esiroyo v. Esiroyo* (1973) East African Law Reports 388.

European Union Directorate General of Trade (2007) *Update : Economic Partnership Agreements*, 19 December. Online: <http://trade.ec.europa.eu/doclib/docs/2007/november/tradoc_136959.pdf>

——(2008) *Interim Economic Partnership Agreements: Questions and Answers*, 27 March. Online: <http://trade.ec.europa.eu/doclib/docs/2008/march/tradoc_138457.pdf>

Exporting Processing Zone Authority (EPZA) (2005) *Horticulture Industry in Kenya 2005*, Nairobi: EPZA. Online: <http://www.epzakenya.com/UserFiles/File/Horticulture.pdf>

Fagan, A. (2006) 'Buying right: consuming ethically and human rights', in Dine, J. and Fagan, A. (eds) *Human Rights and Capitalism*, Cheltenham: Edward Elgar, 115–41.

Garcia, Z. (2004) 'Agriculture, trade and gender', in A. N. Tran-Nguyen and A. Beviglia Zampetti (eds) *Trade and Gender: opportunities and challenges for developing countries*, UN Inter Agency Network on Women and Gender Equality Task Force on Gender and Trade, UNCTAD, New York and Geneva: United Nations.

*Gatimu Kingara v. Muya Gathangari* (1976) Kenya Law Report 265.

Gerreffi, G. and Korzeniewicz, M. (eds) (1994) *Commodity Chains and Global Capitalism*, Westport CT: Praegar.

Gerreffi, G., Humphrey, J. and Sturgeon, T. (2005) 'The governance of global value chains', *Review of International Political Economy* 12(1): 78–104.

Government Lands Act (1915) Chapter 280 of the Laws of Kenya.

Harrison, J. (2007) *The Human Rights Impact of the World Trade Organisation*, Oxford and Portland: Hart Publishing.

Hassim, S. and Razavi, S. (2006) 'Gender and social policy in a global context: uncovering the gendered structure of "the Social"', in S. Hassim and S. Razavi (eds) *Gender and Social Policy in a Global Context: uncovering the gendered structure of "the Social"*, Basingstoke: Palgrave.

Hoskyns, C. and Rai, S. M. (2007) 'Recasting the global political economy: counting women's unpaid work', *New Political Economy*, 12(3): 297–317.

Human Rights Watch (2003) *Double Standards: women's property rights violations in Kenya*, New York: Human Rights Watch. Online: <http://www.hrw.org/reports/2003/kenya0303>

Hunt, D. (2005) 'Some outstanding issues in the debate on external promotion of land privatisation', *Development Policy Review*, 23(2): 199–231.

*I v. I* (1971) East African Law Reports 278.

Ikdahl, I. et al. (2005) *Human Rights, Formalisation and Women's Land Rights in Southern and Eastern Africa*, Studies in Women's Law No. 57, Institute of Women's Law, University of Oslo.

International Labour Office (2007) *Global Employment Trends for Women Brief*, March, Geneva: ILO.

Kabeer, N. (2004) 'Globalisation, labor standards, and women's rights: dilemma of collective (in)action in an interdependent world', *Feminist Economics*, 10(1): 3–35.

Kaplinsky R. (2000) 'Spreading the gains from globalisation: what can be learned from value chain analysis', *IDS Working Paper 110*, Falmer: Institute of Development Studies.

*Karanja v. Karanja* (1976) Kenya Law Review 307.

Kenya Land Alliance (2004) *The National Land Policy in Kenya: critical gender issues and policy statements*, Nairobi: Kenya Land Alliance Issues Paper no. 1.

*Kiarie v. Wanjku* (2007) [Application 8 *John Kinyanjui Kiarie v. Grace Wanjiku Kimani (Nelson Kaburu)* in Chief Magistrates Court of Milimani, February 2006]

Labour Institutions Act (2007) Act 12 of 2007. Online: <http://www.kenyalaw.org/kenyalaw/klr_home>

Labour Relations Act (2007) Act 14 of 2007. Online: <http://www.kenyalaw.org/kenyalaw/klr_home>

Land Control Act (1967) Chapter 302 of the Laws of Kenya. Online: <http://www.kenyalaw.org>

(Lomé I) ACP-EEC Convention of Lomé (1975). Signed at Lomé on 28 February 1975. I.L.M. 14:595. Online: <http://www.acp.int/en/conventions/lome1.htm>

(Lomé II) Second ACP-EEC Convention of Lomé (1975). Signed at Lomé on 28 February 1975. I.L.M. 19:327. Online: <http://www.acp.int/en/conventions/lome2_f.htm>

(Lomé III) Third ACP-EEC Convention of Lomé (1984). Signed at Lomé on 8 December 1984. I.L.M. 24:571. Online: <http://www.acp.int/en/conventions/lome3e.htm>

(Lomé IV) Fourth ACP-EEC Convention of Lomé (1989). Signed at Lomé on 15 December 1989. I.L.M. 29:783. Online: <http://www.acp.int/en/conventions/lome4_e.htm>

Luce, S. (2005) 'The case for international labour standards: a "Northern" perspective', *IDS Working Paper 20*, Falmer: Institute of Development Studies.

Matembe, M. (2002) *Gender, Politics and Constitution Making in Uganda*, Kampala: Fountain Publishers.

McAuslan, P. (1998) 'Making law work: restructuring law relations in Africa', *Development and Change*, 29(3): 525–52.

——(2003) *Bringing the Law Back In: essays in land, law and development*, Basingstoke: Ashgate.

Molyneux M. and Razavi, S. (eds) (2002) *Gender Justice, Development and Rights*, Oxford: Oxford University Press. Muchlinksi, P. (2007) *Multinational Enterprises and the Law*, Oxford: The Oxford International Law Library.

*Muguthu v. Muguthu* (1968) HC Civil Case Number 377. Unreported.

National Land Alliance (2004) The National Land Policy in Kenya: Addressing Historical Injustices.

National Land Policy Secretariat (2007) Draft National Land Policy April Nairobi: Kenyan National Land Policy Secretariat.

Nussbaum, M. (1999) 'Women and equality: the capabilities approach', *International Labour Review*, 138(3): 227–45.

——(2003) 'Capabilities as fundamental entitlements: Sen and social justice', *Feminist Economics*, 9: 33–59.

——(2000) *Women's Capabilities and Social Justice*, Mimeo, Geneva: UNRISD.

Nyamu-Musembi, C. (2006) 'Breathing life into dead theories about property rights: de Soto and land relations in rural Africa', Brighton: Institute of Development Studies, Working Paper 272.

*Obiero v. Opiyo* (1972) East African Law Reports 227.

Occupational Safety and Health Act (2007). Act 15 of 2007. Online: < http://www.kenyalaw.org/kenyalaw/klr_home>

O'Donovan, K. (1985) *Sexual Divisions in Law*, London: Weidenfeld and Nicolson.

Ong'wen, O. (2008) 'Understanding Kenya: post election crisis, land and the Interim EPA', *Trade Negotiations Insights International Centre for Trade and Sustainable Development*, 7(5): 9–10. Online: <http://ictsd.net/downloads/tni/tni_en_7-5.pdf>

Pearson, R. (2003) 'Feminist responses to economic globalisation: some examples of past and future practice', *Gender and Development*, 11(1): 25–34.

——(2007) 'Beyond women workers: gendering CSR', *Third World Quarterly*, 28(4): 731–49.

Pensions Act, Chapter 189 of the Laws of Kenya. Online: <http://www.kenyalaw.org/kenyalaw/klr_app>

Razavi, S. (2003) 'Introduction: agrarian change, gender and land rights', *Journal of Agrarian Change*, 3(1–2), January and April: 2–32.

Registered Land Act (1963). Chapter 300 of the Laws of Kenya. Online: <http://www.kenyalaw.org>

Rittich, K. (2002) 'Feminization and contingency: regulating the stakes of work for women', in J. Conaghan, M. Fischl and K. Klare (eds) *Labour Law in an Era of Globalization*, Oxford: Oxford University Press, 117–36.

*(Rono v. Rono) Mary Rono v. Jane Rono and William Rono* (2002). Civil Appeal no. 66.

Smith, S., Auret, D., Barrientos, S., Dolan, C., Kleinbooi, K., Njobvu, C., Opondo, M. and Tallontire, A. (2004) *Ethical Trade in African Horticulture: gender, rights and participation*, IDS working Papers 223, Falmer: Institute of Development Studies.

Steiner, H. and Alston, P. (2000) *International Human Rights in Context: Law Politics Morals*, Oxford: Oxford University Press.

Stewart, A. (2004) 'Entitlement, pluralism and gender justice in sub-Saharan Africa', in J. Morrison et al. (eds) *Remaking Law in Africa: transnationalism, persons and rights*, Edinburgh: Centre of African Studies. 195.

Tesco (2007) 'Tesco: every little helps Bangladesh develop'. Letter to *The Guardian*, 27 April 2007. Republished with additional information. Online: <http://www.tesco.com/talkingtesco/news/?page=article6>

*The Guardian* (2006) 'How Kenya is caught on the thorns of Britain's love affair with the rose', 13 February 2006.

Traidcraft (2007) *A fresh perspective. Consultation: sourcing vegetables from developing countries.* Traidcraft UK. Online: <http://www.responsible-purchasing.org/assets/files/A%20Fresh%20Perspective.pdf>

Transfer of Property Act (1882). Chapter Group 8 of the Laws of Kenya. Online: <http://www.kenyalaw.org>

Tripp, A. M. (2002) 'The politics of women's rights and cultural diversity in Uganda', in Molyneux, M. and Razavi, S. (eds) *Gender Justice, Development and Rights*, Oxford: Oxford University Press.

Tronto, J. (1993) *Moral Boundaries: a political argument for an ethic of care*, London: Routledge.

Trust Land Act (1939). Chapter 288 of the Laws of Kenya.

United Nations General Assembly (2007) *'Anti Discrimination Committee Urges Kenya to Continue Pursuing Gender Equality'*, 27th July Wom 1644. Online: <http://www.un.org/News/Press/docs/2007/wom1644.doc.htm>

United Nations Research Institute for Social Development (UNRISD) (2005) *Gender Equality: Striving for Justice in an Unequal World*, Geneva: UNRISD.

United States Trade Act (1974). 19 U.S.C. § 2411.

*(Wangari Wanjohi v. Continental Credit Finance) Elizabeth Wangari Wanjohi and Elizabeth Wambui Wanjohi v. Official Receiver and Interim Liquidator (Continental Credit Finance)* (1989) Civil Application NAI No 140 of 1988, *Nairobi Law Monthly* 14 February 1989.

Whitehead, A. and Tsikata, D. (2003) 'Policy discourses on women's land rights in Sub-Saharan Africa: the implications of the re-turn to the customary', *Journal of Agrarian Change*, 3(1–2) January and April: 67–112.

Williams, M. (2003) *Gender Mainstreaming in the Multilateral Trading System: a handbook for policy makers and other stakeholders*, London: Commonwealth Secretariat.

Work Injury Benefits Act (2007) Act 13 of 2007. Online: <http://www.kenyalaw.org/kenyalaw/klr_home>

World Bank (2003a) *Land Policies for Growth and Poverty Reduction*, Washington DC: World Bank.

——(2003b) *The Kenya Strategic Country Gender Assessment* Washington DC: World Bank Africa Region. Online: <http://siteresources.worldbank.org/EXTAFRREGTOPGENDER/Resources/KenyaSCGA.pdf>

——(2007) *Gender and Economic Growth in Kenya: Unleashing the Power of Women*, Washington DC: IBRD and World Bank.

——(2008) *World Development Report: Agriculture for Development*, Washington DC: World Bank. Online: <http://go.worldbank.org/LBJZD6HWZ0>

## Useful websites

Constitution of Kenya
    <http://www.kenyalaw.org/kenyalaw/klr_home>
Divine Chocolate
    <http://www.divinechocolate.com/about/story.aspx>
(ETI) Ethical Trading Initiative Base Code
    <http://www.ethicaltrade.org/Z/lib/base/code_en.shtml>
EUREPGAP
    <http://www.globalgap.org>
Fairtrade Certification
    <http://www.fairtrade.org.uk/what_is_fairtrade/
    fairtrade_certification_and_the_fairtrade_mark/default.aspx>
Kenyan Law Reports
    <http://www.kenyalaw.org>
Kenyan Land Alliance
    <http://www.kenyalandalliance.or.ke>
Lomé Convention (European Commission)
    <http://ec.europa.eu/development/geographical/lomegen_en.cfm>
Ministry of Lands (Government of Kenya)
    <http://www.ardhi.go.ke>
Trade Justice Campaign (Oxfam)
    <http://www.oxfam.org.uk/oxfam_in_action/issues/trade.html>
Women Working Worldwide
    <http://www.poptel.org.uk/women-ww/africaproject.html>
WTO Agriculture Gateway
    <http://www.wto.org/english/tratop_e/agric_e/agric_e.htm>

# Access to medicines versus protection of 'investments' in intellectual property: reconciliation through interpretation?

## Valentina Sara Vadi*

### Introduction

Intellectual property (IP) is a policy device aimed at promoting inventiveness and public welfare. By giving creators exclusive rights to their creations, it provides an incentive for inventors both to invent and to disclose the fruits of their inventiveness. This dual function is captured in Article 15 of the International Covenant on Economic, Social and Cultural Rights (1966; hereinafter ICESCR), which identifies the need to protect both public and private interests in knowledge creation and diffusion (see also Macmillan in this volume).

As the economic pillar of the post-industrial society, intellectual property plays a fundamental role in international relations, and recent developments in international law reflect this socio-economic role (Vadi 2008a). Intellectual property rights have become stronger than ever since the inception of the Agreement on Trade-Related Aspects of Intellectual Property Rights (1994; hereinafter TRIPS Agreement) under the aegis of the World Trade Organization (WTO). In recent years, states have added another layer of protection to intellectual property rights by signing all-encompassing investment treaties. Besides providing extensive protection for investors' rights, investment agreements offer foreign investors direct access to arbitration against a host state. Crucially, this option opens the door to challenging national regulation that allegedly infringes investors' rights.

This chapter is concerned with the combined impact of intellectual property rights and investment agreements upon access to medicines. It first defines the notion of access to medicines. It then explores the interplay between intellectual property and access to medicines in investment law using recent case law. Finally some proposals are put forward in the attempt to reconcile investors' rights with public health in international investment law.

### Access to medicines

Essential medicines are defined by the World Health Organization as 'those drugs that satisfy the priority health care needs of the majority of the population' and that should therefore be available at all times, in adequate amounts and at a price that individuals and the community can afford (WHO 2004). From a legal perspective, access to essential medicines is a core component of the right to health, and is also related to human dignity and the right to life (see UNGA 2004). The status of the right to health in customary international law is a matter of controversy. However, it is generally recognized that states have the duty to protect public health. In addition, the right to health is included in a large number of treaties and other instruments of international relevance. In particular, Article 12 of ICESCR (1966) obliges states to respect, protect and fulfil the right of everyone to the highest attainable standard of health, in particular by addressing ' … the prevention, treatment and control of epidemic, endemic, … and other diseases'.

The ICESCR is legally binding for those states which ratify it, and provides an international mechanism to control the application of its provisions, under which the parties must send periodic reports to the UN Committee on Economic Social and Cultural Rights (UNCESCR) on the measures adopted (see UNCESCR website). In its General Comment No 14 on the 'Right to the Highest Attainable Standard of Health',[1] the Committee recognized that access to essential medicines is part of a state's minimum core obligations 'to ensure the satisfaction of … essential levels of each of the rights enunciated in the Covenant' (UNCESCR 2000: paragraph 43). In other words, if a state does not make essential medicines available, it fails to fulfil its international legal obligations towards the right to health.

The international obligation to secure access to medicine is reinforced by the recent adoption by the Human Rights Council[2] and the General Assembly of the United Nations of the Optional Protocol to the International Covenant on Economic, Social and Cultural Rights. The Protocol would allow persons to petition an international body about the violation of their rights under the Convention.[3] If the Protocol enters into force, it will represent an important step towards the justiciability of economic and social rights at the international level.

In a sense, the right to health is a social right, which states are obliged to fulfil gradually, in a manner compatible with their economic and structural capabilities.[4] The implementation of the right to health, like other economic and social rights, is contingent upon the existence of sufficient resources. However, while that justifies a gradual approach, it should not justify inaction.

## Pharmaceutical patents and investment treaties

Complex and asymmetrical, with inclined planes and slippery converging surfaces, the governance of international knowledge is, like Frank Gehry's postmodernist architecture, disciplined by a number of legal regimes.[5] In the WTO system, the TRIPS Agreement (1994) has secured standards of intellectual property protection similar to those adopted in industrialized countries. These standards have been further enhanced through investment treaties. As intellectual capital exporters, industrialized countries have increasingly used investment treaties in a strategic fashion to incorporate so-called TRIPS-plus[6] commitments that they would not be able to obtain through the WTO.[7]

The policy justification for protecting IP through investment treaties is to open the door to more technology transfers to developing countries. Although the latter would, as net importers of knowledge-based products, benefit from laxer levels of protection, they generally accept TRIPS-plus provisions to obtain favourable concessions in other areas, notably in agriculture (Ryan 1998: 92). Some authors have compared the strategy of promoting such treaties to a new form of imperialism, similar to the ancient Roman military tactics *divide et impera* (Drahos 2003). Under this 'regime shift' (Helfer 2004: 12) knowledge and knowledge-based products have, they argue, been progressively 'feudalized' (Drahos and Braithwaite 2003).

These treaties raise many concerns. First, at the political level, it seems that the discipline provided by investment agreements is imbalanced. While in the multilateral arena, coalitions allow even small and medium-sized countries to enjoy an amplified bargaining power, no such opportunities arise in the context of bilateral negotiations.

Second, at the legal level, as Drahos underlines, 'preferential trade agreements have shifted from being simple tariff-reducing instruments to institution-regulating instruments' (Drahos et al. 2004: 243). Where conflicts arise between treaty provisions and national laws, the regulatory powers of the state may be constrained. For instance, pharmaceutical patents create monopoly rights, and can result in medicines that are unaffordable to the poor. If a host state were to adopt emergency measures to facilitate access to medicines by reducing prices, and corporate profits were to suffer, the state might be accused of breaching its treaty obligations to protect intellectual property rights.

In order to clarify the issues at stake, the following subsections identify some key characteristics of investment treaties that affect access to medicine.

### TRIPS-plus protection

Investment treaties tend to protect intellectual property rights extensively through TRIPS-plus provisions. Investment agreements are negotiated on an ad hoc basis, so such provisions vary. However this concept has generally developed in a cumulative fashion, as negotiators have sought to build up standards based on past experience (Vadi 2007). This chapter focuses on an illustrative sample of three such provisions as they apply to pharmaceutical patents.[8]

### Extended terms

Some investment agreements extend patent terms beyond the 20-year period required under TRIPS. Extending the monopoly period may prejudice the public interest in accessing medicines. As soon as the patent expires, competitors may produce and commercialize the pharmaceutical product. This competition generally leads the prices down and facilitates access to medicines.

There have been few challenges to regulations concerning the duration of patents. In a rare example, the North American Free Trade Agreement (NAFTA) case *Signa S.A. v. Canada* (1996), a Mexican generic pharmaceutical company challenged a Canadian measure concerning the duration of pharmaceutical patents. The company claimed that the extensive protection would have frustrated its legitimate expectations under NAFTA Article 1105, which requires fair and equitable treatment. The parties soon settled their dispute, probably in response to the inception of the TRIPS Agreement, which generally extended the pharmaceutical patent protection to twenty years. As a result there is no publicly available information on the case and whether the filing of the Notice of Intent to Arbitrate had any strategic impact is not known. However, this case demonstrated that corporations can challenge regulatory measures on the grounds that they diminish corporate profits. Also, it is likely that the scarcity of cases in this matter is due not to an absence of conflicts, but to the desire not to transform these conflicts into disputes and to avoid even the relatively limited publicity of arbitration.

## Secondary use

Some investment treaties mandate that patents be available to protect new uses of known products. Such 'secondary-use' patents protect products which offer incremental innovation and improvements over a previously patented product. These improved products are treated as new inventions, eligible for a new patent. In the area of pharmaceuticals, incremental innovations often consist of new and improved methods of administering a medicine or new uses for chemical substances already known.[9] The risk, from a public welfare point of view, is that companies may be encouraged to register 'me-too' drugs, and that the patent lifespan will be excessively prolonged, allowing 'ever-greening' practises by pharmaceutical companies. Such patents may, of course, be challenged. But the cost of that challenge falls on the generic companies – that is, those competitors that produce and/or commercialize the off-patent medicine.

In 2007, the High Court of Chennai (Madras) in the Indian state of Tamil Naidu rejected a challenge by Swiss Novartis against Section 3(d) of the 2005 Indian Patent Law, which blocks patenting of minor improvements in known molecules (*Novartis AG and another v. Union of India and Others*, 2007). Novartis filed the case following the rejection of its patent application on *Glivec*, a leukaemia medicine, on the grounds that the new medicine was insufficiently different from the previous version. First, the company argued that the requirement in Section 3(d) that there be an 'enhancement of the known efficacy' was not sufficiently defined and therefore conferred unguided power on the patent examiner, who could decide applications on a case-by-case basis. As such, the section contravened the equality principle affirmed by Article 14 of the Indian Constitution. The Court rejected this claim, stating that the goal of the provision was clear: for a patent to be granted, it must be shown that the medicine has a better therapeutic effect. Second, the company claimed that the section violated Article 27 of the TRIPS Agreement in not requiring patentability of new uses of the pharmaceutical product. With regard to the issue of compliance with the TRIPS Agreement, the Court held that it lacked jurisdiction, as India is a dualistic country in which treaties are not directly enforceable.

Had the court ruled the other way, Indian companies would have been prevented from manufacturing generic versions of *Glivec*, which they sell for about a tenth of what Novartis charges. This would have left large numbers of patients without access to the treatment.

### Limiting compulsory licensing

Faced with the need to secure access to a particular drug, for example during a public health emergency, a state may choose to issue a 'compulsory licence' to allow those other than the patent holder to produce a medicine. Compulsory licences are issued by competent state authorities to allow the production of a drug without the patent owner's consent. Article 31 of the TRIPS Agreement sets out the conditions under which a compulsory licence will be regarded as a lawful infringement of intellectual property rights.[10] According to the Doha Declaration, each WTO member has the right to grant compulsory licences and 'the freedom to determine the grounds upon which such licences are granted' and 'what constitutes a national emergency or other circumstances of extreme urgency', it being understood that public health crises, including those relating to HIV/AIDS, tuberculosis, malaria and other epidemics, can be so designated (Doha Declaration 2001: paragraph 5). According to a subsequent waiver (General Council of the WTO 2003), countries with no domestic pharmaceutical production capacity could issue compulsory licences to import generic medicines if necessary. In addition, WTO members agreed not to initiate complaints under the TRIPS Agreement and the General Council opened a Protocol of Amendment for signature in order to make the waiver permanent (Doha Ministerial Conference 2001: paragraph 11.1; WTO Council for TRIPS 2005).[11]

However, investment treaties generally limit the grounds on which compulsory licensing may be used. For example, the US–Australia Free Trade Agreement (2004) allows just two grounds for granting compulsory licensing, namely to remedy anti-competitive practices and in the case of national emergency. Moreover, many investment agreements require that right holders be compensated more generously than under TRIPS. The risk is that diverging provisions in different treaty regimes make access to medicines more difficult for the poor.

In January of 2007, Thailand's military government issued compulsory licences on Kaletra, an HIV treatment supplied by US-based Abbott Laboratories, to be distributed to those poorer patients who were cared for by the public health system. The Ministry of Health argued that the Government could not afford to buy the necessary medicines so its measures were consistent with the TRIPS Agreement and the Doha Declaration (Tremblay 2007: 11). The compulsory licence authorized the Government to import generic versions of the drug from India until domestic production came on line.

However, on 1 May 2007, the US Trade Representative placed Thailand on the Priority Watch List, as a country which would not provide an adequate level of protection to intellectual property. This move could open the country up to retaliatory trade measures such as loss of generalized system of preferences (GSP). For its part, Abbott Laboratories announced that it would not register any new medicines in Thailand unless the Government reversed its decision. This was a clear attempt to pressurize Thailand and to inhibit other developing countries from using compulsory licensing.

A number of points for consideration arise from the Thai controversy. First, if health emergencies arise, states are compelled by international law to intervene in a prompt manner. Second, complaints by corporations about lack of nego- tiation before the issuance of compulsory licences are unjustified as Article 31(b) of the TRIPS Agreement explicitly waives such a requirement 'in the case of national emergency or other circumstances of extreme urgency'. Third, it may be questioned what would have happened if Thailand had signed a bilateral investment agreement with the United States. Indeed, the Thai–US talks fell apart at the end of 2006, partly due to a failure to agree on IP issues (see Bilaterals.org 2008).

### Regulatory measures as indirect expropriation

A second key feature of international investment agreements is that they tend to protect foreign assets from expropriation, whether direct (full taking of property) or indirect (de facto taking).[12] Treaty provisions do not generally offer a precise definition of indirect expropriation. Rather, their language tends to encompass a potentially wide variety of state activity that may interfere with an investor's property rights in his investment (Fortier 2003: 1). For example, Article 1110 of the NAFTA (1994) states that:

1. No Party may directly or indirectly nationalize or expropriate an invest- ment of an investor of another Party in its territory or take a measure tan- tamount to nationalization or expropriation of such an investment ('expropriation'), except:[13]

(a) for a public purpose;
(b) on a non-discriminatory basis;
(c) in accordance with due process of law and Article 1105(1); and
(d) on payment of compensation in accordance with paragraphs 2 through 6.

With regard to pharmaceutical patents, the question is whether the granting of compulsory licences and other regulatory measures might be deemed an expro- priation such that it might trigger claims against a host state under an investment treaty. A patent holder might challenge a compulsory licence on the grounds that, for example, it was not for a genuine public purpose, or that it was inadequately compensated. Such measure might be regarded as neutralizing the enjoyment of property rights, thus amounting to indirect expropriation. The success of such claims is more likely in the context of the rise of the 'sole-effect' doctrine: arbitration panels increasingly direct their attention to the question of whether an investor is deprived of a certain economic utility (effect), notwithstanding the nature and the public goal of the given regulatory measure (Brunetti 2003: 150–51). For instance, in *Compania del Desarollo de Santa Elena v. Republic of Costa Rica* (2000), the arbitral tribunal concurred with the claimant that the nature of the public objective pursued by the expropriation could not per se affect the level of compensation. In other words, the question of compensation would not be linked to the legality of taking. The upshot is that, where they are found to be applicable, compensation rules may in some cases be more beneficial to the patent owner than the compulsory license rules.

In some cases, the potential clash between compulsory licensing and the duty to protect public health has been dealt with in side letters. For example, a side letter to the US–Morocco Free Trade Agreement (2004) clarifies that the intellectual property chapter of the Agreement will not prevent the effective utilization of the WTO waiver. This means that in case of public health emergency, states might issue compulsory licences not only to produce pharmaceutical products but also to import these from other countries if they lacked manufacturing capacities. It also states that nothing in the intellectual property chapter of the Agreement shall:

> … affect the ability of either party to take necessary measures to protect public health by promoting access to medicines for all, in particular concerning cases such as HIV/AIDS, tuberculosis, malaria, and other epidemics as well as circumstances of extreme urgency or national emergency.
> (US–Morocco Agreement 2004: Side Letter)

Similarly, when the Central America–Dominican Republic United States Free Trade Agreement (CAFTA–DR) was signed in 2004, a side letter or understanding on intellectual property and public health was included in response to criticism that the intellectual property regulation in the agreement could undermine public health. This understanding states that CAFTA provisions 'do not affect a Party's ability to take necessary measures to protect public health by promoting access to medicines for all' or from 'effective utilization' of the WTO decision on TRIPS (CAFTA–DR 2004: Side Letter).

However, the legal value of these side letters is very uncertain. They may well represent just a declaratory statement rather than a legally binding exception. The risk is that the philanthropic declarations and conflict clauses come to a standstill because of economic pressures exercized by corporations. These may prevent states, especially developing countries, from taking measures to protect public health.

Other investment agreements provide for compulsory licensing in the main text. For instance, Article 1110 of NAFTA (1994) makes clear that provisions on expropriation and compensation do not apply to compulsory licences:

> This Article does not apply to the issuance of compulsory licenses granted in relation to intellectual property rights, or to the revocation, limitation or creation of intellectual property rights, to the extent that such issuance, revocation, limitation or creation is consistent with Chapter Seventeen (Intellectual Property).
>
> (NAFTA 1994: Article 1110.7)

Similarly, the US–Chile Free Trade Agreement (2004) stipulates that the provision on expropriation and compensation does not apply to the issuance of compulsory licences granted in relation to intellectual property rights in accordance with the TRIPS Agreement (Article 10.9.5).

### Investor–state arbitration

At the procedural level, the most notable feature of contemporary investment treaties is their provision for investor–state arbitration. Investor–state disputes generally involve judicial review of governmental conduct that is public law adjudication. Arbitration, though, is a private dispute-resolution mechanism, and presents some characteristics that might not be suitable to public law adjudication. Traditionally, arbitral tribunals are neither open to the public nor accountable to democratic processes. They are not bound by precedents and are not obliged to publish final decisions. They lack the transparency generally afforded by judicial proceedings, yet are empowered to order governments to compensate investors for regulations that hurt them, regardless of the public good that the regulations might serve. Further, there are only limited grounds for annulment.[14]

The flourishing of investor–state disputes in recent years has transformed the landscape of investment protection which had hitherto been dealt with between states (McLachlan et al. 2007: 5). The widespread introduction of a relatively neutral forum of arbitration into international investment relations[15] is regarded as an important mechanism for recognizing and protecting the assets of foreign investors from expropriation, nationalization or other forms of regulation by the host state. As Böckstiegel (2007) points out, the traditional David–Goliath relationship between private investors and states has been replaced, at least procedurally, by a level playing field.

However, in giving their consent to investor–state arbitration in investment treaties, states waive their sovereign immunity and give arbitrators jurisdiction over regulatory disputes – matters of public and even constitutional law (Van Harten 2007a). Many recent arbitral awards have concerned the determination of the appropriate boundary between two conflicting values: the legitimate sphere for state regulation in the pursuit of public goods on the one hand, and the protection of private property from state interference on the other (Vadi 2008c). The extension of characteristics typical of international commercial arbitration, an essentially private-sector-oriented dispute-settlement mechanism, to investment treaty arbitration, an essentially public-oriented enterprise, has proven problematic.

The question that arises is whether the public interest can be adequately protected within a framework aimed primarily at protecting private interests. Prima facie, it seems that the current framework lacks adequate procedural protections for the public interest since it fails to secure transparency, public accountability or third-party participation. Some have proposed procedural reforms to improve the structure of investor–state arbitration (see, for example, Van Harten 2007b). The remainder of this study focuses on how treaty inter-pretation can help to avoid the need for arbitration or, at the minimum, improve the outcomes of arbitration for states seeking to protect public health.

## Reconciliation through interpretation?

Having highlighted the provisions of investment treaties that may conflict with the host state's international obligations to protect public health by ensuring access to essential medicines, we now explore how we might reconcile the different interests at stake using alternate interpretative methods.

### Textual interpretation

Traditional means of treaty interpretation may help arbitrators to find an appropriate balance between the different interests concerned. According to customary norms of treaty interpretation as restated by Articles 31, 32 and 33 of the Vienna Convention on the Law of Treaties (1969), treaties must be inter-preted in good faith. In addition, the intentions of the parties need to be revealed through the ordinary meaning of the terms of the treaty, in their con-text, and in light of its object and purpose.

As seen above, certain treaties expressly provide for clauses that clarify that public health measures, such as compulsory licensing, are not to be considered a form of indirect expropriation. Arbitrators and interpreters are called to inter-pret these clauses in good faith and according to their ordinary meaning. If such clauses are not inserted in the text of the treaty, arbitrators are to apply other customary norms of treaty interpretation, namely teleological interpretation and systemic interpretation.

### Teleological interpretation

If we look at the very rationale of protecting intellectual property rights, we see that intellectual property, which is a special form of property, is never absolute.

On the contrary, the notion that intellectual property serves a social function has wide acceptance in international law, as expressly indicated by Articles 7 and 8 of the TRIPS Agreement and by Article 15 of the International Covenant on Economic, Social and Cultural Rights.

Thus, private interests should not be given more weight than the social welfare. Medicines are not mere investments, but also serve a social function being related to health and life. Importantly, the issuance of compulsory licences should not be considered breach of patent, and consequently breach of treaty, but as the concrete application of a special norm embedded in the regulation of intellectual property rights. The former European Commission on Human Rights adopted this approach when it held in the *SmithKline* (1990) case, that the grant under Dutch law of a compulsory licence in a patented medicine was not a violation of Article 1 of Protocol 1 to the European Convention on Human Rights (1950), which protects the right to property. It considered that the compulsory licence was lawfully issued as it pursued a legitimate aim.

I would argue in favour of interpreting some regulatory measures as intrinsic limits to property. Thus, some compulsory licences can be conceived as inherent limits to pharmaceutical patents, constituting a natural boundary of the right, rather than an exception to the rule. This theory of inherent limitation of property rights would constitute a ground for non-compensation in the event that a compulsory licence was granted.[16]

### Systemic interpretation

If looking at the object and purpose of the treaty does not help, another criterion of treaty interpretation requires adjudicators to take into account 'any relevant rules of international law applicable in the relations between the parties' (Vienna Convention 1969: Article 31(3)(c)). Pursuant to this rule, '[e]very treaty provision must be read not only in its own context, but in the wider context of general international law, whether conventional or customary' (Sinclair 1984: 139).

Indeed, NAFTA expressly requires that 'A Tribunal established under this Section shall decide the issue in dispute in accordance with this Agreement and applicable rules of international law' (NAFTA 1994: Article 1131(1)), and NAFTA tribunals appear to have used WTO authorities for the purpose of interpreting NAFTA Chapter 11 provisions (Vadi 2008b).

The TRIPS Agreement is not the only international treaty which regulates IP: a number of international organizations such as the World Intellectual Property Organization play an active role in this area, determining a sort of 'institutional density' (Raustiala 2006). If WTO law is taken into account in interpreting investment treaties, it seems there is no reason to object to the consideration of other treaty regimes.

The problem is that while the national judge knows the law that has to be applied to the case and applies it even if the parties have invoked different rules (*iura novit curia*), arbitrators generally consider only the investment agreements and the legal arguments expressly made by the parties (*secundum alligata et probata*). Still, it may be questioned whether arbitrators can legally ignore international law. I would argue that the splendid isolation of investment arbitration from international law has to come to an end. This is not arbitral activism, or something that goes against arbitral ethics. On the contrary, it is a natural consequence of arbitrators' duty to interpret investment agreements in a systemic fashion (McLachlan 2005: 279).

The obverse of the same coin is that arbitrators should acknowledge their responsibility as cartographers of the international legal order. If arbitral awards are referred to as persuasive precedent[17] then arbitrators must realize their determinant role not only with regard to the single dispute but also with regard to the possible influence that their reasoning may have on subsequent arbitral panels.

## Conclusions

Adopting a humanist approach, which puts the human being at the heart of contemporary law (Abi-Saab 2008), this study argues that states should put the well-being of their populations at the heart of policymaking. Public health, *salus publica*, lies at the very heart of state sovereignty, as the basic duty of government is maintaining and enhancing the well-being of its people (Loughlin 2003: 7).

The Doha Declaration and the proposed Amendment to the TRIPS Agreement suggest that the international trade system has already moved towards the adoption of a human-rights approach to trade. Similarly, investment law should be coherent with human-rights law.

*De lege lata*, according to customary rules of treaty interpretation, treaties must be interpreted not only according to their strict textual meaning but also in good faith, in context and in the light of their object and purpose. Moreover, treaties must be interpreted taking account of any relevant rules of international law applicable in the relations between the parties. As investment law increasingly intersects with other sets of international law norms, it is necessary to rethink carefully this interplay and to adopt a holistic approach.

Furthermore, the conflict of norms between intellectual property and public health seems to be a spurious one: intellectual property is a policy device aimed at promoting inventiveness and public welfare. Therefore, intellectual property rights should not be considered as absolute rights, but should be interpreted in the light of their goals and limits. This paper does not contend the legitimacy of intellectual property, but it proposes an equilibrate understanding of property rights, according to the constitutional traditions of many states and the case law of human-rights courts such as the European Court of Human Rights.

*De lege ferenda*, there should be more dialogue and interaction between different regulatory networks in order to promote access to essential medicines. Increasing awareness of the issue should drive international lawmakers to legislate coherently in a manner consistent with their human-rights obligations.

# Notes

* Earlier versions of this contribution were presented at the Fifth Seminar of the Garnett PhD School on *Global Governance & Regionalism*, held at the University of Geneva, Switzerland, on 6 December 2007 and at the Socio-Legal Studies Association Conference on *Justice, Power and Law in the Pursuit of Development*, held at Birkbeck College, University of London on 10 December 2007. The author would like to thank Dr. Amanda Perry-Kessaris, Professor Ernst-Ulrich Petersmann, Professor Francesco Francioni, Professor Gabrielle Marceau and Professor Bronwen Morgan for their comments on earlier drafts, and for their encouragement.

1 General Comments are authoritative interpretations of specific treaty provisions. While General Comments are not legally binding, they are influential in shaping the opinion of states.

2 'The Human Rights Council is an inter-governmental body within the UN system made up of 47 States responsible for strengthening the promotion and protection of human rights around the globe' (Human Rights Council website).

3 The Optional Protocol is annexed to United Nations General Assembly resolution A/RES/63/117, which recommends that the Optional Protocol be opened for signature in 2009.

4 The distinction between civil and political rights on the one hand and social and economic rights on the other is usually explained in terms of their distinct historical origin. 'First generation' civil and political rights are associated with the liberal ideals promoted by the French and American revolutions in the eighteenth century. 'Second generation' economic, social and cultural rights derive from the socialist ideals in the late-nineteenth century. The distinction also revolves around the perceived role of the state. Civil rights demand freedom from state interference, whereas economic and social rights require active measures by the state. In the past century, the ideological conflict between East and West during the Cold War determined the division of the International Bill of Rights into two separate instruments, namely the ICCPR and the ICESCR. Given the interconnectedness of the two sets of rights and the changed political arena, the need for such a dichotomy has been put into question (Raes 2002).

5 International knowledge governance may be defined as the international regulation of knowledge creation and diffusion.

6 Under the TRIPS Agreement, WTO Member States are free to institute more extensive IP protection than is required by the Agreement, provided that such protection does not contravene its provisions (Article 1.1).

7 Bilateral investment treaties are agreements between two countries for the reciprocal encouragement, promotion and protection of investments in each other's territories by companies based in either country.

8 For a complete analysis of the contents of such agreements, see Vadi (2007).

9 The TRIPS Agreement protects all forms of innovation in Article 27(1) but is silent about the patentability of new uses of known substances.

10 Article 31 Other Use Without Authorization of the Right Holder.
Where the law of a Member allows for other use (7) of the subject matter of a patent without the authorization of the right holder, including use by the government or third parties authorized by the government, the following provisions shall be respected:
    (a) authorization of such use shall be considered on its individual merits;
    (b) such use may only be permitted if, prior to such use, the proposed user has made efforts to obtain authorization from the right holder on reasonable commercial terms and conditions and that such efforts have not been successful within a reasonable period of time. This requirement may be waived by a Member in the case of a national emergency or other circumstances of extreme urgency or in cases of public non-commercial use. In situations of

national emergency or other circumstances of extreme urgency, the right holder shall, nevertheless, be notified as soon as reasonably practicable. In the case of public non-commercial use, where the government or contractor, without making a patent search, knows or has demonstrable grounds to know that a valid patent is or will be used by or for the government, the right holder shall be informed promptly;

(c) the scope and duration of such use shall be limited to the purpose for which it was authorized, and in the case of semi-conductor technology shall only be for public non-commercial use or to remedy a practice determined after judicial or administrative process to be anti-competitive;

(d) such use shall be non-exclusive;

(e) such use shall be non-assignable, except with that part of the enterprise or goodwill which enjoys such use;

(f) any such use shall be authorized predominantly for the supply of the domestic market of the Member authorizing such use;

(g) authorization for such use shall be liable, subject to adequate protection of the legitimate interests of the persons so authorized, to be terminated if and when the circumstances which led to it cease to exist and are unlikely to recur. The competent authority shall have the authority to review, upon motivated request, the continued existence of these circumstances;

(h) the right holder shall be paid adequate remuneration in the circumstances of each case, taking into account the economic value of the authorization;

(i) the legal validity of any decision relating to the authorization of such use shall be subject to judicial review or other independent review by a distinct higher authority in that Member;

(j) any decision relating to the remuneration provided in respect of such use shall be subject to judicial review or other independent review by a distinct higher authority in that Member ...

11 In December 2007 the WTO Members agreed to a further two-year extension of the deadline to 2009 (General Council of the World Trade Organization 2007). As the Amendment has to be ratified by two thirds of the WTO Member States to come into force, the waiver will remain in force until then.

12 For a review of expropriation under international law see UNCTAD (2000).

13 This provision is particularly powerful because it includes protection from measures that are merely 'tantamount to' nationalisation or expropriation.

14 For a critique of international commercial arbitration and of securities arbitration, see McLaughlin and Perry-Kessaris in this volume.

15 For a detailed assessment of the neutrality and transparency of international arbitration see Dezalay and Garth (1996).

16 Interestingly, this inherent limitation analysis was adopted by the American Supreme Court in *Lucas v. South Carolina Coastal Council* (1992: 2899–2900).

17 Although there is no such rule as *stare decisis* in investment arbitration, usually arbitrators do make reference to previous cases. See for instance *Malaysian Historical Salvors v. The Government of Malaysia* (2007).

# References

Abi-Saab, G. (2008) 'Droit international et humanisme juridique: quelles perspectives?', in H. Ruiz Fabri et al. (eds) *Select Proceedings of the European Society of International Law*, vol. 1, Oxford: Hart Publishing.

Bilaterals.org (2008) *US Postpones FTA Talks with Thailand*, 6 November 2006. Online: <http://www.bilaterals.org/article.php3?id_article=6404 > (Accessed on 23 July 2008.)

Böckstiegel, K. H. (2007) 'Enterprise v. State: the New David and Goliath?', *Arbitration International*, 23: 93–104.

Brunetti, M. (2003) 'Introduction', *International Law Forum de Droit International*, 5: 150.

(CAFTA-DR) Central America–Dominican Republic–United States Free Trade Agreement 2004. Online: <http://www.ustr.gov/Trade_Agreements/Regional/CAFTA/Archive_Section_index/Section_Index.html>

*Compania del Desarollo de Santa Elena v. Republic of Costa Rica* (2000), ICSID Case No. ARB/96/1, Final Award of 17 February 2000, 15 (1) ICSID Review-FILJ (Spring 2000) 169–204.

Dezalay, Y. and Garth, B. S. (1996) *Dealing in Virtue: International Commercial Arbitration and the Construction of a Transnational Legal Order*, Chicago: University of Chicago Press.

(Doha Declaration) Doha WTO Ministerial 2001 Declaration, Adopted 14 November 2001. Online: <http://www.wto.org/english/thewto_e/minist_e/min01_e/mindecl_e.htm>

Doha Ministerial Conference (2001) Implementation–Related Issues and Concerns, Decision of 14 November 2001, WT/MIN(01)/17, paragraph 11.1.

Drahos, P. (2003) *Expanding Intellectual Property's Empire: The Role of FTAs*. Online: <http://www.grain.org/rights/tripsplus.cfm?id=28#.>

Drahos, P. and J. Braithwaite (2003) *Information Feudalism – Who Owns the Knowledge Economy?* New York: The New Press.

Drahos, P. et al. (2004) 'Pharmaceuticals, intellectual property and free trade: the case of the US–Australia Free Trade Agreement', *Prometheus*, 22.

Fortier, L. Y. (2003) 'Caveat Investor: the meaning of "Expropriation" and the protection afforded investors under NAFTA', 20 *News From ICSID*.

General Council of the World Trade Organization (2003), Implementation of Paragraph 6 of the Doha Declaration on the TRIPS Agreement and Public Health, WT/L/540, Decision of the General Council of 30 August 2003. Online: <http://www.wto.org/english/tratop_e/trips_e/implem_para6_e.htm>.

——(2007), Amendment to the TRIPS Agreement – Extension of the Period for the Acceptance by Members of the Protocol Amending the TRIPS Agreement, Decision of 18 December 2007, WT/L/711. Online: <http://docsonline.wto.org:80/DDFDocuments/t/WT/L/711.doc>

Helfer, L. R. (2004) 'Regime shifting: the TRIPS Agreement and new dynamics of international intellectual property lawmaking', *Yale Journal of International Law*, 29: 1.

(ICESCR) International Covenant on Economic, Social and Cultural Rights, UNGA Resolution 2200 (XXI) 16 December 1966, entered into force on 3 January 1976 (999 UNTS 171).

Loughlin, M. (2003) *The Idea of Public Law*, Oxford University Press: Oxford.

*Lucas v. South Carolina Coastal Council* 112 S. Ct. 2886 (1992)

*Malaysian Historical Salvors, Sdn, Bhd v. The Government of Malaysia*, Award on Jurisdiction, 17 May 2007, ICSID Case No ARB/05/10.

McLachlan C. (2005) 'The principle of systemic integration and Article 31(3)(c) of the Vienna Convention', *International and Comparative Law Quarterly*, 54: 279–319.

——(2008) 'Investment treaties and general international law', *International and Comparative Law Quarterly*, 57: 361–401.

McLachlan C., Shore, L. and Weiniger, M. (2007) *International Investment Arbitration*, Oxford: OUP.

(NAFTA) North American Free Trade Agreement, signed in 1992, entered into force on 1 January 1994.

*Novartis AG and another v. Union of India and Others*, unreported, High Court of Judicature at Madras, 6 August 2007.

Raes, K. (2002) 'The philosophical basis of social, economic and cultural rights', in Van der Auweraert et al. (eds) *Social, Economic and Cultural Rights*, Maklu: Antwerpen, 43–53.

Raustiala, K. (2006) 'Density and conflict in international intellectual property law', *UC Davis Law Review*, 40: 1021–39.

Ryan, M. (1998) *Knowledge Diplomacy – Global Competition and the Politics of Intellectual Property*, Brookings Institution Press: Washington DC.

*Signa v. Canada* (1996) Notice of Intent to Submit a Claim to Arbitration Under Section B of Charter 11 of the North American Free Trade Agreement, New York 4 March 1996.

Sinclair, I. (1984) *The Vienna Convention on the Law of Treaties*, Manchester: Manchester University Press.

*SmithKline and French Laboratories Ltd. v. The Netherlands*, Appl. No. 12633/87, 4 October 1990, 66 D.R.70 (1990).

Tremblay, J.F. (2007) 'Drug patent struggles in Asia', *Chemical & Engineering News*, 85: 11.

(TRIPS) Agreement on Trade–Related Aspects of Intellectual Property Rights, Annex C of the Agreement Establishing the World Trade Organization, done at Marrakesh on 15 April 1994, 33 ILM 1144. Online: <http://www.wto.org/english/tratop_e/trips_e/t_agm0_e.htm>

(UNCESCR) UN Committee on Economic, Social and Cultural Rights (2000), *General Comment* n. 14, adopted on May 2000 (E/C.12/2000/4).

(UNCTAD) United National Conference on Trade and Development (2000) *Taking of Property*, UNCTAD Series on issues in international investment agreements, New York and Geneva: UNCTAD. Online: <http://www.unctad.org/en/docs/psiteiitd15.en.pdf>

(UNGA) United Nations General Assembly (2004) Resolution, The Right of Everyone to the Enjoyment of the Highest Attainable Standard of Physical and Mental Health (A/RES/58/173) 10 March 2004.

—— (2008) Resolution 63/117, Optional Protocol to the International Covenant on Economic, Social and Cultural Rights (A/RES/63/117) 10 December 2008.

United States–Australia Free Trade Agreement 2004. Online: <http://www.ustr.gov/Trade_Agreements/Bilateral/Australia_FTA/Final_Text/Section_Index.html>

United States–Chile Free Trade Agreement (2004). Online: <http://www.ustr.gov/Trade_Agreements/Bilateral/Chile_FTA/Final_Texts/Section_Index.html>

United State–Morocco Free Trade Agreement (2004) Online: <http://www.ustr.gov/Trade_Agreements/Bilateral/Morocco_FTA/Section_Index.html>

Vadi, V. (2007) 'Access to essential medicines and international investment law: the road ahead', *Journal of World Investment & Trade*, 505–32.

——(2008a) 'Sapere Aude! Access to knowledge as a human right and a key instrument to development', *International Journal of Communications Law and Policy*, 12: 346–68.

——(2008b) 'Towards arbitral path coherence and judicial borrowing: persuasive precedent in investment arbitration', *Transnational Dispute Management*, 5: 1–16.

——(2008c) 'Cultural heritage and international investment law: a stormy relationship', *International Journal of Cultural Property*, 15(1): 1–23.

Van Harten, G. (2007a) 'The public-private distinction in the international arbitration of individual claims against the state', *International and Comparative Law Quarterly*, 56: 371–94.

——(2007b) *Investment Treaty Arbitration and Public Law*, Oxford University Press: Oxford.

Vienna Convention on the Law of Treaties, done at Vienna on 23 May 1969, entered into force on 27 January 1980, United Nations Treaty Series Vol. 1155, p.331.

WHO (2004) The World Medicines Situation, Geneva: WHO.

(WTO) Agreement Establishing the World Trade Organization (1994) done at Marrakesh on 15 April 1994, 33 ILM 1144. Online: <http://www.wto.org/english/docs_e/legal_e/04-wto.pdf>

WTO Council for Trade–Related Aspects of Intellectual Property Rights (2005) 'Implementation of Paragraph 11 of the General Council Decision of 30 August 2003 on the Implementation of Paragraph 6 of the Doha Declaration on the TRIPS Agreement and Public Health' (IP/C/41), 6 December 2005.

## Useful websites

Human Rights Council
<http://www2.ohchr.org/english/bodies/hrcouncil>
(NAFTA) North American Free Trade Area Secretariat
<http://www.nafta-sec-alena.org/en/view.aspx>
(UNCESCR) UN Committee on Economic, Social and Cultural Rights
<http://www.unhchr.ch/html/menu2/6/cescr.htm>
(WTO) World Trade Organisation TRIPs Gateway
<http://www.wto.org/english/tratop_e/TRIPS_e/TRIPS_e.htm>

# Chapter 5

# Development, cultural self-determination and the World Trade Organization

*Fiona Macmillan*

## 'Development': setting the scene

The concept of development comes with a complex and, arguably, somewhat dubious baggage. It was born, as Tony Anghie (2000: 243) has argued, at the end of the colonial period and elevated into a 'science' based on a notion of uniform and neutral economic rationality under which 'advanced' or 'developed' countries would aid 'backward' or 'developing' or 'less-developed' countries to bridge the economic gap (Alessandrini 2007: Chapter 1). By some lucky co-incidence, bridging this economic gap would have the side effect of providing developed countries with access to raw materials in 'developing' countries as well as access to new markets (Arrighi 1994, Alessandrini 2007).

Since this instrumental and pragmatic emergence, the concept of development has, at least in some quarters, itself developed in two notable ways. First, it has transcended its purely economic focus, moving to a more holistic, but also highly contested, concept with a variable content (e.g. World Commission on Culture and Development 1996, Sen 1999). Second, and consequentially, it has transcended its focus on the gap between so-called advanced and so-called backward countries. In this process of transcendence it has become a ubiquitous carrier of multiple meanings. The problem, of course, with ubiquitous carriers of multiple meanings is that the loss of focus implied by this very ubiquity tends to deprive them of much in the way of substantial meaning.

At the end of the previous century and in the early stages of this century, there has been a tendency, which is particularly apparent in international agreements, to refer not simply to 'development' but to 'sustainable development'. There seems to be some kind of loose consensus that this refers to development that satisfies the needs of the present while not compromising the ability of future generations to satisfy their needs. While this seems to tell us something about the meaning of the qualifier 'sustainable', it still leaves us with the problem of the meaning of 'development'. Thus, appeals to 'sustainable development' do little to clarify the situation. Further, attempts to understand concepts of development, or sustainable development, through an examination of their use in international legal instruments are not necessarily enlightening, as this chapter seeks to show by focusing on the relationship between two international agreements, both of which purport to be grounded in the concept of sustainable development. The chapter will seek to demonstrate that the two agreements, the United Nations Educational, Scientific and Cultural Organization (UNESCO) Convention on the Protection and Promotion of the Diversity of Cultural Expressions (2005; hereinafter 'Convention on Cultural Diversity') and the Agreement Establishing the World Trade Organization (1994; hereinafter 'WTO Agreement') seem unlikely to be appealing to a common concept of development, sustainable or otherwise. A possible consequence of this finding is that a mismatch exists between concepts of development used in the realm of public international law and in the realm of international economic law.[1] If such a mismatch exists, it is likely to be contributing to the hollowing of the concept of development in international law discourse.

As is clear from the famous UNESCO study, *Our Creative Diversity* (World Commission on Culture and Development 1996), the UNESCO Convention on Cultural Diversity (2005) is based on a broad concept of development, which transcends economic development and is focused on the enhancement of effective freedom of choice for individuals, embracing concepts such as 'access to the world's stock of knowledge ... access to power, the right to participate in the cultural life of the community' (World Commission on Culture and Development 1996: Introduction). In other words, it owes much to Amartya Sen's (1999) famous exploration of 'development as freedom' (see also Faundez in this volume). The provenance of the concept of development in the WTO Agreement (1994), which provides the legal framework holding together the multilateral agreements that comprise the WTO, is less clear. Nevertheless, in a notable departure from the Preamble to the General Agreement on Trade and Tariffs (1947), which is otherwise largely reproduced in the preamble to the WTO Agreement, sustainable development has made its way into the first paragraph of the WTO Agreement.[2] Despite the attractiveness of the idea, the association in this chapter of the WTO regime with the regime established under the UNESCO Convention is not purely random, nor is it merely based on the coincidence of the expression 'sustainable development' in both legal instruments. Since it has always been clear that the specific motivation for the UNESCO Convention was an attempt to remedy the lack of a so-called cultural exception in WTO law (Hahn 2006: 515–20, Graber 2006: 554–55), it follows that this Convention must purport to address common factual (if not legal) territory to that traversed in the WTO Agreement.

Since it appears that the protection of cultural diversity is the key aspect of the concept of development or sustainable development in the UNESCO Convention, the specific business of this chapter is to consider the relationship between the international legal regime established under the Convention and the international copyright system, which is embedded in the law of the WTO by virtue of its Agreement on Trade-Related Intellectual Property Rights (1994; hereinafter 'TRIPs Agreement'; see also Vadi in this volume).[3] In order to examine this relationship, the chapter looks at six issues. First, it considers the extent to which international law, both before and after the coming into force of the UNESCO Convention (2005), confers a 'right' to cultural diversity. It is argued that the UNESCO Convention may be regarded as articulating and building upon rights previously laid down in the human rights covenants to the Charter of the United Nations. A particular concern of the chapter becomes, therefore, whether the relationship between the UNESCO Convention and the international copyright system is likely to show any marked differences from the relationship that has existed to date between the human rights covenants and the copyright system. As a basis for arguing that some relationship should exist between the UNESCO Convention and the copyright system, the next section offers some views on the extent to which the concept of culture in the Convention interacts with the concept of culture with which copyright is concerned. The chapter then turns to a more detailed analysis of the relationship between copyright and cultural diversity in the fourth section, followed by a consideration of the extent to which the entrenching of the international copyright system in the WTO has affected this relationship. The sixth section broadens this consideration by arguing that other provisions of WTO law exacerbate the negative effects of the international copyright system on cultural diversity. Finally, the chapter comments upon the extent to which there is a clash between the 'right' to cultural diversity, if it exists, and the international copyright system. The chapter concludes with some observations on the significance of this clash in relation to attempts to understand the content of the expressions 'development' and 'sustainable development' in international law.

## Cultural diversity as a (human) right?

Prior to the coming into force of the UNESCO Convention on 18 March 2007, international legal obligations with respect to cultural diversity could only be gleaned from the composite effect of a range of provisions found in the human rights covenants to the Charter of the United Nations. The provisions of these covenants that may be argued to operate together in order to create a right to cultural self-determination are Articles 1, 19 and 27 of the International Covenant on Civil and Political Rights (1969; hereinafter 'ICCPR') and Article 15 of the International Covenant on Economic Social and Cultural Rights (1966; hereinafter 'ICESCR'). When these provisions are analyzed it can be seen that it is probably more appropriate to characterize their composite effect as creating, if anything, a right to cultural self-determination, which in turn suggests the valorization of cultural diversity.

The general right to self-determination is laid down in ICCPR Article 1.1, which provides:

> All peoples have the right of self-determination. By virtue of that right they freely determine their political status and freely pursue their economic, social and cultural development.

As can be seen, this right is conferred on '[p]eoples' rather than individuals and, obviously, it leaves open the somewhat delicate question of how such entities might be identified or defined. While 'peoples' may, presumably, be constituted by the citizens and residents of a particular nation state, it is also clear from Article 1.3 that this is not the only method of constituting a 'people'.[4] It appears to be the case that ethnic, religious or linguistic groups are not necessarily 'peoples' for the purpose of Article 1.1 since Article 27 confers a range of somewhat more limited rights on such groups:

> In those States in which ethnic, religious or linguistic minorities exist, persons belonging to such minorities shall not be denied the right, in community with the other members of their group, to enjoy their own culture, to profess and practice their religion, or to use their own language.

The individual rights that contribute to this composite right of cultural self-determination are laid out in ICCPR, Article 19:

1. Everyone shall have the right to hold opinions without interference.
2. Everyone shall have the right to freedom of expression; this right shall include freedom to seek, receive and impart information and ideas of all kinds, regardless of frontiers, either orally, in writing or in print, in the form of art, or through any other media of his choice.

These are complemented by ICESCR, Article 15:

1. The States Parties to the present Covenant recognize the right of everyone:
   a) To take part in cultural life;
   b) To enjoy the benefits of scientific progress and its applications;
   c) To benefit from the protection of the moral and material interests resulting from any scientific, literary or artistic production of which he is the author.
2. The steps to be taken by the States Parties to the present Covenant to achieve the full realization of this right shall include those necessary for the conservation, the development and the diffusion of science and culture.
3. The States Parties to the present Covenant undertake to respect the freedom indispensable for scientific research and creative activity.
4. The States Parties to the present Covenant recognize the benefits to be derived from the encouragement and development of international contacts and co-operation in the scientific and cultural fields.

As is not infrequently the case with provisions of this sort in international instruments, the exact ambit of ICESCR is not entirely clear. One example of this is the right in Article 15.1(a) '[t]o take part in cultural life', which is obviously of some significance in the context of a right to cultural self-determination. However, it is Article 15.1(c) that has attracted particular debate. This is because it is frequently argued that this provision supports the characterization of intellectual property rights as human rights.[5] A similar argument is frequently made with respect to the precursor of Article 15.1(c), Article 27.2 of the Universal Declaration of Human Rights (1948; hereinafter 'UDHR'). This is not surprising since ICESCR, Article 15.1, is clearly based upon Article 27 of the UDHR, which provides:

1. Everyone has the right to freely participate in the cultural life of the community, to enjoy the arts and to share in scientific advancement and its benefits.
2. Everyone has the right to the protection of the moral and material interests resulting from any scientific, literary or artistic production of which he is the author.

It is evident that neither Article 27.2 of the UDHR nor ICESCR, Article 15.1(c) necessarily mandate intellectual property protection in the form in which it currently prevails. It is also clear that whatever means are chosen to implement the rights in Article 27.2 and Article 15.1(c), respectively, those rights must be balanced against the other rights laid down in Articles 27 and 15. This is a matter to which this chapter will return.

The rather loose-fitting garment clothing a right to cultural self-determination, which is produced by knitting together these various provisions, may have taken on a more structured appearance as a result of the UNESCO Convention on the Protection and Promotion of the Diversity of Cultural Expressions of 2005. It is evident from both its Preamble and its operative provisions that the Convention firmly lodges itself within the human-rights camp, even if it does not go so far as to create a new human right.[6] So far as the Preamble is concerned, amongst an enormous list of other things, it declares itself to be, in the words of the first five paragraphs:

*Affirming* that cultural diversity is a defining characteristic of humanity,
*Conscious* that cultural diversity forms a common heritage of humanity and should be cherished and preserved for the benefit of all,
*Being aware* that cultural diversity creates a rich and varied world, which increases the range of choices and nurtures human capacities and values, and therefore is a mainspring for sustainable development for communities, peoples, and nations,
*Recalling* that cultural diversity, flourishing within a framework of democracy, tolerance, social justice and mutual respect between peoples and cultures, is indispensable for peace and security at the local, national and international levels,
*Celebrating*, the importance of cultural diversity for the full realization of human rights and fundamental freedoms proclaimed in the Universal Declaration of Human Rights and in other universally recognized instruments.

The location of the Convention within the stable of human rights instruments, which is suggested in the Preamble, is reinforced by a number of the operative provisions of the Convention. Two such provisions are of particular note in this respect. One is the first of the Convention's so-called guiding principles in Article 2.1, which provides:

Cultural diversity can be protected and promoted only if human rights and fundamental freedoms, such as freedom of expression, information and communication, as well as the ability of individuals to choose cultural expressions, are guaranteed. No one may invoke the provisions of this Convention in order to infringe human rights and fundamental freedoms as enshrined in the Universal Declaration of Human Rights or guaranteed by international law, or to limit the scope thereof.

The other relevant article, however, provides the clearest invocation of the authority and relevance of the pre-existing human rights instruments. This is Article 5.1, which is concerned with the obligations of the parties to the Convention:

The Parties, in conformity with the Charter of the United Nations, the principles of international law and universally recognized human rights instruments, reaffirm their sovereign right to formulate and implement their cultural policies and to adopt measures to protect and promote the diversity of cultural expressions and to strengthen international cooperation to achieve the purposes of this Convention.

By drawing together the various strands from the UDHR and the Covenants to the UN Charter that make up the composite right to cultural self-determination, the UNESCO Convention may be conceptualized as a particular, if rather Byzantine, instantiation of the right to cultural self-determination. Certainly, it gives more concrete form to the idea that the promotion and protection of cultural diversity should be the subject of international legal obligations. But is this new form likely to be more successful than its forerunners in counterbalancing the effects of the international copyright system, which is now so firmly entrenched within the system of international economic law operating under the auspices of the WTO?

## The concept of 'culture'

Before moving on to the question of the operation and effect of the WTO agreements in the arena of cultural self-determination, it is necessary to put some flesh on the bones of the concept of 'culture' in relation to which this right of self-determination exists. In fact, there is a great deal of flesh to play around with here: 'culture' being an expression of enormous potential width and diversity. The words 'culture' or 'cultural' appear, without any definition, in the UDHR and in both the UN Covenants. Not much by way of refinement can be gleaned from the rather general terms in which the expressions are used in the ICCPR. However, both the UDHR and ICECSR offer some context for assessing the meaning of these expressions. So far as UDHR, Article 27.1 is concerned, direct reference is made to 'the arts' and to 'scientific advancement'. Some help in divining the meaning of 'culture' and 'cultural' may also be provided by Article 27.2 and its reference to 'scientific, literary or artistic production'. Similar expressions are used in ICECSR, Article 15.1. It is unclear how much should be read into it, but it is also interesting to note that sub-Articles 2, 3 and 4 of Article 15 contrast the concepts of 'science' and 'culture', and of 'scientific research' and 'creative activity'.

The UNESCO Convention (2005) also gives some form to the concept of culture with which it is concerned, although it is noticeable that the definitions involve some circularity because they all invoke the notion of culture in order to define it. This, possibly inevitable, circularity is not the only indication that the drafters of the Convention experienced considerable difficulty pinning down the central concept with which they were concerned.[7] It is also evident that each attempt at definition gives rise to other definitional problems that call for further elucidation (and circularity). Article 4 of the Convention defines its central concept of 'cultural diversity' as 'the manifold ways in which cultures and groups and societies find expression', including 'diverse modes of artistic creation, production, dissemination, distribution and enjoyment, whatever the means and technologies used'. 'Cultural content' is 'the symbolic meaning, artistic dimension, and cultural values that originate from or express cultural identities'. 'Cultural expressions ... result from the creativity of individuals, groups and societies, and ... have cultural content'. Article 4 also deals with the more concrete aspects of cultural expressions. It defines 'cultural activities, goods and services' as those that 'embody or convey cultural expressions, irrespective of the commercial value they may have'. Cultural activities are, however, distinguished from cultural goods and services on the basis that they 'may be an end in themselves, or they may contribute to the production of cultural goods and services'. The production and distribution of these cultural goods and services may be undertaken by 'cultural industries'.

The interest manifested by the Convention in the production of cultural goods and services by cultural industries suggests a clear, if unarticulated, link with copyright law. While it is clear that copyright would not apply to the full range of cultural expressions and activities with which the Convention is concerned, there is a reasonably marked overlap between those things that would appear to fall within the definition of cultural goods and services in the Convention and the range of works protected by copyright law. As is envisaged in the Convention, this also raises the question of the role of the 'cultural industries' in the copyright arena. Of course, the cultural industries are not involved in the production of all the cultural goods and services protected by copyright. Indeed, on the creative side much production is done by individuals or groups that would hardly feel comfortable with the sobriquet 'cultural industry'. On the other hand, there are some copyright cultural goods and services that are more obviously the product of the cultural industries, the clearest example of these being films and broadcasts, which rely on the collaboration of a wide range of creative activities under the auspices of a 'cultural industry'. One might also argue that the production of a book or a CD in a commercially available form is a collaboration between the quintessential individual in the garret and a publisher, the latter of which might reasonably be described as being part of a cultural industry. Even where the cultural industries cannot be said to be involved in the production of copyright goods and services, they have a clear role in their distribution. These roles of the cultural industries in the production and distribution of certain types of cultural goods and services are subject to generous protection by copyright law. This protection sits alongside, often uncomfortably, the protection that copyright offers to individual creators. The ensuing tension between creative or cultural interests and business interests lies at the heart of copyright's relationship with the concept of cultural self-determination.

## Copyright and culture

The international copyright system, now embedded in the international trading system as a consequence of the TRIPs Agreement (1994), has operated at least in relation to some types of copyright-protected 'cultural goods and services' as a fetter on cultural diversity and self-determination.[8] This effect has been produced by certain aspects of copyright law itself, allied with aspects of behaviour in the market for 'cultural goods and services'.

So far as copyright law is concerned, the threat that it poses to cultural diversity and self-determination is a consequence of the process by which it commodifies and instrumentalizes the cultural outputs with which it is concerned. There are five interdependent aspects of copyright law that have been essential to this process.[9] The first and most basic tool of commodification is the alienability of the copyright interest. A second significant aspect of copyright law, making it an important tool of trade and investment, is its duration. The long period of copyright protection increases the asset value of individual copyright interests (Towse 1999: 91). Third, copyright's horizontal expansion means that it is progressively covering more and more types of cultural production. Fourth, the strong commercial distribution rights,[10] especially those which give the copyright holder control over imports and rental rights, have put copyright owners in a particularly strong market position, especially in the global context. Finally, the power of the owners of copyright in relation to all those wishing to use copyright material has been bolstered by a contraction of some of the most significant user rights in relation to copyright works, in particular fair dealing/ fair use and public interest rights. Allied to these characteristics of copyright law are the development of associated rights, in particular the right to prevent measures designed to circumvent technological protection,[11] which has no fair-dealing type exceptions and which, as we know now, is capable of a quite repressive application.[12]

Viewed in isolation from the market conditions that characterize the cultural industries, copyright's commodification of cultural output might appear not only benign but justified by both the need for creators to be remunerated in order to encourage them to create[13] and the need for cultural works to be disseminated in order to reap the social benefits of their creation.[14] However, viewed in context the picture is somewhat different. Copyright law has contributed to, augmented or created a range of market features that have resulted in a high degree of global concentration in the ownership of intellectual property in cultural goods and services. Five such market features, in particular, stand out (for a fuller discussion, see Macmillan 2006). First is the internationally harmonized nature of the relevant intellectual property rights.[15] This dovetails nicely with the second dominant market feature, which is the multinational operation of the corporate actors who acquire these harmonized intellectual property rights while at the same time exploiting the boundaries of national law to partition and control markets. The third relevant feature of the market is the high degree of horizontal and vertical integration that characterizes these corporations. Their horizontal integration gives them control over a range of different types of cultural products. Their vertical integration allows them to control distribution, thanks to the strong distribution rights conferred on them by copyright law.[16] The fourth feature is the progressive integration in the ownership of rights over content and the ownership of rights over content-carrying technology. Finally, there is the increasing tendency since the 1970s for acquisition and merger in the global market for cultural products and services (Bettig 1996: 37ff; see also Smiers 1999: 119). Besides being driven by the regular desires (both corporate and individual) for capital accumulation (Bettig 1996: 37), this last feature has been produced by the movements towards horizontal and vertical integration, and integration of the ownership of rights over content and content-carrying technology.

So far as cultural diversity and self-determination are concerned, the consequences of this copyright-facilitated aggregation of private power over cultural goods and services on the global level are not happy ones. Through their control of markets for cultural products the multimedia corporations have acquired the power to act as a cultural filter, controlling to some extent what we can see, hear and read.[17] Closely associated with this is the tendency towards homogeneity in the character of available cultural products and services (see also Bettig 1996). This tendency, and the commercial context in which it occurs, has been well summed up by the comment that a large proportion of the recorded music offered for retail sale has 'about as much cultural diversity as a McDonald's menu' (Capling 1996: 22). It makes good commercial sense in a globalised world to train taste along certain reliable routes, and the market for cultural goods and services is no different in this respect to any other (Levitt 1983: 92).[18] Of course, there is a vast market for cultural goods and services and, as a consequence, the volume of production is immense. However, it would obviously be a serious mistake to confuse volume with diversity.

The vast corporate control over cultural goods and services also has a constricting effect on what has been described as the intellectual commons or the intellectual public domain.[19] The impact on the intellectual commons manifests itself in various ways (see further Macmillan 2002b, Macmillan 2005a and Macmillan 2006). For example, private control over a wide range of cultural goods and services has an adverse impact on freedom of speech. This is all the more concerning because control over speech by private entities is not constrained by the range of legal instruments that have been developed in Western democracies to ensure that public or governmental control over speech is minimised (see further Macmillan Patfield 1996: 199 and Macmillan 2005a). The ability to control speech, arguably objectionable in its own right,[20] facilitates a form of cultural domination by private interests. This may, for example, take the subtle form of control exercised over the way we construct images of our society and ourselves.[21] But this subtle form of control is reinforced by the industry's overt and aggressive assertion of control over the use of material assumed by most people to be in the intellectual commons and, thus, in the public domain. The irony is that the reason people assume such material to be in the commons is that the copyright owners have force-fed it to us as receivers of the mass culture disseminated by the mass media. The more powerful the copyright owner the more dominant the cultural image, but the more likely that the copyright owner will seek to protect the cultural power of the image through copyright enforcement. The result is that not only are individuals not able to use, develop or reflect upon dominant cultural images, they are also unable to challenge them by subverting them.[22] Coombe describes this corporate control of the commons as monological and, accordingly, destroying the dialogical relationship between the individual and society (Coombe 1998: 86). Some remnants of this dialogical relationship ought to be preserved by copyright's fair dealing/fair use right. It is, after all, this aspect of copyright law that appears to be intended to permit resistance and critique (Gaines 1991: 10). Yet the fair-dealing defence is a weak tool for this purpose and becoming weaker (see further Macmillan 2006).

These constrictions of the intellectual commons (or public domain) affect its vibrancy and creative potential. They also tend to undermine the utilitarian/development justification for copyright, which is increasingly seen as the dominant justification for copyright protection, especially in jurisdictions reflecting the Anglo-American bias on these matters. As is well known, the general idea underlying this justification is that the grant of copyright encourages the production of the cultural works, which is said to be essential to the development process.[23] However, the consequences of copyright's commodification of cultural goods and services, as described above, seem to place some strain on this alleged relationship between copyright and development – at least if development is construed in the broad sense indicated in Section 1 of this chapter, which was embraced by the World Commission on Development and Culture and subsequently reprised in the UNESCO Convention. The edifice of private power that has been built upon copyright law has deprived us all to some extent of the benefits of this type of development. As Waldron comments, '[t]he private appropriation of the public realm of cultural artifacts restricts and controls the moves that can be made therein by the rest of us' (Waldron 1993: 885). This is hardly a reflection of a world in which effective freedom of choice is enhanced, and in which individuals enjoy such things as 'the right to participate in the cultural life of the community' (UNESCO; see further Macmillan 1998 and Macmillan 2002a). It seems worth noting briefly that increases in the duration of copyright protection, such as those which have occurred in the European Union countries[24] and in the United States,[25] are hardly helping.

### Contribution of the TRIPs Agreement

The impact of copyright on cultural self-determination and diversity, which has been described above, was already well established before the advent of the WTO in 1994. The question that is now addressed is whether the establishment of the new multilateral trading framework under the auspices of the WTO has exacerbated the tensions between the protection of copyright and the right to cultural self-determination. In part, the answer to this question depends on the effects of the TRIPs Agreement (1994).

If the arguments made in this chapter concerning the relationship between copyright and cultural self-determination and diversity are persuasive then it is difficult to conceive of the TRIPs Agreement as contributing in a positive way to this relationship. This can hardly be a surprise. The conclusion of the TRIPs Agreement was formally driven by the United States. Lying, however, behind the government of the United States as formal actor was a formidable coalition of US-based multinational corporate interests that were pushing for a strong system of rights to protect their trading interests (Blakeney 1996: Chapter 1 and Sell 2003: especially Chapters 5 and 6). The upshot of this activity is a multilateral agreement, the very name of which reflects its gestation and instrumentality. That is, since the arrival of the TRIPs Agreement, intellectual property law has been explicitly configured as being about 'rights' in relation to 'trade'. For those who would want to see copyright bolstering the fundamental role of cultural products as having a value in their own right, rather than a purely instrumental role, some comfort might be taken from the fact that the Agreement refers to 'trade related aspects' of intellectual property and thereby suggests that there may be some other aspects – but it is cold comfort. Not only is the TRIPs Agreement the dominant normative instrument of international intellectual property law, its location within the suite of WTO agreements means that it is an integral part of what is emerging as the pre-eminent system of international law-making (see further Kennedy 1995: 671 and Macmillan 2004: 115). These two aspects of the TRIPs Agreement are, of course, intrinsically related. The systemic legal dominance and concomitant strong enforcement procedures of the WTO are a large part of the reason that the TRIPs Agreement has acquired the ability to define the parameters of intellectual property law discourse.[26] While it is true that some of the most important steps down the instrumental/trade-related road were taken before the advent of the TRIPs Agreement, at least in the Anglo-Saxon model of copyright law, the TRIPs Agreement has provided an authoritative consolidation and normalization of that approach.

The copyright provisions of the TRIPs Agreement are, more or less, the same as those already laid down in the Berne Convention for the Protection of Literary and Artistic Works (1869).[27] Therefore there are not enormous differences between the legal framework of international copyright law before and after TRIPs. Yet the reification of intellectual property rights as trade rights, capable of enforcement through a system of trade retaliation, seems to be emphasizing certain aspects of the international copyright landscape at the expense of others. This perception is reinforced by two further factors. The first is that the TRIPs Agreement has shown itself to be a useful uniform basis upon which to negotiate bilateral investment treaties, which may strengthen the oligopolistic nature of the market for cultural goods and services (Drahos 2002: 791). Indeed wrapped up in this observation is the further suggestion that the TRIPs Agreement might be even better characterized as an investment agreement than as a trade agreement (Macmillan 2005b: 115). (Either way, its capacity to nourish cultural self-determination and diversity seems rather limited.) The second factor reinforcing the nature of the change in the international copyright landscape is that the interpretation and enforcement of international copyright law is now in the hands of trade law experts, who are not necessarily experts in intellectual property law or practice.

The WTO panel in *US – Section 110(5) of US Copyright Act* (2000; hereinafter '*US Copyright*') does not do much to relieve concerns about the effect of the TRIPs Agreement on the current trajectory of copyright law. This case considers the so-called three step test for the validity of national copyright exceptions in Article 13 of the TRIPs Agreement.[28] It is of some importance in the present context because the width of exceptions to the copyright interest determines the strength of the copyright holder. As a result of the incorporation of the provisions of the Berne Convention into the TRIPs Agreement (see above), [MS-Office1] the TRIPs Agreement contains a range of exceptions. These include the general exception provision in Article 9(2) of the Berne Convention, which contains its own version of a three-step test for exceptions. The WTO panel in *US Copyright* decided that Article 13 of the TRIPs Agreement was an embodiment of the minor exceptions doctrine that formed part of the Berne Convention. The panel does not explain why, if the minor exceptions doctrine was already part of the Berne Convention and (therefore) of the TRIPs Agreement, it was necessary to repeat it in Article 13. Thus it missed the opportunity to consider the possibility that Article 13 was intended to add, or could be construed as adding, something to the existing body of law. Interestingly enough, buried in the somewhat objectionable arguments of the European Union in *US Copyright* are the seeds of a suggestion as to what the 'something' possibly added by Article 13 might be. The European Union argued that the requirements of the first step, that exceptions must be confined to 'certain special cases', required justification of the exception by reference to a legitimate policy purpose. Such a legitimate policy purpose might, for example, include the need to balance the interests of copyright owners and users in certain cases. This argument might be bolstered by reference to the objective stated in Article 7 of the TRIPs Agreement, which speaks about intellectual property rights being used in a manner which is 'conducive to social and economic welfare, and to a balance of rights and obligations'. Not only was this article ignored in *US Copyright*, but the whole concept of copyright as a balance between rights and obligations was overlooked. Once this balance is lost then copyright's potential as a tool of cultural domination and homogenization is unconstrained by any mechanism internal to copyright law.

### The rest of the WTO

The TRIPs Agreement, which imposes minimum legal standards with respect to national intellectual property protection, is somewhat aberrant in the context of the overall WTO stable of agreements. This is because, unlike the TRIPs Agreement,[30] the other WTO multilateral agreements are dedicated to reducing national barriers to trade using three main tools, which are the reduction of tariffs, the reduction of non-tariff barriers and 'the elimination of discriminatory treatment in international trade relations' (WTO Agreement 1994: Preamble). The elimination of discriminatory treatment is effected through the principles of national treatment and most favoured nation (MFN) treatment.[31] Taken together these two principles provide that a WTO member state may not create a trade disadvantage *vis a vis* domestic goods and services for like goods or services coming from another WTO member state, nor may they discriminate between like goods and services coming into their jurisdiction from more than one other member state.[32] The WTO agreements laying down obligations pursuant to the principles of national treatment and MFN treatment are subject to a range of exceptions allowing governments to take steps that would amount to breaches of these principles in some cases involving pressing national priorities, but the exceptions are limited and narrowly drawn.

In terms of the picture painted above of cultural domination by private actors, a national government may wish to take steps at the national level to ameliorate the effects of the oligopolistic markets for cultural goods and services. For example, it may wish to attempt to prevent the swamping of local culture as the result of the homogenizing effect of global media and entertainment oligopolies by providing for quotas, local content restrictions or subsidies for local cultural production.[33] All these sorts of devices run the risk of falling foul of WTO rules. The Agreement which has the capacity to be the particular culprit is the General Agreement on Trade in Services (1994; hereinafter 'GATS').[34] Due to the somewhat unusual nature of the GATS as a bottom-up liberalizing agreement,

WTO members are only bound by the liberalizing provisions of GATS if, and to the extent that, they have accepted obligations in the relevant sector.[35] There is not yet any general agreement or protocol on liberalization of obligations in the audio-visual sector,[36] which is the sector in which the cultural effects of the copyright-induced oligopolies are most keenly experienced (for example, Dunkley 2001: 183–87, Macmillan 2002b, Macmillan 2006, Grantham 2000). However, some WTO members have undertaken relevant obligations and there is considerable international political pressure for more liberalization in this sector (see further Graber 2006: 569–70, Dunkley 2001, Grantham 2000, Hahn 2006: 526).

Once commitments are made under GATS, derogations from the principles of MFN treatment and national treatment are allowed if they are contained in the relevant member's GATS schedules.[37] Otherwise, the regime is strict and the range of exceptions laid down in Article XIV quite narrow compared, for example, to the older General Agreement on Trade and Tariffs (1947 and 1994; hereinafter 'GATT').[38] As under the GATT, to make out an exception under the GATS it is necessary to show not only that the subject matter of the relevant measure falls within one of the specific classes of exceptions, but also that it complies with the so-called *chapeau*, with which the Article commences. Specifically, Article XIV provides as follows:

> Subject to the requirement that such measures are not applied in a manner which would constitute a means of arbitrary or unjustifiable discrimination between countries where like conditions prevail, or a disguised restriction on trade in services, nothing in this Agreement shall be construed to prevent the adoption or enforcement by any member of measures:

a) necessary to protect public morals or to maintain public order;
b) necessary to protect human, animal or plant life or health;
c) necessary to secure compliance with laws or regulations which are not inconsistent with the provisions of this Agreement including those relating to:
   (i)  the prevention of deceptive and fraudulent practices or to deal with the effects of a default on services contracts;
   (ii) the protection of the privacy of individuals in relation to the processing and dissemination of personal data and the protection of confidentiality of individual records and accounts;
   (iii) safety;
d) inconsistent with Article XVII [national treatment], provided that the difference in treatment is aimed at ensuring the equitable or effective imposition or collection of direct taxes in respect of services or service suppliers of other Members;
e) inconsistent with Article II [MFN treatment], provided that the difference in treatment is the result of an agreement on the avoidance of double taxation or provisions on the avoidance of double taxation in any other international agreement or arrangement by which the member is bound.

As is apparent, there is no specific exception in Article XIV that relates to cultural diversity or self-determination.[39] The closest one might get to this would be an expansive reading of paragraph (a) on the basis that measures designed to protect human rights might fall within it. The WTO Appellate Body decision in *US – Measures Affecting the Cross-Border Supply of Gambling and Betting Services* (2005; hereinafter 'Cross Border Gambling'), which considered the meaning and application of Article XIV(a), suggests that such a result is possible. In its decision the Appellate Body quoted with apparent approval the definitions given to 'public morals' and 'public order', respectively, in the panel decision (Appellate Body, paragraph 296). According to the panel, the former 'denotes standards of right and wrong conduct maintained by or on behalf of a community or nation' (Panel, paragraph 6.465). The latter expression is qualified by footnote 5 of the GATS, which provides that '[t]he public order exception may be invoked only where a genuine and sufficiently serious threat is posed to one of the fundamental interests of society'. Taking this into account, the panel found that '"public order" refers to the preservation of the fundamental interests of a society, as reflected in public policy and law' (Panel, paragraph 6.467). The panel found, and the Appellate Body agreed, that since the various measures in question were concerned with preventing 'money laundering, organized crime, fraud, underage gambling and pathological gambling', they were concerned with protecting either or both of public morals or public order (Panel, paragraph 6.486; Appellate Body, paragraph 296). This reasonably expansive reading tends to suggest that measures necessary for protecting human rights would have a chance of falling within the exception. Even if (and it is a reasonably big 'if') this is so, however, there are some other issues that arise with respect to the utility of the exception in relation to measures designed to protect or promote cultural self-determination or diversity.

One problem, which plagues many of the WTO exceptions, is the restrictive interpretation that has been given to the word 'necessary'. Early WTO jurisprudence interpreted 'necessary' in the context of the GATT exceptions as requiring that there be no alternative measures that are consistent, or more consistent, with GATT.[40] The status of this approach was opened to some doubt in a range of cases concerning the GATT,[41] and by *Cross-Border Gambling* in the context of Article XIV of the GATS. The effect of these more recent cases was summarized by the Appellate Body in *Dominican Republic – Measures Affecting the Importation and Internal Sale of Cigarettes* (2004 and 2005; hereinafter '*Dominican Cigarettes*'). It noted that a measure is 'necessary' to achieve a certain result if another WTO-consistent measure is not 'reasonably available' (paragraph 69, quoting the Appellate Body in *Cross-Border Gambling* at paragraph 307). The Appellate Body went on to point out that:

> [I]n assessing whether a proposed alternative to the impugned measure is reasonably available, factors such as the trade impact of the measure, the importance of the interests protected by the measure, or the contribution of

the measure to the realization of the end pursued, should be taken into account in the analysis. The weighing and balancing process of these three factors also informs the determination whether a WTO-consistent alternative measure which the Member concerned could reasonably be expected to employ is available, or whether a less WTO-inconsistent measure is reasonably available.

(*Dominican Cigarettes* 2005: paragraph 70)

This reappraisal of the meaning of 'necessary' certainly lowers the bar for its application, although in the area of cultural self-determination and diversity there is some difficulty in predicting in advance whether other WTO-consistent measures might be 'reasonably available'.

Another hurdle in exempting measures designed to protect cultural self-determination and diversity is posed by the *chapeau* to Article XIV. As is evident on its face, it is concerned with the application of the measures in question. Somewhat less obvious is exactly what standards that application must attain in order to comply with the *chapeau*. This question was the subject of analysis in *United States – Import Prohibition of Certain Shrimp and Shrimp Products* (1998; hereinafter '*Sea Turtles*'), in which it was considered in relation to the almost identical wording in GATT, Article XX.[42] In the *Sea Turtles* case the Appellate Body acknowledged the difficulty in interpreting the expressions 'arbitrary discrimination' and 'unjustifiable discrimination' in the absence of any *chapeau* criteria for assessing arbitrariness or unjustifiability. This is presumably the reason for the Appellate Body's reference to the shifting line of equilibrium that must be marked out when applying the *chapeau* 'so that neither of the competing rights [of WTO members] will cancel out the other and thereby distort and nullify or impair the balance of rights and obligations constructed by the Members themselves in that Agreement' (paragraph 159).

Of course, one of the problems with this shifting line is that it makes it difficult to predict when a measure will fall foul of the *chapeau*. It may, however, be concluded from the Appellate Body Report in *Sea Turtles* that measures offending general principles of fairness constitute arbitrary discrimination, while those distinguishing between different WTO members without regard to their differing circumstances amount to unjustifiable discrimination.[43] In considering whether either type of discrimination was manifested by the relevant measure, the Appellate Body considered both the application of the measure and the fact that the US had not attempted to negotiate a corresponding multilateral treaty obligation. The emphasis that the Appellate Body placed on the latter factor suggests that a measure having extraterritorial effect can only escape being unjustifiably discriminating where it is based on a treaty obligation.[44] Theoretically, this sounds quite hopeful for human-rights measures based on multilateral treaty obligations. The problem, however, is the uncertain treaty status of the right to cultural self-determination and diversity. As the first part of this paper sought to show, it is possible to create this right from the composite effect of a number of treaty provisions. However, it would hardly be an exaggeration to say that its provenance as a broad 'right' is somewhat doubtful. Even in the UNESCO Convention there is little in the way of formal treaty obligations that might be sufficient to convince a WTO dispute-settlement panel that the strictures laid down in *Sea Turtles* have been met. In fact, the most likely effect of the UNESCO Convention is not on the operation of the exceptions to the GATS, but rather as a political device to constrain its signatory states from undertaking new GATS obligations that may lead to conflicts with the provisions of the Convention. The extent to which it will be effective for this purpose is likely to be a reflection on the countervailing political and strategic imperatives.

Looking at the WTO as a whole, it does not seem unreasonable to conclude that the TRIPs Agreement strengthens a copyright system that facilitates the growth of private oligopoly power over cultural output and the consequent cultural effects of this oliogopoly power, while other WTO agreements potentially forbid governments of WTO member states to take ameliorating action or action aimed at correcting the resulting market distortions.

## The rights clash?

So at the international-law level one is left with, on the one hand, the swathe of human-rights treaties and conventions that address themselves to rights of cultural self-determination and diversity, and on the other, the WTO. As argued above, the combined operation of the WTO agreements appears to fly in the face of international legal norms valorizing cultural self-determination and diversity. Is it correct to describe the relationship between these two systems of international law obligations as clashing? If so, what is the nature of this clash? This chapter concludes by examining the question of a rights clash from three different perspectives: (a) a normative perspective; (b) a formal legal perspective; and (c) a consideration of systemic governance (or political) issues at the international level.

### Normative questions

#### Does free trade promote cultural diversity?

The first of the issues raised by what is described here as the normative perspective addresses, in essence, the extent to which one might look so hard at the trees that one misses the wood. It will be recalled that the UNESCO Convention specifically refers to the need for cultural interchange in order to stimulate cultural diversity (see UNESCO Convention, Articles 1 and 7). Might it be, therefore, that a trading system that is geared to promote trade in cultural goods and services in fact serves that very end? (For an example of this argument, see Hahn 2006: 520–21.) Advocates of this argument sometimes suggest that the real problem with the WTO is the absence of multilateral rules on competition operating under the auspices of the WTO that might restrain the oligopolistic conduct (for example, Germann 2006).

A possible problem with this argument is that it may underestimate the real spiritual parentage of the WTO in the doctrine of comparative advantage. This doctrine postulates that resources will be most optimally allocated if each country concentrates on producing and trading those goods and services that it is best placed, for whatever reason, to produce. It is true, of course, that all countries and societies automatically generate cultural artefacts and that probably no particular country has a comparative advantage in this respect. However, some countries have comparative, if not absolute, advantage in the generation of the commodi-fied forms of culture that are capable of being traded in the form of goods or services. It is, of course, these countries that are swamping the global culture with their output. Dunkley puts a similar argument leading to rather the same result:

> Cultural embodiment in services such as audio-visuals reverses many tradi-tional free trade assumptions. For instance, Free Traders always argue against governments attempting to rectify a trade deficit in any one sector because this will be countered by a surplus in another sector. In audio-visuals, however, this could mean constantly being subject to someone else's culture, and the idea that we should console ourselves with the thought of people in other countries wearing jumpers made of Aussie wool is a non-sense … In a world where even culture and entertainment are commodified and mass-marketed, free trade in these sectors is likely to mean that only countries possessing comparative advantage can have the privilege of retaining their national identities, which in my view is socially outrageous and should be resisted (Dunkley 2001: 184–85).

It seems reasonable to argue that we would need to move the WTO a long way away from its present form before we could celebrate its ability to create a vibrant and diverse trade in cultural artefacts.

### Does copyright promote cultural diversity?

There is strong belief in some quarters that copyright protection is essential to cultural diversity and self-determination.[45] Indeed, the provisions of the UN Covenants are frequently cited as a basis for the granting of intellectual property protection. This is particularly so with respect to ICCPR, Article 27, which is used to found a claim to intellectual property rights for Indigenous peoples. Similarly, as is all too well known, Article 27.2 of the Universal Declaration on Human Rights is frequently used as a justification for the granting of intellectual property rights.

This question is tied up with the questions of both formal legal conflict and systemic governance and is further addressed below. Perhaps, for the moment, it might be noted that if copyright is necessary for the promotion of cultural diversity and self-determination, then something has gone wrong and we need to look very carefully again at the shape of copyright law and consider whether there are parts that we might want to jettison or change dramatically – that is, some of the parts considered in more detail above (see the fourth section of this chapter) – if we want it to serve the objective of cultural diversity and self-determination.

## Formal legal issues

The origins of the UNESCO Convention, as a response to the absence of a cultural exception in the WTO agreements (see further Hahn 2006: 515–20 and Graber 2006: 554–55), make it clear that its framers understood at least some dimensions of the potential conflict between the WTO agreements and the UNESCO Convention. This is most obviously the case in relation to the GATS and the GATT.[46] However, the framers of the UNESCO Convention seem to have underestimated the potential impact of intellectual property rights on cultural diversity. The Convention Preamble recognizes 'the importance of intellectual property rights in sustaining those involved in cultural creativity'. The reasons for this largely positive attitude to the role of intellectual property rights in securing cultural diversity are unclear. The original UNESCO Universal Declaration on Cultural Diversity (2001; hereinafter 'UNESCO Declaration') upon which the Convention was based, included in its action plan the need to ensure the protection of copyright but 'at the same time upholding a public right of access to culture, in accordance with Article 27 of the Universal Declaration of Human Rights' (paragraph 16). The Declaration also drew a parallel in its Article 1 between biological diversity and cultural diversity. In the light of this, it is interesting to note that the framers of the Convention on Biological Diversity (1992) were far more anxious about the role of intellectual property in securing biological diversity. Its Article 16.5 provides:

> The Contracting Parties, recognizing that patents and other intellectual property rights may have an influence on the implementation of this Convention, shall cooperate in this regard subject to national legislation and international law in order to ensure that such rights are supportive of and do not run counter to its objectives.

By contrast, the UNESCO Convention seems to envisage no conflict.

It seems possible that, if there is a legal conflict between the UNESCO regime and the WTO regime, this might occur at either the domestic level or at the international level. In order to deal with this, Article 20.1 of the UNESCO Convention introduces the concept of 'mutual supportiveness' between various treaty obligations undertaken by its parties. It goes on to provide that 'when interpreting and applying other treaties to which they are parties or when entering into other international obligations, Parties shall take account of the relevant provisions of this Convention'. All this is to occur without 'subordinating this Convention to any other treaty'. However, it is unclear how much impact this will have when the UNESCO Convention rubs up against WTO obligations.[47] Perhaps, as noted already, its main effect will be to halt or retard the giving of further GATS commitments in sectors likely to impact on cultural diversity, such as the audio-visual sector. In general, however, it seems likely that the concepts in Article 20.1 are not up to the task of resolving many potential conflicts. This likelihood seems to be accepted in the UNESCO Convention, which squarely faces the question of formal legal conflict in Article 20.2, which provides that 'Nothing in this Convention shall be interpreted as modifying rights and obligations of the Parties under any other treaties to which they are parties.'

In considering the effect of Article 20.2 it should be borne in mind that if there was a formal legal conflict between the UNESCO Convention and a WTO agreement, the likely forum for the airing of the dispute would be a WTO dispute-settlement proceeding. This is primarily because the WTO has become the pre-eminent system for international dispute resolution. However, it is also because of the very weak Conciliation Procedure laid down in the Annex to the UNESCO Convention, which Hahn describes as 'worth mentioning only as being reminiscent of the very early days of modern international law' (Hahn 2006: 533). Rather depressingly, Article 20.2 of the UNESCO Convention is the perfect let-out for the WTO, should it ever need it. There have been occasions when the WTO Appellate Body has shown itself willing to take into account international agreements emanating from outside the WTO, although it has always found a way to ensure that this does not, so far as it is concerned, lead to a systemic conflict between the WTO agreements and international agreements that are exterior to it and that might influence the outcome of its deliberations.[48] This is relatively easy where the agreements predate the WTO agreements, but new techniques might be necessary for agreements that postdate the WTO agreements, unless (of course) they have a provision like Article 20.2. However, having said all this, it is far from clear that the UNESCO Convention could ever lead to the sort of legal conflict with the WTO agreements that would require reliance on Article 20.2 by the WTO dispute-resolution bodies. This is because the UNESCO Convention requires very little in the way of positive acts from its adherents.[49] For reasons that are located in their generality, one would also be hard put to find a formal legal conflict between any of the provisions of the UN Covenants and the provisions of any WTO agreement.

The clash, if there is one, is some sort of overall systemic conflict in which two systems, viewed in their entirety, produce results that cannot coexist with any comfort. This is what is referred to in this chapter as an issue of systemic governance or, more simply, politics.

## Systemic governance/politics

It has just been argued that Article 20.2 of the UNESCO Convention would make life easy for a WTO panel should it ever be faced with a conflict between a

WTO agreement and the UNESCO Convention. However, the need for such a consideration is unlikely ever to arise, and not just because of the fact that there is little in the way of positive obligations with respect to cultural diversity in the UNESCO Convention. In fact, the need for such a consideration is unlikely to arise because the system of human rights/public international law conventions and the system of WTO agreements are systemically divided so that there is no legal mechanism for an interface between the two systems. Further, there appears to be very little, if any, space in the WTO system for a consideration of international human-rights norms. As noted above, one possible space arises in the context of the interpretation of exceptions to WTO obligations – and even here the jurisprudential basis for this assertion has to be accepted as being extremely thin.[50] Such an opportunity could only arise if there was a relevant exception that invited the consideration of human-rights norms. In the GATS it is far from clear that any such exception exists. After the *US Copyright* case there seems to be little scope of reading such an opportunity into the relevant provisions of the TRIPs Agreement, unless there is some reassessment in the light of Article 7.

Assuming that, in normative terms, there is some sort of clash between the human-rights system in general, and the UNESCO Convention in particular, and the WTO system, then that clash is happening in a space between the two systems – a space that has been neglected in the bifurcated system of international governance represented by the systems of public international law and international economic law (see further Macmillan 2004). It is clear that this is a political issue as well as a legal one.[51] So how might or should the problems raised by this issue be resolved? One approach might be to rely upon the political high ground of human rights. Generally speaking, describing a right as 'human' seems to invest it with some form of moral urgency, which makes it incontrovertible or irresistible. The implication must be that when a human right comes into conflict with some other right, the irresistible moral superiority of the human right must be recognized and respected. However, the position is not clear when we are talking about human rights and copyright, which is capable of being constructed as a species of human right. Of course, we might deal with this problem of moral high ground by having a closer look at the human-rights credentials of copyright. This would be likely to show us that some of the most objectionable aspects of copyright are not mandated by a human-rights approach to it. Further, the reification of intellectual property rights as trade rights does little to improve their human-rights credentials.

Another approach might be to incorporate the human-rights agenda into the trade liberalization agenda. Despite the persuasive commentators who have argued to the contrary (for example Petersmann 2002: 621, Trachtman 2002: 77) this is neither sensible nor desirable. Such an approach is, in Alston's words, 'a form of epistemological misappropriation' (Alston 2002: 815, 826). The WTO is not an appropriate body to oversee the protection of human rights, including those relating to cultural diversity and self-determination (see further Macmillan 2004). This creates some difficulties in relation to suggestions that a link might be created by inserting a cultural exception into the WTO agreements,[52] or even the ingenious device of a procedural clause in the form of a WTO Ministerial Decision (Graber 2006: 572–73). If we think that the human-rights approach is a better approach than the trade-related approach, then one choice would be to pit the political power of human-rights law and rhetoric against the WTO system. But this is a problematic choice: the hollowed-out concept of the human, stripped of race, religion, ethnic affiliation, the empty 'human' essential to the universality of the human in human-rights laws, seems a weak and meaningless abstraction to pit against the powerful concept of the global market delivering economic benefits to all (Orford 2005: 179).

So where does this leave the concept of development as a workable tool of international law and politics? Its significance in the conflict between cultural self-determination and diversity, on the one hand, and the demands of the international copyright system, on the other, seems to have been largely overlooked. Perhaps it has fallen into the same neglected legal and political space in which this conflict seems to be taking place. But is it also the case that international legal and political contestation over the meaning of development more generally has fallen into this same space? This is not a palatable thought. If the concepts of development employed in the system of WTO law and the system of public international law operating under the auspices of the UN are as diverse as this case study of approaches to cultural self-determination suggest then, for as long as the WTO continues to be the pre-eminent system of international dispute resolution, we are faced with a predominant concept of development that is uncomfortably close to the universal economic rationality with which development started its late colonial life.

## Notes

1 For an account of this distinction between public international law and international economic law, see Macmillan (2004).

2 The *Parties* to this Agreement, *Recognizing* that their relations in the field of trade and economic endeavour should be conducted with a view to raising standards of living, ensuring full employment and a large and steadily growing volume of real income and effective demand, and expanding the production of and trade in goods and services, while allowing for the optimal use of the world's resources in accordance with the objective of sustainable development, seeking both to protect and preserve the environment and to enhance the means for doing so in a manner consistent with their respective needs and concerns at different levels of economic development ...

3 See Agreement Establishing the World Trade Organization, Annex 1C.

4 CCPR, Article 1.3 provides:

The States Parties to the present Covenant, including those having responsibility for the administration of Non-Self-Governing and Trust Territories, shall promote the realization of the right of self-determination, and shall respect that right, in conformity with the provisions of the Charter of the United Nations.

5 A similar argument has been made, pursuant to CCPR, Article 27, in relation to the conferring of intellectual property rights on indigenous peoples.

6  For an assessment of the relationship between the UNESCO Convention and existing international human-rights obligations, see Graber 2006: 553, 560–63.

7  However, for a more generous assessment of Article 4, see Graber 2006: 558.

8  For a fuller version of this argument see, e.g., Macmillan 2002a: 99–118, Macmillan 2002b: 483–92, Macmillan 2005a: 35–65, Macmillan 2006: 46–69.

9  For a fuller version of this argument see Macmillan 1998: 71, Macmillan 2002a and Macmillan 2002b.

10  See especially the TRIPs Agreement, which enshrines rental rights in relation to computer programmes, films and phonograms (Articles 11 and 14(4)); Article 7, WIPO Copyright Treaty 1996; and Articles 9 and 13, WIPO Performances and Phonograms Treaty 1996.

11  See, for example, Article 11, WIPO Copyright Treaty 1996; Article 6, EU Directive on Copyright in the Information Society (2001); section 1201, US Copyright Act of 1976.

12  See, for example, *Universal City Studios, Inc. v. Corley* (2001) and the discussion of this case in Macmillan 2002b.

13  See, however, Towse (2001), especially Chapters 6 and 8, in which it is argued that copyright generates little income for most creative artists. Nevertheless, Towse suggests that copyright is valuable to creative artists for reasons of status and control of their work.

14  For arguments about the importance of copyright in securing communication of works, see van Caenegem 1995: 322 and Netanel 1996: 283.

15  Through, for example, the Berne Convention (1886), Articles 9 to 14 of the TRIPs Agreement, the WIPO Copyright Treaty (1996) and the WIPO Performances and Phonograms Treaty (1996).

16  For a discussion of how the film entertainment industry conforms to these features, see Macmillan 2002b.

17  See further: Macmillan 2006 and, in relation to the film industry, Macmillan 2002b: 488–89. See also Capling 1996: 21–24, Abel 1994a: 52, Abel 1994b: 374, 380.

18  Cf. Gray 1998: 57–58. However, Gray's view seems to be that diversity stimulates globalization, which must be distinguished from the idea that globalization might stimulate diversity.

19  This is a concept that has become, unsurprisingly, a central concern of intellectual property scholarship: see, e.g., MacQueen and Waelde (eds) 2007.

20  See, for example, the discussion of the justifications for the free-speech principle in Barendt (2005).

21  See further, for example, Coombe 1998: 100–129, which demonstrates how even the creation of alternative identities on the basis of class, sexuality, gender and race is constrained and homogenized through the celebrity or star system.

22  See, for example, *Walt Disney Prods v. Air Pirates* (1978 and 1979). On this case, see Waldron 1993: 841 and Macmillan 2006. See also Chon 1993: 97, Koenig 1994: 803 and Macmillan Patfield 1996.

23  For a good example of a statement of this rationale, see the Preface to World Intellectual Property Organization (1978). For discussion of this rationale, see, e.g., Waldron 1993: 850ff and Macmillan Patfield 1997: 113.

24  As a result of Council Directive 93/98/EEC, 1993 OJ L290/9.

25  As a result of the Bono Copyright Term Extension Act (1998), held to be constitutionally valid in *Eldred v. Ashcroft* (2003).

26  Although, as Sell (2003)shows, important changes in discourse, such as the move from intellectual property 'privileges' to intellectual property 'rights', began to occur much earlier than the Uruguay Round of trade negotiations (Chapter 3).

27  Article 9.1, TRIPs Agreement (1994) incorporates Articles 1 to 21 of the Berne Convention, except Article 6*bis* (moral rights) by reference. Articles 10 to 14 of the

TRIPs Agreement add some further obligations. In particular, Articles 11 and 14.4 broaden the exclusive rights of the copyright holder by the addition of rental rights in relation to computer programs, films and phonograms. However, neither of these provisions are unique in international copyright law: see Article 7, WIPO Copyright Treaty 1996 and Articles 9 and 13, WIPO Performances and Phonograms Treaty 1996.

28 The TRIPs Agreement (1994) provides:

Members shall confine limitations and exceptions to exclusive rights to certain special cases which do not conflict with a normal exploitation of the work and do not unreasonably prejudice the legitimate interests of the right holder (Article 13).

30 The aberrant nature of the TRIPs Agreement is also manifested in its particularly uncertain relationship to the doctrine of comparative advantage that grounds the concept of free trade upon which the WTO is (very loosely) based: see Reichman 1993: 171, 175. On the doctrine of comparative advantage, see elsewhere in this chapter.

31 In fact both these principles make an appearance in the TRIPs Agreement, Articles 3 (MFN) and 4 (national treatment), but their significance in this context appears to be limited to the requirement that national legal entities (human or artificial) are all to be regarded as being alike.

32 Consistently with the WTO's somewhat inconsistent approach, WTO law and practice embrace a number of derogations from these principles. For example, the GATS (1994) permits measures that are inconsistent with MFN(Article II) and the exceptions for customs unions in GATT (Article XXIV) and GATS (Article V) involve inconsistencies with both principles.

33 That is, some of the types of devices envisaged by the UNESCO Convention (Article 6).

34 Although the GATT (1994) and the WTO Agreement on Subsidies and Countervailing Measures (1994) may also have a part to play. The difficulties posed by these agreements are comparable, if not identical, to those posed by the GATS. In relation to the GATT, it should be noted that it has, in Article IV, a special regime in relation to films permitting internal quantitative measures, however pressure has been applied by the US to force other WTO members to abandon Article IV regimes (see Hahn 2006: 515, 522–23).

35 GATS, Articles VI & XVI. In relation to the process of progressive liberalisation, see Article XIX.

36 Cf. the GATS Annexes on Air Transport Services, Financial Services, Negotiations on Maritime Transport Services, Telecommunications, and Negotiations on Basic Telecommunications.

37 GATS, Article II and Annex on Article II Exemptions (MFN), Article XVII (national treatment). MFN exemptions should, in principle, not exceed 10 years: GATS, Annex on Article II Exemptions, paragraph 6.

38 The GATT has had two lives: one as a freestanding agreement (GATT 1947) and the other as one of the WTO-covered agreements (GATT 1994). However, the general exceptions in GATT Article XX have remained the same throughout.

39 For a summary of the history of the debate in the WTO over the absence of a cultural exception, see Hahn 2006 and Graber 2006: 554–55.

40 See *United States – Standards for Reformulated & Conventional Gasoline*(1996); *Thailand – Restrictions on the Importation of and Internal Taxes on Cigarettes* (1990). Until *European Communities – Measures Affecting Asbestos and Products Containing Asbestos* (2001; hereinafter *Asbestos Products*), this had proved an insurmountable bar to the application of Article XX(b): see further Macmillan 2001: 99–100.

41 *Asbestos Products* (2001); *Korea – Measures Affecting Imports of Fresh, Chilled and Frozen Beef* (2000); *Dominican Republic – Measures Affecting the Importation and Internal Sale of Cigarettes* (2004 and 2005).

42 The only difference between the *chapeaus* to GATS, Article XIV and GATT, Article XX is that the former refers to "trade in services" where the latter uses "international trade". This difference is not material for present purposes.

43 This is some improvement on the construction of the *chapeau* in *Reformulated Gasoline* (1996), which made it difficult to tell the difference between the meaning of the *chapeau* and the general principle of non-discrimination on which GATT obligations are based. On the construction of the *chapeau*, see further Macmillan 2001: 101–3.

44 For a discussion of the uncertainty that now surrounds the fate of unilateral measures under the *chapeau* to GATT, Article XX see Macmillan 2001: 103–8.

45 For a weaker statement of this general idea, see the Preamble to the UNESCO Convention.

46 Even though some commentators take the view that it might be possible to argue that culturally diverse products are not 'like products' and would, therefore, not fall within the prohibitions arising under those agreements. For a very optimistic assessment of this argument, see Hahn, 2006: 549–52.

47 For a fuller analysis of Article 20 of the UNESCO Convention (2005), see Hahn 2006: 539–46 and Graber 2006: 564–67.

48 The classic example of this is *Sea Turtles* (1998). For a full analysis of this case, see Macmillan 2001: 88–96 and 108–10.

49 For a compelling critique of the UNESCO Convention on, inter alia, this basis, see Germann 2006. See also Graber 2006: 563–65 and Hahn 2006: 533.

50 Such authority as exists would, presumably, be derived from the Appellate Body in *Sea Turtles* (1998).

51 Assuming that the political and the legal can be separated in any meaningful way, which is a large and possibly unwarranted assumption, especially in the context of international law.

52 Even if this were politically viable in the current international climate, which seems unlikely given the opposition of the US to the conclusion of the UNESCO Convention (2005): see, for example, Graber 2006: 560, Hahn 2006: 522–25.

# References

Abel, R. L. (1994a) *Speech and Respect*, London: Stevens and Son/Sweet and Maxwell.

——(1994b) 'Public freedom, private constraint', *Journal of Law and Society*, 21: 374, especially 380.

Agreement on Subsidies and Countervailing Measures (1994), Annex 1A of the Agreement Establishing the World Trade Organization, done at Marrakesh on 15 April 1994, 33 ILM 1144. Online: <http://www.wto.org/english/docs_e/legal_e/24-scm.pdf>

Alessandrini, D. (2007) *Developing Countries and the Multilateral Trade Regime: the failure and promise of the WTO's Development Mission*, PhD Thesis, University of London.

Alston, P. (2002) 'Resisting the merger and acquisition of human rights by trade law: a reply to Petersmann', *European Journal of International Law*, 13: 815–26.

Arrighi, G. (1994) *The Long Twentieth Century: money, power and the origins of our times*, London: Verso.

Barendt, E. (2005) *Freedom of Speech*, Oxford: Oxford University Press.

Berne Convention for the Protection of Literary and Artistic Works (1869) completed at PARIS on 4 May 1896, revised at BERLIN on 13 November 1908, completed at

BERNE on 20 March 1914, revised at ROME on 2 June 1928, at BRUSSELS on 26 June 1948, at STOCKHOLM on 14 July 1967, and at PARIS on 24 July 1971, and amended on 28 September 1979. Online: <http://www.wipo.int/treaties/en/ip/berne/trtdocs_wo001.html>

Bettig, R. (1996) *Copyrighting Culture: the political economy of intellectual property*, Boulder: Westview Press.

Blakeney, M. (1996) *Trade Related Aspects of Intellectual Property Rights*, London: Sweet and Maxwell.

Bono Copyright Term Extension Act (1998) s505. Online: <http://www.copyright.gov/legislation/s505.pdf>

Capling, A. (1996) 'Gimme shelter!', *Arena Magazine*, February/March: 21–24.

Chon, M. (1993) 'Postmodern "progress": reconsidering the copyright and patent power', *DePaul Law Review*, 43: 97.

Convention on the Protection and Promotion of the Diversity of Cultural Expressions (2005). Online: <http://unesdoc.unesco.org/images/0014/001429/142919e.pdf>

Coombe, R. (1998) *The Cultural Life of Intellectual Properties*, Durham/London: Duke University Press.

Copyright Act (1976) United States Code Title 17. Online: <http://www.copyright.gov/title17>

*(Cross-Border Gambling) US – Measures Affecting the Cross-Border Supply of Gambling and Betting Services* (2005). WT/DS285/R, 10/11/2004; WT/DS285/AB/R, 7/4/2005. Online: <http://www.wto.org/english/tratop_e/dispu_e/cases_e/ds285_e.htm>

*Dominican Republic – Measures Affecting the Importation and Internal Sale of Cigarettes* (2004 and 2005), WT/DS302/R, 26 November 2004; WT/DS302/AB/R, 25 April 2005. Online: <http://www.wto.org/english/tratop_e/dispu_e/302abr_e.doc>

Drahos, P. (2002) 'BITS and BIPs: bilateralism in intellectual property', *Journal of World Intellectual Property*, 4: 791.

Dunkley, G. (2001) *The Free Trade Adventure: the WTO, the Uruguay Round & globalism – a critique*, London & New York: Zed Books.

*Eldred v. Ashcroft* (2003) 123 S Ct 769

*European Communities – Measures Affecting Asbestos and Products Containing Asbestos*, WT/DS135/R, 18 September 2000, WT/DS135/AB/R, 12 March 2001. Online: <http://www.wto.org/english/tratop_e/dispu_e/135abr_e.pdf>

EU Directive on the harmonisation of certain aspects of copyright and related rights in the information society (2001/29). Online: <http://eur-lex.europa.eu/LexUriServ/LexUriServ.do?uri=CELEX:32001L0029:EN:HTML>

Gaines, J. (1991) *Contested Culture: the image, the voice and the law*, Chapel Hill/London: University of North Carolina Press.

(GATS) General Agreement on Trade in Services (1994) Annex 1B of the Agreement Establishing the World Trade Organization, done at Marrakesh on 15 April 1994, 33 ILM 1144. Online: <http://www.wto.org/english/docs_e/legal_e/26-gats.pdf>

(GATT) General Agreement on Tariffs and Trade (1994). 15 Apr. 1994, Marrakesh Agreement Establishing the World Trade Organization, Annex 1A, 1867 U.N.T.S. 187, 33 I.L.M. 1153 (1994). Online: <http://www.wto.org/english/docs_e/legal_e/06-gatt.pdf>

Germann, C. (2006) 'Towards a "cultural contract" against trade related cultural discrimination' (Draft Paper, 26 June 2006, on file).

Graber, C. (2006) 'The new UNESCO Convention on Cultural Diversity: a counter-balance to the WTO?' *Journal of International Economic Law*, 9: 553, 560–63, 572–73.

Grantham, B. (2000) '*Some Big Bourgeois Brothel': contexts for France's culture wars with Holly-wood*, Luton: University of Luton Press.

Gray, J. (1998) *False Dawn: the delusions of global capitalism*, New York: New Press.

Hahn, M. (2006) 'A clash of cultures? The UNESCO *Diversity Convention* and international trade law', *Journal of International Economic Law*, 9: 515, 522–23.

(ICCPR) Covenant on Civil and Political Rights (1969) adopted and opened for signature, ratification and accession by United Nations General Assembly resolution 2200A (XXI) of 16 December 1966, entry into force 23 March 1976. Online: <http://www.unhchr.ch/html/menu3/b/a_ccpr.htm>

(ICESCR) Covenant on Economic, Social and Cultural Rights (1966). Adopted and opened for signature, ratification and accession by United Nations General Assembly resolution 2200A (XXI) of 16 December 1966. Online: <http://www.unhchr.ch/html/menu3/b/a_ICESCR.htm>

Kennedy, D. (1995) 'The international style in postwar law and policy: John Jackson and the field of international economic law', *American University Journal of International Law and Policy*, 10: 671.

Koenig, D.M. (1994) 'Joe Camel and the First Amendment: the dark side of copyrighted and trademark-protected icons', *Thomas M. Cooley Law Review*, 11: 803.

*Korea – Measures Affecting Imports of Fresh, Chilled and Frozen Beef* (2000), WT/DS161/R & WT/DS169/R, 31 July 2000, WT/DS161/AB/R & WT/DS169/AB/R, 11 December 2000. Online: <http://www.wto.org/english/tratop_e/dispu_e/cases_e/ds169_e.htm>

Levitt, T. (1983) 'The globalisation of markets', *Harvard Business Review*, 61: 92.

Macmillan, F. (1998) 'Copyright and culture: a perspective on corporate power', *Media and Arts Law Review*, 10: 71.

——(2001) *WTO and the Environment*, London: Sweet and Maxwell, 99–100.

——(2002a) 'Copyright and corporate power', in R. Towse (ed.), *Copyright and the Cultural Industries*, Cheltenham, UK and Northampton, MA, USA, Edward Elgar.

——(2002b) 'The cruel ©: copyright and film', *European Intellectual Property Review*, 483–92.

——(2004) 'International economic law and public international law: strangers in the night', *International Trade Law and Regulation*, 6: 115.

——(2005a) 'Commodification and cultural ownership', in J. Griffiths and U. Suthersanen (eds), *Copyright and Free Speech: comparative and international analyses*, Oxford: Oxford University Press.

——(2005b) 'Looking back to look forward: is there a future for human rights in the WTO?' *International Trade Law and Regulation*, 6: 115.

——(2006) 'Public interest and the public domain in an era of corporate dominance', in B. Andersen (ed.), *Intellectual Property Rights: innovation, governance and the institutional environment*, Cheltenham, UK and Northampton, MA, USA: Edward Elgar.

Macmillan Patfield, F. (1996) 'Towards a reconciliation of copyright and free speech', in E. Barendt (ed.), *Yearbook of Media Law and Entertainment Law*, Oxford: Clarendon Press.

——(1997) 'Legal policy and the limits of literary copyright', in P. Parrinder, W. Chernaik and W. Gould (eds), *Textual Monopolies: literary copyright and the public domain*, London: Arts and Humanities Press.

MacQueen, H. and Waelde, C. (eds) (2007) *Intellectual Property: the many faces of the public domain*, Cheltenham, UK and Northampton, MA, USA: Edward Elgar.

Netanel, N.W. (1996) 'Copyright and a democratic civil society', *Yale Law Journal*, 106: 283.

Orford, A. (2005) 'Beyond harmonization: trade, human rights and the economy of sacrifice', *Leiden Journal of International Law*, 18: 179.

Petersmann, E. U. (2002) 'Time for a United Nations "Global Compact" for integrating human rights into the law of worldwide organizations: lessons from European integration', *European Journal of International Law*, 13: 621.

Reichman, J. H. (1993) 'The TRIPs component of the GATT's Uruguay Round: competitive prospects for intellectual property owners in an integrated world market', *Fordham Intellectual Property, Media & Entertainment Law Journal*, 4: 171.

Sell, S. K. (2003) *Private Power, Public Law: the globalization of intellectual property rights*, Cambridge: Cambridge University Press.

Sen, A. (1999) *Development as Freedom*, New York: Anchor Books.

Smiers, J. (1999) 'The abolition of copyrights: better for artists, Third World countries and the public domain', in R. Towse (ed.) (2002) *Copyright in the Cultural Industries*, Cheltenham, UK and Northampton, MA, USA: Edward Elgar.

*Thailand – Restrictions on the Importation of and Internal Taxes on Cigarettes* (1991), 37S/200, DS10/R, adopted 7 November 1990, 29th Supp BISD 200 (1991) Online: <http://www.wto.org/english/tratop_e/envir_e/edis03_e.htm>

Towse, R. (1999) 'Copyright, risk and the artist: an economic approach to policy for artists', *Cultural Policy*, 6: 91.

——(2001) *Creativity, Incentive and Reward: an economic analysis of copyright and culture in the information age*, Cheltenham, UK and Northampton, MA, USA: Edward Elgar.

Trachtman, J. P. (2002) 'Institutional linkage: transcending "trade and … "', *American Journal of International Law*, 96: 77.

(TRIPs) Agreement on Trade-Related Aspects of Intellectual Property Rights, Annex C of the Agreement Establishing the World Trade Organization, done at Marrakesh on 15 April 1994, 33 ILM 1144. Online: <http://www.wto.org/english/tratop_e/trips_e/t_agm0_e.htm>

(UDHR) Universal Declaration of Human Rights (1948) G.A. res. 217A (III), U.N. Doc A/810 at 71. Online: <http://www.un.org/Overview/rights.html>

UN Convention on Biological Diversity (CBD) (1992). 31. I.L.M. 818.

(UNESCO Declaration) UNESCO Universal Declaration on Cultural Diversity (2001). Adopted by the 31st Session of UNESCO's General Conference, Paris, 2 November 2001. Online: <http://unesdoc.unesco.org/images/0012/001271/127160m.pdf>

*United States – Import Prohibition of Certain Shrimp & Shrimp Products* (1998), WT/DS58/R, 15 May 1998, WT/DS58/AB/R, 12 October 1998. Online: <http://docsonline.wto.org/imrd/directdoc.asp?DDFDocuments/t/WT/DS/58ABR.doc>

*United States – Standards for Reformulated & Conventional Gasoline* (1996), WT/DS2/R, 29 January 1996; WT/DS2/AB/R, 29 April 1996. Online: <http://www.wto.org/english/tratop_e/envir_e/edis07_e.htm>

*Universal City Studios, Inc v Corley* (2001), US Court of Appeals for the Second Circuit, 28 November 2001.

*(US Copyright) US – Section 110(5) of US Copyright Act* (2000) WT/DS/160/R, 15/6/2000. Online: <http://www.wto.org/english/tratop_e/dispu_e/cases_e/ds160_e.htm>

van Caenegem, W. A. (1995) 'Copyright, communication and new technologies', *Federal Law Review*, 23: 322.

Waldron, J. (1993) 'From authors to copiers: individual rights and social values in intellectual property', *Chicago-Kent Law Review*, 69: 841.

*Walt Disney Prods v. Air Pirates*, 581 F 2d 751 (9th Cir, 1978), *cert denied*, 439 US 1132 (1979).

World Commission of Culture and Development (1996) *Our Creative Diversity*, Paris, UNESCO, 1996.

WIPO Copyright Treaty (1996) adopted in Geneva on 20 December 1996. Online: <http://www.wipo.int/treaties/en/ip/wct/>

(WIPO) World Intellectual Property Organization (1978) *Guide to the Berne Convention for the Protection of Literary and Artistic Works*, Geneva, WIPO, 1978.

WIPO Performances and Phonograms Treaty (1996) adopted in Geneva on 20 December 1996. Online: <http://www.wipo.int/treaties/en/ip/wppt>

(WTO) Agreement Establishing the World Trade Organization (1994) done at Marrakesh on 15 April 1994, 33 ILM 1144. Online: <http://www.wto.org/english/docs_e/legal_e/04-wto.pdf>

## Useful websites

GATS Gateway (WTO)
<http://www.wto.org/english/tratop_e/serv_e/serv_e.htm>
TRIPS Gateway (WTO)
<http://www.wto.org/english/tratop_e/TRIPS_e/TRIPS_e.htm>
(UNESCO) United National Educational, Scientific and Cultural Organization Cultural Diversity Website
<http://www.unesco.org/culture/diversity>
(WIPO) World Intellectual Property Organization
<http://www.wipo.int>
(WTO) World Trade Organization
<http://www.wto.org>

# Chapter 6

# Liberalisation and environmental legislation in India

*Kanchi Kohli and Manju Menon*

## Introduction

India committed itself to the protection of its environment in the 1980s when it set up a Ministry of Environment and Forests (MoEF) and passed a range of legislation. In 1991 India committed itself to the New Economic Policy, a programme of liberalisation. As this chapter explains, the tension between economy and environment has produced increasing conflict ever since.

## The growth thrust

> [India's] goals can only be achieved by a considerable increase in national income and our economic policy must, therefore, aim at plenty and equitable distribution. We must produce wealth, and then divide it equitably. How can we have a welfare state without wealth?

The above quotation is from a speech made by Jawaharlal Nehru, India's first Prime Minister, in 1955. Back then, it was an aspiration fitting a new-born socialist democracy emerging from over four centuries of colonial rule. The quotation was recycled by the Indian Finance Minister during his presentation of the country's budget for 2008–9. Today this statement symbolizes 'business as usual': growth and accumulation of wealth are taken-for-granted goals. It is also believed that the country's land, water, ecological spaces and biodiversity should be used 'optimally' for economic growth. To achieve this, new partnerships with the private sector and multilateral agencies are to be encouraged, and mammoth investments are to be invited at all costs. Meanwhile, the number of people displaced from their original homes stands at 60 million (Fernandes 2008), and the 2007–8 Economic Survey, which is a precursor to the budget, highlights that the United Nations Development Programme (UNDP) Global Human Development Report (2007) ranked India in 128th position among the countries with medium human development out of 177 countries of the world, as against 126th in the previous year.

The position adopted by the present government of India with respect to the environmental degradation caused by development projects is supported by the Kuznet's curve. Simon Kuznet originally developed his theory in the 1960s to explain why inequalities increase when a country begins to develop economically, but later the wealth begins to 'trickle down' and incomes begin to equalize. Kuznet's curve was somewhat arbitrarily applied to environmental situations. The argument goes that a certain amount of degradation of natural resources is essential while a country is achieving its growth aspirations. After a threshold, when basic 'physical needs' are met, interest in a clean environment rises (Richmond et al. 2007).

Having placed this econometric tool at the centre of environmental governance, successive Indian governments have systematically dismantled the legal and policy framework established to protect the environment since the 1970s.

## Forms

The 1980s and early 1990s brought in some elaborate regulations for the protection of the environment and the livelihoods of people dependent on natural resources in India,[1] which are implemented by the MoEF. It is often argued that, although not directly oriented towards conservation of natural resources, some of these laws nonetheless allow the location and operation of industrial and development processes to be regulated to minimize the destruction of forests, wetlands, coasts and biodiversity.

This phase began with the enactment of the Forest Conservation Act (1980), which laid down the assessment and approval procedure before allowing for diversion of officially recorded forest land for non-forest use. In 1996, through an order of the Supreme Court of India (*N. Godavarman Thirumulpad v. Union of India*), the scope of this legislation was extended to any area which satisfied the dictionary definition of forest, irrespective of its ownership or management.

Soon after came the Environment (Protection) Act (EPA) in 1986. This law introduced much needed spirit and direction to the central government's efforts to conserve the country's environment. An especially powerful provision in this legislation, section 3(2)(v), allowed the promulgation of two important regulatory notifications in the early 1990s.

The first was the Coastal Regulation Zone (CRZ) Notification (1991), prohibiting and/or restricting indiscriminate industrial and infrastructural expansion in sensitive areas all across the coastline. The Notification also mandated the setting up of Coastal Zone Management Authorities and the preparation of Coastal Zone Management Plans to ensure the mandate is delivered.

The second was a notification under the EPA known as the Environment Impact Assessment Notification (1994). With this came a much needed regulatory framework under which impacts of development and industrial projects would be fully assessed, debated in public through a mandatory public-hearing process and, finally, appraised at the central government level. This procedure was meant to make the environmental and social impacts of projects and public opinion regarding them an important component of environmental decision-making.

More recently came India's Biological Diversity Act (2002). The process for formulating this legislation had started much earlier following India becoming a signatory to the United Nations' Convention on Biological Diversity (CBD), 1992 (see further Kotsakis in this volume). Based on the principles of conservation, sustainable use and equitable sharing of benefits, the Act laid down clear procedures to be followed by those seeking to access the country's biological resources and traditional knowledge. The legislation also entrusted the central government with specific duties towards conservation of the above.

The current operation of these acts needs no speculation: they have been turned into efficient tools of exploitation. There are clear statistics to indicate how over the last decade and a half, forest environment and biodiversity clearance regimes have increasingly been driven towards conditional approvals, rather than rejections. So the original intention of these acts requires some scrutiny: were they brought into force to ensure conservation and protection of natural resources or were they meant to regulate access to these 'resources' to exploit and turn into profits?

Both environment and forest clearances for development projects are granted along with a set of conditions that have to be followed by project proponents. These conditions are intended to cover the gaps in the initial impact assessments. For instance, the 1997 environment clearance of the construction of the Mumbai–Pune expressway road project, in the western state of Maharashtra (see Mumbai–Pune Expressway website), laid out conditions which allowed for *ex post facto* assessment of project components. One of the most ecologically fragile and vulnerable sections of the project was a bypass through Lonavala–Khandala forming part of the Western Ghats forests. The MoEF issued an environment clearance for the expressway as a whole, with a condition that an EIA for the bypass would be carried out separately, and a separate clearance would be granted. This was absurd since the project could only be completed with the bypass. The decision as to whether to issue a clearance ought to have been taken in light of the overall impact of the project, including the bypass. In the end, the Maharashtra State Road Development Corporation (MSRDC) and MoEF waived the requirement of an EIA to be commissioned on the grounds that the investment was below Rs 50 crores, which was the limit prescribed in the EIA notification at that time.

Many of the conditions attached to clearances are based on so-called management and mitigation models. The implementation of these is impractical in local contexts and can actually worsen local environmental and social conditions. For instance, one of the conditions imposed on the Lower Subansiri Hydroelectric Project is the conversion of the entire catchment area upstream into a Protected Area under the Wildlife (Protection) Act of 1972 (see Subansiri Project website). While construction on the project has begun, the state of Arunachal Pradesh and the Centre are embroiled in litigation over this condition, which is seen as being unfair and blocking off the catchment area from the several livelihood uses to which it is put by the local people (Vagholikar 2005). By using conservation offsets, such as the declaration of a Protected Area, rather than focusing on direct protection of forest and wildlife, regulators only add to the impact of the project. Furthermore, if these conditions are suspended or withdrawn by the regulators, the primary negative impact of the project will remain unaddressed. Sometimes conditions are impossible to fulfil. For instance, a clearance might make it mandatory for small-scale industries or industries in industrial estates to develop green belts of 'adequate' width and length to offset the pollution that will be caused by factories. But despite such conditions being decided upon by regulators and the department concerned, based on project documents, there are several instances in which project authorities report back to the MoEF through their compliance reports that they do not have enough land/space to develop such green belts.

Clearances and approvals are decided upon using a narrow range of technical expertise in the fields of engineering, management and administration. The expert committees that study project documents and recommend the granting of clearance are populated by technocrats and bureaucrats. A 2005 assessment of the expert committees overseeing clearances revealed that, in breach of clear guidelines on committee compositions, the committees comprised only one wildlife expert and no-one from the social sciences or anthropology. Furthermore, 28 out of 59 members were from government-affiliated institutions or agencies set up directly under government departments/ministries (Kalpavriksh 2005, Kohli and Menon 2005).

## Flaws

### Forest

The MoEF has, by its own admission, allowed 1.14 million hectares of India's forest land to be diverted to non-forest in the period between the promulgation of the Forest (Conservation) Act (1980) and early 2007. Permissions for forest clearance have been granted to developers of roads, industries, dams, mines and so on. What is also interesting to note is the trend of massive up-scaling of the diversion to non-forest use in the last four to five years. For instance, approximately 0.3 million hectares, a quarter of all land cleared in the 26 years during which the Act has been implemented, were cleared by the MoEF in the four years between 2003 and 2007 (Kohli and Menon 2008). Some of the high-impact projects that have received forest clearance are dam projects like Indira Sagar Irrigation Project (Andhra Pradesh),[2] Athirapilly Hydroelectric Project (Kerala), industrial projects such as the Lafarge Cement Plant (Meghalaya), mining projects within Kudremukh National Park (Karnataka), and infrastructure projects such as the Dhamra Port near Bhitarkanika Wildlife Sanctuary (Orissa) and the Mumbai–Pune Expressway (Maharashtra).

Violations of environmental law and clearance conditions have also been abundant. There are a large number of damage reports and fines imposed by state forest departments and litigation in these matters is growing. For example, clear forest and environment conditions about tree felling and muck dumping were imposed in awarding environmental clearances for the construction of the Parbati Stage II Hydroelectric Project in the northern state of Himachal Pradesh. Nevertheless, the State Forest Department officials have had to issue notices and impose fines on the project proponents, National Hydro Power Corporation (NHPC) and its subcontractors. These fines are levied for the violation of the Forest Conservation Act by the illegal cutting of trees, or by indiscriminate dumping of debris in the forest. The fines run to approximately Rs 34 million from three forest divisions where the construction activity related to the project has been undertaken. The payment of the fines imposed by the state government cannot undo the environmental and social damage caused by project violations. The project continues to be under construction despite repeated and continuing irregularities (Kalpavriksh and Lok Vigyan Kendra 2008; see also Parbati Project website).

## Environmental impact assessments

The situation with respect to clearances under the EIA Notification (1994) is even more bleak. The environment clearance process became a mandatory requirement in 1994 and went through thirteen amendments in its 12-year existence till 2006. Each amendment (barring a few) diluted the law and its spirit.[3]

The fourteenth amendment, which took place in 2006, almost totally dismantled the original intent and potential of the Notification as an effective tool of environmental decision-making. The 2006 notification came about as part of a broader programme to 're-engineer' the regulatory framework affecting investment. That programme was in turn triggered by the lessons from a World Bank-funded Environment Management Capacity Building Project;[4] and by certain recommendations of the 2002 Govindarajan Committee on investment reforms (Kohli and Menon 2008, Planning Commission 2006).[5] The most significant of the Govindarajan Committee recommendations for the purposes of this chapter was that:

> ... Re-engineering of regulatory processes prescribed under various legislations, regulations, etc., is necessary to simplify the procedures for grant of approvals, reduce delays and ground level hassles and simplify the regulation of projects during their operational phase ...
> (Kohli and Menon 2008, Planning Commission 2006).

A number of recommendations from various high-level committees also endorsed these changes, resulting in a significant deregulation of the environment sector. For example, the report of the High Level Committee on the National Mineral Policy states:

> If investment in mining activity is to be encouraged on a large scale then the problem of procedural delays and time overruns will need to be addressed.

It is more than two and a half decades since the FCA came into operation and discussions that have taken place in various fora to streamline the procedures for forest clearance have been largely in vain. In the Committee's view, immediate action is now required[.]

(Hoda Committee 2006)

This recommendation was translated into the National Mineral Policy (2008), which states:

The Central Government in consultation with State Governments shall formulate the legal measures necessary for giving effect to the new National Mineral Policy, 2008, to ensure basic uniformity in mineral administration across the country and to ensure that the development of mineral resources keeps pace, and is in consonance with the national policy goals[.]

While the sectoral policies were being drafted to give short shrift to environmental regulations, the central government also came out with a National Environment Policy (2006). The policy was criticized in its draft form thus:

... instead of mainstreaming environmental concerns into all development activities and sectors (its stated goal), it 'mainstreams' the current notion of unbridled development into even the limited environmental regulation we have.

(Lele and Menon 2005)

The above committee reports and policy statements could not have got the root causes of the problem more wrong. Government and project proponents continue to be concerned by delays in the granting of clearances. But those delays are only symptomatic of the importance given to impact-assessment studies in project decision-making. Environmental clearances are project-specific, not sectoral, and they come downstream in the decision-making process. In their haste to start construction of projects, proponents present shoddy, factually incorrect and inadequate assessments and bypass mandatory public-hearing procedures. These shortcuts are challenged in courts or by petitioning the regulators. In effect, most 'delays' are caused by attempts by the project proponents or government to circumvent legal procedures and undermine or ignore local concerns about the project.

Because delay in the granting of clearances was identified as the main hurdle faced by investments in various sectors such as mining and real estate projects, a new environment clearance regime was brought into force. This reduced the time period for granting of clearance but did not do anything to improve the quality of EIAs, nor of the public-hearing and compliance-monitoring procedures. The results of these changes are clear. In the first 15 months of its existence (September 2006 to December 2007) the MoEF cleared 1,736 projects.

This averages out to more than 100 projects a month. In comparison, the MoEF granted clearance to just 4,016 development and industrial projects in the 20-year period of 1986–2006. It also remains to be seen what levels of compliance will be achieved with the much higher rate of clearance, not least because compliance rates under the old 'slow' rate of clearance were rather dismal. The increased rate of clearance is likely to place an unbearable administrative burden on the Ministry.

The new EIA Notification (MoEF 2006) allows for a 'lesser' process for the real estate and construction sector. Projects under these categories are to be appraised on the basis of information provided in an Appraisal Form. The requirements for an EIA and public hearing have been dispensed with for these projects.

### Coastal zones

If the EIA Notification went through 13 amendments before it was totally reorganized to fit into the growth agenda, the Coastal Regulation Zone (CRZ) Notification had to wait for 19 amendments. The Notification of 1991 was subject to review by the M. S. Swaminathan Committee in 2004 so that it could be made more 'scientifically sound'. The minutes of the committee's meetings and the content of the draft notification issued by MoEF in May 2008, make clear the intentions of the government to undo the protection mechanism and make coastal areas freely available to development projects. The process followed by the committee has come under severe criticism from fish-worker groups, coastal communities and environmental groups (Menon et al. 2007).

The newly proposed Coastal Management Zone Notification allows for re-defining the coastal zone, thus making it open to development projects. As Sridhar et al. (2008) explain:

CRZ-I areas under the CRZ Notification were initially defined as areas where no activities would be permitted, until several dilutions were introduced to change this. The proposed CMZ Notification is extremely regressive and establishes that various activities will be allowed in these sensitive ecosystems as long as they are recorded in the 'Integrated Coastal Zone Management Plans' (ICZMP). These are therefore no longer no-development zones and hence no longer protected as in the CRZ Notification.

As local communities and public-interest groups have increasingly sought to engage in participatory decision-making, the central and various state governments have gone about shrinking these spaces and clamping down on dissent, sometimes using brutal force. The public hearing is a single point where there is a formal interaction between the project proponents and local community and civil society representatives. However, where there are strong objections from the side of local people, the state has been known all too often to respond by deploying its law-and-order machinery. Public hearings of the highly controversial Sethusamudram Ship Channel Project (SSCP; see project website) in southern India saw direct clashes between the local police and the fisherfolk objecting to the project. A similar instance took place at the public hearing for the Gare Mines in Chhatisgarh state which were proposed for exploitation by a large industrial giant in India, the Jindal Group, in early 2008 – the police *lathi-* (baton-) charged the protesting public.

Amendments to the EIA and CRZ Notification have narrowed their remit and watered down their effect, especially in relation to transparency, access to information and public participation in decision-making. A response to an application filed under the Right to Information Act (2005), seeking information regarding the process of drafting of amendments, revealed the true intention behind the amendments: the Prime Minister's Office had ordered that:

> the amended version of the EIA notification be sent to this Office, Planning Commission and *major industry associations* … The Ministry of Environment and Forests is also requested to complete consultations *with the major industry associations* within a month's time and submit the final draft EIA notification to this office. [Emphasis added.]

### Biodiversity

India's commitment to initiating a process of drafting overarching legislation to regulate access to biological resources and ensure its conservation began when it signed the United Nations' Convention on Biological Diversity (1992). This was around the same time that the country began its liberalisation programme. It took ten years for the Biological Diversity Act (2002) to appear, and during that time the very perception of what constitutes biodiversity – the intrinsic values of biodiversity, encapsulating the cultural and spiritual elements as well as basic livelihood use – has changed drastically.

In the more than five years since the law has been in place, the National Biodiversity Authority (NBA) set up under it has granted close to 260 approvals for access towards research, commercial exploitation and intellectual property rights (IPRs). As of March 2008, 232 of these approvals were solely for IPRs such as patents. These rights stem from a trade regime and rely on unnatural exclusive, private, monopolized control over wild and domesticated species of flora and fauna. They seek to convert the intrinsic value of biological diversity and the traditional knowledge associated with it into a 'resource' which can be manipulated and controlled. The ethical debate around this has been in existence for decades. However, it takes on a new life when we consider that these approvals are in conflict with the objectives laid out for the parent legislation: none of the IPR applications seeks either to conserve or to use sustainably the biological resource accessed.

Only extremely rarely has benefit-sharing for local communities been found in approvals granted by the NBA. The only form of benefit mentioned is royalties, which are paid at the NBA level of a five per cent royalty if the patent is licensed/transferred, or five per cent of net sales of the company in the case of commercial production. There is no mention about community ownership of genetic resources and, in the absence of clear guidance on ownership of resources, there is always scope for confusion in sharing the benefits.[6]

The legislation mandates that approvals be done only after 'consultation' (but not prior and informed consent) with Biodiversity Management Committees (BMCs), which are to be set up at the local community level (s. 41 BD Act 2002). As per the information available on the NBA website, only 646 BMCs are in place (in a country of 500,000 villages), 621 being from the southern state of Karnataka. Moreover, there are no guidelines in place for a sound and informed system of setting up the BMCs and empowering them with roles of decision making (Kohli 2008).

As with the clearances granted under other environmental regulations, the Biological Diversity Act has granted approvals in the shortest possible time. In August 2007, an expert committee of the NBA met for one day to examine applications related to IPRs. The committee looked at 161 such applications and recommended approval. The NBA proved equally efficient when it met in November of the same year and managed to take note of the Committee's comments in a single one-day meeting for which it also had additional items on the agenda.

Undoubtedly a legal regime to 'regulate' access to and use of life forms and associated knowledge has been established, and has begun yielding results. While there has been zealous use of the provisions for access to biological resources, the provisions binding the government to conservation and equity remain unused.[7]

## Solutions

The faulty or non-implementation of the EIA and CRZ Notifications has resulted in several high-impact projects being located in ecologically sensitive areas and has caused social impacts such as land alienation, loss of livelihoods, forced displacement, ill health and disease, cultural degradation and sudden demographic changes, thus impoverishing local communities.

Of the large hydropower projects proposed to be built in Northeast India, those few that have been granted clearance by the MoEF and currently under construction are already demonstrating severe environmental and social impacts. For example, the Teesta V hydroelectric project in Sikkim state has caused problems such as decreased agricultural productivity, pollution due to blasting, drying up of water sources due to tunnelling, damage to houses and buildings, and a steep increase in the incidence of sexually transmitted diseases due to the non-implementation of the condition that all labourers employed on the project should be screened and treated for communicable diseases before they are given work permits (Menon and Vagholikar, unpublished).

The non-implementation of the CRZ Notification has resulted in rampant industrialization and urbanization of the coast. For example, the highly environmentally degrading shrimp-farming industry was allowed to thrive in the 1990s, and the tourist facilities which have mushroomed all along the coast have disturbed turtle-nesting beaches such as Morjim beach in Goa and dried up fresh water aquifers (Equations 2005). The tsunami of 2004 proved beyond doubt that the non-implementation of appropriate coastal protection measures enhanced the vulnerability of the Indian coastline and coastal dwellers to natural disasters (Joshi 2005). The fish-worker communities of India, who depend completely on the coast for their survival but at the same time have no formal individual ownership of coastal spaces, have been pitted against the real-estate mafia, Special Economic Zone (SEZ) developers, thermal and nuclear power and other projects. As an activist friend described, the fisher communities are caught between the tsunami of development from the landward side and natural disasters from the sea (Nityanand Jayaraman, Corporate Accountability Desk, personal communication).

As disquiet over the environmental impacts of large projects has grown, so clearances have been subject to conditions aimed at mitigating those impacts. Conditions requiring the creation of new protected areas for wildlife conservation, the reservation of forest areas to compensate for losses due to projects and the treatment of reservoir catchment areas are some of the most common conditions. Yet these measures are never discussed with local communities before they are recommended, and the implementation of these measures results in exacerbating the social impacts of the projects for local communities. For example, forest-dwelling communities are displaced for the creation of government-declared Protected Areas, and agriculture/shifting cultivation and other forest uses are restricted or prohibited when new forest lands are taken over for reservation or catchment-area treatment (Menon and Kohli, unpublished).

## Conclusion

The complete failure of successive governments to ensure that the environment and livelihoods of India's natural-resource-dependent communities are protected is one of the causes of intense conflict in many areas of the country today. Environmental regulations have been turned into 'access legislations' allowing the state to occupy any land under the guise of 'public purpose', without regard for democratic decision-making processes.[8] Thus more and more people are being alienated from their lands and their homes. In the conflict between liberalisation and environmental protection, liberalisation is the current victor. Communities involved in the bloody struggle to protect their homelands and livelihoods are now not only at the forefront of a national social movement. They are also redefining the environmental movement.

## Notes

1 A list of Indian environmental legislation, as well as the complete texts, can be found at the MoEF website.

2 Indira Sagar Irrigation Project is also called the Polavaram Project.
3 For a detailed critique of the erosion of the EIA Notification, see Kohli and Menon (2005).
4 Project ID P043728. The Project Documents can be found on the Environmental Management Capacity Building Technical Assistance Project website. The Bank's own Project Performance Assessment Report of the Project is predominantly negative. In summary:

> ... outcome was moderately unsatisfactory; risk to the development outcome was significant; Bank performance was unsatisfactory; and Borrower performance was unsatisfactory[.]
> (Environmental Management Capacity Building Technical Assistance Project website).

5 For an assessment of the role played by World Bank-led 'investment climate discourse' in triggering the erosion of the Notification and of the consequences for foreign investors, civil society actors and government officials, see Perry-Kessaris (2008).
6 These observations are based on an analysis of approval letters available on the NBA website.
7 Some of the provisions that could bring about conservation of biodiversity are those relating to the declaration of Biodiversity Heritage Sites (s. 37 BD Act 2002), developing and determining mechanisms of equitable sharing of benefits accruing from access, or taking measures for protection of people's knowledge.
8 The draconian Land Acquisition Act (1894) also contributes to this process.

## References

Biological Diversity Act (2002) Online: <http://envfor.nic.in/divisions/biodiv/act/bio_div_act.htm>

(Environment Impact Assessment Notification) Ministry of Environment and Forests Notification (1994) S.O.60(E) (Amended 2004) on Environmental Impact Assessments.

Environment Protection Act (1986) Central Act No. 29 of 1986. Online: <http://envfor.nic.in/legis/env/eprotect_act_1986.pdf>

Equations (2005) Impacts of the Tsunami in the Andaman Islands. Bangalore: Equations.

Fernandes, W.(2008) 'Sixty years of development-induced displacement in India: scale, impacts and search for alternatives', in H. M. Mathur (ed.) India: Social Development Report, Delhi: Oxford University Press, 89–102.

Forest Conservation Act (1980) Central Act No. 69 of 1980. Online: <http://envfor.nic.in/legis/forest/forest2.html>

Govindarajan Committee (2002) 'Report on reforming investment approvals and implementation procedures', New Delhi: Department of Industrial Policy and Promotion.

Hoda Committee (2006) Report of High Level Committee on the National Mineral Policy, New Delhi: Planning Commission. Online: <http://planningcommission.nic.in/reports/genrep/rep_nmp.pdf>

Joshi, P. (2005) The Naked Coast. Outlook, 17 January 2005.

Kalpavriksh (2005) 'Why are the Expert Committees of Ministry of Environment and Forests dominated by ex-bureaucrats, politicians and engineers?' Open Letter to the Ministry of Environment and Forests No. 4. Dated 8 April 2005. Online: <http://www.kalpavriksh.org/campaigns/campopenletter/EIA%20Committees%20Open%20Letter,%20final,%207.4.05.doc>

Kalpavriksh and Lok Vigyan Kendra (2008) *Compliance and Monitoring of Environment Clearance Conditions of Parbati State II Hydro Electric Project in Himachal Pradesh: a case study.* Unpublished.

Kohli, K. (2008) 'India's Biodiversity Regime: All Access, No Benefit-sharing'. *Eco Newsletter.* Volume 23, Issue 8, 28 May 2008. Online: <http://www.cbdalliance.org>

Kohli, K. and Menon, M. (2008) Legalised Destruction: Environment Protection Laws reduced to a travesty of their mandate. Down to Earth, 15 February 2008.

——(2005) *Eleven Years of Environment Impact Assessment Notification, 1994: a status report.* Pune: Kalpavriksh, Just Environment Trust, and Environment Justice Initiative.

Land Acquisition Act, Central Act No. 1 of 1894.

Lele, S. and Menon, A. (2005) 'Draft NEP: a flawed vision'. SEMINAR 547. Online: <http://dlc.dlib.indiana.edu/archive/00001615>

Menon, M. and Kohli, K. (2007) 'Environmental decision making: whose agenda?' *Economic and Political Weekly*, 42(26) June 30.

——'River valley projects and clearance regimes related to environment and forests', unpublished draft.

——(2008) 'Re-engineering the legal and policy regimes on environment' *Economic and Political Weekly*, 43(23) 7 June.

Menon, M., Rodriguez, S. and Sridhar, A. (2007) 'Coastal Zone Management Notification '07 – better or bitter fare?' Produced for the Post-Tsunami Environment Initiative Project, ATREE, Bangalore. Online: <http://www.atree.org/CZM_Notif_Crit_Aug07.pdf>

Ministry of Finance (Government of India) (2008) Economic Survey 2007–8. Online: <http://indiabudget.nic.in/es2007–8/esmain.htm>

(MoEF) Ministry of Environment and Forests (1991) Notification under section 3(1) and section 3(2)(v) of the Environment (Protection) Act, 1986 and rule 5(3)(d) of the Environment (Protection) Rules, 1986 declaring coastal stretches as coastal regulation zone (CRZ) and regulating activities in the CRZ. New Delhi, 19 February 1991 (Coastal Regulation Zone (CRZ) Notification) Online: <http://envfor.nic.in/legis/crz/crznew.html>

——Notification (1994) S.O.60(E) on Environmental Impact Assessments. Online: <http://envfor.nic.in/legis/eia/so-60(e).pdf>

——Notification (2006) Notification S.O. 1533(E) on Environmental Impact Assessments. Online: <http://envfor.nic.in/legis/eia/so1533.pdf>

National Mineral Policy (2008) Online: <http://mines.nic.in/NMP2008.pdf>

*N. Godavarman Thirumulpad vs Union of India* WP (C) No. 202/95 and WP (C) No .

Perry-Kessaris, A. (2008) *Global Business, Local Law: the Indian legal system as a communal resource in foreign investment relations,* Aldershot: Ashgate.

Planning Commission (2006) National Mineral Policy: Report of High Level Committee. New Delhi: Government of India. Online: <http://planningcommission.nic.in/reports/genrep/rep_nmp.pdf>

Richmond, A. and Zencey, E. (2007) 'Environmental kuznets curve', in Cutler J. Cleveland (ed.) *Encyclopaedia of Earth*, Washington, D.C.: Environmental Information Coalition, National Council for Science and the Environment. Online: <http://www.eoearth.org/article/Environmental_kuznets_curve> (Accessed 21 July 2008.)

Right to Information Act (2005) Central Act No. 22 of 2005.

Sridhar, A., Menon, M., Rodriguez, S. and Shenoy. S. (2008) Coastal Management Zone Notification '08 – The Last Nail in the Coffin. ATREE, Bangalore. Online: <http://www.atree.org>

UN Convention on Biological Diversity (CBD; 1992) 31. I.L.M. 818.
(UNDP) United Nations Development Programme (2007) Human Development Report. New York: UNDP. Online: <http://hdr.undp.org/en/media/HDR_20072008_EN _Complete.pdf >
Vagholikar, N. (2005) 'Damming our wildlife', *Sanctuary Asia*, 25: 1.

## Useful websites

(ATREE) Ashoka Trust for Research in Ecology and the Environment
   <http://www.atree.org>
Environmental Management Capacity Building Technical Assistance Project (World Bank)
   <http://web.worldbank.org/external/projects/main?pagePK=64283627&piPK=73230 &theSitePK=40941&menuPK=228424&Projectid=P043728>
Kalpavriksh Environment Action Group
   <http://www.kalpavriksh.org/>
Ministry of Environment and Forests (Government of India)
   <http://www.envfor.nic.in>
Mumbai–Pune Expressway (Government of Maharastra)
   <http://www.msrdc.org/Projects/Mumbai_Pune_Expr.aspx>
(NBA) National Biodiversity Authority of India
   <http://www.nbaindia.org>
Parbati Project
   <http://www.nhpcindia.com/hp/parbati2hp.htm>
Sethusamudram Channel Project
   <http://sethusamudram.gov.in>
Subansiri Project
   <http://www.nhpcindia.com/Projects/English/Scripts/Prj_Introduction.aspx?vid=23>

# Accountability mechanisms of multilateral development banks: powers, complications, enhancements

*Suresh Nanwani**

## Introduction

Multilateral Development Banks (Mdbs) such as the World Bank and the ADB are mandated to promote and finance the economic development of borrowing or developing countries. They lend primarily to governments in more than 150 developing countries through project loans, programme loans, private-sector investments including equity investments, and technical assistance intended to benefit billions of people.[1] Their lending operations cover various sectors, including transport and communications; finance; energy; water, sanitation and flood protection; law, justice and public administration; and agricultural and natural resources (see also the chapters by Decker and Hammergren in this volume).

In recent decades, MDBs have increasingly encouraged external participation in MDB policymaking and practice. For example, the World Bank has begun to emphasize the value of greater collaboration with civil-society organizations in achieving development results. The Asian Development Bank (ADB) has similarly stressed its commitment to working with its civil society[2] partners to promote economic growth. These banks have gradually enabled NGOs to raise their concerns from dialogue to consulting and collaborating through gateways such as the World Bank Participation and Civic Engagement Group and Global Civil Society Team and the ADB NGO and Civil Society Centre. At the same time, individuals affected by poorly-designed and/or implemented projects have increasingly vocalized their grievances and demanded a response from the MDBs.[3] These developments have been buttressed by the creation of 'accountability mechanisms' – that is, gateways for private individuals and civil society groups to file claims with these and other banks (see Table 7.1).

This chapter tracks the evolution of these mechanisms and assesses their effectiveness by focusing in particular on the accountability mechanisms of the World Bank and ADB. The World Bank's Inspection Panel, established in 1993, is of particular interest because it was the first, and remains the most experienced (World Bank 1993). The ADB's Accountability Mechanism, established in 2003 to replace its original 1995 Inspection Function policy, is of special interest due to its innovative use of both problem-solving and investigation phases (ADB 1995 and 2003).

## Powers

Over the years, Mdbs and other financial institutions have created a range of opportunities for claimants to file complaints. The options include investigation (at the World Bank Inspection Panel, the IDB's Independent Investigation Mechanism and ADB's Inspection Function), problem-solving (Compliance Advisor/Ombudsman Office at IFC and MIGA; hereinafter 'CAO Office') and combined investigation and problem-solving (at the accountability mechanisms in ADB, EBRD, AfDB, Japan Bank for International Cooperation [JBIC] and Overseas Private Investment Corporation, USA [OPIC]).

The range of powers held by MDB accountability mechanisms is well illustrated through a comparison of the World Bank Inspection Panel with its rather more flexible and innovative younger counterpart the ADB Accountability Mechanism. In particular, the ADB Accountability Mechanism has an innovative two-stage process which begins with a 'consultation' (problem-solving) phase, followed by a 'compliance review' (investigation) phase.

### Problem-solving

The problem-solving stage at the ADB is carried out by the Special Project Facilitator (SPF). Problem-solving is carried out through informal means such as facilitation and mediation, with the intention of addressing the problems on the ground. In some cases, matters are dealt with to the satisfaction of the complainant at this stage.

An example is the complaint against the Community Empowerment for Rural Development Project (CERDP), which aimed to address social exclusion in rural Indonesia through a range of training and infrastructural improvements (see CERDP SPF Website and CERDP Project Website). Three NGOs and villagers from five villages in the project area filed a complaint alleging, among other things, improper sequencing of project components and inadequate public participation in project planning and design. The SPF found the signatories from the five villages to be the complainants. He could not accept the three NGOs as complainants but noted that they had an important role as intermediaries between the complainants and his office (ADB 2005b: 2). The SPF carried out a review and assessment with the result that five village agreements on infrastructure issues such as roadway construction and non-infrastructure matters such as participation in decision-making were signed by the villages, the government and ADB. The SPF concluded his monitoring of these agreements in May 2006. The three NGOs stated that, had they been complainants, they 'would have withdrawn from the consultation process and filed a request for

*Table 7.1* Establishment of MDB accountability mechanisms

| Date | MDB | Mechanism |
|------|-----|-----------|
| 1993 | World Bank (International Bank for Reconstruction and Development and International Development Association) | World Bank Inspection Panel |
| 1994 | Inter-American Development Bank (IDB) | Independent Investigation Mechanism |
| 1995 | Asian Development Bank (ADB) | Inspection Function (replaced by Accountability Mechanism in 2003) |
| 1999 | International Finance Corporation (IFC) and Multilateral Investment Guarantee Agency (MIGA) | Compliance Advisor/ Ombudsman Office |
| 2003 | European Bank for Reconstruction and Development (EBRD) | Independent Recourse Mechanism |
| 2004 | African Development Bank (AfDB) | Independent Review Mechanism |

compliance review'. However, they found that the 'villagers were quite satisfied with the agreements that were reached' (ADB 2005b: 12).

By contrast, the Sri Lankan claimants in the Southern Transport Development Project (STDP) were entirely dissatisfied with the problem-solving stage of the ADB Accountability Mechanism. The purpose of the project was to improve transport links between Colombo and the southern regions of Sri Lanka by building a 128 kilometre highway (see STDP website). The claim stemmed from a change of trace for which required studies and consultations were not properly done, as well as adverse effects including loss of homes and livelihoods, damage to the environment and resettlement problems. The claimant was a local NGO (Joint Organization of the Affected Peoples on Colombo-Matara Highway) representing 28 individuals living in the project area.[4]

The claimants went through the consultation stage from June 2004 to January 2005. The SPF could not establish whether a change of highway trace was justifiable, and recommended a course of action which included exploring a change in trace and recruiting an international facilitator for intensive facilitation/mediation (ADB 2006: 3). The international facilitator terminated the consultation process because he considered it unlikely that the parties would agree to a mediated settlement. He concluded that 'resolution in this case may only be effectively sanctioned within the forum of the judicial system' and the claimants' 'perceived issues are incapable of resolution within the forum of a mediated settlement'. In February 2005 the SPF informed the claimants that the consultation process was concluded (ADB 2005a: 10). The claimants felt that 'the facilitation [had] failed and that is indicative of the lack of want of ADB to make it work, as well as an illustration of [the OSPF mediator's] incomplete grasp of the issues and misrepresentation of the facts' and 'failure to carry out a proper mediation process in a professional manner'. A civil society advocacy group criticized the consultation process, alleging that the 'SPF walked away from the process without completing its job … The SPF failed in its basic duty to be responsive to Affected Persons Complaints' (ADB 2006: 9). The claimants referred the claim for compliance review while they were at an advanced stage of the consultation process.[5] This is the only claim to date to have passed through both stages of the ADB Accountability Mechanism.

## Investigation

The investigation function of an accountability mechanism focuses on the institution's conduct, in particular on whether it has complied with its policies and procedures in designing and/or implementing projects. At the ADB this function is carried out by the Compliance Review Panel (CRP), a permanent three-member body similar to the World Bank Inspection Panel.[6] A common thread running through MDB accountability mechanisms is that they tend to have limited competence to review the internal law of their parent institution.

The investigating panels under the World Bank and ADB accountability mechanisms are required to check that the institution has adhered to its internal law, that is, its 'operational policies and procedures' (World Bank 1993 and CRP 2004: 32). At the World Bank, these are to be found in the Operations Manual, which covers strategies, products and project requirements. The project requirements include analysis, financial, and disclosure matters and 11 safeguard policies on, among others things, involuntary resettlement, indigenous peoples, environmental assessment and dam safety. The Operations Manual is updated regularly to reflect changing priorities. For example, 2005 saw the introduction of an additional safeguard policy piloting the use of borrower (country) systems to address environmental and social safeguard issues in Bank-supported projects.

Similarly, the internal law of the ADB is to be found in its Operations Manual, consisting of 'bank policies', which are short, focused statements of operational policies approved by the Board of Directors, and 'operational policies', which set out procedural requirements and guidance on the implementation of policies. The ADB Operations Manual also details a wide range of business products and instruments, safeguard policies (environmental considerations, involuntary resettlement and indigenous peoples), analyses, financial and public communications policy.[7]

The accountability mechanisms at other institutions have widely varying remits. For example, the EBRD accountability mechanism (Independent Recourse Mechanism) is limited to monitoring compliance with the Bank's environmental, social and public information policies (see EBRD IRM website). By contrast, where the AfDB has no internal policies on a matter its accountability mechanism is enabled to consider compliance with the policies of other institutions. For example, in the *Bujagali Hydropower Project and Bujagali Interconnection Project* claim,[8] the AfDB accountability mechanism noted the absence of safeguard policies for indigenous peoples and safety of dams, and concluded that since the institution uses the policies and procedures of another institution (the World Bank) on these subject matters, the panel would need to refer to them in its investigation (AfDB Independent Review Mechanism 2007: 20).[9]

Importantly, accountability mechanisms typically are not enabled to review the consistency, adequacy or suitability of these policies and procedures (see World Bank 1996, ADB 2003: paragraph 72(vi), AfDB 2004: paragraph 14(viii), EBRD 2004: paragraph 19(f)). Nor may they typically review matters relating to procurement irregularities, corruption, fraud or housekeeping matters such as personnel, administrative and financial matters. For example, in the World Bank and ADB such matters are dealt with by separate offices.

### Recommendations and monitoring

Accountability mechanisms at ADB, EBRD and AfDB provide for outcomes reached through problem-solving and investigation to be monitored. These bodies are also allowed to make recommendations, so that the institution's Boards of Directors can then make a decision on the remedial actions that Management should take to ensure project compliance. So the CRP annually monitors Management's implementation of the remedial actions for a period of up to five years, during which time it consults with concerned stakeholders including the claimants regarding the status of implementation (CRP 2004: 9).

For example, the CRP investigating the Sri Lankan STDP claim found violation of seven operational policies and procedures, including those relating to environmental considerations, gender and development, benefit monitoring and evaluation, and involuntary resettlement. It made two categories of recommendations: project-specific (to bring the project back to compliance) and general (to address issues which may cause difficulties in ensuring compliance of ADB-assisted projects with Bank policies for development effectiveness) (CRP 2005a: 60). The Board approved the Panel's recommendations in July 2005. Since 2006 the Panel has been annually monitoring Management's implementation of the Board-approved remedial measures, and reporting to the Board and posting its monitoring reports on the website. The claimants were generally pleased that their efforts in claiming violation of certain Bank policies were confirmed by the Panel (CRP 2006: 6). One NGO agreed that the CRP's investigation of this claim was 'very successful'. However, it also noted that 'the international advocacy communities do not receive extra safeguard unless the management properly implement the course of action as a result of the CRP report' (NGO Forum on ADB: 2006).

Importantly, the issue of implementation is not addressed at the World Bank accountability mechanism, where the investigative function (and only this function) is performed by the Inspection Panel. The Panel is restricted to acting as a fact-finder. It can neither make recommendations nor monitor Management's remedial action plans in projects which it finds to be out of compliance.

## Complications

A number of general observations can be made about accountability mechanisms at World Bank and the Asian Development Bank. First, most of the claims filed with World Bank and the ADB accountability mechanisms relate to infrastructure projects including highways and roads, dam construction and power plants. Second, the policies which have most often been found to be violated include those relating to involuntary resettlement, environment and social issues, indigenous peoples, project supervision and disclosure of information. Third, of all MDB accountability mechanisms, the World Bank Inspection Panel has been the most scrutinized by civil society and scholars, because of its role as a pioneer of these mechanisms, its vast experience in handling cases from borrowing countries worldwide, and the clarifications made during the two Board-level reviews. The remainder of this section focuses on some more complex observations which centre on the topics of access, justice and politics.

### Empowerment through access ...

Accountability mechanisms are primarily intended to serve as internal governance tools to enhance institutional development effectiveness. For example, the 'objective of the [World Bank Inspection] Panel's function is not listed' in the resolution under which it was created (Shihata 1994: 36), but World Bank President Lewis Preston has stated that the 'Panel is part of the Bank's evolving policy of improving its effectiveness' (Shihata 1994: v). In contrast, the ADB Accountability Mechanism makes it expressly clear that one of its principles is to 'enhance ADB's development effectiveness and project quality' (ADB 2003: 14).

One aspect of the 'effectiveness' or 'quality' of projects which has grown in importance over the years is the extent to which they negatively impact upon the interests of people. These so-called project-affected people are unable to obtain damages at the national level because MDBs are afforded immunity from local jurisdiction (Suzuki and Nanwani 2005: 206). Although the immunity of states has evolved from absolute to relative immunity, the immunity of MDBs 'has remained absolute, barring exceptions allowed under specific provisions mandated by the nature of the organization or of the dispute in question' (Gaillard and Pingel-Lenuzza 2002: 3).[10] Consequently, project-affected persons only have recourse at a national level if MDBs waive their immunities to court proceedings or agree to organize some form of dispute settlement.

A second aspect of project 'effectiveness' and 'quality', only relatively recently recognized, is the extent to which projects align with the various public interests typically supported by civil society actors. Indeed, civil society played a catalytic role in creating the World Bank Inspection Panel, the first MDB accountability mechanism established in 1993 (Van Putten 2006: 79).[11] Although civil society did not actively contribute to the establishment of the original ADB Inspection Function in 1995, 'concerns about independence, credibility, transparency and information dissemination, and effectiveness of the Inspection Function' led to considerable pressure during the review process which resulted in its replacement in 2003 by the Accountability Mechanism (ADB 2003: 1).

Accountability mechanisms are clearly designed to empower members of the public by providing them with a degree of access to the inner workings of development banks. How and to what extent do the mechanisms fulfil this goal?

### Bringing complaints

These mechanisms allow those people who are affected by a project to bring complaints to the Banks through a formalized system. As stated by World Bank President James Wolfensohn, by 'giving private citizens – and especially the poor – a new means of access to the Bank, [the Inspection Panel] has *empowered and given voice to those we most need to hear*' (Umaña 1998: vii; emphasis added). Claims to both World Bank and ADB accountability mechanisms may be made in local languages, and grievance procedures are explained in short, non-technical brochures, with translations in many local languages.

The claim relating to the Jamuna Bridge Project is a good illustration of accountability mechanisms as gateways for the masses. The project aimed to connect two halves of Bangladesh by building a bridge across the river Jamuna. It was co-financed by the ADB, the International Development Association (IDA) of the World Bank Group and the JBIC (see Jamuna Bridge Project Website).

A complaint was filed with the World Bank Inspection Panel in August 1996 by a local NGO, the Jamuna Char Integrated Development Project, representing about 3,000 dwellers in *chars* (islands) in the project area.[12] The claimants stated that they wanted the project to continue, but they objected to the fact that they were not taken into account in the planning, designing and implementation of the resettlement and environment measures adopted by the World Bank. The Inspection Panel report stated that the claim was eligible, and found that the claimants were 'uninformed and out of the design and appraisal stages of the project, including the environmental and resettlement plans aimed at mitigating adverse effects on people and nature'. The Panel further noted that the Bank had 'omitted to identify and incorporate *char* people specifically during design and appraisal of the project', and that the claimants 'should have been identified *ex-ante* as a particularly vulnerable group' (World Bank Inspection Panel 1996: 15–17).

However, the Panel did not recommend an investigation of this project. It found that an Erosion and Flood Policy, which had been 'issued after the Request was filed could constitute an adequate and enforceable framework' such that Management would be able 'to comply with the policies and procedures relevant to the Requesters' concerns' (World Bank Inspection Panel 1996: 18; see also Bissell 2001: 122). The Board of Directors asked the Panel to monitor Management's follow-up action. The Panel duly made a report in August 1998 (World Bank Inspection Panel, 1998). It was not asked to make any further reports.

In this case, the Inspection Panel served as a significant gateway to justice, empowering about 3,000 *char* dwellers to voice their grievances and be heard. However, the claimants found it difficult to get information on how the Panel operated, especially since they had no access to the Internet. They also found it a 'daunting task' to fulfil the criteria set by the Inspection Panel (Dulu 2003: 98–99). While the claimants welcomed the Panel's role in monitoring and supervising the action plan, they were 'frustrated' by the Panel's 'failure to follow up on the outcome of the action plan and to see it through its completion' (Dulu 2003: 108).

### Registering views

Accountability mechanisms enable the public at large, including civil society groups, to present their views on projects. For example, public hearings are carried out as part of World Bank and ADB accountability mechanisms. During its monitoring of the implementation of the Board's decision, the CRP consults with concerned stakeholders and obtains information from the public regarding the status of implementation, as in the STDP claim where local and international NGOs prepared a report for the CRP's use in its monitoring task.

However, members of the public are not always willing to contribute to the work of the accountability mechanisms, as the history of the complaint relating to the Chashma Right Bank Irrigation Project (Stage III) demonstrates. This ADB-supported project is designed to irrigate and drain a semi-arid area in north-western Pakistan by diverting the Indus river at the Chashma Barrage (see Chashma Project website). A request for inspection was lodged in 2002 by a number of local civil society actors (see Chashma Project Compliance Review Panel website). The Project was investigated under the erstwhile Inspection Function and found to be in violation of a range of policies relating to flood and erosion protection, project benefit monitoring and evaluation, environmental impacts, socio-economic and cultural impacts, involuntary resettlement, incorporation of social dimensions, and supplementary financing of cost overruns.

The new Accountability Mechanism, which includes a monitoring function, was introduced shortly thereafter, and the Board of Directors of the ADB mandated the Compliance Review Panel (CRP) to monitor the project and ensure that it was brought back into compliance. However, the requesters disengaged themselves from the monitoring process, failing to provide comments on Management's action plan and 'boycott[ing]' ADB processes including CRP field visits (CRP 2005b: 5). The Panel does, however, have access to reports published by other NGOs and, in its field monitoring visits, continues to interact as much as possible with those who are affected by the implementation of the Board-approved remedial actions.

### Bar on individual claims

One significant barrier to access is that individual claims are not allowed to be presented under any MDB accountability mechanism other than the IFC/MIGA's

CAO Office (CAO 2008: 12). At the World Bank and ADB, claims must be filed by a community of persons such as an organization, association, society or other grouping of individuals, and claimants must consist of any two or more persons in the territory of the borrowing country. Under the ADB accountability mechanism, provision is also made allowing the claimants to be in an ADB member country adjacent to the borrowing country. So long as the claimants give their authority, claims may be made by a local representative of the affected group or, in 'exceptional cases', by a non-local representative. Of all the claims filed with these mechanisms, only one has involved a non-local representative. That claim related to the Western Poverty Reduction Project in China and was filed with the Inspection Panel by the London-based international NGO International Campaign for Tibet. The Panel found the claim eligible within the 'exceptional circumstances' test, noting that the Campaign was serving in a representative capacity for the local Tibetans affected by the project and had their authorization, and that appropriate local representation was not available.[13]

Table 7.2 provides a breakdown of 153 claims filed or registered with seven MDB accountability mechanisms. It should be noted that several claims are filed on the same projects.[14]

At the World Bank, the decision to exclude single-party claims stemmed from fears that such a right 'could open the door to frequent, frivolous requests causing unwarranted disruption' (Shihata 2000: 59). These fears appear to be baseless since figures from CAO's ombudsman (problem-solving) function show that of the 70 complaints it has received over the past nine years (CAO 2007: 50–52) only 11 are filed by individuals, and of those seven have arisen from a single project (the BTC Main Export Pipeline Project) (CAO 2008).

### ... to justice?

Although the World Bank and ADB accountability mechanisms are citizen-driven grievance systems, their basic documents do not expressly refer to the terms 'justice', 'people empowerment' or 'law'. These terms are however implicit

*Table 7.2* Claims with MDB accountability mechanisms to 1 June 2008

|  | Years of operation | Claims filed or registered |
| --- | --- | --- |
| World Bank Inspection Panel | 15 | 52 |
| IDB Independent Investigation Mechanism | 14 | 5 |
| ADB Inspection Function (1995–2003) | 8 | 8 |
| ADB Accountability Mechanism (from 2003) | 5 | 12 |
| IFC and MIGA Ombudsman | 9 | 70 |
| EBRD Independent Recourse Mechanism | 4 | 5 |
| AfDB Independent Review Mechanism | 2 | 1 |

or given a limited meaning in the operation of these mechanisms. On justice, the World Bank and ADB accountability mechanisms are silent in their constituent documents. The Panel is tasked to present to the Board of Directors its findings on whether the Bank has complied with all relevant Bank policies and procedures as a fact-finding body (World Bank 1993, 1996 and 1999). It is not a judicial forum and cannot award damages. At ADB, the policy clearly specifies that the CRP's findings and recommendations are 'not adjudicative' and that compliance review is 'not intended to provide judicial-type remedies, such as injunctions or money damages' (ADB 2003: 15). In short, the MDB accountability systems mechanisms were never intended to function as judicial bodies.

Although the World Bank and ADB accountability mechanisms are investigative and advisory, they are required to operate according to certain rules of administrative justice. The constituent documents or the accompanying operational procedures spell out rules of administrative justice such as the right to be heard through 'holding public meetings in the project area' (World Bank Inspection Panel, 1994a and CRP 2004: 8), giving opportunities to a wide range of stakeholders to provide their views[15] or considering 'any information received from the requester and the public' (ADB 2003: 30) during the CRP's monitoring of the Board-approved remedial actions for the project. Also, the ADB accountability mechanism has given claimants due process by providing them with the opportunity to comment, at the same time as ADB Management (namely, the President and Vice-Presidents), on the CRP's draft investigation report before the report is finalized.

## Wider repercussions

As the following examples demonstrate, complaints made to accountability mechanisms can have far-reaching consequences, whether intended or otherwise.

The Pangue/Ralco hydroelectric dam project involved the construction of a hydroelectric dam on the Biobío river in Chile with the support of the International Finance Corporation (IFC), part of the World Bank Group. A claim was filed with the World Bank Inspection Panel alleging that the IFC had violated its own and World Bank policies during the course of the project. The claim was filed by a local NGO (Gruppo de Acción, GABB), with help from various international NGOs, representing itself and others, including the Pehuenche Indian people. The claimants were aware that the claim was outside of the Panel's jurisdiction, but wished to highlight the need for an accountability mechanism to cover the activities of the IFC and MIGA. A petition was also sent to the World Bank President and to the Board of Directors of the IFC to 'persuade them either to extend the Inspection Panel's jurisdiction to the IFC or authorize an independent inspection of some sort, assuming that the Inspection Panel would not have jurisdiction' (Hunter, Opaso and Orellana 2003: 127). The Panel declined to register the claim on the grounds of lack of jurisdiction: its mandate restricted it to the review of projects financed by IBRD or IDA only. It forwarded the claim to the World Bank President who initiated an 'impartial internal review' (the Hair Investigation) of the environmental and social concerns of the project (Udall 1997: 54). The claim was an ingenious attempt to attract international attention to the problems of the Pangue project. It galvanized an NGO campaign for the creation of an accountability mechanism for IFC and MIGA, helping to secure the addition of the problem-solving function (ombudsman) at the Compliance Advisor/Ombudsman office in 1999. Two claims on the Pangue project were filed in 2000 and 2002 and the ombudsman resolved these claims and closed them in 2005 and 2006 respectively (see CAO Pangue website).[16]

Similarly dramatic external repercussions flowed from the Arun III Hydroelectric Project. As noted by an Inspection Panel member who investigated this case, the 'greatest impact of the claim' was the cancellation of the World Bank's participation in this project. From this flowed proclamations of victory among advocacy NGOs and claimants,[17] and expressions of dismay from the Government of Nepal (Bissell 2003: 37 and 39). A longer-lasting effect was the establishment of the World Commission on Dams (WCD) in 1998 'with the Bank as a co-initiator' (Bissell 2003: 40). The Commission was an 'independent, international, multi-stakeholder process which addressed the controversial issues associated with large dams' (see WCD Website).

### Politicization

#### Management-Panel dynamics

In the early years of the World Bank Inspection Panel's operation, claimants and civil society groups were concerned that Management-Panel dynamics were impeding the operation of the Panel and preventing claimants from playing a pivotal role. For example, in some cases,[18] the Bank's Management responded to claims made to the Panel by proposing plans for remedial action or mitigation. This then prompted the Board of Directors to refuse to authorize the Panel to carry out an investigation. In this way, the activities of the Panel were short-circuited and the claimants were excluded from the Panel process.

Such was the situation in the first claim to be heard by the Inspection Panel which related to the proposed Arun III Hydroelectric Project in Nepal. The request was filed by four requesters, two of whom 'asked for anonymity'[19] and authorized the other two requesters to represent them. The requesters claimed to be directly and adversely affected by the violation of five World Bank policies (on economic evaluation of investment operations, disclosure of information, environmental assessment, involuntary resettlement and indigenous peoples) in the design and appraisal of this project. The Panel was authorized by the Board to carry out an investigation, but Management then made an action plan for remedial measures to improve project design and bring the project back into compliance. The Panel found violation of three policies that it was authorized to investigate (environmental assessment, indigenous peoples and involuntary resettlement) and found that Management's proposed remedial measures 'appear to be adequate if and as long as they continue with the applicable operative directives, and appropriate follow-up mechanisms are introduced' (World Bank Inspection Panel 1995: 5).

In a second example of the impact of Board-Panel dynamics, the Board of Directors was unable to decide whether it would authorize the Panel to investigate the 1996 Yacyretá claim. The Argentine representative on the Board of Directors objected to the investigation and lobbied support from the borrowing countries to support the opposition. A split emerged between donor and borrowing countries. No formal vote was taken, but if it had been, the Panel's recommendation would likely have been approved as the donor countries hold a majority of votes. The Board postponed its decision for about three weeks. An intensive NGO campaign ensued, including a letter to the World Bank President by 26 NGOs stating that if 'a claim as strong and compelling as that presented in Yacyretá is turned away by the Board, it may be difficult for NGOs to continue to support the Panel process' (Treakle and Peña 2003: 76). After presentation by Management of an 'action plan', the Board authorized the Panel to carry out 'review and assessment', short of an 'investigation' (Udall 1997: 38).

Happily, the problem of Management-Panel dynamics appears to be a thing of the past as Management-generated action plans to pre-empt investigations were resolved in the Board's second review, resulting in the 1999 Conclusions.[20] Since this review, the Board of Directors has approved without objections all of the Panel's recommendations for investigations and has not restricted the Panel's investigative mandate.

### Claimant–government dynamics

Some claimants have voiced concerns about the response of government to the bringing of claims in accountability mechanisms. For example, in the Southern Transport Development Project (STDP) claim, some claimants and project affectees alleged that they had faced discrimination from the government of Sri Lanka because they had used the accountability mechanism to obtain compensation payments. The CRP took up this issue in its monitoring report and stated that 'there should be no penalty against those who avail of grievance mechanisms' (CRP 2006: 6).

The World Bank Inspection Panel also encountered fears of discrimination or reprisals among claimants in the Yacyretá Hydroelectric Project in Argentina/Paraguay in 1996. Here the requesters claimed confidentiality of names due to fear of reprisals. In its ongoing investigation of the Proposed Private Power Generation Project in Uganda, the Inspection Panel has stated in its eligibility report its concern by 'the reports of pressure and fear among at least some of the affected people who signed the Request to the Panel. The Panel trusts that the Bank will take appropriate steps to ensure that the concerns turn out to be not well-founded' (World Bank Inspection Panel 2007: 20).

## Enhancements

Richard Bissell, former Inspection Panel member and former ADB CRP member, has commented that access is a major riddle for modernizing democratic movements, including accountability mechanisms. He has remarked that the Resolution establishing the Inspection Panel 'laid out a legalistic blueprint for obtaining access to the panel' (2001: 114), thus undermining to some degree the goal of enfranchising the poorest of the poor.

As the examples cited in this chapter demonstrate, the relationship between the accountability mechanisms and those who submit claims to them has been mixed. The voices of claimants have been heard and addressed in the Bank's design and implementation process (Jamuna Project claim). Claimants have managed to stop bank financing for a project (Arun III Project claim) and even to trigger the creation of a new accountability mechanism (Pangue Project claim). But along the way they have sometimes found the mechanisms to be politicized, their positions marginalized and their ability to access the mechanisms constrained. So, claimants have responded by boycotting some processes (Chashma claim), and declaring themselves to be broadly satisfied with others (CERDP claim, STDP claim).

At the ADB, the recent introduction of a dual problem-solving and investigation approach has helped to ensure that the Accountability Mechanism is more relevant to complainants than was its predecessor. Participation has been improved in some instances, for example by allowing claimants to comment on the CRP's draft reports during the investigation and giving claimants and civil society the opportunity to provide inputs during the CRP's monitoring. But there is room for improvement in all the accountability mechanisms.

First, the number of projects about which civil society actors have concerns dramatically outweighs the number of claims presented to World Bank and ADB accountability mechanisms. As of 1 June 2008 only 72 claims had even been presented to the mechanisms of these two institutions, and in only a few of those had violations been found. Meanwhile, the Bank Information Center, USA lists on its website eight problem projects at the World Bank and two at ADB (see BIC, USA website) and other NGOs such as Bretton Woods Project, Oxfam Australia and NGO Forum on ADB have also flagged their concerns on a number of other projects (Oxfam Australia, 2007). One explanation for the disparity is that access to these mechanisms by affected people and civil society is still overly restricted. MDBs can address this issue by allowing advocacy NGOs with a legitimate interest to bring claims on problem projects for compliance reviews. These NGOs might also provide a suitable external forum for hearing and addressing the concerns of NGOs so that development effectiveness might be improved.

Second, accountability mechanisms should consider increasing outreach activities, singly and jointly, in borrowing countries, especially those with problem projects, and to a wider civil society audience such as the World Social Forum. Joint outreach will help people understand the roles of different accountability mechanisms and assist them in accessing these mechanisms in problem projects co-financed by multiple MDBs. They can also promote mandatory dissemination on their mechanisms by project staff from an early stage, such as fact-finding to provide better access to disenfranchised people. In cases in which similar claims in the same project are filed with multiple mechanisms for compliance review, such as the Bujagali Hydropower Project with the AfDB and World Bank accountability mechanisms, the claimants will still have to go through separate reviews by these mechanisms. However, there can be cooperation agreements between these mechanisms to facilitate investigation, information sharing and hiring consultants to reduce costs (AfDB 2007: 20). In the case where one mechanism is carrying out a problem-solving exercise while another carries out a compliance review, these different processes may cause confusion to the affected people, who have to be conversant with the different rules and procedures in addressing their complaints, and these mechanisms would have to be clear in managing people's expectations.

Third, in claims before MDB accountability mechanisms where procurement matters or allegations of fraud and corruption are raised, the mechanisms could, after highlighting that these matters are not within their remit, take proactive roles by referring them to the relevant offices in the institution, and record in their reports the responses received on actions to be taken by these offices. This could contribute towards the institution's curbing of corruption on projects tainted with corruption allegations. MDB management practices on handling corruption in particular have undergone increasing scrutiny from MDB member countries and the enhancement of development, for example in the United States House Committee on Financial Services (see Lugar 2005 and United States House Committee on Financial Services 2007).

Fourth, the MDBs could enhance their panels' competence in determining violations of bank policies by having regard during their policy reviews to the recommendations of civil society, and to best practice from other MDBs and other treaty organisations. For example, when the IFC updated its environmental and social safeguard policies in 2004, it took into account civil society's inputs on best practices. Similarly, the ADB has received a wide range of views during its consultation on the ongoing Safeguard Policy Update and has issued a second draft of the Policy in order to respond to these views. Such developments have been welcomed by NGOs (see ADB Safeguard Policy Update Website and BIC, USA 2008).[21]

Fifth, MDB accountability mechanisms could act collectively to simplify the documents and procedures necessary to make a complaint. This could be done at the annual meetings of accountability mechanisms of MDBs and other financial institutions (such as Export Development Canada, JBIC and OPIC), at which they exchange views on their own activities. Harmonization would be particularly useful in the event of joint referrals by claimants on co-financed projects. The resulting efficiencies would be very much in accordance with the commitments made by MDBs, states and civil society actors in the Paris Declaration on Aid Effectiveness (2005). MDBs may consider allowing individual claims to be filed, as has the CAO Office of the IFC and MIGA, without any negative impact on their operations. They might also allow claimants to respond to the panel's draft investigation report, thereby ensuring that their voices are heard during the accountability procedures.

Finally, panel credibility (including independence) is crucial for effective operation of MDB accountability mechanisms. Hunter notes that, in its early days, the Inspection Panel was viewed by civil society networks as either legalistic or too closely aligned to the institution, even to the point that some critics believed the Panel was 'not worth engaging', but that over the years the Panel has achieved credibility to critics outside the World Bank (2003: 208). This experience indicates to other MDB accountability mechanisms that panel credibility is critical to their efforts to be more responsive in handling citizen claims. Without it, citizens and civil society will not come expecting justice, empowerment, or adherence to internal laws.

## Notes

* The author thanks Dr Richard E. Bissell, Professor Leslie Moran, Dr Eisuke Suzuki and Ms Mishka Zaman for their comments in the preparation of this chapter as well as Ms Josefina C. Miranda and Ms Marie Antoinette Virtucio for their research assistance. The views expressed in this chapter are those of the author and do not reflect the views of the Asian Development Bank.

1 See for example IBRD Articles of Agreement, Article I (iii); IDA Articles of Agreement, Article I and Agreement Establishing the Asian Development Bank, Article I. The World Bank lent about $24.7 billion in its fiscal year 2007 (World Bank 2007: 55) and ADB approved loans, technical assistance and grants amounting to $11 billion in 2007 (ADB 2008: 23).

2 Civil society is not a monolithic group and acts through diverse forms and channels. In the context of MDB lending operations, the term 'civil society' is used to refer to formal or informal groups including individuals adversely affected by bank projects and advocacy NGOs supporting them or acting on their own in demanding greater transparency in bank operations and decision-making in policy formulation or review (Nanwani: 2008).

3 Examples of MDBs are the International Bank for Reconstruction and Development (IBRD), the International Development Association (IDA), the International Finance Corporation and Multilateral Investment Guarantee Agency and the regional development banks for Africa, Asia, Europe and Latin America. The focus of this chapter is on the accountability mechanisms at the World Bank (consisting of IBRD, which aims at middle income and creditworthy countries, and IDA, which targets the world's poorest countries) and ADB.

4 The Joint Organization of the Affected Peoples on Colombo-Matara Highway was acting as an umbrella organization for two local groups, Gama Surakeema Sanvidhanaya (GSS) and United Society for Protection of Akmeemana (USPA). Its request that the identities of 25 individuals be kept confidential was honoured by the Special Project Facilitator (SPF) and the Compliance Review Panel (CRP). The GSS and USPA had earlier filed separate claims under the previous Inspection Function. The Board Inspection Committee constituted under the Inspection Function found their claims to be eligible but not a sufficient basis for an inspection to be authorized. There were also two other claims relating to this project filed in 2001 and 2002 but

the Board Inspection Committee deemed them ineligible on the basis that there was no reasonable evidence presented that the affected community's rights and interests had been or were likely to be directly, materially and adversely affected by the Bank's conduct as a result of its failure to comply with its operational policies and procedures (see ADB Inspection Function website).

5 The CRP noted that, while the same project had been subject to a prior inspection request (see above) and would, therefore, normally have been excluded for submission to the Panel (ADB 2003: 18), in this case new evidence had been provided to the CRP including new information on issues of adequacy of environmental and social assessments for the final trace of the highway.

6 If the consultation process is not purposeful to the claimants, or the claim is held ineligible by the SPF, or if the consultation process has reached an advanced stage and there are concerns on compliance issues, the claimants can file a request for a compliance review with the CRP.

7 For the World Bank, these operational policies and procedures consist of 'the Bank's Operational Policies, Bank Procedures, and Operational Directives, and similar documents issued before these series were started, and does not include Guidelines and Best Practices and similar documents or statements' (World Bank 1993). Since 1992, the World Bank has been replacing its Operational Directives with Operational Policies and Bank procedures. For ADB, these operational policies and procedures relate to 'the formulation, processing, or implementation of an ADB-assisted project. … They are included in the current OM [Operations Manual], the Project Administration Instructions (PAIs), and the New Business Processes (NBP)' (ADB 2003: paragraph 143). PAIs outline the policies and procedures to be followed by ADB staff involved in the administration of ADB-financed loan and technical assistance projects. The New Business Processes are contained in 'Business Processes for the Reorganized ADB', published in December 2001 to guide staff in the provision of ADB's services and products until formal instructions and guidelines are issued through modifications in the Operations Manual.

8 A compliance review panel commenced its, still ongoing, investigation in October 2007. For updates see the AfDB Independent Review Mechanism Register website.

9 It is interesting to note that there is a division of internal law application for public and private sector operations at AfDB's accountability mechanism while the ADB and EBRD mechanisms do not make such a differentiation between public and private sector operations. The AfDB's Independent Review Mechanism refers to the following in the case of projects financed by any AfDB Group entity: for a sovereign guaranteed project, the Bank's 'operational policies and procedures in respect of the design, appraisal and/or implementation of such project', and in the case of private sector or non-sovereign guaranteed projects, 'social and environmental policies and safeguards' (AfDB 2004: paragraphs 11 (i) and (ii)).

10 For example, Article 50(1) of the ADB Charter prescribes that its immunity does not extend to 'the exercise of its powers to borrow money, to guarantee obligations, or to buy and sell or underwrite the sale of securities.' For World Bank immunities see IBRD Articles of Agreement, Chapter VII, Section 3 and the IDA Articles of Agreement, Chapter VIII, Section 3.

11 Apart from MDBs, JBIC, Japan International Cooperation Agency (JICA) and OPIC introduced their accountability mechanisms in 2003, 2004 and 2004 respectively.

12 The claimants chose to use the World Bank Inspection Panel rather than the newly formed ADB Inspection Function because the former was more established and the World Bank had acted as the lead development agency since the pre-investment studies were conducted in the 1980s.

13 This case caused considerable controversy at the World Bank and was the first time that the Board of Directors invoked its own authority to request an investigation of

the case by the Inspection Panel, a residual right provided in the resolution establishing the Panel. A similar right is provided in the ADB Accountability Mechanism on filing a request with the CRP.

14 For example, the Yacyretá Hydroelectric Project with the World Bank and IDB accountability mechanisms, the Southern Transport Development Project (STDP) with the ADB Inspection Function and ADB Accountability Mechanism and the Baku-Tbilisi-Ceyhan [BTC] Main Export Pipeline Project with the CAO Office and EBRD's IRM.

15 The Inspection Panel can 'request written or oral submission on specific issues from the Requester, affected people, independent experts, government or project officials, Bank staff, or local or international non-governmental organizations' under its Operating Procedures (1994: 45(c)). The ADB's CRP can, during its investigation, consult 'the Board member representing the country concerned and representatives of interested nongovernmental organizations, all of whom will be given an opportunity to record their views' under its Operating Procedures (2004:para. 38 (i)).

16 For detailed information on the nature, procedure and outcome and so on of claims addressed by the CAO, see its review of its work: CAO 2006.

17 Although one requester reportedly stated in an interview that the requesters were 'not fully satisfied' with the outcome of the investigation (Udall 1997: 28).

18 See for example the Rondônia Natural Resources Management Project in Brazil in 1995, the Yacyretá Hydroelectric Project in 1996, and the Itaparica Resettlement and Irrigation Project in Brazil in 1997.

19 The Panel accepted these two claimants as 'anonymous' although technically the matter should have been treated as keeping the names of the requesters confidential, as 'anonymous' complaints are excluded. The ADB accountability mechanism also does not allow anonymous complaints, though claimants can request that their names be kept confidential (CRP Operating Procedures 1994:para. 22 (e)).

20 The 1999 Conclusions of the Board's Second Review of the Inspection Panel is also sometimes referred to as the 1999 Clarifications of the Board's Second Review of the Inspection Panel; see the Inspection Panel's Annual Report (August 1, 2000 to July 31, 2001) where both titles are used at pp. 43 and 44.

21 However, some NGOs have advocated the incorporation of free prior informed 'consent' (rather than 'consultation') as stated in the United Nations Declarations on the Rights of Indigenous Peoples adopted in September 2007 by the General Assembly. See for example Forest Peoples Programme 2008.

# References

ADB (1995) 'Establishment of an Inspection Function', Manila: Asian Development Bank. Online: <http://www.adb.org/Documents/Policies/Inspection/inspection_policy.pdf>

——(2003) 'Review of the Inspection Function: establishment of a new ADB Accountability Mechanism', Manila: Asian Development Bank. Online: <http://www.adb.org/Documents/Policies/ADB_Accountability_Mechanism/ADB_accountability_ mechanism.pdf>

——(2005a) 'Special Project Facilitator Final Report. Southern Transport Development Project', March 2005, Manila: Asian Development Bank. Online: <http://www.adb.org/Documents/SPF-Reports/SRI/26522/SF-SRI-1711.pdf>

——(2005b) 'Review and Assessment Report of the Special Project Facilitator on the Community Empowerment Rural Development Project in Indonesia', April 2005, Manila: Asian Development Bank. Online: <http://www.adb.org/Documents/SPF-Reports/INO/32367/cerdp-final-rar.pdf>

——(2006) 'Office of the Special Project Facilitator's Annual Report 2005', Manila: Asian Development Bank. Online: <http://www.adb.org/Documents/Others/IN36-06.pdf>

——(2008) *Annual Report 2007*, Manila: Asian Development Bank. Online: <http://www. adb.org/Documents/Reports/Annual_Report/2007/default.asp>

AfDB (2004) 'Independent Review Mechanism Resolutions B/BD/2004/9 and F/BD/ 2004/7' (June 30, 2004.) Tunis: African Development Bank. Online: <http://www. afdb.org/fileadmin/uploads/afdb/Documents/Compliance-Review/00157746-EN -BOARD-RESOLUTION-B-BD-2004-9-F-BD-2004-9-ENGLISH.PDF>

AfDB Independent Review Mechanism (2007) 'Eligibility report for Compliance Review of Bujagali Hydropower Project/Bujagali Interconnection Project in Uganda, Compliance Review Request No. RQ2007/1', Tunis: African Development Bank. Online: <http:// www.afdb.org/fileadmin/uploads/afdb/Documents/Generic-Documents/23754315-EN-CRMU-ELIGIBILITY-REPORT-BUJAGALI-PROJECT-WEB.PDF?bcsi_scan_B90AE 85AF6AB15C6=0&bcsi_scan_filename=23754315-EN-CRMU-ELIGIBILITY-REPORT-BUJAGALI-PROJECT-WEB.PDF>

Bank Information Centre, USA (BIC USA) (2008). ADB agrees to NGO demand for second draft of Safeguard Policy Update Online: <http://www.bicusa.org/en/ Article.3765.aspx>

Bissell, R. E. (2001) 'Institutional and procedural aspects of the Inspection Panel', in G. Alfredsson and R. Ring (eds) *The Inspection Panel of the World Bank: a different complaints procedure*, Kluwer Law International.

——(2003) 'The Arun III Hydroelectric Project, Nepal', in D. Clark, J. Fox and K. Treakle (eds) *Demanding Accountability: civil-society claims and the World Bank Inspection Panel*, Lanham, Maryland: Rowman and Littlefield.

CAO (2007a) *CAO Annual Report 2006–07*, Washington DC: World Bank. Online: <http://www.cao-ombudsman.org/html-english/documents/CAO_AR0607_Eng.pdf>

——(2007b) *CAO Operational Guidelines*, Washington DC: World Bank. Online: <http://www. cao-ombudsman.org/html-english/documents/WEBEnglishCAO06.08.07Web.pdf>

——(2008) 'Summary of BTC Pipeline complaints from 2003 to March 2008', Washington DC: World Bank. Online: <http://www.cao-ombudsman.org/html-english/documents/CurrentBTCComplaintTracker_updated March08.pdf>

Compliance Advisor Ombudsman (CAO) (2006) 'A retrospective analysis of CAO interventions: trends, outcomes and effectiveness', Washington DC: World Bank. Online: <http://www.cao-ombudsman.org/html-english/documents/ RetrospectiveAnalysisonCAOEffectiveness_final_9May06.pdf>

Compliance Review Panel (CRP) (2004) *Compliance Review Panel Operating Procedures*. Manila: Asian Development Bank. Online: <http://ocrp.asiandevbank.org/dir0035p .nsf/alldocs/ELLN-6NC8A4?OpenDocument>

CRP (2005a) 'Final report to ADB Board of Directors: CRP Request No. 2004/1 on the Southern Transport Development Project' (June 22, 2005). Online: <http://www. compliance.adb.org/dir0035p.nsf/attachments/STDP-CRPFinalReport-12Jul05.pdf/ $FILE/STDP-CRPFinalReport-12Jul05.pdf>

——(2005b) 'Supplementary report to Annual Monitoring Report 2004–5: implementation of remedial actions on the Inspection Request on the Chashma Right Bank Irrigation Project (Stage III) in Pakistan' (December 21, 2005). Manila: Asian Development Bank. Online: <http://www.compliance.adb.org/dir0035p.nsf/ attachments/ChashmaMonitoringSuppRpt2005-Final-26Jun06-rev.pdf/$FILE/Chashma MonitoringSuppRpt2005-Final-26Jun06-rev.pdf>

——(2006) 'Annual Monitoring Report 2005–6 on the Southern Transport Development Project in Sri Lanka' (July 11, 2006). Online: <http://www.compliance.adb.org/dir0035p.nsf/attachments/STDP-MonitoringReport2006.pdf/$FILE/STDP-Monitoring Report2006.pdf>

Dulu, M. H. (2003) 'The experience of Jamuna Bridge: issues and perspectives', in D. Clark, J. Fox and K. Treakle (eds) *Demanding Accountability: Civil-Society Claims and the World Bank Inspection Panel*, Lanham, MD: Rowman and Littlefield.

European Bank for Reconstruction and Development (EBRD), 2004. Independent Recourse Mechanism Rules of Procedure (April 6, 2004).

Forest Peoples Programme (2008) Inquiries, Comments, and Suggestions on the Safeguard Policy Statement (second draft). Online: <http://www.adb.org/Safeguards/Forest-12Feb2008.pdf>

Gaillard, E. and Pingel-Lenuzza, I. (2002) 'International organizations and immunity from jurisdiction: to restrict or to bypass', *International and Comparative Law Quarterly*, 51.

Hunter, D. B. (2003) 'Using the World Bank Inspection Panel to defend the interests of project-affected people', University of Chicago Journal of International Law, 4: 201.

Hunter, D. B., Opaso, C. and Orellana, M. (2003) 'The Biobío's legacy: institutional reforms and unfulfilled promises at the International Finance Corporation', in D. Clark, J. Fox and K. Treakle (eds) *Demanding Accountability: civil-society claims and the World Bank Inspection Panel*, Lanham, MD: Rowman and Littlefield.

Lugar, R. (2005) 'Opening statement for Hearing on the Review of the Anti-Corruption Strategies of the Regional Development Banks by US Senate Committee on Foreign Relations Chairman Richard G. Lugar' (April 21, 2005) Washington DC: United States Senate. Online: <http://foreign.senate.gov/testimony/2005/LugarStatement050421.pdf>

Nanwani, S. (2008) 'Holding multilateral development banks to account: gateways and barriers', *International Community Law Review*, 10: 200.

NGO Forum on ADB (2006) *NGO Forum on ADB Annual Report 2005*. Online: <http://www.forum-adb.org/pdf/Campaign%20Materials/Annual%20Reports/Annual%20Report%202005.pdf>

Oxfam Australia (2007) *Safeguarding or disregarding? Community experiences with the Asian Development Bank's safeguard policies*, Fitzroy, Victoria: Oxfam Australia. Online: <http://www.oxfam.org.au/campaigns/development-banks/docs/SafegardingDisregardingOA07.pdf>

Paris Declaration on Aid Effectiveness (2005) High Level Forum Paris, February 28 to March 2 2005. Online: <http://www.worldbank.org/harmonization/Paris/FINALPARISDECLARATION.pdf>

Shihata, I. F. I. (1994) *The World Bank Inspection Panel*, New York: Oxford University Press.

——(2000) *The World Bank Inspection Panel: in practice*, 2nd edn, New York: Oxford University Press.

Suzuki, E. and Nanwani, S. (2005) 'Responsibility of international organizations: the accountability mechanisms of multilateral development banks', *Michigan Journal of International Law* 27(1): 177–225.

Treakle, K. and Peña, E. D. (2003) 'Accountability at the World Bank: what does it take? Lessons from the Yacyretá Hydroelectric Project, Argentine/Paraguay', in D. Clark, J. Fox and K. Treakle (eds) *Demanding Accountability: civil-society claims and the World Bank Inspection Panel*, Lanham, MD: Rowman and Littlefield.

Udall, L. (1997) *The World Bank Inspection Panel: a three year review.* Washington, D.C.: The Bank Information Center.

Umaña, A. (ed.) (1998) *The World Bank Inspection Panel. The First Four Years (1994–1998).* Washington, D.C.: World Bank.

US House Committee on Financial Services (2007) *Full Committee Hearing on The Role and Effectiveness of the World Bank in Combating Global Poverty* (May 2007). Washington DC: United States House of Representatives. Online: <http://www.house.gov/apps/list/hearing/financialsvcs_dem/ht052207.shtml>

Van Putten, M. (2006) '*Policing the World*', *Accountability Mechanisms for Multilateral Financial Institutions and Private Financial Institutions.* The Netherlands: Tilburg University and Canada: McGill University.

World Bank (1993) The World Bank Inspection Panel Resolution No. IBRD 93–10 and Resolution No. IDA 93–96 (22 September 1993). Washington D.C.: World Bank. Online: <http://siteresources.worldbank.org/EXTINSPECTIONPANEL/Resources/ResolutionMarch2005.pdf>

——(1996) Review of the resolution establishing the Inspection Panel 1996 clarification of certain aspects of the resolution (17 October 1996). Washington D.C.: World Bank. Online: <http://siteresources.worldbank.org/EXTINSPECTIONPANEL/Resources/1996ReviewResolution.pdf>

——(1999) *1999 Clarification of the Board's Second Review of the Inspection Panel.* Washington D. C.: World Bank. Online: <http://siteresources.worldbank.org/EXTINSPECTIONPANEL/Resources/1999ClarificationoftheBoard.pdf>

——(2007) *The World Bank Annual Report 2007.*

World Bank Inspection Panel (1994a) *The Inspection Panel's Operating Procedures* (19 August 1994).

——(1995) *World Bank Investigation Panel Report, Arun III Proposed Hydroelectric Project* (22 June 1995).

——(1996) Report and Recommendation to the Executive Directors of the International Development Association on Request for Inspection. Bangladesh: Jamuna Bridge Project (Credit 2569-BD) (November 1996).

——(1998) Report on Progress on Implementation of the Erosion and Flood Action Plan. Request for Inspection. Bangladesh: Jamuna Bridge Project (Credit 2569-BD), (14 August 1998).

——(2007) Report and Recommendation on Request for Inspection. Uganda: Private Power Generation Project (Proposed) (May 2007). Online: <http://siteresources.worldbank.org/EXTINSPECTIONPANEL/Resources/UgandaeligibrepoMay3FINAL.pdf>

## Useful websites

ADB Inspection Function
  <http://www.adb.org/Inspection/default.asp>
AfDB Independent Review Mechanism Register
  <http://www.afdb.org/en/about-us/structure/independent-review-mechanism/requests-register/>
Bank Information Center, USA (BIC, USA)
  <http://www.bicusa.org/en/Institution.Projects.5.aspx> and
  <http://www.bicusa.org/en/Institution.Projects.2.aspx>

CERDP SPF
  <http://www.adb.org/SPF/cerdp-complaint-registry.asp>
CERDP Project
  <http://www.adb.org/Projects/project.asp?id=32367>
Chashma Right Bank Irrigation Project
  <http://www.adb.org/Projects/Chashma/default.asp>
Chashma Project Compliance Review Panel
  <http://ocrp.asiandevbank.org/dir0035p.nsf/alldocs/ELLN-6NHABE?Open-
  Document>
(CAO) Compliance Advisor/Ombudsman Pangue Project
  <http://www.cao-ombudsman.org/html-english/complaint_pangue.htm>
EBRD Independent Recourse Mechanism (IRM)
  <http://www.ebrd.com/about/integrity/irm/about/index.htm>
Jamuna Bridge Project
  <http://go.worldbank.org/MQJUEMCXH0>
Southern Area Infrastructure Project
  <http://www.adb.org/Projects/project.asp?id=26522>
(WCD) World Commission on Dams
  <http://www.dams.org/>
World Bank Inspection Panel
  <http://www.inspectionpanel.org>

# Community participation in biodiversity conservation: emerging localities of tension

*Andreas Kotsakis*

The 1992 Convention on Biological Diversity has created a path of interaction between the local and the global, the consequences of which are now beginning to emerge. In a 2007 message, the executive secretary of the Convention characterized indigenous and local communities as 'environmental managers with immense ecological knowledge' and 'crucial partners' in both conservation and the sustainable use of biodiversity (Djoghlaf 2007).[1] This statement reveals a belief that these communities can make a significant contribution to the project of biodiversity conservation. It also signifies the emergence of a new locality to form a significant part of the legal discourse produced by the Convention. Combining elements of natural-resource management and community participation, this new locality aspires to become a multi-stakeholder multiplicity of plants, animals and people. In fact it is a site of confusion in which meanings of environment, nature and community are at once imposed from above and contested from below.

This chapter explores two significant, interrelated, aspects of the establishment of this link between 'biodiversity' and 'community'. First, it argues that this link suggests a discursive and spatial shift in the focus of biodiversity conservation activities and debates,[2] from the global and the North, towards the local and the South. These newly delineated discursive and spatial boundaries offer an alternative to the state regulation and, subsequently, market mechanisms which failed to deal with the complexities of the 'environment and development' debate (Li 2005). Second, this chapter argues that this linking of biodiversity to community is part of a tendency in environmental discourse to extend the management of biodiversity as a system of biological and genetic (biogenetic) resources: hence the ubiquitous use of the term 'community-based natural resource management' when referring to community approaches to conservation.

Drawing these two arguments together, this chapter concludes that even as the conceptions of biodiversity and community are employed to include local, rural or indigenous communities within an emerging global environmental discourse, they may, through their inherent contradictions and conflicts, actually serve to exclude them. This is because, although this form of community participation discourse ascribes a political and cultural 'otherness' to the traditional community, symbolized by the image of the biodiversity 'steward', it also forcibly attaches a 'managerial' – biological and economic – approach to the environment. The first section outlines the 'managerial' approach that dominates current biodiversity thinking. Next, some of the difficulties posed by the entry of community-based approaches into biodiversity discourse are exposed. Finally, the last section describes three primary effects stemming from the link between biodiversity and community; effects that extend beyond the confines of the biodiversity discourse to pose questions regarding the role of a newly created locality in the development of international environmental law in the era of sustainable development.

## Managerialism

The Biodiversity Convention has promulgated a 'managerialist' understanding of biodiversity in which biological and economic constructs are combined to conceptualize biodiversity not simply as an ecosystem, but as a system of (biological and genetic) resources. The guiding principles of the Convention appear to descend from an original call expressed in the very first sentence of the proceedings of the 'Forum on BioDiversity', held in 1986 by the American Academy of Sciences: 'biological diversity must be treated more seriously as a global resource, to be indexed, used, and above all, preserved' (Wilson and Peter 1988: 3). These three functions (indexing, use, conservation) are mirrored in three main objectives (conservation, sustainable utilization and fair and equitable benefit sharing) eventually adopted in the Biodiversity Convention (Article 1).[3]

### Economic influences

For economists, biodiversity is 'biogenetic capital', a profitable system of biogenetic resources. Advances in the fields of biology and ecology are making it possible to use this system sustainably, and 'in ways that can relieve both human suffering and environmental destruction' (Wilson and Peter 1988: 3). This last observation echoes the economic and biological understandings of biodiversity promoted by the Convention: biodiversity conservation is presented as worthwhile because it is for the mutual benefit of both the environment and humanity.[4]

In addition to mapping out the operation of the, then new, concept of biodiversity, the proceedings of the 1986 Forum on Biodiversity develop a specific understanding of biodiversity as a global resource. This understanding is pushed further under the Biodiversity Convention, which treats biodiversity as a resource that can be sustainably managed to provide multiple benefits to be (re-) distributed amongst various parties (CBD 1992: Article 15). From its early origins, biodiversity has always been intertwined with sustainable development. The Biodiversity Convention originated at the same United Nations Environment Programme (UNEP) session which saw the release of the so-called Brundtland report which introduced the concept of sustainable development (World

Commission on Environment and Development 1987), and the final text was agreed and signed during the 'Earth Summit' at Rio in 1992. Ten years later, the CBD Strategic Plan formally conceptualized biodiversity as the 'living foundation of' and an 'essential instrument for achieving' sustainable development, further legitimizing the economic understanding of biodiversity (UNEP/CBD/COP VI/26 2002).

This economic understanding of biodiversity rests on the assumption that a simple relationship is common to all natural resources: the sustainable utilization of biogenetic resources will create the necessary political and financial support for their conservation, so long as the benefits derived are shared equitably and are enough to finance conservation. Those benefits have increased exponentially since the development of biotechnology made the utilization of genetic resources a profitable reality. Kathleen MacAfee (1999) is critical of this mechanism of 'selling nature to save it', but it has proved successful in garnering political support for environmental initiatives in the developing world, as evidenced by the near-global membership of the Biodiversity Convention.

The influence of economics is apparent in the expression of the Convention's primary objective of 'conserving biodiversity', which is directed towards maintaining a sustainable stock of biogenetic capital, rather than, for example, the preservation of any fixed environmental standard. This signals a further departure from old-style 'command and control' methods of environmental regulation. The focus of the Convention's current programme of work expands upon the other two objectives of utilizing this biogenetic capital and distributing the benefits in a fair and equitable manner. Those objectives are addressed in the negotiation for a new international regime regulating the access to and utilization of these biogenetic resources (ABS regime).[5] The increased attention afforded to this process seems to support the idea that an economic approach, focusing on the management of this valuable biogenetic capital, remains a priority for the parties to the Convention.

### Biological influences

The Biodiversity Convention defines biodiversity in broad, strictly biological terms, as 'variability among living organisms from all sources; this includes diversity within species, between species and of ecosystems' (CBD 1992: Article 2). As McConnell (1996) reminds us, this biological understanding was defended 'fiercely' from the outset of the Convention negotiations, despite the reticence of the negotiators:

> Because the phrase 'conservation of biological diversity' was so cumbersome a proposal to revert to the shorter, traditional concept of 'nature conservation' appealed to many delegates who had no deep knowledge of the subject. But this was fiercely attacked by the few scientific experts present who had a hard but eventually successful task in convincing the ignorant

majority that biological diversity was the correct term. Very soon everyone was using the shortened form – biodiversity – but with as yet little clear understanding of its meaning.[6]

The science of biology is used to categorize natural components that may be considered as biological or genetic resources. The scientific experts in charge of promoting the concept of biodiversity on the international stage clearly intended to distinguish the term 'biodiversity' from the rest of environmental discourse, to create a separate field of inquiry.

The legal definition of biodiversity adopted in the Convention text draws heavily on the biological approach. It is extremely broad and abstract, perhaps unhelpfully equating diversity with variability, but certainly equating biodiversity with the sum total of all life on earth, minus humanity. As such, it legitimizes a certain 'bio-based environmentalism'.[7]

According to the biological interpretation, biodiversity is constantly quantified, categorized, stratified, classified and specialized, creating an intricate network of organisms and ecosystems under the sole discursive control of the biodiversity expert.[8] While humanity is not excluded from the legal definition of biological resources,[9] it is restricted to the position of the outside adjudicator of the value of these resources. Thus, the boundary between 'external' nature and 'internal' humanity is reinforced, strengthening a limited understanding of environmental issues as issues pertaining solely to an outside nature, an 'other' outside of humanity's social and cultural existence.

### An invitation to manage

The Convention and related documents set clear conceptual boundaries to what constitutes legitimate environmental knowledge and, consequently, action.[10] The resulting biodiversity 'managerialism' focuses on biological and economic interpretations of biodiversity to the exclusion of other – namely social and cultural – considerations. Thus a complex and multi-layered environmental concern over the loss of biodiversity is transformed into a specific interest in promoting the appropriate management of a newly discovered biogenetic capital.[11] So, an 'invitation' to participate in the discourse of biodiversity such as that extended by the Convention's secretary can be read as an invitation to become a bio-diversity manager – to utilize the available biogenetic capital based on technical knowledge provided by the Convention.

Since the articulation of environmental concerns in terms of biodiversity necessitates a combined economic and biological understanding of the problem, the entry of the local and indigenous communities into the biodiversity discourse in turn assists in the ever wider dissemination of this specific, dominant conception of biodiversity. Local communities are invited to participate in the pursuit of sustainable development via this conception of a sustainably used and profitable biogenetic capital; the becoming of a 'biodiversity manager'.

## Difficulties in community participation

After a long history of environmental rhetoric oscillating in a futile manner between the competing state and market-based paradigms, community-based approaches are generally considered a 'third way' of sorts in environmental regulation. Past failures of both state and market approaches have led to a certain level of cynicism and resignation:

> [C]ommunities could not do a worse job than corporations, states, multi-lateral agencies and development experts who have caused an extraordinary amount of human and environmental damage (Brosius et al. 2005: 1).

The viability of a community-based approach to conservation was acknowledged as early as 1992, when Principle 22 of the Rio Declaration introduced an obligation to protect indigenous and local communities;[12] and Agenda 21 dedicated a separate chapter to calling for the 'empowerment' of indigenous communities, their 'participation in the national formulation of policies' and their 'involvement, at the national and local levels, in resource management and conservation strategies' (CSD 1992: Paragraphs 26(3)(a)-(c)).

The promise of sustainable development further complicates this 'third way', as participation seems to be equated with a complete regeneration of economic, political and historical agency previously denied to these communities. However, the Biodiversity Convention focuses rather more narrowly on the twin issues of the traditional dependence of these communities on their surrounding biodiversity and the protection of their traditional knowledge to improve biodiversity conservation. In this limited context, community participation in biodiversity discourse was originally hampered by a conflict between the national orientation of the original treaty text and an increasing emphasis on the local in subsequent biodiversity discourse. The global ABS regime (see below) aims to resolve this conflict. But a deeper obstacle, in the form of the idealisation of these local and indigenous communities as ecologically wise 'stewards', shows no signs of being resolved.

### From the national to the local

As Le Prestre has astutely noted, the loss of biodiversity may be considered a 'world-wide' – as opposed to a global – problem, in the sense of being 'experienced by all countries, but resolved in a way that is largely national' (Le Prestre 2002: 4). The Biodiversity Convention appears to follow this blueprint, leaving implementation almost exclusively to national initiatives.[13] Any global aspirations are limited to a Preamble recognition that 'the conservation of biological diversity is a common concern of humankind'. The Convention includes no global standards of biodiversity, nor global lists of protected areas, nor appendices of protected species; essentially no substantive, binding standards to be measured or legal obligations to be enforced against signatory states. In fact, in order to comply with the provisions of the Convention, national governments must merely report that they consider themselves to be in compliance, for example by adopting a national biodiversity conservation strategy that it deems to be 'effective for meeting the objectives of the Convention'. Second, the Convention reaffirms the principle of national sovereignty over the created biogenetic capital (CBD 1992: Articles 26 and 3). Third, the 'fair and equitable' sharing of benefits from the sustainable utilization of genetic resources[14] will take place at the national level, as the text identifies national governments as competent authorities for implementing the Convention. Consequently, the Convention objective of 'benefit sharing' refers to redistribution between, and not within, states.[15]

Local and indigenous communities are specifically in a paragraph on the protection of 'traditional, knowledge, innovation and practices', which falls within the Convention's objective of biodiversity conservation (CBD 1992: Article 8(j)). This protection seems to be afforded simply on the basis of what has been called a 'founding assumption' that:

> [P]eople who live close to the resource and whose livelihoods depend on it have more interest in sustainable use and management than do state authorities and or distant corporations (Li 2005: 428).

Second, the Preamble of the Convention recognizes the 'traditional dependence of … communities embodying traditional lifestyles' on local biological resources. Thus the assumption that proximity to the biological resources increases knowledge and interest in their sustainable use is reinforced. Furthermore, these communities are expected to take biodiversity more seriously in exchange for this recognition of their traditional knowledge and local interests. This limited construction of a community-based approach is far removed from the empowerment described in Agenda 21 or the 'devolution to local polities' (Rose 2008: 213) frequently discussed in the 'communities and conservation' literature.

The Convention text eschews hitherto popular terms such as 'common heritage', which had been used to signify the global character of environmental problems. This retreat from earlier global aspirations directs the action towards the national level, so the state-centric character of international environmental law is retained. The lack of a local element, beyond the emphasis on the protection of traditional knowledge, makes it difficult to understand how community-based approaches came to such prominence in biodiversity discourse, as exemplified by the endorsement of local and indigenous communities by the Convention's executive secretary (see above). However, the language surrounding the Convention has shifted over time in subtle, yet important ways, from the original state-centric approach.

The first major step towards a genuine focus on community participation was the recognition of local and indigenous communities as stakeholders in the context of the non-binding Bonn Guidelines (2002) regulating access to genetic resources and benefit sharing.[16] Under the guidelines, these communities are stakeholders to be engaged in securing prior informed consent of the local population for an outsider to gain access to a genetic resource, and the terms on which the benefits of commercial utilization of the resource will be shared. Second, the steadily increasing importance of the role of community in biodiversity discourse was further signified by the creation and continued operation of two separate working groups devoted to local and indigenous communities.[17] Third, the Biodiversity Convention has adopted the non-binding Akwé: Kon Guidelines (2004). These introduce provisions for the participation by, and taking into account of the needs and concerns of, local and indigenous communities in the design and implementation of development projects (Secretariat of the CBD 2004). Again, close proximity to the harmful effects of these projects is the major criterion for intervention. The last major step towards the local is the evolution of the non-binding Bonn Guidelines into the negotiation of a fully-fledged, possibly binding, international regime for the regulation of Access and Benefit Sharing (ABS) (UNEP/CBD/COP VII/19 2004). Under that regime, recognized stakeholders would presumably join national governments at the centre of the stage. The ability to share in the benefits derived from the sustainable utilization would support a community-based approach to the management of the biogenetic capital of biodiversity, creating a direct path for the pursuit of sustainable development.

Despite all these steps, and in contrast to the early declarations included in Agenda 21, biodiversity discourse continues to reserve a fairly limited role for these communities. The emphasis is on specific and restricted economic rights surrounding the redistribution of benefits from the sustainable utilization of biogenetic capital. The suggestion is that being able to profit from a conveniently located resource can in itself be a solution to a host of political and social problems faced by these communities. Second, as we have seen, the Convention seems to trap these communities in a procedural 'limbo' by recognizing them as stakeholders, but not right holders, in a number of legal processes. The extent of that 'stake' remains unclear, but it is certainly understood as something less than a right.

### Communities as traditional 'stewards' of biodiversity

At the 'point of entry' into biodiversity discourse, local and indigenous communities seem to embody a nostalgic ideal of 'small, localised communities that can operate in harmony with nature' (Philippopoulos-Mihalopoulos 2007: Chapter 5) and 'reified models of cohesive, village-located societies with tight tribal structures' (Wilder 1997: 222). This notion of local or indigenous community is habitually used to remind and warn the outside 'observer' – usually urban societies in the global North and South – of their own alienation from their environment. As Wilder (1997) observes, this 'tendency to thematize indigenous peoples is a phenomenon that is peculiar to advanced world societies' (216).

Much of the discourse around 'communities and conservation' assumes that a local community consists of a small spatial unit with a homogeneous social structure, guided by shared norms (Agrawal and Gibson 1999). This is a timeless and de-contextualized entity, existing in parallel to mainstream history, linked to a static, local environment and characterized by rigid and unchanging social and cultural structures. Traditional practices of resource management are, by extension, thought to be small-scale, homogenous, not resource-intensive, isolated from external influences and naturally geared towards self-sustainability. The result is a

> persisting myth that tends to romanticize human communities and their abilities to apply wisdom and foresight in their relationships with their resources and each other (Baland and Platteau 1996: 183).

This community 'nostalgia' for a localized past in harmony with nature (Phi-lippopoulos-Mihalopoulos 2007) is encapsulated in the image of the biodiversity 'steward': 'what is blessed in the "other" is nothing but the opposite of our own society; it is the hidden solution to our own anxieties' (Bruckner 1986: 103). Furthermore, community is defined as in perpetual opposition, especially in relation to the past failures of the state and the market. Although local communities enter into the field of biodiversity as something to be admired, they must ultimately be reconciled and integrated into a pre-existing discourse. For the image of a 'traditional steward' is not consistent with that of the 'biological and economic manager' so beloved of biodiversity discourse.

This nostalgic construction of community leaves little scope for change. Paradoxically, its members must remain within the nostalgic 'stewardship' construction if they are to continue to be recognized as this specific form of (local, indigenous or rural) community, while at the same time adopting the managerial approach required by the biological and economic understanding inherent in biodiversity discourse. These communities are 'required to play on the ethnicity attributed to them' and adhere to their homogeneous, ecologically-wise stewardship (Wilder 1997: 242). Being bound to the image of the traditional steward and an externally-constructed, continuously imposed, history of harmonious local co-existence with nature, they are also constantly located on the outside of modern and urban societies. In this way, their political and historical agency is severely hampered. They are less likely to influence, and even less likely to initiate, law-making that affects them. Ultimately, even at the moment of their participation, these communities become trapped in a historical limbo, unable to shed their traditional identity or move completely forward into a new managerial role. Despite all the steps achieved in engineering community participation, they remain excluded, 'noble savages' locked outside the city gates.

## Effects of linking community and biodiversity

Despite the difficulties outlined above, the 'entry' of community into biodiversity discourse has changed the conceptual and physical geography of the field. An alternative 'map' of local community has been grafted onto a pre-existing 'map' of biodiversity by enabling first a shift in focus towards the developing world free from the controversies that have plagued past attempts, and second, the rejection of the 'protected area' as the primary target of biodiversity regulation, in favour of a more open 'multi-stakeholder locality'. However, the conflicts and uncertainties inherent in the discursive link between biodiversity and community have produced a 'locality of tension'. Here, understandings of biodiversity and community are contested through an emerging third – and perhaps unintended – effect: the emergence of direct pathways between the local and the global.

## A new discursive territory and the reversal of causality

The first section of this chapter examined how biodiversity discourse focuses on the loss of biogenetic resources: if biodiversity is simply a biological resource or system of resources or biogenetic capital then it can only be effectively understood in biological and economic terms. In this way, the relatively open discursive territory implied by terms such as 'nature' or the 'environment' is replaced by the bounded territory of biodiversity, under the strict control of the biologist and the economist.

The creation of this new discursive territory is supported by the extensive knowledge and information functions of the Biodiversity Convention. These include a separate permanent scientific body, a 'clearing-house mechanism' for the collection and dissemination of biodiversity information, as well as the 'global taxonomy initiative', which coordinates classification activities (CBD 1992: Articles 25 and 18(3)). These mechanisms attempt to position the Convention as an 'overseer' of knowledge production regarding the conservation and utilization of biogenetic resources, a global site for the creation of the new discursive territory of biodiversity. Despite reaffirmations of national sovereignty over resources, biodiversity experts have become the interpreters of the new environmental reality of biogenetic capital, arbitrators of 'appropriate' biodiversity management, and, ultimately, the sovereigns of this new discursive territory.

This new territory was primarily understood from a global perspective and was often the source of generalizing claims about the relationship between two fictional entities, such as a global humanity and a global biodiversity:

> the primary cause of decay of organic diversity is not direct human exploitation or malevolence, but the habitat destruction that inevitably results from the expansion of human populations and human activities (Ehrlich 1988: 21).

Overexploitation or over-consumption is conceptually associated with the consumerist societies of the North, while 'uncontrolled' human encroachment on the environment through population growth is discursively linked with the sprawling, uncontrolled metropolises of the South, complete with images of *favelas*, illegal logging and rising pollution and waste. By universalizing claims regarding the impact of population on biodiversity, the focus of the biodiversity discourse turned to the South, the area with the largest expansion of human population.

Biodiversity loss is now thought to be caused by the over-population of the South, not over-consumption of the North. As the location of 'problematic' population growth and rapid habitat destruction, the South became the new location of major biodiversity loss. A range of simplistic, reactionary and highly controversial solutions were proposed to deal with the newly defined problem, such as that 'the growth of the human population must be halted' (Ehrlich 1988).[18]

This awkward and reactionary development has been short-circuited by the entrance of community into biodiversity discourse. The South is reimagined as the location of the majority of biogenetic capital, and hence of the solution to the problem of biodiversity loss. This profitable discovery came at a 'price': managerialism, without which the concept of biogenetic capital cannot be understood. The result is that the South as a whole (and its local communities more specifically) bear both the responsibility for and the solution to a major environmental disaster such as biodiversity loss.

### From protected areas to a multi-stakeholder locality

The second geographical shift produced by linking community with biodiversity is the rejection of the protected area or the natural reserve as the primary mechanism for biodiversity conservation. The designation of a natural reserve or protected area, whereby certain territories are 'walled-off' and granted special legal protection, especially from human intrusion, remains one of the most direct ways in which environmental law can influence the physical environment. The idea of separating nature and humanity originates in an excessively biological focus, which conceptualizes the health of the natural environment as independent from, or even in conflict with, humanity. The nature reserve represents a conceptual walling-off of nature, an attempt to preserve a single, Northern conception of nature as a repository of nebulous environmental values that appear lost to urban populations. It is an impossible attempt to rid nature of social and cultural elements, precisely because the ideal of 'pristine' nature, much like the ideal of a local or indigenous community, is in itself a social construction of Northern societies that consider themselves alienated from nature. This process remains a largely state-centric process, as environmental treaties hold national governments responsible for designating and maintaining protected areas. Indeed, the environmental credentials of national governments are often measured by the extent of these protected areas. Moreover, the strict boundaries and regulations of these protected areas have often been directed specifically against local and indigenous communities. Environmentalists have in turn regarded those communities as utilitarian, short-sighted, ignorant of the intrinsic environmental value of their land. Their stewardship role had been seen in the past as an obstacle to the institution of rational resource managerialism (Agrawal and Gibson 1999: 631).[19]

As the notion of community entered into biodiversity discourse, so the previously walled-off protected area was transformed into a multi-stakeholder locality, the site of multiple interactions between nature and humanity. It is now more than a natural landscape to be protected from encroachment. It is a profitable place with the last reserves of biogenetic resources and a local population that could manage them sustainably to its own benefit. Conceptual and physical boundaries around these protected areas were torn down, opening them up to the possibility of sustainable utilization and drawing the South into an environmental discourse that had previously sought to keep local and indigenous communities at arm's length. Biodiversity regulation today refers not just to the protection of plants and animals, but to complex interactions between plants, animals and humans.

## A locality of tension

The main consequence of the establishment of a link between community and biodiversity appears to be the creation of an open, multi-stakeholder space for sustainable development and community participation. But it remains very much a work in progress, its exact contours unclear. What is certain is that it is a locality of tension.

The introduction of community into biodiversity reflects a tendency in international environmental law to operate through successive uncritical acceptances and steadfast idealizations of ecological concepts. Early environmental law focused on the protection of a nebulously defined environment, idealizing the intrinsic value of the natural landscape and life devoid of human intervention, as exemplified by the state-sponsored designation of protected areas and natural reserves. Under the influence of sustainable development, environmental law aimed to create the conditions for the sustainable management of a natural capital (which in the context of biodiversity was transformed into biogenetic capital) as a panacea to the woes of state-sponsored environmentalism. The last step in this process of uncritical adoption appears to prioritize 'generic, model-type ideas' (Brosius et al 2005: 2) of local and indigenous communities, idealizing a perceived local relationship with nature as an environmental solution to alleviate the failures of both the state and the market.[20]

The steward and the manager are equally external constructions and the unnecessary dualism they engender leads to unclear and defective participatory initiatives. Lisa Wilder has discussed this problematic duality in relation to the granting of native titles to Aboriginal communities.[21] She concludes that 'if an indigenous people is successfully to claim surviving rights and interests in land, it must clothe itself with the requisite authenticity', presenting an alternative, traditional conception of land that nevertheless persists in today's modern society (1997: 240). However, by articulating such land claims in an accessible, 'modern' form or even resorting to proceedings in a court of law, claimants can do damage to them: 'it is not clear how much change a society can tolerate before the court will regard it as *insufficiently authentic* to support a claim of surviving title' (Wilder 1997: 240; emphasis added). The more modern they become, the less indigenous, the less worthy of the 'privileges' allowed under community participation mantras they will appear. In reality, local communities are fluid structures that can co-evolve according to changes in the local environments and perceptions.[22] Indeed, there are many parts of the world where, far from being a timeless enclave of authenticity, indigenous community has been subjected to the power of numerous globalizing and centralizing discourses (colonialism, imperialism, cosmopolitanism, economic globalization), resulting in violence, assimilation and dispossession.

It is in these parts of the world in particular where the goal of empowerment through the sustainable development of biogenetic capital seems to overwhelm the procedural stakes offered by biodiversity discourse. Community-based approaches must cater to the interests of communities at least as much as they cater to the perceived interests of biodiversity. But while there is much discussion of how these communities will assist the effectiveness of conservation, little attention is paid to ensuring that biodiversity conservation will in turn assist these communities. This is an especially significant omission since the promise of sustainable development, by way of Rio and Johannesburg, has drastically increased expectations.

In theory, the local can now filter more easily to the international level. Even from a marginal position community has voice, and can fight back, contest and manipulate the discursive shifts and outcomes. But as they oscillate between the images of the steward and the manager, these 'stakeholder' communities have little real chance of introducing their own definition of conservation and development priorities into the discourse.

Until a balance between the role of manager and the role of steward is found and communities can construct and implement their own imagined future, the link between community and biodiversity will continue to create a tension at the local level, and to allow that tension to filter up to the global level. As long as the manager is described as global, rational and scientific, and the steward as local, spiritual and traditional, the entry of community into biodiversity will remain incomplete. Left unchecked, enforced managerialism and tribalism will eventually institutionalize communities as opposite, un-evolving and un-evolved 'other' to our modern selves; an addition to the beautiful landscape.

## Notes

1 For a critique of the implementation of the Convention in India, see Kohli and Menon in this volume.
2 For a presentation of the concepts of environmental discourse, paradigms and discursive shifts see Dryzek (2007).
3 The Convention's programme of work continues to revolve around this set of objectives, a fact which points to the importance of these initial discursive workings.
4 This influential approach was first established and further developed in McNeely et al (1990) and Reid et al (1993).
5 For the current draft under negotiation see the COP Decisions section of the CBD website.
6 The head of the UK delegation at the 1987 UNEP governing council, Fiona McConnell, recalls this incident from the start of the negotiations for the Biodiversity

Convention. Environmental experts delineated their domain and protected their privileged position from the beginning (1996: 5).

7 On the possibilities for alternative ecological articulations see Forsyth (2003). For more radical perspectives see Lopez (2007).

8 For an initial examination of the development of the scientific field of conservation biology that deals specifically with the issue of biodiversity see Sarkar (2005). For a more detailed analysis see Norton (2002). For an early imagining of this scientific field see Soule (1986).

9 'Biological resources includes genetic resources, organisms or parts thereof, populations or any other biotic component of ecosystems with actual or potential use or value to humanity' (Article 2, CBD).

10 On how the production of scientific knowledge regarding nature affects environmental intervention see Litfin (1994: Chapter 2).

11 On the notion of 'discursive works-ups' that transform broad environmental concern into resource managerialism see Luke (1999). Luke expands this notion to include the 'three Rs': resources, recreation and risk.

12 'Indigenous people and their communities and other local communities have a vital role in environmental management and development because of their knowledge and traditional practices. States should recognize and duly support their identity, culture and interests and enable their effective participation in the achievement of sustainable development' (UNCED 1992, Principle 22).

13 For example, the two main treaty provisions regarding *in situ* (Article 8, CBD) and *ex situ* (Article 9, CBD) conservation oblige Parties to 'adopt national plans and measures. ... as far as possible and appropriate'.

14 One of the Convention's three objectives set out in Article 1 and further explained in Article 15.

15 For example: 'Each Contracting Party shall take ... measures ... with the aim of sharing in fair and equitable way ... the benefits arising from the commercial and other utilisation of genetic resources with the Contracting Party providing such resources' (Article 15(7) CBD).

16 These guidelines were a response to accusations of 'biopiracy', for more on which see Shiva (1998: 484) and Svarstad (2002).

17 These are the working group on Article 8(j) and the working group on ABS established by UNEP/CBD/COP V/26 (2000).

18 For example, by 1996, influential commentators Reaka-Kudla et al. were discussing both overexploitation and over-consumption on equal footing with overpopulation.

19 For a description of such problems encountered by local communities in a US setting see Duane (1997).

20 Throughout these shifts in legal discourse, the reductionisms are clear; from the reduction of nature initially to a beautiful landscape and subsequently to natural capital, to the reduction of complex localities to a rigidly structured and unevolving traditional community.

21 Of which *Mabo and others v. Queensland* (No. 2) (1992) is the most prominent case.

22 This is an argument put forward by 'grassroots' social movements that link different localities. The social movement literature is vast, but for some representative examples see Escobar (2004), Escobar et al. (2002) and Flitner (1998).

# References

Agrawal, A. and Gibson, C. C., (1999) 'Enchantment and disenchantment: the role of community in natural resource conservation', *World Development*, 27: 629–49.

Baland, J. M. and Platteau, J. P. (1996) *Halting Degradation of Natural Resources: is there a role for rural communities*, Oxford: FAO/Oxford University Press.

Brosius, J. P., Lowenhaupt Tsing, A. and Zerner, C. (eds) (2005) *Communities and Conservation: histories and politics of community-based natural resource management*, Walnut Creek: AltaMira Press.

Bruckner, P. (1986) *The Tears of the White Man: compassion as contempt*, New York: The Free Press.

Commission on Sustainable Development (CSD) (1992) Agenda 21. Online: <http://www.un.org/esa/sustdev/documents/agenda21/english/agenda21chapter1.htm>

Djoghlaf, A. (2007) Message from the Executive Secretary on the Occasion of the International Day of the World's Indigenous people, 9 August 2007. CBD. Online: <http://www.cbd.int/doc/speech/2007/sp-2007-08-09-indigenous-en.pdf>

Dryzek, J. S. (2007) 'Paradigms and discourses', in D. Bodansky, J. Brunnée and E. Hey (eds), *The Oxford Handbook of International Environmental law*, Oxford: Oxford University Press.

Duane, T. P. (1997) 'Community participation in ecosystem management', *Ecology Law Quarterly*, 24: 771–97.

Escobar, A., Rocheleau, D. and Kothari, S. (2002) 'Environmental social movements and the politics of space', *Development*, 45(1): 28–53.

Escobar, A. (2004) 'Beyond the Third World: imperial globality, global coloniality and anti-globalization social movements', *Third World Quarterly*, 25(1): 207–30.

Flitner, M. (1998) 'Biodiversity: of local commons and global commodities', in M. Goldman (ed.) *Privatizing Nature: political struggles for the global commons*, London: Pluto Press.

Forsyth, T. (2003) *Critical Political Ecology: the politics of environmental science*, London and New York: Routledge.

McAfee, K. (1999) 'Selling nature to save it? Biodiversity and green developmentalism', *Environment and Planning D: Society and Space*, 17: 133–54.

Le Prestre, P. G. (2002) *Governing Global Biodiversity: the evolution and implementation of the convention on biological diversity*, Aldershot: Ashgate.

Li, T. (2005) 'Engaging simplifications: community-based natural resource management, market processes, and state agendas in upland Southeast Asia', in J. P. Brosius, A. Lowenhaupt Tsing and C. Zerner (eds) (2005) *Communities and Conservation: histories and politics of community-based natural resource management*, Walnut Creek: AltaMira Press.

Litfin, K. (1994) *Ozone Discourses: science and politics in global environmental cooperation*, New York: Columbia University Press.

Lopez, B. (ed.) (2007) *The Future of Nature: writing on a human ecology from ORION magazine*, Canada: Milkweed Editions.

Luke, T. W. (1999) 'Eco-managerialism: environmental studies as a power/knowledge formation', in M. Hajer and F. Fischer (eds) *Living with Nature: environmental politics as a cultural discourse*, Oxford: Oxford University Press.

*Mabo and Others v. Queensland* (No. 2) [1992] HCA 23; (1992) 175 CLR 1 F.C. . Online: <http://austlii.law.uts.edu.au/au/cases/cth/high_ct/175clr1.html>

McConnell, F. (1996) *The Biodiversity Convention: a negotiating history*, London: Kluwer Law International.

McNeely, J. A., Miller, K. R., Reid, W. V., Mittermeier, R. A. and Werner, T. B. (1990) *Conserving the World's Biological Diversity*, Gland and Washington: IUCN, WRI, CI, WWF-US, the World Bank.

Norton, B. G. (2002) *Searching for Sustainability: interdisciplinary essays in the philosophy of conservation biology*, New York: Cambridge University Press.

Philippopoulos-Mihalopoulos, A. (2007) *Absent Environments: theorising environmental law and the city*, London: UCL.

Reaka-Kudla, M. L., Wilson, D. E. and Wilson, E. O. (eds) (1996) *Biodiversity II: understanding and protecting our biological resources*, Washington, D.C.: Joseph Henry Press.

Reid, W. V., Laird, S. A., Meyer, C. A., Gamez, R., Sittenfield, A., Janzen, D. H., Gollin, M. A. and Juma, C. (1993) *Biodiversity Prospecting: using genetic resources for sustainable development*, World Resources Institute, USA.

Rose, J. (2008) 'Community-based biodiversity conservation in the Pacific: cautionary lessons in "regionalising" environmental governance', in M. I. Jeffery, J. Firestone and K. Bubna-Litic (eds), *Biodiversity Conservation, Law + Livelihoods: bridging the North-South divide*, New York: Cambridge University Press.

Sarkar, S. (2005) *Biodiversity and Environmental Philosophy: an introduction*, Cambridge: Cambridge University Press.

Secretariat of the Convention on Biological Diversity (CBD) (2004) 'Akwe: Kon Voluntary guidelines for the conduct of cultural, environmental and social impact assessments regarding developments proposed to take place on, or which are likely to impact on, sacred sites and on lands and waters traditionally occupied or used by indigenous or local communities', Montreal. Online: <http://www.cbd.int/doc/publications/akwe-brochure-en.pdf>

Shiva, V. (1998) *Biopiracy: the plunder of nature and knowledge*, Dartington: Green Books.

Soule, M. E. (1986) *Conservation Biology: the science of scarcity and diversity*, Sunderland, Mass.: Sinauer.

Svarstad, H. (2002) 'Analysing conservation-development discourses: the story of a biopiracy narrative', *Forum for Development Studies*, 63(1): 63–92.

UNCED (1992) Rio Declaration on Environment and Development. Online: <http://www.unep.org/Documents.Multilingual/Default.asp?DocumentID=78&ArticleID=1163&l = en>

UNEP/CBD/COP V/26 (2000) Decision on access to genetic resources. Online: <http://www.cbd.int/decisions/?id=7168>

UNEP/CBD/COP VI/24 (2002) 'Bonn Guidelines on access to genetic resources and the fair and equitable sharing of the benefits arising from the sustainable utilisation of biodiversity'. Online: <http://www.cbd.int/abs/bonn.shtml>

UNEP/CBD/COP VI/26 (2002) Decision on strategic plan for the Convention on Biological Diversity. Online: <http://www.cbd.int/decisions/?id=7200>

UNEP/CBD/COP VII/19 (2004) Decision on access and benefit-sharing as related to genetic resources. Online: <http://www.cbd.int/decisions/?id=7756>

United Nations Convention on Biological Diversity (CBD) (1992) 31. I.L.M. 818.

Wilder, L. (1997) 'Local futures? From denunciation to revalorization of the indigenous other', in G. Teubner (ed.) *Global Law without a State*, Aldershot: Dartmouth.

Wilson, E. O. and Peter, F. M. (eds) (1988) *BioDiversity*, Washington, D.C.: National Academy Press.

World Commission on Environment and Development (1987) *Our Common Future*, Oxford: Oxford University Press.

## Useful websites

(CBD) Convention on Biological Diversity
    <http://www.cbd.int/>
(UNEP) United Nations Environment Programme
    <http://www.unep.org>

# Chapter 9

# Stock exchanges in East Africa: something borrowed, something new?

*June McLaughlin**

## Introduction

The rapid integration of international financial markets has been one of the starkest examples of globalization. The impressive rise of private capital flows to emerging markets, from $25 billion in 1990 to $300 billion in 2005, has been a key feature of this trend … [But] Africa's 'frontier markets' – those outside South Africa – still receive a tiny fraction of emerging markets investment and the widespread reaction in Africa has been of disappointment (Moss et al. 2007: 1).[1]

It has long been argued that a good investment climate[2] is built upon a sound legal and financial infrastructure that supports stock exchanges such as credible securities laws, share trading systems, and dispute-resolution schemes (Anyanwu 2006: 64–67). For example, in their Communiqué on Africa issued at Gleneagles in July 2005, the G8 Heads of State stated that:

… African countries need to build a much stronger investment climate: we will continue to help them do so, including through the promotion of a stable, efficient and harmonized legal business framework.

This chapter focuses on the regulation of investments made through the emergent (and future) stock exchanges of Kenya, Uganda, Tanzania, Rwanda and Burundi, which together form the East African Community (EAC). Stock exchanges such as the New York Stock Exchange (NYSE) and the London Stock Exchange (LSE) have served as prototypes for legal and financial standards of most emerging exchanges, including those in East Africa. Britain's influence in this part of Africa cannot be discounted, but East African exchanges tend to draw more on US models of regulation.

Empirical research in support of the 'legal origins' theory suggests that a country's history of legal transplantation – whether civil or common law – greatly influences how securities markets are controlled (Pistor et al. 2003). In particular, those developing countries which transplant laws, including securities law, from common-law systems such as the US and the United Kingdom, tend to have better economic prospects than those transplanting from civil-law systems such as France (La Porta et al. 2006: 27).[3] So it perhaps bodes well that East African nations with active stock exchanges have their (modern, not traditional) legal origins in common law.

This chapter explores the likely future of East African reliance on US models of securities exchange using the example of dispute resolution. That future is made uncertain because US securities law is itself in a state of turmoil.

## Overview of stock exchanges

A stock exchange (otherwise known as a 'capital' or 'securities' market) is a financial system.[4] Like any kind of market – fruit, flower or fish – it brings buyers and sellers together.

### Functions and features

Exchanges can occur electronically or in bricks and mortar buildings. Companies sell equity, known as 'shares', while governments sell debt, known as 'bonds'. When a company sells shares (or a country sells bonds) this is referred to as 'raising capital' – that is, raising money by selling shares (/bonds) to investors. The company (or government) can then use the investment money for designated purposes, such as expanding a physical plant (/responding to an economic recession) and so on. Once sold by the company or government on an exchange, shares and bonds can be sold on again and again (Walker 2007). Other participants in the market include broker-dealers: firms which charge a commission for facilitating the buying and selling of shares and bonds.

Both the investor and the issuer of the share (or bond) hope that the share or bond will appreciate in value. Such appreciation takes place when the general market sees the company (or country) performing in a way likely to result in increased dividends to the shareholder (or when there is increased likelihood that the country will repay its debt), for example by turning a profit (or supporting economic growth). Because the supply of shares is limited, the value of shares in well-performing companies appreciates.

Stock exchanges profit from the fees they charge to all participants in the share-trading process.[5] Exchanges around the world compete to attract business by claiming to offer the most dependable, transparent and efficient service to buyers and sellers. For instance, the London Stock Exchange boasts that it:

has built on more than 300 years of integrity, expertise and market knowledge to become one of the world's foremost equity exchanges. ... The Exchange is the most international of all the world's stock exchanges, with ... companies from over 60 countries admitted to trading on its markets ... The BBC and CNN all broadcast from the studios inside the

Exchange [and] 3118 firms trade on its markets, more than any other exchange in Europe.

(LSE website)

### Regulation

Exchanges operate within a legal and regulatory infrastructure which is designed to enable the monitoring of market participants, scrutinising of financial and sales practices and the settlement of disputes. These functions are typically performed by a government body know as a 'securities commission' or 'capital market authority', which issues rules and enforces them through investigations and fines with a view to ensuring that the exchange operates transparently and efficiently.[6] For example:

the mission of the United States Securities and Exchange Commission [SEC] is to protect investors, maintain fair, orderly, and efficient markets, and facilitate capital formation.

(SEC website)

Similarly, the Capital Markets Authority of Uganda (CMAU):

is an autonomous body responsible for promoting, developing and regulating the capital markets industry in Uganda, with the overall objectives of investor protection and market efficiency.

(CMAU Website)

One of the primary concerns of any securities regulator is to identify and eliminate fraud in their exchange in order to protect the confidence of market participants.[7] So, like many such authorities, the Capital Markets Authority of Uganda has the power to investigate suspected violations of rules, which may in turn lead to fines, suspension of licences and even incarceration (Capital Markets Authority Act 2000: Part II).[8]

Importantly for the purposes of this chapter, complaints involving investors (consumers) usually inhabit a special place in the regulatory infrastructure: they are handled by a separate dispute-resolution division which is overseen by the regulatory authority, but which has distinct powers and duties. The matter of how disputes between brokers and their consumers tend to be resolved is addressed in greater detail below. First, we explore the development of stock exchanges in East Africa.

## Stock exchanges of East Africa

### Rationale

The development of securities exchanges may seem an irrelevant, absurd fancy given the degree of poverty experienced in some emerging markets. A simple comparison of the 2007 per capita Gross National Incomes (GNI) of the United States (US$ 46,040) with that of Kenya (US$ 640), Tanzania (US$ 410), Uganda (US$ 370), Rwanda (US$ 320) and Burundi (US$ 110) is enough to remind us of the chasm across which the stock markets are stretched (source: World Bank Data and Statistics website). At the minimum, an exchange must be supported by a sound economy and a credible financial system if it is to support economic growth (N'Zue 2006: 139). Some have even suggested that stock market development and economic growth are negatively correlated, so that governments may be wasting resources by starting exchanges (Stiglitz 1994).

For others, the benefits of stock exchanges to economic development are clear: they attract investment, both domestic and foreign (Adjasi et al. 2006). As such, stock markets are one of the keys to filling the chasm. Specifically, they are said to 'serve as a source of long-term capital for financing investment'; they increase the range of options to those who wish to save, allowing them to diversify their risk; and they enable 'continuous monitor[ing] of the corporate sector' (Moss et al. 2007: 3).

Putting debates cautiously to the side, for the purposes of the present, fundamentally legal, analysis, it is necessary to accept that these institutions are a central feature of many governments' strategies for economic revival (Moss 2003: 5). 'At the behest of local governments, and with some donor encouragement, Africa has also expanded the number of its domestic stock exchanges from five in the late 1980s to fifteen today.' However, these exchanges 'still receive a tiny fraction of emerging markets investment'. The problem, according to Todd Moss and his colleagues at the Centre for Global Development, is 'mostly one of size' (Moss et al. 2007: 1). They simply have not yet achieved the critical mass of activity necessary to grow at speed.

A range of organizations seek to support the development of these stock exchanges. For instance, the World Bank/International Finance Corporation (IFC) Global Capital Markets Development Department 'helps countries deepen their securities markets and make them more transparent and accessible to investors' (website). Similarly, the US Securities and Exchange Commission joins with the US Agency for International Development (USAID) each year, to conduct an International Institute for Securities Market Development (USAID 2005). For example, in 2007, the SEC reported that it had:

> completed its 17th Annual International Institute for Securities Market Development ... at SEC headquarters in Washington, D.C. Attendance included 174 senior securities officials from 74 foreign jurisdictions ... Approximately 100 speakers made presentations at the Institute ... Presentation topics included financial reporting, disclosure, auditing and accounting issues, broker dealer regulation, self-regulatory organizations, compliance and supervision, investigatory techniques, remedies and penalties as well as the challenges to securities regulators in emerging markets.
>
> (SEC 2008)

Such activities tend to reinforce the influence of US securities practice in emergent markets.

## Emergence

The Nairobi Stock Exchange (NSE) has a relatively long history. The informal dealing of shares began in Kenya in the 1920s. In 1954, the NSE was only open for trading for residents of the European Community. After independence from Britain in 1963, Africans and Asians were then permitted to deal in securities. It was not until 1991 that the exchange was modernized with the current regulatory structure. It is the only one of the East African stock exchanges to be run as a private, rather than government-owned, enterprise (*The East African* 2008). Today shares are traded electronically and information on share prices and company statements is accessible online. At the time of writing the NSE was listing 46 companies (NSE website).

The Dar es Salaam Stock Exchange (DSE) in Tanzania was established in 1996. 'Trading is conducted ... under an Automated Trading Electronic System ... which matches bids and offers using an electronic matching engine.' Matched bids are then displayed on monitors on the trading floor and in a public gallery. Clearing, settlement and share registration are also conducted electronically (DSE website). At the time of writing the DSE was listing 14 companies, as well as supporting the trading of five corporate bonds and eight Government of Tanzania bonds.

The Uganda Securities Exchange (USE) was established in 1997. Unlike the Nairobi or Dar es Salaam stock exchanges, it uses a manual system which relies on the 'Continuous Open Outcry Auction Trading System'. Representatives of brokers 'converge at the trading floor and trade by shouting their orders to a board writer ... A trade is effected when a bid and an offer are matched' (USE website). Such a system is a common starting point for exchanges which usually go on to trade shares electronically. In January 2007, Stanbic Bank Uganda Ltd issued an initial public offering on the USE. This was a milestone for the exchange as there are few companies listed and each additional company increases the viability of the exchange. At the time of writing, the USE is listing 11 companies (USE website).

The Rwanda Over the Counter Market (ROTCM) was established in January 2008 by the Capital Market Advisory Council (CMAC) of Rwanda (CMAC 2008). 'Over the counter' trading involves direct trades between buyers and sellers without the involvement of a securities exchange – companies need not be listed on the exchange in order for their shares to be traded, and the exchange need not publish share prices. As the CMAC explains:

> The Rwanda OTC market operates a dual trading process. Firstly members trade securities directly with investors and among themselves. Secondly, open outcry trading sessions are conducted at the trading floor of the OTC

market at the CMAC Secretariat every day from 9:00 a.m. to 12:00 p.m. At the open outcry trading floor, members' representatives get together and trade between each other.

OTC markets have been the precursors to securities exchanges around the world and are particularly attractive where trades are likely to be small.[9] The very basic level of the market for – and regulation of – such trading is illustrated by the fact that the CMAC issued a brochure to educate the public about the exchange, including details of the seven steps required to sell/buy shares (2008). That document, along with a slim handbook, represented the sum total of the rules covering trades on the market. In May 2008 it was reported that the CMAC was still in search of a consultant to establish a legal and regulatory framework for the market (Ruburika 2008).

### Region-wide developments

Kenya, Uganda and Tanzania are currently working toward linking their stock exchanges.[10] There are plans to harmonize securities regulations across the East African Community. So, when Burundi eventually establishes a capital market it will be able simply to adopt the harmonized rules rather than drafting its own (Riungu 2008). Furthermore, the East African Securities Exchange Association (EASEA) has been instrumental in driving an effort to allow companies and investors from any nation to participate in any exchange (see EASEA Committee on Mass Cross-Listing 2005).[11] Such 'cross-listing' will allow companies to seek capital wherever it might be found, without being considered a foreign entity for regulatory purposes (EASRA website).[12]

There is already one regional exchange in Africa. The Bourse Régionale des Valeurs Mobilières (BVRM) is made up of the eight nations that comprise the French-speaking West African Economic and Monetary Union (WAEMU) that is Benin, Burkina Faso, Cote D'Ivoire, Guinea Bissau, Mali, Niger, Senegal and Togo. A similar exchange on a larger scale, with more nations involved and potentially more languages, would require a great deal of political will. However, it would immediately remove the obstacles to stock exchange development that now plague the many and disparate exchanges on the continent: ill-liquidity and fragmentation (Yarty et al. 2007).

### Regulation

The typical regulations governing activities on the exchange itself – those involving brokers and dealers, not consumers (investors) – are present in East Africa. It is not clear if such regulation is necessary, given the lack of activity. Indeed, as Friedman and Grose have noted, there is no need to transplant international best practice all in one go 'if the rules are not relevant for the efficient conduct of the market or if the market is not sufficiently mature to absorb them' (2006:

8). Nonetheless, with the exception of Rwanda, activities on East African exchanges are covered by an abundance of regulation.

The terrain which remains largely unmapped is that of dispute resolution. And as East African exchanges interlink, it is important to note that it is unclear in what forum any resulting cross-border disputes would be resolved. It is the stated mission of the Emerging East African markets to attract foreign investment from outside of the region (DSE 2006). Those investors are likely to require a dispute-resolution method that does not rely on local courts. Arbitration is the dispute-resolution choice for international commercial parties (Beechey 2006). So it is a natural choice for exchanges endeavouring to attract foreign investors. As we shall see, it is also a problematic one.

## Resolving securities disputes

Conflicts are a common derivative of investment activity in securities exchanges. For instance, disputes may arise over allegations of fraud or misrepresentation by a stockbroker, unauthorized trading in an account, or simple confusion over why money was lost on a 'sure' investment. Hence, the World Federation of Stock Exchanges (WFE) requires that its 51 members have a functioning dispute-resolution system. In this section we trace the history of, and current controversy over, the often emulated American model of securities arbitration.

### Securities arbitration

In the US, most disputes over stock-exchange transactions were historically dealt with through the courts. However, as Jill Gross explains, the NYSE has a long relationship with arbitration, beginning 'in the late 1790s, when NYSE clerks ruled on disputes over mismatched trades'. By 1871, the NYSE was 'using internal arbitration to resolve disputes between members, and in 1872 expanded its use to disputes between consenting customers and member firms'. Today the NYSE sports an Arbitration Department.[13] Contracts between consumers and brokers have long included pre-dispute arbitration agreements (PDAAs) which specify that disputes are to be resolved by specialized securities arbitration. By the 1960s, brokerage firms had begun to enforce these agreements 'against their customers' wishes'. By this time there were two specialist securities arbitration options for the resolution of consumer disputes: the NYSE Arbitration Department and the National Association of Securities Dealers, which had adopted its own Code of Arbitration (Gross 2006: 336–37).

The brokerage industry has long argued that a lack of expertise in securities law would impair the abilities of judges and juries to decide disputes appropriately. It fought long and hard to convince courts that arbitration was the more suitable process for resolution of investor disputes. But the US courts resisted promoting general commercial arbitration, as well as securities arbitration, as an alternative to litigation. Eventually, in *Shearson/American Express, Inc.*

*v. McMahon* (1987), the US Supreme Court held that mandatory arbitration clauses included in account agreements entered into between customer and broker were valid and binding. Customers were, therefore, obliged to go to arbitration before they would be permitted to seek redress in the courts. Today, some disputes are resolved through a range of other methods including mediation and ombudsman services (Gross 2006).[14] However,

> [f]ollowing these Supreme Court decisions, most customer disputes with their broker-dealers have been resolved in an arbitration forum sponsored by a securities SRO – either NASD-DR or the NYSE Arbitration Department.
>
> (Gross, 2006: 337)

Until 2007, the USAID-sponsored International Institute for Securities Markets Development mentioned above brought in US dispute-resolution specialists to lecture delegates on the virtues of US-style dispute resolution. It is significant that at the same time the US Congress was preparing legislation declaring this type of dispute resolution to be unfair and illegal (USAID 2005).

Even before the recent economic crisis, the use of arbitration as a method for resolving securities disputes was under siege:

> [R]eforms designed to alleviate investors' concerns transformed a formerly quick and informal process into a system resembling litigation ... [S]ecurities arbitration was more expensive and slower than ... [expected], and required a mastery of many rules and procedures. Moreover, the securities industry, in a classic case of "be careful what you wish for," started doubting the wisdom of its preference for binding arbitration and sought judicial intervention to overturn arbitration awards.
>
> (Gross 2006: 330–31)

Moreover, since the summer of 2007, the US Congress has debated the introduction of an Arbitration Fairness Act (AFA), which would amend the Federal Arbitration Act (1925). The proposed legislation is a response to growing concern among legislators over the high cost, lack of due process and tales of abuses surrounding arbitration. It seeks to address the growing use by business of arbitration as a mandatory dispute-resolution forum in its dealings with individual consumers. In so doing, it goes to the heart of securities arbitration.

'The bill opens with seven "findings" that set forth the drafter's assessment of the problem to be addressed by the legislation' (Caron and Schreiberg 2008: 15). These suggest that the Arbitration Act was intended to relate to business dealings, and fails to take into account the significant imbalances in bargaining power that are characteristic of consumer interactions. Accordingly, section 2(b) would render invalid and unenforceable pre-dispute arbitration agreements requiring arbitration of a consumer dispute. Furthermore, section 2(c) states that 'the validity or enforceability of an agreement to arbitrate shall be determined by the court, rather than the arbitrator' (Caron and Schreiberg 2008: 15–17). So, should the AFA be introduced as law, arbitration clauses in contracts between brokerage firms and individuals would become invalid and unenforceable.

The Securities Industry and Financial Markets Association (SIFMA) responded to the proposed legislation through a white paper defending the use of arbitration in securities transactions, the subtitle of which – 'The success story of an investor protection focused institution that has delivered timely, cost-effective, and fair results for over 30 years' – speaks for itself. In the paper, SIFMA emphasizes that securities arbitrations are open to public scrutiny, their procedural fairness is safeguarded through regulation, and they are faster and cheaper than litigation. Statistics are adduced to demonstrate that, other forms of consumer relationships aside, the use of arbitration in securities transactions is inherently fair. The paper concludes that 'the use of pre-dispute securities arbitration agreements is fair to investors and serves the public interest' (SIFMA 2007).

Despite protestations from business, 'it is thought – particularly given the outcome of the recent elections in the United States – that … [it] will be introduced early in … 2009' (Caron and Schreiberg 2008: 15). This does not mean that securities arbitrations between broker and consumer would no longer occur, only that they will no longer be mandatory, regardless of what the consumer-broker contract may say. However, such securities arbitrations might well be less common. One consideration is that the negotiations which would have to occur between a consumer and a broker over whether to have a securities arbitration in a given situation would incur transaction costs. Furthermore, confidence in the suitability of securities arbitration as the primary method of dispute resolution in the sector could be undermined by the debate surrounding the AFA.

## Alternatives

A limited range of dispute-resolution processes are acceptable to the financial community. If securities arbitration should come to be regarded as unacceptable, what other choices might there be, in particular for developing exchanges?

### Ombudsman

Economic actors in the US, the UK and continental Europe all employ alternatives to litigation to resolve at least some forms of financial dispute (Cirelli 2003). In the United Kingdom the Financial Ombudsman Service (FOS), a public body, is available for investors with a complaint (see FOS website). The fact that an ombudsman is used in place of arbitration is probably because there are relatively few investor disputes in the UK, and because the UK authorities adopt a fundamentally different approach to business regulation, as compared to the US. It is unclear whether an ombudsman might be suited to an East African context. Another alternative is international commercial arbitration.

## International commercial arbitration

Much of the current legal literature regards arbitration as contributing positively to the prospects of developing economies (Amundsen 2003: 400). In short, arbitration (whether international or domestic) is expected to supplement often overloaded local courts, thereby providing the dispute-resolution capacity and investor confidence necessary to support securities transactions. Of particular interest for the purposes of this chapter is the question of whether it might be desirable to bend the existing structures of international commercial arbitration to the task of resolving securities disputes in the emergent exchanges of East Africa.

Public systems for dispute resolution gain legitimacy from the state. Private systems such as arbitration – which to some extent rely on parties being repelled by state institutions – must build their own legitimacy by selling merits of their personnel, processes, location and so on. This point is well illustrated by the language used by the American brokerage industry in its battle for the supremacy of securities arbitration over litigation (see above).

The recurrent use of international commercial arbitration underscores its legitimacy and encourages parties to respect and comply with arbitral awards (Mitchell 2002 and Rogers 2005). As Dezalay and Garth (1996) explain, the legitimacy of international commercial arbitration was solidified in the 1970s in the context of a boom in international economic activity such as foreign direct investment and trade, which was increasingly occurring between independent (post-colonial) parties. This period saw a number of high-profile nationalizations (in, for instance, Libya, Iran, Ethiopia and Chile) which required dispute resolution to determine the matter of compensation. International commercial arbitration was the answer. Arbitration processes have gradually harmonized, a development which many in the field regard as efficient and therefore welcome (Kaufmann-Kohler 2003: 1333).

But international commercial arbitration clauses, just like their domestic securities counterparts, can become a tool used against the weaker party, very similar to the threat of litigation – a costly, time-consuming process best avoided (Norton 2004). International commercial arbitration procedures – including arbitrator, expert and translation fees – are perhaps prohibitively expensive, especially to a party from a developing country.

Furthermore, international commercial arbitration is open to the charge that, as a private justice system, it lacks the kinds of checks and balances which ensure impartiality in courts (Mattli 2001). This concern is all the more pressing for those who regard international commercial arbitration as just another legal transplant (Sempasa 1992) – a system developed and often administered outside of the developing world. For example, Dezalay and Garth (1996) have shown that lawyers on both sides of arbitrations have increasingly tended to be American, less likely to be European and rarely to originate from developing countries.

The concept of 'party autonomy' is regularly carted out to defend against criticisms of arbitration (Lew et al. 2003). The argument goes that the parties to the contract freely choose the procedural rules, the seat of arbitration, the arbitral venue and so on. But this 'defence' disregards the possibility that some parties, and their legal advisors, may lack the necessary experience to negotiate fully on these matters, especially in emerging stock markets (Blackaby 2006).[15]

The idea that arbitration is inaccessible and unrepresentative clearly has currency, since it is directly challenged by the International Court of Arbitration (ICA) at the International Chamber of Commerce (ICC). Its website boldly asserts that:

> ICC arbitration is there for everybody in business. It is accessible to companies of all sizes, not just major corporations in the industrialised countries. Arbitration fits all legal systems and cultures. No one national legal tradition predominates.

However, it is possible to find signs of openness and diversity. For example, in 2007 the ICC held a conference in Bahrain on the 'role of arbitration in economic development and in relation to Sharia law and the Islamic finance industry' (ICC website). There is also a clutch of nascent international arbitration centres in developing countries such as India, Sri Lanka and Egypt. They are by no means dominant in the market. Nor are the arbitrators from such countries. But this may change.

At a minimum, the rich experience of international commercial arbitration might serve as a reference point for emerging exchanges seeking dispute-resolution schemes to safeguard confidence among local and foreign investors.

## Conclusion

Stock exchanges facilitate the raising of capital in developed and developing countries. In order to do this, however, they must engender investor confidence. This is achieved through the establishment of basic financial and technological infrastructures as well as proper regulatory regimes.

While the East African exchanges have adopted much of the US-style securities regulation, they have developed none of its dispute-resolution mechanisms. The current controversy over the fairness of securities arbitration in the US may temper emerging exchanges' interest in replicating it.

As mature exchanges face a credit crisis, and a revolution in their dispute-resolution schemes, emerging exchanges must mould their own future. Might East Africans be creating a distinct, unique and, most importantly, successful hybrid of old and new?

## Notes

\* This chapter would not have been possible without the generous editorial efforts and contributions of Amanda Perry-Kessaris.

1 For an analysis of the impact of stock market liberalization on the performance of capital markets in emerging economies see de la Torre et al. (2007).

2 The term 'investment climate' refers to the environments in which investments, indirect (for example, on the stock market) and direct (for example, by opening a subsidiary),

foreign and local, occur. For detailed statistical analysis of investment climates around the world, see World Bank Investment Climate Capacity Enhancement Website. For a critique of 'investment climate discourse', see Perry-Kessaris (2008: Chapter 2).

3 For a more detailed analysis of the relationship between legal origins and securities exchanges, explored through the example of Mexico, see Alvarez-Macotela (2008).

4 For an introduction to the history, key players and basic instruments involved in global financial flows see Singh 1999: Part One.

5 For example, the fees charged by the USE are set out in Schedule 8 of its Listing Rules (2003).

6 There is always a risk that regulations may be perverted to protect the regulator, rather than the public (Shleifer 2005: 446–49). So, rather than protect investors from dodgy brokers, a capital markets authority might create and enforce rules simply to keep all the wheels in motion so everyone involved makes money. One might argue that this is precisely what happened with the current financial crisis: rather than ending the issuance of bad debt instruments, US regulators perpetuated the practice, leaving investors to suffer major losses when the entire scheme imploded. As a result the very existence of a capital markets regulator is under review in the US Congress.

7 One of the most important recent expressions of the need to maintain transparency in securities exchanges was the Sarbanes-Oxley Act (2002), which was a response to revelations of corporate and accounting fraud in relation to companies such as Enron.

8 Details of enforcement litigation undertaken by the US SEC can be found on its website.

9 This strategy of establishing capital markets in order to attract investment but not ever grow to the point where they list companies was discussed in 2002 when a World Bank Development Research Group released a Policy Research Working Paper discussing the movement of stocks from exchanges in emerging economies to more international centres (Claessens et al. 2002). The authors argued that with the development and growth of international financial centres, companies will seek to raise capital in the most advantageous location – not necessarily the local exchange. Countries with smaller markets should link trading and settlement systems with global exchanges.

10 A United Nations report on commodities exchanges in Africa called on the African Union to play a bigger role in the development of exchanges (UNCTAD, 2005). This role would include organizing workshops and conferences.

11 This move mirrors global trends which have seen a number of mergers of exchanges in search of economies of scale (Walker, 2007). An example is that between the London Stock Exchange and Borsa Italiana S.p.A in 2007.

12 The East African Member States Securities Regulatory Authorities (EASRA), an association of regulatory authorities in the region, is reportedly also working to help Burundi – which does not as yet have a stock exchange – to join it in the near future (EASRA website).

13 The NYSE has thus spanned the full range of arbitrations: from entirely ad hoc to the use of formal rules, to the full institutionalized model.

14 The Financial Industry Regulatory Authority (FINRA), formerly the National Association of Securities Dealers, has been offering mediation as an alternative to arbitration since 1989 (Gross 1996: 331).

15 There are differences between commercial arbitration and the type of arbitration that is conducted for BIT disputes. However, it is often the same players involved, the same lawyers, the same arbitrators, and the procedures are similar (Blackaby 2006).

# References

Adjasi, C. and Biekpe, N. (2006) 'Stock market development and economic growth: the case of selected African countries', *African Development Review*, 18:144–61.

Alvarez-Macotela, O. S. (2008) *Securities law and informal redress: an institutional analysis of equity market development in Mexico (1975–2005)*, PhD Thesis, Norwich: University of East Anglia.

Amundsen, J. (2003) 'Membership has its privileges: the confidence-building potential of the New York Convention can boost commerce in developing nations', *Wisconsin International Law Journal*, 21(2): 383–409.

Anyanwu, J. (2006) 'Towards the promotion of investment in Africa', *African Development Review*, 18: 42.

(AFA) Arbitration Fairness Act (2007) S. 1782 110th Congress. Online: <http://thomas.loc.gov/home/gpoxmlc110/h3010_ih.xml>

Blackaby, N. (2006) 'Investment arbitration and commercial arbitration (or the tale of the dolphin and the shark)', in J. Mistelis and L. Lew (eds) *Pervasive Problems in International Arbitration*, The Netherlands: Kluwer Law.

Capital Markets Authority Act (2000) Cap. 84 of the Laws of Uganda. Online: <http://www.cmauganda.co.ug/onlinefiles/uploads/CMA/Downloads/laws_&_regulations_CMA_ACT_CAP_84.pdf>

Caron, D. S. and Schreiberg, S. (2008) 'Anticipating the 2009 U.S. "Fairness in Arbitration Act"', *World Arbitration & Mediation Review* 2(3): 15–22. Online: <http://works.bepress.com/david_caron/75>

Cirelli, S. (2003) 'Financial markets and banking disputes', *American Review of International Arbitration* 14: 263.

Claessens, S., Klingebiel, D. and Schmukler, S. (2002) 'Explaining the migration of stocks from exchanges in emerging economies to international centers', World Bank Policy Research Working Paper No. 2816, Washington D.C.: World Bank. Online: <http://ssrn.com/abstract=296960>

(CMAC) Capital Markets Advisory Council (Rwanda) (2008) 'National public education about the Rwanda OTC market'. Brochure. Online: <http://cmac.org.rw/downloads/CMAC%20brochure.doc>

de la Torre, A., Gozzi, J. C. and Schmukler, S. L. (2007) 'Stock market development under globalization: whither the gains from reforms?' World Bank Policy Research Working Paper No. 4184. Online: <http://go.worldbank.org/R5XO1Y86C0 >

Dezalay, Y. and Garth, B. S. (1996) *Dealing in Virtue: international commercial arbitration and the construction of a transnational legal order* Chicago: University of Chicago Press.

EASEA Committee on Mass Cross-Listing (2005) Report submitted 17 November 2005 in Arusha, Tanzania. Online: <http://www.nse.co.ke/newsite/pdf/report_on_cross_listings_ea.pdf>

(FAA) Federal Arbitration Act (1925) 9 U.S.C ss. 1–16. Online: <http://www.law.cornell.edu/uscode/html/uscode09/usc_sup_01_9_10_1.html>

Friedman, F. B. and Grose, C. (2006) 'Promoting access to primary equity market: a legal and regulatory approach', World Bank Working Paper No. 44343. Washington D.C.: World Bank. Online: <http://go.worldbank.org/7T947F2HM0>

Gross, J. (2006) 'Securities mediation: dispute resolution for the individual investor', *Ohio State Journal on Dispute Resolution*, 21(2). Online: <http://ssrn.com/abstract= 1026355>

Harvard Law Review (2008) 'Recent proposed legislation', *Harvard Law Review*, 121(8): 2262–69. Online: <http://www.harvardlawreview.org/issues/121/june08/recentlegislation/arbitration_fairness_act2007.pdf>

Kaufmann-Kohler, G. (2003) 'Globalization of arbitral procedure', *Vanderbilt Journal of Transnational Law*, 26: 1313.

La Porta, R., Lopez De Silanes, F. and Shleifer, A. (2006) 'What works on securities laws?', *The Journal of Finance*, 61: 1.

Lew, J., Mistelis, L. and Kroll, S. (2003) *Comparative International Commercial Arbitration*, The Hague: Kluwer.

Mitchell, S. M. (2002) 'A Kantian system? democracy and third-party conflict resolution', *American Journal of Political Science*, 46: 749.

Moss, T. (2003) *Adventure Capitalism*, New York: Palgrave Macmillan.

Moss, T., Ramachandran, V. and Standley, S. (2007) 'Why doesn't Africa get more equity investment? Frontier stock markets, firm size and asset allocations of global emerging market funds', Centre for Global Development Working Paper 112, Washington D.C.: Centre for Global Development. Online: <http://www.cgdev.org/files/12773_file_Moss_Rama_Standley_Portfolio_Africa.pdf>

Norton, J. (2004) 'Encouraging capital flows and viable dispute settlement frameworks under the Monterrey Consensus', *Law & Business Review of the Americas*, 10: 65.

N'Zue, F. (2006) 'Stock market development and economic growth: Evidence from Cote d'Ivoire', *African Development Review*, 18: 123–43.

Perry-Kessaris, A. (2008) *Global Business, Local Law: the Indian legal system as a communal resource in foreign investment relations*, Aldershot: Ashgate.

Pistor, K., Keinan, Y., Kleinheisterkamp, J. and West, M. D. (2003) 'Evolution of corporate law and the transplant effect: lessons from six countries', *The World Bank Research Observer*, 18(1): 89–112.

Rogers, C. (2005) 'Emerging dilemmas in international economic arbitration: the vocation of the international arbitrator', *American University International Law Review*, 20: 1007.

Riungu, C. (2008) 'Burundi set to join East African capital markets body' *The East African*, 16 August 2008. Online: <http://www.theeastafrican.co.ke/news/-/2558/457006/-/s321tlz/-/index.html>

Ruburika, S. (2008) 'Rwanda: capital market to become more attractive' *allAfrica.com* 28 May 2008. Online: <http://allafrica.com/stories/200805290997.html>

Sarbanes-Oxley Act (2002) Pub. L. 107–204, 116 Stat. 745, enacted 30 July 2002. Online: <http://www.sec.gov/about/laws/soa2002.pdf>

(SEC) Securities and Exchange (2008) 'Report to the U.S. Agency for International Development (USAID) Concerning Technical Assistance to USAID Cooperating Countries Interagency Agreement (IAA) Between USAID and the SEC for the Quarter Ending June 30, 2007'. Online: <http://pdf.usaid.gov/pdf_docs/PDACJ844.pdf>

*Shearson/American Express Inc. v McMahon* (1987) 482 U.S. 220.

Shleifer, A. (2005) 'Understanding regulation', *European Financial Management*, 11: 439.

(SIFMA) Securities Industry and Financial Markets Association (2007) 'White paper on arbitration in the securities industry'. Online: <http://www.sifma.org/regulatory/pdf/arbitration-white-paper.pdf>

Singh, K. (1999) *The Globalisation of Finance: a citizen's guide*, London: Zed Books.

Stiglitz, J. (1994) 'The role of the state in financial markets', Proceedings of the World Bank Annual Conference on Development Economics 1993, Washington, D.C.: World Bank. Online: <http://go.worldbank.org/SM7YJE9UG0>

*The East African* (2008) 'Rwanda to open "Over the Counter" stockmarket' 15 January 2008. Online: <http://www.rwandagateway.org/article.php3?id_article=7858>

UNCTAD Secretariat (2005) 'Progress in the development of African commodity exchanges'. Report to the 2nd Extraordinary Session of the African Union Conference of Ministers of Trade 21–24 November 2005 in Arusha, Tanzania. Addis Ababa:

African Union. Online: <http://www.africa-union.org/trade%20and%20industry/ Arusha/Commodities/UNCTAD_Exchanges.pdf>
(USE) Uganda Securities Exchange (2008) *Annual Report 2007*, 30 June 2008. Online <http://www.use.or.ug/documents/USE_Annual_Report_2007.pdf>
USE (2003) Listing Rules 2003. Online: <http://www.use.or.ug/documents/ USE_Listing_Rules_Sep_2003_FPC.pdf>
Yarty, C. and Adjasi, C. (2007) 'Stock market development in Sub-Saharan Africa: critical issues and challenges', IMF Working Paper WP/07/209. Washington D.C.: IMF. Online: <http://imf.org/external/pubs/ft/wp/2007/wp07209.pdf>

## Useful websites

(CMAU) Capital Markets Authority of Uganda
   <http://www.cmauganda.co.ug>
(CMAK) Capital Markets Authority of Kenya
   <http://www.cma.or.ke>
(CMSA) Capital Markets and Securities Authority (Tanzania)
   <http://www.cmsa-tz.org>
(CMAC) Capital Markets Advisory Council (Rwanda)
   <http://www.cmac.org.rw/>
(DSE) Dar Es Salaam Stock Exchange
   <http://www.dse.co.tz/index.php>
(EASRA) East African Member States Securities Regulatory Authorities
   <http://www.cma.or.ke/index.php?option=com_content&task=view&id=112&Itemid= 123>
(FOS) Financial Ombudsman Service (UK)
   <http://www.financial-ombudsman.org.uk>
(LCIA) London Court of International Arbitration
   <http://www.lcia-arbitration.com/>
(LSE) London Stock Exchange
   <http://www.londonstockexchange.com>
(NSE) Nairobi Stock Exchange
   <http://www.nse.co.ke/>
(NYSE) New York Stock Exchange
   <http://www.nyse.com>
(SEC) United States Securities and Exchange Commission
   <http://www.sec.gov>
(USE) Uganda Securities Exchange
   <http://www.use.or.ug>
World Bank/IFC Global Capital Markets Development Department
   <http://www.ifc.org/ifcext/economics.nsf/Content/GCMD-Capital_Markets_ Development>
World Bank Investment Climate Capacity Enhancement
   <http://go.worldbank.org/JRAYKKJSL0>
(WFE) World Federation of Exchanges
   <http://www.world-exchanges.org>

# Chapter 10

# Rule-of-law assistance discourse and practice: Japanese inflections

*Veronica L. Taylor*

## Introduction

The 'rule of law' continues to gain momentum as an organizing principle for global financial transfers, and so scholarly attention has turned to updating the intellectual history of the field. Scott Newton (2006) suggests that we have witnessed a continuum of five distinct periods of foreign aid or donor-propelled legal reform worldwide, namely: a pre-history of colonial legal development (to the 1960s); the inaugural moment of US legal development cooperation (1965–74); the critical moment (1974–89); the revivalist moment (1989–98); and the 'post' moment (1998 to the present). Similarly, but using slightly different taxonomy, David Trubek has declared this present period to be a 'third moment' of law and development (Trubek and Santos 2006: 1).

Trubek argues that we now see the emergence of a new paradigm of law and development, fuelled in part by critical reaction to the neo-liberal policies of the 1990s. Rather than focusing on private law enhancement in the service of market strengthening, 'the [new] concept of development … [has been] expanded to include law reform as *an end in itself*' (Trubek and Santos 2006: 9; emphasis in the original). Trubek suggests that this new paradigm is shaped by two key ideas: the importance of the role of state intervention when markets fail and the redefinition of 'development' to encompass not only economic growth, but also social goals such as human freedom, in the style of Amartya Sen's definition of rule of law (Trubek and Santos 2006: 8, Santos 2006: 265).

For evidence of the emergence of the 'third moment' paradigm, Trubek turns to some of the apparently changed priorities within World Bank documents and financed projects. Among other things, he cites examples of the Bank's explicit recognition of the failures of transplants and top-down methods; rejection of a one-size-fits-all approach and stress on the need for context-specific project development based on consultation of all 'stakeholders'; awareness that legal reform requires a long time-horizon and cannot be carried out quickly; recognition of the importance of the rule of law for poorer segments of the population; support for rule-of-law projects that deal with labour rights, women's rights and environmental protection; and its acceptance of the need to make access to justice an explicit dimension of judicial reform projects (Trubek 2006: 92).

Thus, for Trubek, the 'third moment' is characterized by a new commitment to critique, and a greater willingness to accommodate local conditions and national diversities (Trubek and Santos 2006: 9). On this view, the 'third moment' is an opportunity to review, correct, critique and perfect legal reform in the service of development. Trubek is cautiously optimistic that this 'third moment' heralds donor-funded legal reform initiatives around the world that are more nuanced and (potentially) more successful than those of previous decades, although '[i]t is premature to say that [they] presage real change' (Trubek and Santos 2006: 92).

The 'third moment' thesis is deeply attractive, but it is also contestable on a number of levels. One key question is whether the thesis and the normative assumptions that underpin it are supported by 'thick' descriptions of how contemporary donor-funded legal reform is proceeding worldwide (see, for example, Arnscheidt et al. 2008, Bergling et al. 2009). For me, an especially important missing component in the 'third moment' story is the rise of Asia, both as a target region for contemporary rule-of-law assistance (see Berger 2004) and as a source of distinct models of legal reform, whether domestic or as part of donor-assistance activities in the region.

Shifting the focus to Asia has a number of implications for how we view contemporary practice in the field of rule-of-law assistance. First, thinking about Asia as a locus of rule-of-law reform draws attention to the range and diversity of external donor interventions now carried out in the name of 'rule of law'. It becomes clear that there has been a significant diversification of types and modes of rule-of-law assistance, which now range from long-standing programmes of institutional reform and democratization (Indonesia) through to legal assistance for World Trade Organization (WTO) accession and market-strengthening (China and Vietnam), post-conflict reconstruction (Timor Leste, Cambodia), disaster relief for the poorest countries or regions (Bangladesh or Aceh) and finally fragile state construction during an ongoing conflict (Afghanistan; see the chapters by McAuslan and Sahovic in this volume).

Second, Asian examples remind us that subsuming rule-of-law programmes within military activities throughout Asia has been a hallmark of the last decade, fuelled by civil unrest and the effects of the (former) US Bush Administration's 'war on terror'. Conventional military activities, such as 'standing-up' police forces, prison systems, prosecution services and courts, have morphed into delivery of law reform and dispute resolution at the local level, independently of civilian development projects. This is now a pattern traceable from Timor Leste and Aceh, through the Provincial Reconstruction Teams in Iraq and Afghanistan, to the creation of a military-style 'standing corps' of civilian legal professionals in the US (United States Institute for Peace 2009, Taylor 2009).

Third, focusing on Asia reveals new, regional rule-of-law actors. For example, we see the emergence of Asian rule-of-law donors. Beyond multilateral donors such as the World Bank and the IMF, regional financial institutions have been important. The Asian Development Bank, for example, has long been a significant donor and an intellectual resource for legal reform programming within the region (see Pistor and Wellons 1999). At the bilateral level, Japan and South Korea have also assumed new roles as rule-of-law assistance providers, in order to meet their own political and economic goals. China, through Macau, is actively seeking to advance its influence on the Portuguese-speaking legal world, particularly in Africa. Taiwan and Singapore function as de facto models of legal reform within the region, in particular for China and Indonesia respectively, while Singapore has also emerged as a regional legal training and educational centre (Taylor, in press). Thailand continues to be a legal model and reference point for the Lao PDR and for Cambodia. What we do not yet understand is how elites within these relatively new Asian donor and 'model' institutions conceive rule-of-law assistance and how, in the delivery phase, they reconcile global concepts and narratives with their own national policy priorities and recipient needs and preferences.

Fourth, the Asia experience is noteworthy for its complex, multidirectional flows of 'rule of law' or legal reform. For example, China is simultaneously a recipient of rule-of-law donor assistance (donors include Japan, the EU and the US) and an emerging superpower in the process of remaking its own legal system. And while trying to achieve a functioning distribution of 'rule of law' domestically, China also acts as an important point of reference for other developing legal systems. More proactively, it is now a major economic force and aid provider in Africa and Central Asia and has begun to provide legal technical assistance to developing countries.

These new – or newly prominent – streams of rule-of-law assistance from and within Asia prompt a second question: is there any necessary link between development and rule-of-law assistance in Asia, either as an intellectual field or in practice? We might also ask Trubek, '*Whose* moment of law and development is this?' Responses may vary according to where we sit within the Asian matrix of rule-of-law assistance, and whether we employ the conventional western/ global framework of analysis or adopt local perspectives (see, for example, Peerenboom 2004, Perry-Kessaris 2008, Gillespie and Peerenboom 2009). In this chapter I suggest that these kinds of questions represent challenges to the 'third moment' thesis. I seek to illustrate this by exploring one under-studied aspect of rule-of-law assistance in Asia: Japan's evolving experience as a rule-of-law donor.

Having rebuilt its own economy in the second half of the twentieth century – initially with multilateral financing and foreign aid assistance – Japan grew to become the world's second largest economy. By the 1990s it had begun to export rule-of-law assistance to Asia. While they were familiar with the approaches of other multilateral and bilateral donors, Japanese governmental and legal elites initially avoided the formulations 'law and development' and 'rule of law', opting instead to label their activities 'legal technical assistance' [*hoseibishien*].

A distinctive national discourse developed about the origins, aims and characteristics of Japanese legal technical assistance which was, in its 'first moment', not framed as either economic or as explicitly developmental in nature. By 2008, however, Japan had entered its 'second moment' as a donor. A new political debate about the definition, delivery and geographic targets for legal technical assistance emerged and there were indications that some elites wished to recast the activity as a more explicitly economic initiative and to locate projects within the multilateral donor discourse of 'rule of law assistance'. At the same time, a recurrent thread in the policy discourse underscores the need for 'Japanese-style assistance' (see Kurokawa 2008: 1)

Japan's 'first' and 'second' moments of legal technical assistance contain a very different mix of elements from those sketched in the Trubek typology. Japan clearly monitors the dominant western donor initiatives and discourses in legal reform, but is forging a rather different path, substantively and geographically. I suggest that reviewing Japan's approach to legal technical assistance since 1996 is important, both as a significant caveat to universal applicability of the 'third moment' thesis and because it suggests ongoing tension between a western/globalized vision of rule-of-law assistance and the political imperatives at the national/local level.

## The Japanese trajectory of rule-of-law assistance

Japan is a relatively late entrant to the rule-of-law assistance surge of the late-twentieth century. Its formal program of ODA-funded legal technical assistance began in 1996 and was targeted at developing economies in Asia that were commercially important markets for Japan, particularly Vietnam, Cambodia, Indonesia and China. Although Japan's outright ranking as the world's largest bilateral provider of ODA (official development assistance) has fallen, it remains a dominant source of development funding in Asia and Central Asia, the primary shareholder in the Asian Development Bank and the second largest shareholder in the World Bank after the United States.

The domestic mandate for Japan's move into legal technical assistance derives from Japan's ODA Charter, first approved as a Cabinet policy directive in 1992 and then significantly revised in 2003 to deliver better 'strategic value, flexibility, transparency and efficiency' in Japan's ODA spending (Official Development Assistance Charter 2003; hereinafter 'ODA Charter'). Newly incorporated in those revisions was an explicit reference to requiring recipient countries to exercise good governance, and a commitment to providing cooperation 'for institution building including development of legal systems'. The policy priority areas identified in the 2003 revision were poverty reduction, sustainable growth (explicitly defined to include protection of intellectual property rights and standardization); global issues such as terrorism and international organized crime; and peace building. The priority regions for Japanese ODA were defined as Asia (particularly South Asia, Central Asia and the Caucuses), Africa, the Middle

East, Latin America and Oceania (ODA Charter 2003: 2–7). However, to date legal technical assistance has been carried out primarily in South East Asia and Central Asia.

The 2003 revision was driven by rapid geopolitical changes in the 1990s, including a policy switch by multilateral development banks from Washington Consensus-style policies to poverty reduction. During the same period, Japan experienced a prolonged recession of historic severity, and public support for ODA dropped from 43.2 per cent in 1990 to 19 per cent in 2003 (Sunaga 2004: 3–4). Some factions of the ruling Liberal Democratic Party began to push for an ODA policy emphasizing national interest, and Japan's private sector continued to lobby for a return to tied aid so as to align better with national commercial interests (see Keidanren 2007). Japanese NGOs, on the other hand, remained strongly in favour of both continuing and increasing the value of untied ODA. The 2003 Charter attempted to strike a compromise, paying some deference to the ruling party's views but preserving untied ODA (Sunaga 2004: 4, 6).

The 2003 Charter ensured that the status of legal technical assistance was boosted, and its future was secured, when it established 'institution building including development of legal systems' as an ODA priority activity. In so doing, it bolstered recommendations in a policy document issued in 2001 by the Justice System Reform Council. The Council was created in 1998 as part of the most intense domestic legal reform for Japan since the Occupation (1947–53) and Meiji (1868–1912) periods. Under the heading 'Legal technical assistance for developing countries should be promoted', the document points out that:

Utilizing its own experience in having adopted modern legal systems from other countries and having established the legal system as well as the administration of that system in conformity with the circumstances of the country, Japan has been providing legal technical assistance by accepting trainees from Asian and other developing countries, dispatching professionals and conducting on-site seminars in the fields of civil law, commercial law and criminal justice. Such assistance is important in order for Japan to play a positive role as a member of the international society and also to contribute to the development of smooth economic activities in private sectors in the advancing globalization of society and the economy.

Therefore, the government, lawyers and bar associations should cooperate as appropriate and continue to actively promote support for legal technical assistance for developing countries.

(Justice System Reform Council 2001: Chapter II, Part 3.3)

Inscribed into both justice system reform policy and into the revised ODA Charter, legal technical assistance – hitherto a modest voluntary effort by a small number of Japanese legal academics and government lawyers – now had secure ongoing government funding.

## Japanese rule-of-law actors and projects

Japan's legal technical assistance funding comes primarily from an ODA budget that is distributed across multiple government ministries and agencies. The Ministry of Foreign Affairs (MOFA) administers more than half of this. Its agency, the Japan International Cooperation Agency (JICA) is one of several direct recipients and to date a key umbrella for legal technical assistance projects. Programming in this area involves multiple government and non-government players, including: the Cabinet Secretariat; the Ministry of Foreign Affairs; JICA; the Ministry of Justice; the International Civil and Commercial Law Centre (ICCLC, now Foundation); the Ministry of Finance; the Ministry of Economy, Technology and Industry (METI); the Japanese Federation of Industries (Keidanren); the Japan Federation of Bar Associations (see Nichibenren 2002); the Supreme Court; and Japanese university law faculties, particularly the regional national universities, Nagoya, Kyushu and Kobe. As the list suggests, legal technical assistance in Japan is predominantly a public-sector-led enterprise, although the government does solicit financial support from the private sector. Business, in turn, is able to call for project priorities (see Keidanren Subcommittee on Corporate Law 2004).

Legal technical assistance projects have, at least until 2008, also been treated as pro-bono or public service for the purposes of staffing. The national development agency, JICA, has relatively few legally-trained staff so must co-opt academics, prosecutors, judges and attorneys. Despite (or perhaps due to) the small size of the Japanese legal professions, volunteering for legal technical assistance work is the norm. The projects and their implementers build on the self-perception of legal professionals as an elite, charged with the support and advancement of a national mission. In the case of attorneys, this fits well with the foundational provision Article 1(1) of the Practising Attorney Law (1949, as amended), which explicitly defines the mission of Japanese attorneys as public service and the upholding of human rights. Furthermore, the legal technical assistance wave is exciting for Japanese lawyers, prosecutors and judges because it offers an opportunity to be internationally engaged and important without directly incurring the systemic capital expense of increasing the size of the legal profession or establishing global legal practices.

The combination of a small-scale legal profession and a unitary legal system facilitated a high degree of interpersonal cooperation during Japan's 'first moment'. JICA convenes several legal coordination committees with outside membership; the universities sponsor frequent seminar series and symposia on law and development; and the Ministry of Justice publishes a regular newsletter for the field, *ICD News: law for development*. These same players also coordinate the staffing of projects, allowing what one commentator calls the 'all Japan' approach to delivering the necessary mix of legal professionals to counterpart countries (Inaba 2008: 3). In private, Japanese legal professionals engaged in legal technical assistance are dismissive of American corporatized rule-of-law delivery, believing their 'national' Japanese model to be more altruistic and responsive:

> To date, the Ministry of Justice has, based on our national experience of the Meiji era, aimed at not directly transplanting our national legal system, but – through repeated consultative with the counterpart country – the 'unforced legal technical assistance' suited to the needs and conditions [of that country]. Due to appreciation and understanding of this approach, among the many donors that conduct legal technical assistance, our national assistance is particularly highly valued by target countries.
>
> (Kurokawa 2008: 3)

Japanese altruism may indeed be the overriding norm here, but the mode of delivery is also structurally induced by the limited supply of legal professionals. The national bar pass rate is artificially pegged to just above replacement levels in all branches of the profession and, while the 70 per cent of legally-educated applicants who are not permitted to pass each year would be prime candidates for building out new areas of legal practice and/or consulting, there is no sign that legal elites in Japan plan to loosen their grip on the definition or accreditation of 'lawyers'.

A corollary of this is that the expanded 'second moment' of legal technical assistance sketched below is problematic without sufficient personnel. The short-term 'fix' proposed is to ease personnel regulations for judges and dig deeper into the public service to court clerks and institutional staff, in order to populate projects (Kurokawa 2008: 3) while 'hoping' that more volunteers will appear (Yabuki 2008: 16).

The 'second' moment changes sketched below will require rethinking of Japanese modalities. Thus the ad hoc, voluntary response to recipient requests is likely to be replaced by Japanese diagnostic determinations about what is needed, a more strategic deployment of resources and a formal mechanism for inter-agency cooperation established at the Cabinet level (Kurokawa 2008: 2).

### 'First moment' projects and characteristics

The first 'moment' of Japan's official contemporary legal technical assistance commenced with the work of Emeritus Professor Akio Morishima, former Dean of the Law Faculty of Nagoya University. An acquaintanceship with the Minister of Justice in Vietnam led to a request to provide advice on legislative drafting, which he did under the auspices of cultural exchange in 1992 (Morishima 2000). This was followed by training courses for Vietnamese officials in Japan from 1994 and the formal commencement of legal technical assistance to Vietnam as ODA in 1996. The core of the Vietnam project in its first phase was a ten-member Japanese team on Civil Code drafting chaired by Morishima and working with Vietnamese counterparts. The final draft of the Civil Code was adopted by the National Assembly of Vietnam in May 2005, replacing the Civil Code of 1995. Further requests followed from Cambodia and from Mongolia in 1994 to the Japan Federation of Bar Associations and from the Ministry of Justice in the Lao PDR in 1996. In 1999, the Japanese and Cambodian governments agreed to draft a new Civil Code and Code of Civil Procedure for Cambodia.

Individual Japanese projects during this 'first moment' were broadly similar to those supported by other donors, including the usual components of legislative drafting; institutional support for economic policy, such as direct assistance to the competition authority in Indonesia; judicial training on decision-writing and the selection and publication of case decisions; law-enforcement mechanisms, especially in relation to intellectual property rights; computerization and legal education, including short-course training in-country, project-based skills transfer and scholarship support for advanced legal study in Japan (Taylor 2005). In scale and significance, however, the code-drafting projects in Vietnam and Cambodia were the most important legal technical assistance projects carried out by Japan (Yamashita and Tanaka 2003) and they established what Japanese commentators see as distinctive characteristics and national practices.

## Japanese narratives of the 'first moment'

Japanese legal elites describe the rise of legal technical assistance through three different narratives: government-sponsored stories about law in the service of Japanese modernity; Japan's response to recipient countries' desire for a non-western form of legal reform; and questions about how to reconcile Japan's own reception of modern law and its new role as provider of legal technical assistance. Running in parallel to each of these discourse threads is a self-critical comparison with Western bilateral and multilateral donors.

### Law in the service of Japanese modernity

In government sources, and in some scholarly writing, the Japanese law-and-development story begins with the foreign legal experts invited to Meiji Japan (1868–1912) in the latter half of the nineteenth century, to teach law and to advise on the drafting of European-style codified positive law (Riles 2001). Japanese political leaders during the same period dispatched their best and brightest young men to Europe, in order to make an exhaustive study of comparative legal models. Decades of laborious statutory drafting and redrafting followed, resulting in the promulgation of hybrid codes that draw on multiple sources. There followed decades of 'reception' of the new legal concepts, professionalization of the Bench and Bar and then legal self-reliance (see Araki 2001).

Now in the role of assistance provider, Japanese Code-drafting projects explicitly reference both this kind of historical sequencing and the civil law *mentalité.* In Cambodia, the Japanese Taskforce on the Civil Code was chaired by Professor Morishima and the Japanese Taskforce on the Civil Procedure Code by Professor Takeshita. Morishima and Takeshita placed great emphasis on the orderly development of law, beginning with the code framework for private and commercial law. Critical of other donors, who encouraged patchwork development of specific legislation aimed at attracting foreign investment, Japanese actors maintained that specific laws on security interests in property, or on insolvency, could only make sense once the code framework was established (Taylor 2005). The unspoken premise here is that Japan's nineteenth-century codification served the country well, at least until the post-World War Two Occupation reforms of the 1950s, and then until the intensive statutory reforms of the 1990s and 2000s. Thus, conversational claims such as that (Professor) 'Morishima is the Boisonnade of Vietnam' explicitly tie together the 'foreign legal advisor', code-drafting and voluntary adoption of modern European law as phases of Japan's state-building with an implicit expectation that the rapid military and economic development of the twentieth century that followed in Japan can be emulated. This is a mythic narrative of abstracted modernity in which the key themes are self-reliance, collaboration, and voluntary choices by local decision-makers, elements that seem subordinated in twenty-first century rule-of-law assistance (Taylor, in press).

This historical discourse also weaves in cultural attributes, such as a Japanese 'preference' for alternate dispute resolution (ADR), which marks Japan as an 'Asian' country, well placed to assist neighbours seeking to avoid the litigious excesses of the United States. As system insiders know, however, the historical pattern in Japan is that ADR was created and manipulated by the state to curb citizen litigation during economic downturns and social crises (Tanase 2001, Haley 1991, Upham 1998): this is an invented tradition of non-litigiousness.

This kind of sanitized legal-development narrative conceals Japan's historical use of law as a tool of social control, both at home and during its colonization of Asia. In the early-twentieth century, this meant implementing variations of newly-minted Japanese law in the colonies of Korea, Formosa and Manchuria, while carefully studying local law and custom in order to create concentric circles of indigenous, local colonial and imperial law (Wang 1992, Dudden 2004). Not all Japanese legal reform was coerced; Thailand made a careful study of Japan on a voluntary basis before embarking on its own codification and legal modernization drive (Kagawa 2002).

Nor was Japanese legal development tempered and gradual, although the historical narrative is largely silent about the ways in which war, social conflict and the toxic side effects of modernization influenced the trajectory of the legal system. Convulsive legal change occurred, for example, when the post-World War Two Occupation introduced market-oriented commercial law, as well as democratic institutions that create new possibilities for challenging the state. Regulatory law was subordinated to the needs of big business during the economic take off period of the 1950s and subsequent high growth from the 1960s to the 1980s, and consumer protection and fully-developed intellectual property rights were delayed until the 1990s (Hirowatari 2000). However, legal (and litigated) clashes between citizens and the government continued to target regulatory lapses and harmful business practices in areas such as the environment, labour, gender equity and civil rights during the twentieth century, in some cases successfully (Feldman 2000). Even today, the statutory gaps that remain in respect of protection from discrimination, redress for wartime wrongs and protection of human rights are routinely challenged through public-interest litigation.

### Responding to a call for a non-Western form of legal reform

Japanese legal technical assistance projects, of course, are intended to stabilize rather than challenge the local system. Common to these projects is a strong emphasis on recipient autonomy in selecting and requesting the form of assistance. The projects in Vietnam and Cambodia took several years of round-table collaborative discussion before the Japanese partners were satisfied that the local counterparts had sufficient understanding of the laws and the drafting issues to make informed choices about what their code provisions should contain (Taylor 2005). This echoes a kind of legal 'memory' of Japan's nineteenth-century (Meiji) legal modernization, instituted as a result of US gunboat diplomacy, but then implemented autonomously. Japanese participants place a high value on the freedom to fashion a national legal identity, or 'independent development' (*jiritsu hatten*) (Inaba 2008: 4).

Not surprisingly, a core theme of the first-moment projects has been an emphasis on legal education. On the Japanese side, the foundations of this approach lie in the 1980s policy outlined by (then) Prime Minister Nakasone which emphasized development of human resources within Japan's strategically important markets. Student scholarships in law at Japanese universities that are targeted at Central Asian republics such as Mongolia and Uzbekistan and the newly marketized economies of China and Vietnam are illustrative (see, for example, Aikyo 2008). The content of customized programmes at the graduate level for these students has tended to be doctrinal and/or practical. At Nagoya, for example, the LLM and PhD programmes have been delivered in English, with a long-term plan to build cohorts of graduates who are also fluent in Japanese and able to use Japanese legal materials at an advanced level. Although some 'perspectives' courses are available, there is relatively little theoretical 'law and development' content and branding. This is both a pragmatic choice, given the educational backgrounds of the students, and also probably reflects some Japanese ambivalence about Anglo-American 'law and development' scholarship, the degree to which it reflects Japanese policy priorities and its applicability in an Asian context.

The educational emphasis within legal technical assistance in the 1990s also supported the emergence of 'Asian law' as a formal field of research and teaching in Japanese universities. To be sure, Japanese legal scholars do not see Asian law and legal technical assistance as fungible fields (e.g. Imai, Morigiwa and Inoue 1999, Yasuda 2000 and Kaneko 1998), but there is no doubt that government funding for ODA also played a role in universities hiring young faculty in law with backgrounds in Asian languages and/or area studies, the Center for Asian Legal Exchange (CALE) at Nagoya University, the Asian Law Center at Kyushu University and the Faculty of International Cooperation at Kobe University being leading examples.

## From receiver of law to provider of legal assistance

The third strand of legal technical assistance discourse in Japan is linked to the Justice System Reform policies of the late 1990s. A clear theme in this policy initiative is the charge that the rule of law never really took root in Japan, either during Meiji or after the Occupation reforms (cf. Haley and Taylor 2004, Hamada 2008: 5). Not surprisingly, thoughtful academics in Japan have tremendous difficulty reconciling the apparent contradiction of their own country's justice system 'failure' and the success of its economy with the standard rule-of-law claim that highly developed legal systems are indispensable elements in economic growth. Providing an account of modern law as the central, propelling factor in Japan's industrialization is taxing, largely because this is a modernist fiction. Certainly Japan had sophisticated civil, commercial and procedural law, and plenty of it, but as Haley (1991) and Upham (1987) have argued, it was the strong reliance on informal means of ordering and the government control of formal law and processes that really distinguished Japan until at least the mid-twentieth century.

Japanese legal history raises real questions about how much law is necessary for development (or modernization) and at what point, and how much predictability business really seeks (as opposed to claiming that it seeks) in a transitional economy. Leading Japanese legal sociologist Takao Tanase argues that 'law was not a precondition of the modernization in Japan, at least to the degree that the sweeping statement of "the law as a prerequisite for modern society" implies' (Tanase 2001: 192). Rather, he suggests, the Justice System Reform narrative employs a standard modernist technique: simultaneous denial and affirmation of (Japanese) legal culture and legal institutions. This leads to, and indeed requires, more modern law (Tanase 2001: 187–98).

This tension between the historical development narrative in Japan and the Western donor rhetoric of rule-of-law assistance runs through Japan's first 'moment' of legal technical assistance. The tension involves self-critique, as well as considerable ambivalence about Western donor approaches. A common self-criticism by Japanese practitioners during this period is that Japan's legal technical assistance lacks clear objectives and measurable outcomes. By this they often mean a clear normative statement of priorities.

For example, Japanese legal technical assistance to date is noticeably agnostic on economic theory, particularly neoliberal or new institutional economics (NIE) ideas (see Sakumoto, Kobayashi and Imaizumi 2003, Kobayashi 2001). Instead Japanese lawyers in the field seem to accept the market economy as meaningful but also to understand the diverse and hybrid features of US, European and Japanese capitalisms (see Hall and Soskice 2001). They have been reluctant to present the evolution of Japanese commercial law as a causal factor in Japan's rise as an economic superpower, being more concerned with how law and legal institutions in Japan were historically moulded to the political and economic priorities of the day (see, for example, Hirowatari 2000). The lack of a dominant economic theory in Japanese legal technical assistance is not simply a normative preference. Legal education in Japan is not interdisciplinary at either the undergraduate or graduate level, so very few lawyers are trained in economics. Similarly, Japan's legal technical assistance projects are seldom staffed with members from a business background, although they may utilize the local presence of entities such as the Japan External Trade Organization (JETRO) or Japanese businesses.

A further domestic criticism by Japanese business and taxpayers was that the ODA efforts are invisible and lack direct, tangible benefits for Japan.[1] Japanese legal technical assistance is vulnerable to this claim in part because projects to date have not focused on metrics in the style of other donors (see Taylor 2007). Nor do they employ elaborately designed project evaluation (see SIDA 2009).

The absence of a rigid or normative framework can, of course, be useful. If, for example, you want to engage with Myanmar on legal reform, not having an overarching concern with human-rights norms can be convenient. But it can also be felt as a void. So, for example, the Scandinavian design elements of gender equity and human rights which are clearly tracked in Japan's evolving ODA policy (see JICA 2003) are also attractive to some Japanese legal technical assistance academics and practitioners (Nagoya, undated). Japan's pragmatic, low-profile approach is also vulnerable to the charge that insufficient attention is given to partnering with NGOs, both at home and abroad (Kawai and Takagi 2001: 13).

## New global pressures and Japan's 'second moment'

Since 2008, the beginning of what we could call Japan's 'second moment', the political nature of Japan's technical legal assistance has become more apparent. Japan's first-moment practitioners sometimes claimed in conversation that Japan's ODA (including legal technical assistance) was distinct from that of other countries because it had no instrumental motive; it was simply a response to a genuine request from recipients. To the extent that rule-of-law assistance is a form of ODA, however, it is more accurate to view it as having multiple main purposes: diplomatic (including security), developmental, humanitarian relief, commercial and cultural (Lancaster 2006: 13). Since the 1990s, bilateral aid has also performed the additional tasks of promoting economic and social transitions (including legal reform), promoting democracy, addressing global issues, mitigating conflicts and managing post-conflict transitions (Lancaster 2006: 13). Donors mix, shift and frequently obscure the nature and relative priority of their goals. Japan's 'first moment' of legal technical assistance could be coded as a mix of cultural (student scholarships and in-country training) and economic transition – providing foundational legal infrastructure such as codes. However, policy discourse suggests that a 'second moment' of legal technical assistance has begun since 2008, as part of which policy objectives become more sharply defined.

The first indicator of a shift to a 'second moment' was the geographic expansion of Japanese legal-reform projects. Work in Vietnam, Cambodia, Lao PDR, Indonesia and China is now joined by a significant focus on Central Asia and a projected build-out to Africa. All of these countries and regions appeared in the revised ODA Charter of 2003, but the Central Asian focus was underscored in the 'Silk Road' policy launched in 2004 with (then) Foreign Minister Yoriko Kawaguchi's visit to the region and then the conclusion of a series of bilateral trade agreements with governments in that region (Len et al. 2008)

The second indicator that legal technical assistance in Japan was changing was when it became the focus of the ruling Liberal Democratic Party's Legal Affairs Committee, which unveiled 'Strategic Vision for Our Country's Legal Technical Assistance that we can take Pride in Before the World' in June 2007 (Liberal Democratic Party 2007). This was subsequently fed into Cabinet policy deliberations and reappeared in the Cabinet-level 13th Annual Forum on Economic Cooperation, held in January 2008, at which legal technical assistance was recognized as 'an important form of foreign economic cooperation, which going forward, requires strategic attention' (Inaba 2008: 3).

The keyword in these policy documents is *economic* cooperation, a bilateral aid objective that was not foregrounded in 'first moment' projects. An immediate practical example is given in the White Paper on Official Development Assistance, which describes capacity building for young bureaucrats in Tashkent and the development of an Uzbekistan commentary on bankruptcy law and strengthening of civil and administrative statutes in order to support business activity (2007: 161).

A new project that illustrates the convergence between commercial and educational interests is the Legal Information Research Center, home of an East Asia legal translation database being developed at Nagoya University in cooperation with the Ministry of Justice (Aikyo 2008: 23). Initially a Japanese Government attempt to respond to the demands of Japanese business exporters for reliable official translations into English of Japan's key statutes, the project has now become a platform for developing an interoperable database of statutes and legal terminology in Japanese, Chinese, Korean and English. An important feature of the latest iteration of the project is the ability to add annotations to statute provisions and so, in effect, create a narrative of statutory and legal-system history around shared doctrinal areas of law. A related project based at Nagoya is the build-out of a collaborative library collection and catalogue covering legal materials from Asia (Aikyo 2008: 20–23). Again, these are both cultural and educational projects but are intended to furnish important commercial intelligence about key markets in Asia, and to promote Japanese law as a relevant resource and standard.

At the trade-policy level, Saadia Pekkanen suggests that Japan in the last decade has sought to enhance its trade competitiveness by engaging in 'aggressive legalism' (2008). Exporting legal services and technical know-how through legal technical assistance is not 'aggressive' in the Pekkanen sense of juridifying trade disputes and manipulating rules legalistically for national advantage, but it is an alternative example of harnessing law as a technology to improve the business environment for Japanese companies in Asian emerging markets.

The continued emphasis on education in this 'second moment' of legal technical assistance is consistent with cultural objectives of bilateral aid – that is, positioning Japan as an 'Asian' donor and emphasizing the cultural similarities and complementarities between the Japanese and recipient legal systems and institutional counterparts. Running through much of the new programming is a nationalist sense that '[i]t is important for us to try to extract ourselves from the "Leave Asia, Enter Europe" situation' (Aikyo 2008: 23). Allied to this is a keen understanding that at least some of the 'wider diffusion of the rule of law being proposed, while laudable, is in essence a new plan for the worldwide export of American lawyers' (Hamada 2008: 6).

Viewed politically, the second-moment projects in legal technical assistance are intended to help Japan assert its 'global player' role in relation to other world powers, particularly China, by emphasizing its Asian credentials. By directing legal technical assistance towards Central Asian countries that remain relatively low priorities for the United States (Len 2005), Japan gains 'market share' in a region that is proximate to China and Russia. Importantly, it also contributes to the legal infrastructure in places where Japan – and its competitors – have a direct interest in securing natural resources and bolstering their own energy security.

Thus far, the 'second moment' looks endogenous, with Japanese elites independently determining the new policy direction. However, woven through the second-moment conceptions is a clear sense that legal technical assistance is also a forum for global competition and policy dialogue. So, legal technical assistance and capacity building formed part of the Justice and Interior Affairs meeting agenda at the June 2008 G8 meeting, requiring Japan to show strategic thinking and commitment (Kurokawa 2008: 3). The sense of global competition also comes through in Kurokawa's observation – as a key policy player in the Ministry of Justice – that legal technical assistance has the advantage of being a type of ODA where 'You can see the international assistance provider's face' (Kurokawa 2008: 4).

## Whose 'moment'?

The Japanese trajectory of legal technical assistance suggests that (the) experience(s) of 'law and development' in Asia may vary, depending on the actors.

Within the United States, of course, 'law and development' resonates with academic lawyers both as an established field of study and as the lived experience of 'first-generation' practitioners. At the same time, neither scholarship nor practice have remained static, so the formula has been displaced in rhetoric and practice by 'rule of law assistance'. Trubek concedes this by subtitling his 'third moment' of law and development 'Rule of Law II' (Trubek 2006: 89), and by recognizing that:

> The contemporary 'Rule of Law' enterprise took shape in a very different *conjuncture* [from that of the development policy of the 1950s and 1960s]. By the 1990s when ROL really became big business, major changes had occurred in the world economy and world politics. International trade had grown substantially. The spread of industry in the 'third world' and the success of export-led growth in Asia, plus the globalization strategies of major transnational corporations and rapid deregulation of capital markets, significantly increased the degree of world economic integration.
>
> … The vision of a world of partially closed national economies and state-controlled national markets gave way to a vision of a fully open global economy with minimal state involvement and free flows of goods and capital across national boundaries. This vision affected thinking about development in very profound ways, creating a new development paradigm with important implications for the law reform agenda.
>
> (Trubek 2006: 83)

Trubek is primarily thinking of how the World Bank operationalizes (multiple) versions of rule of law internally, but of course 'rule of law' as label and construct has a life independent of World Bank usage (see Decker in this volume). Indeed, if Linn Hammegren (in this volume) is correct, we should be cautious about overemphasizing the extent to which the Bank actually exerts hegemonic influence on rule-of-law discourse and practice worldwide. In a new set of case studies edited with Per Bergling and Jenny Ederlov, I have also argued that, in practice, even allowing for some convergence, the animating ideas and modalities of rule-of-law programming are diverse across donors and geographies (Bergling et al. 2009).

The diversity of circumstances in which rule-of-law assistance is deployed is very visible in Asia, where disaster relief, pre-post-conflict peacekeeping, post-conflict reconstruction, institutional reform and democratization and ratification of global trade agreements are all drivers for donor-assisted legal reform (see Decker in this volume). Although we may, following Trubek, continue mentally to classify the donor intervention as 'development assistance', a better working hypothesis for the twentieth century might be that rule-of-law assistance has become decoupled from *development* as the sole or primary objective and that security, commercial, humanitarian and cultural outcomes may be equally, if not more, important.

Japan's legal technical assistance over the last two decades, as I have described it above, would seem to support that hypothesis. This empirical reality, of course, is unlikely to affect the taxonomy of the field in the United States, where the 'third moment' of law and development also functions as intellectual branding by energetic scholar-entrepreneurs. However, at the very least, it should alert us to the possibility that a 'third moment' is not universal, and that developments in Asia bear closer analysis precisely because they do not converge with our own experience.

## Note

1 See Decker (in this volume) for similar concerns in relation to World Bank rule-of-law projects in fragile states.

## References

Aikyo, M. (2008) 'Nagoya daigaku to hoseibishien jigyō / kenkyū' [Nagoya University research and initiatives on legal technical assistance] *Jurisuto* [*Jurist*], 1358 (June): 17–25.

Araki, M. (2001) *Japan's ODA Policy* (Mar. 27, 2001). Online: <http://www.jica.go.jp/english/scholarship/previous_seminar/2001_sp/lecture/araki>

Arnscheidt, J., van Rooij B. and Otto, J. M. (eds) (2008) *Law Making for Development: explorations into the theory and practice of international legislative projects*, Leiden: Leiden University Press.

Basic Outline of National Legal Technical Assistance (2008) *Wagakuni hoseibishien ni kansuru kihonteki kangaekata* [Basic Outline of National Legal Technical Assistance] (Dai 13 kai kaigai keizaikyōryoku kaigigōijikō) Heisei 20 nen 1 gatsu 30 nichi [13th Foreign Economic Cooperation Meeting Heads of Agreement 30 January 2008]. Online: <http://202.232.58.50/jp/singi/kaigai/dai13/13besshi.pdf>

Berger, M. T. (2004) *The Battle for Asia: from decolonization to globalization*, London, New York: RoutledgeCurzon.

Bergling, P., Ederlov J. and Taylor V. L. (eds) (2009) *Rule of Law Promotion: global perspectives, local applications*, Uppsala: Iustus.

Dudden, A. (2004) *Japan's Colonization of Korea: discourse and power*, Honolulu: University of Hawaii Press.

Feldman, E. A (2000) *The Ritual of Rights in Japan: law, society and health policy*, Cambridge: Cambridge University Press.

Gillespie, J. and Peerenboom, R. (2009) *Regulation in Asia: pushing back on globalization*, London: Routledge.

Haley J. O. and Taylor, V. L. (2004) 'Rule of law in Japan', in R. Peerenboom (ed.) *Asian Discourses of Rule of Law*, New York, London: RoutledgeCurzon.

Haley, J. O. (1991) *Authority without Power: law and the Japanese paradox*, Oxford: Oxford University Press.

Hall, P. A and Soskice, D. (eds) (2001) *Varieties of Capitalism*, Oxford: Oxford University Press.

Hamada, K. (2008) 'Nihon ni okeru hō no shihai ni tsuite' [On the rule of law in Japan] *NBL*, 873: 4–8 (January).

Hirowatari, S. (2000) 'Post-war Japan and the law: mapping discourses and legalization and modernization', *Social Science Japan Journal*, 3(2): 155.

Imai H., Morigiwa Y. and Inoue T. (eds) (1999) Henyō suru ajia no hō to tetsugaku [Asian law and philosophy in flux], Tokyo: Yuhikaku.

Inaba K. (2008) 'Hoseibishien jigyō no ima' [Current legal technical assistance initiatives'], *Jurisuto* [*Jurist*], 1358: 2–8 (June).

JICA: Japan International Cooperation Agency (2003) Japan International Cooperation Agency Annual Report 2003. Online: <http://www.jica.go.jp/english/publication/annual/2003/index.html>

Justice System Reform Council (2001) *Recommendations of the Justice System Reform Council – For a Justice System to Support Japan in the 21st Century*, 12 June 2001. English Translation of the Final Report. Online: <http://www.kantei.go.jp/foreign/judiciary/2001/0612report.html>

Kagawa, K. (2002) *Masao Tokichi den: hoseibishien kokusaikyōryoku no senkusha* [Biography of Tokichi Masao, pioneer in international cooperation and legal technical assistance], Tokyo: Shinzansha.

Kaneko Y. (1998) Ajiahō no kanōsei [The potential for Asian law], Okayama City: Daigakukyōikushuppan.

Kawai M. and Takagi S. (2001) Japan's Official Development Assistance: Recent Issues and Future Directions 4 (World Bank Policy Research, Working Paper No 2722) Online: <http://papers.ssrn.com/sol3/papers.cfm?abstract_id=634433>

Keidanren (2007) 'Nippon Keidanren [Japan Business Federation]: recommendations on Japan's International Cooperation Policy and expectations on the new JICA'. Online: <http://www.keidanren.or.jp/english/policy/2007/040.html>

Keidanren Sub-committee on Corporate Law (2004) Committee on Economic Law, Nippon Keidanren [Japan Business Federation] 'The benefits of translating Japanese laws into foreign languages', 14 June 2004. Provisional English translation. Online: <http://www.keidanren.or.jp/english/policy/2004/051.html>

Kobayashi M. (ed) (2001) *Ajiashokoku no shijōkeizaika to shakaihō* [Market transitions in Asian countries and social law], Tokyo: Institute of Developing Economies.

Kurokawa, H. (2008) *'Ōkiku kawaru hoseidoseibishien'* [Major changes to legal technical assistance], *ICD News: Law for Development* 36: 1–4 (Sept) Tokyo: International Cooperation Department Research and Training Institute Ministry of Justice.

Lancaster, C. (2006) *Foreign Aid: diplomacy, development, domestic politics*, Chicago: University of Chicago Press.

Len, C. (2005) 'Japan's Central Asian Diplomacy: motivations, implications and prospects for the region', *The China and Eurasia Forum Quarterly*, 3(3): 127–49.

Len, C. et al. (eds) (2008) *Japan's Silk Road Diplomacy: paving the way ahead*, Central Asia-Caucasus Institute and Silk Road Studies Program, Washington DC, Johns Hopkins SAIS. Online: <http://www.isdp.eu/files/publications/books/08/cl08japansilk.pdf>

Liberal Democratic Party (2007) *'Sekai ni hokoru, Wagakuni hoseibishien no senryaku bijiyon'* 'Strategic vision for our country's legal technical assistance: [one that] we can take pride in before the world'. Online: <http://www.jimin.jp/jimin/seisaku/2007/seisaku-012.html>

Morishima, A. (2000) Hoseibishien to nihon no hōritsugaku [Legal technical assistance and law studies in Japan] *Hikakuhō kenkyu*, 62: 120–36, cited in Yoichi Shio, 'Japanese legal technical assistance: basic codes drafting assistance and the discourse of Japanese legal modernization' (unpublished, on file with author).

Nagoya, (undated) 'Legal assistance in Asia: structuring a paradigm for countries in transition'. Online: <http://tla.nomolog.nagoya-u.ac.jp>

Newton, S. (2006) 'The dialectics of law and development, in D. M. Trubek and A. Santos (eds) *The New Law and Economic Development*, Cambridge, Cambridge University Press, 174–202.

Nichibenren [Japan Federation of Bar Associations] (2002), *Nichibenren ni okeru hoseibishien* [Legal technical assistance by the Japan Federation of Bar Associations], Unpublished Submission to the 14th Session of the Internationalization Sub Committee, Justice System Reform Secretariat, Prime Minister's Office, 14 May 2002, Professor Noboru Kashiwagi, Chair. Online: <http://www.kantei.go.jp/jp/singi/sihou/kentoukai/kokusaika/dai14/14gijiroku.html/>

Official Development Assistance Charter (2003) (Unofficial Translation). Online: <http://www.mofa.go.jp/policy/oda/reform/revision0308.pdf>

Peerenboom R. (ed.) (2004) *Discourses on Rule of Law in Asia*, London, New York: Routledge-Curzon.

Pekkanen, S. M. (2008) *Japan's Aggressive Legalism: law and foreign trade politics beyond the WTO*, Stanford: Stanford University Press.

Perry-Kessaris, A. (2008) *Global Business, Local Law: the Indian legal system as communal resource in foreign investment relations*, Aldershot: Ashgate.

Pistor, K. and Wellons, P. (eds) (1999) The Role of Law and Legal Institutions in Asian Economic Development, New York: Oxford University Press.

*Practicing Attorney Law* (or Lawyers' Law) (1949, as amended). Law No. 205 of 1949. Online: <http://www.nichibenren.or.jp/en/about/pdf/practicing_attorney_law.pdf>

Sakumoto, N., Kobayashi, M. and Shinya I. (eds) (2003) *Law, Development and Socio-Economic Changes in Asia*, Tokyo: Institute of Developing Economies.

Santos, A. (2006) 'The World Bank's uses of the "rule of law" promise in economic development', in Trubek, D. M. and Santos, A. (eds) *The New Law and Economic Development: a critical appraisal*, New York: Cambridge University Press, 253–300.

SIDA (2009) About the Department of Democratic Governance. Online: <http://www.sida.se/?d=502&language=en_US>

Sunaga, K. (2004).The Reshaping of Japan's Official Development Assistance (ODA) Charter, FASID Discussion Paper on Development Assistance No 3, Online: <http://www.mofa.go.jp/policy/oda/reform/paper0411.pdf>

Tanase, T. (2001) 'The empty space of the modern in Japanese law discourse', in D. Nelkin and J. Feest (eds) *Adapting Legal Cultures*, Oxford: Hart Publishing 187–98.

Taylor, V. L. (2009) 'Frequently asked questions about rule of law (why the answers matter and why they are so elusive)', *Hague Journal of Rule of Law*, 1: 46–52.

——(in press) 'Legal education as development', in S. Steele (ed.) *Legal Education in Asia*, Melbourne: Routledge.

——(2007) 'The Law Reform Olympics: measuring technical legal assistance in transition economies', in T. Lindsey (ed.) *Law Reform in Developing and Transitional States*, London: Routledge.

——(2005) 'New markets, new commodity: Japanese legal technical assistance', *Wisconsin International Law Journal*, 23(2):2 51–81.

Trubek, D. M. (2006) 'The "rule of law" in development assistance: past, present and future', in D. M. Trubek and A. Santos (eds) *The New Law and Economic Development: a critical appraisal*, New York: Cambridge University Press, 74–94.

Trubek, D. M. and Santos, A. (2006), 'Introduction: the third moment in law and development theory: the emergence of a new critical practice', in D. M. Trubek and A. Santos (eds) *The New Law and Economic Development: a critical appraisal*, New York: Cambridge University Press, 1–18.

United States Institute for Peace (2009) *Recruitment of Rule of Law Specialists for the Civilian Response Corps*: USIPeace Briefing by Scott Carlson and Michael Dziedzic. Online: <http://www.usip.org/pubs/usipeace_briefings/2009/0106_rol_crc.html>

Upham, F. K. (1998) 'Weak legal consciousness as invented tradition', in S. Vlastos (ed.) *Mirror of Modernity: invented traditions of modern Japan*, Berkeley: University of California Press, 48–64.

Upham, F. (1987) *Law and Social Change in Postwar Japan*, Cambridge, Massachussetts: Harvard University Press.

Yabuki, K. (2008) *'Nihonbengoshi rengōkai to kokusaishihō shienkatsudō'* [Japan Federation of Bar Associations and International Activities to Support Justice] *Jurisuto* [*Jurist*], 1358: 9–16 (June).

Yamashita, T. and Tanaka, K. (2003) *Brief Introduction of Japan's Legal Assistance and the ICD*. Online: <http://www.moj.go.jp/ENGLISH/RATI/ICD/icd-02.pdf>

Yasuda, N. (2000) Tōnanajiahō [An Introduction to Southeast Asian Law] Tokyo: Nihonhyōronsha.

Wang, Tay-Sheng (1992) *Legal Reform in Taiwan under Japanese Colonial Rule* (1895–1945), Seattle: University of Washington Press.

White Paper on Official Development Assistance (2007) *Seifu kaihatsu enjo (ODA) hakusho 2007ban: 'Nihon no kokusai kyōryoku'* [2007 White Paper on Official Development Assistance (ODA): 'Japan's International Cooperation']. Online: <http://www.mofa.go.jp/mofaj/gaiko/oda/shiryo/hakusyo/07_hakusho_pdf/pdfs/07_hakusho_020203.pdf>

Riles, A. (ed.) (2001) *Rethinking the Masters of Comparative Law*, Oxford: Hart Publishing.

## Useful websites

Japan Federation of Bar Associations
<http://www.nichibenren.or.jp/en/index.html>
Liberal Democratic Party of Japan
<http://www.jimin.jp>

# Rule of law or Washington Consensus: the evolution of the World Bank's approach to legal and judicial reform

*Julio Faundez*

Since the 1980s, the World Bank has played a major role in promoting and implementing legal and judicial reform. Its innovative work in this area has contributed to bringing about a major shift in the way development specialists regard law and judicial institutions. The Bank's work in this area is also widely respected because, unlike other international agencies, it has made a serious effort to offer intellectual justification for its involvement in legal reform. Thus, today, any serious intellectual discussions on the role of legal systems in promoting markets, the link between institutions and economic growth, the concept of legal empowerment or the relationship between equity and development cannot afford to ignore the voluminous literature produced by the World Bank on these topics. But as well as being influential and highly respected for its role in the promotion of legal and judicial reform, the work of the Bank in this area has also been the target of severe and often well-deserved criticism. Some critics question the legitimacy of the Bank's involvement in this area of policy, as it is an area that is often regarded as highly political (Nader 2006, Ngugi 2006, Tshuma 2000). Others point out that the conceptualization and the means employed by the Bank to implement legal and judicial reform projects are inadequate as they fail to take into account the specific features of the countries in which the reforms are implemented (Alford 2000, Faundez 2001 and 2005, Dezalay and Garth 2002, Upham 2002). There are still other critics who claim that the reform process, though desirable, is a long and difficult process, since neither legal behaviour nor social practices can be changed overnight (Carrothers 2003, Davis 2004, Davis and Trebilcock 2001, Hammergren 2003). Thus, in different ways and from different perspectives, most critics raise questions about the legitimacy, methodology and efficacy of the Bank's involvement in legal and judicial reform.

Bank critics raise issues that deserve serious consideration. Their criticism, however, is often overly general and, as such, ignores the evolution of the Bank's approach to legal and judicial reform. Indeed, the Bank's approach has not been static. It has undergone an interesting evolution that is worth recounting because it shows the overriding influence of the Washington Consensus on the reform process. Indeed, although over the years there has been enormous pressure to shift the reform process towards a comprehensive approach that takes into account social and political dimensions of the law, the Bank has, in the end, resolutely stuck to the principles of economic deregulation and liberalization embodied in the Washington Consensus (Williams 1999). This outcome, however, was not inevitable. Indeed, as the materials in this chapter show, although initially the reform process was aimed solely at creating rules and institutions to further the process of economic liberalization, the Bank soon came to the realization that it was unrealistic to expect that legal reform could be successfully carried out without also taking into account the institutional framework within which law is embedded. It was thus that the governance agenda became part of the process of legal reform. The linkage between law and governance brought about an extraordinary expansion of the scope of legal reform. Indeed, after the Bank linked governance with legal reform there was virtually no area of the law that could reasonably be excluded from the reform process. This development naturally diluted the Bank's original intention to circumscribe legal reform exclusively to the economic sphere. It also provided the Bank with an excellent opportunity to re-conceptualize the nature of the reform process and to place it within a broader framework of development. Although the Legal Department made some efforts in this direction – and even invited Amartya Sen (Sen 2006) to provide intellectual backing – in the event, the governance and legal reform agendas were placed firmly in the hands of Bank economists, who, espousing novel theories about the relationship between institutions and economic growth, restored the original link between legal reform and the Washington Consensus. Some would probably argue that, given the trends prevailing in the global economy and the central role that the Bank has played in peddling the Washington Consensus, this outcome is not surprising. Yet those who are genuinely interested in ensuring that law and legal institutions make a positive contribution not only to economic but also to social and political development will probably find it difficult to celebrate an outcome that circumscribes legal and judicial reform within such narrow limits. Moreover, those interested in the promotion of a democratic rule of law also have reasons to be concerned. Indeed, although law is today correctly seen as part of governance, the governance agenda, as currently conceived by the Bank, pays scant attention to the complexity of legal and institutional reform and neglects basic aspects of the legal system without which a democratic rule of law is not feasible. Within this framework, the place assigned to law is largely restricted to restraining governments and facilitating commercial intercourse. Under these circumstances, it is unlikely that the Bank's much-flaunted objective of strengthening the rule of law to empower citizens and ensure their effective participation in development has a serious chance of success (World Bank 2004). The Bank's failure, probably welcomed by its critics, will have dire consequences for international efforts to promote the rule of law and democratization.

This chapter is divided into five sections. The first describes how the legal-reform process became part of the Bank's development agenda and why its original objectives were relatively modest. The second section examines some of the persistent difficulties encountered by the Bank in the implementation of its judicial-reform projects. The third section assesses the Bank's response to these difficulties and, in particular, highlights the Bank's failure to take seriously Amartya Sen's suggestion that it should carry out an in-depth study of the link between law and development. The fourth section explains how Bank economists have successfully managed to tame the unruly governance agenda, placing it firmly at the service of the Washington Consensus. This process has had the effect of reinvigorating the demands for deregulation, as exemplified by the prescriptions and rankings found in *Doing Business*, the Bank's most successful publication. The fifth section explores the link between *Doing Business* and legal reform.

## A cautious start

The Bank's involvement in legal and judicial reform dates back to the late 1980s and was preceded by considerable debate within the Bank (Faundez 1997). Those who advocated bringing law into the Bank's agenda had to overcome two related questions. First, whether there exists a link between legal reform and economic development, the Bank's main objective under its Charter; and second, even if law does have a bearing on development, whether the Bank should intervene in an area of policy that hitherto had been regarded as highly political. The shift in the paradigm of development economics from a state-centred to a market-based approach – as embodied in the Washington Consensus – made it easy to overcome these objections. The Consensus required a massive institutional transformation, which, naturally, could not ignore the legal dimension. The need to bring about this transformation was underscored by two factors: the failure of structural adjustment policies in developing countries, which was widely attributed to the weakness of their institutions, rather than to the nature of the policies prescribed by these programmes; and the end of the Cold War and the subsequent transition to a market economy in Russia and other countries hitherto under the military, political and economic influence of the Soviet Union.

As Klaus Decker explains in his contribution to this volume, Ibrahim Shihata, the General Counsel, had the task of setting out the parameters of the Bank's involvement in legal reform (see also Barron 2005: 13, Santos 2006: 269–71). Shihata's approach was low-key, but unambiguous. Legal reform, according to Shihata, was meant to serve the overriding objective of transforming state-centred development policies into market-based policies. Thus, Shihata and his team in the Legal Department proposed that legal rules and institutions should be market-friendly so that the two key institutions of a market economy – private property and contract – could function unencumbered either by arbitrary state action or by undue influence of local elites. In order to achieve this objective, Shihata called for a legal system based on general rules that are effectively enforced, authoritatively interpreted by an independent judiciary and, when necessary, amended through legitimate procedures. Any similarity between the type of legal system required by developing and transition countries and some strands of legal positivism was not coincidental, but intentional. Indeed, it was only by putting forward a narrow positivistic and formalistic conception of law that Shihata could reassure his senior colleagues, as well as officials from developing and transition countries, that the Bank's involvement in legal reform did not entail an expansion of the Bank's brief into areas hitherto deemed political. The determination to avoid contaminating legal reform with political issues is borne out by the fact that the first documents in which the Bank justified its involvement in legal and judicial reform carefully avoided any mention of contested concepts such as democracy or human rights (see also Hammergren in this volume).

The Bank's initial strategy conceived the legal system as a purely procedural mechanism with no particular political orientation and neutral in relation to moral and ideological issues. This notion was ideally suited for the purpose of spreading and consolidating at a global level the market-based policies prescribed by the Washington Consensus (Williamson 1999; Srinivasan 2000). These policies included deregulation, privatization, trade and financial liberalization, openness to direct foreign investment, reorientation of public expenditure, fiscal discipline and tax reform. The policies and assumptions underlying the Washington Consensus were easy to understand and, initially, even appealing since the preceding development paradigm, centred on the state and based on import substitution, had failed to deliver growth and was rapidly becoming redundant in a world dominated by corporations with global production and marketing strategies. The Washington Consensus also had a strong international underpinning since following the end of the Cold War market-based policies came to be regarded as the only viable alternative for securing better development outcomes. Countries reluctant or hesitant to embrace the Washington Consensus were soon brought into line by means of tough conditions attached to World Bank and IMF loans. An important factor that contributed to persuading developing countries to accept the new economic paradigm was the radical transformation of international legal institutions. Indeed, the establishment of the WTO in 1995, along with the vast network of investment treaties and regional trade agreements, enhanced the legitimacy of the new economic paradigm, as these legal instruments replicated and further developed the prescriptions of the Washington Consensus.

This favourable background enabled the Bank to launch a major process of legal and institutional reform aimed at dismantling old state structures, shrinking state bureaucracies and establishing new rules and institutions to regulate foreign investment, international trade, competition policy and capital markets. The reform process was initially quite successful as, one after another, most developing and transition countries requested assistance to adapt their legal institutions to the requirements of the new economic policy. During this period Bank officials played a key role in advising and assisting governments in drafting economic legislation, establishing competition commissions and setting up new structures to regulate the financial sector. Thus, during this initial phase, the Bank's cautious conceptualization of legal reform seemed to be amply justified. Indeed, although the Washington Consensus envisaged a drastically reduced role for the state in the economy, it also called for a corresponding strengthening of legal systems to ensure adequate protection for property rights and prompt enforcement of contracts. The expectation was that this dual transformation would release market forces from the constraints imposed by excessive state intervention and that a rejuvenated legal system, acting as a neutral arbiter, would facilitate the operation of the market, bringing about growth and prosperity.

During the initial phase of the legal-reform process, the Bank was careful to point out that new laws had to take into account and respect prevailing institutions. In particular, the Bank noted the importance that legal culture and other traditions have in shaping legal institutions (World Bank 1995). During this phase, the Bank also assigned a major role to legal experts in the process of designing and implementing programmes of legal reform. At first, most of these experts were drawn from international law firms based in Washington, London and New York, although the Bank was careful to advise developing countries to diversify their pool of legal consultants to ensure that their legal advice was sensitive to local conditions. Matters worsened as the Bank reform portfolio expanded to include judicial reform. While it is relatively easy to import, copy or impose legal rules, reforming complex legal institutions, such as national judiciaries, is far from simple. Since the initial strategy envisaged legal systems that would promptly enforce the law, the Bank could not avoid taking on board the task of reforming judiciaries. Unfortunately, however, the Bank plunged into this area of reform without adequate preparation (Faundez 2005).

Instead of making an effort to understand the specific institutional features of judiciaries country-by-country or even region-by-region, it assessed the quality of judiciaries in developing countries in terms of an ideal model of how judiciaries in well-ordered and mature capitalist societies should work. Unsurprisingly, the picture that emerged from this exercise was bleak, as the Bank found that courts in developing countries are not always independent from the government, that judges are regularly influenced by special interests, that powerful parties often misuse civil and criminal procedure, that court officials are corrupt, that members of the legal profession do not always observe their code of ethics, that laws are not easy to find and courts' decisions are mostly unreported, that courts do not consistently apply sound principles of interpretation, that judges do not have adequate support systems, that Ministers of Justice tend to undermine judicial independence, and that Finance Ministers regularly deny resources to the justice sector since they do not regard justice as a priority sector.

The Bank's bleak diagnosis of the state of the judiciary in developing countries was perhaps useful as a starting point, but insufficient to launch a global process of judicial reform. Judiciaries are complex institutions that operate within a constellation of state institutions in a variety of social and political environments. They cannot be easily changed or replaced without affecting the operation and behaviour of other institutions and actors. Therefore, before embarking on projects to improve judiciaries, it is necessary to have a reasonable understanding of their role and place in the country targeted for reform. It is necessary to understand how the legal system in that country works and how its various components relate to each other. In particular, it is important to bear in mind that different legal traditions operate in different ways and that what may appear as a failing from the perspective of one tradition could well be regarded as a virtue from the perspective of another tradition (Chodosh 2002, Finnegan 2006, Jensen 2003). When carrying out assessments of court performance, account should also be taken of the role of the legal profession and of the way legal education is structured. It is also essential to take into account political and social developments in the country targeted for reform and to understand how political institutions have evolved, how effective they are, how they interact with one another, whether the government effectively controls the whole of the country's territory, what political and ethnic cleavages exist and the impact they may have on political and legal processes, how groups excluded from the exercise of basic civil and political rights manage their community affairs and how they relate to public authorities. This type of inquiry is undoubtedly difficult and costly. Yet, if the objective is to achieve sustainable improvements in the justice system of a country, it is unavoidable.

## Judicial reform: obstacles and outcomes

The available evidence suggests that the Bank did not carry out the type of inquiry outlined above before launching its ambitious judicial reform projects (Faundez 2001 and 2005, Lerrick 2002, Messick 1999). In the absence of adequate country assessments it is difficult to discern the criteria employed by the Bank in designing its reform projects. As a consequence, most projects include long lists of activities without indicating priorities and set unrealistic timetables for completion. These activities include building infrastructure for courts, designing and implementing automated information systems, modernizing the organizational and functional capabilities of courts, establishing career paths for judicial and administrative personnel, strengthening the transparency of the judicial branch, introducing alternative dispute-resolution mechanisms to improve access to justice, establishing programmes to promote awareness of the legal needs of disadvantaged groups, especially aimed at women, young people and indigenous people, implementation of mobile court programmes, establishing legal-aid clinics, strengthening public defenders' offices and improving the efficiency of judicial services for small businesses.

This daunting list of activities – drawn largely from a World Bank project in Honduras – is found in most judicial reform projects (World Bank 2005c; see also Honduras Project website). While it is undisputable that judiciaries in most developing countries would benefit from improvement in all these areas, it is unrealistic to assume that progress can be made simultaneously in all these areas, without taking into account the social conditions and institutional framework in recipient countries. Indeed, I am certain that anyone familiar with Honduras' political and legal systems would regard the aims of this project as overambitious and unrealistic. Even assuming that progress could be made in all these areas at the same time, it is unlikely that the World Bank, or for that matter any external agency, has the expertise, experience or capacity to bring such an ambitious programme of reform to a successful conclusion.

Despite the conceptual shortcomings identified above, Bank projects have had some positive outcomes. Although the Bank has been reluctant to carry out a full independent evaluation of its work in legal and judicial reform, useful information about the outcomes of projects can be found in its Implementation Completion Reports (ICRs) – evaluations (available on the Bank's website) prepared upon completion of projects by Bank officials not involved in the design or implementation of the projects. For example, the ICR for a project in Morocco reveals that court delays in commercial courts were significantly reduced and that the enforcement of judgments registered an improvement of 66 per cent (World Bank 2004a). A project in Tanzania was found to have enhanced the government's capacity to formulate a coherent policy towards the justice sector, to have provided a catalyst for the emergence of a national consensus on the importance of the legal system as a means to further the process of development and to have prompted the government to begin investing in the physical and logistical infrastructure of the legal system (World Bank 2001; see also Tanzania Project website.). In Ecuador, court-annexed mediation centres introduced by the Bank's project were found to have inspired the government to adopt this model on a national scale. Moreover, the ICR for Ecuador claims that the legal-aid clinics introduced by the project contributed to reduce the probability of severe physical violence against women by 17 per cent and also increased the probability of their children attending school by 4.8 per cent (World Bank 2003b).

These are impressive claims and, despite the lack of rigour of the method employed to compile the evidence, I have no reason to believe that they are unjustified. The question, however, is whether the positive outcomes brought about by Bank projects are firmly linked to national development priorities and whether they are sustainable. Have commercial courts in Morocco continued to make progress in reducing delays? Has their good practice filtered through to other courts in the country? Does legal reform continue to play such an important role in Tanzania's development strategy? Are court-annexed mediation centres in Ecuador still part of the country's national policy? I do not know the answer to these questions, but I would not be surprised if the interest of local officials and judges in the reform process decreased shortly after the completion of these projects as they became embroiled in other equally important matters.

Securing the sustainability of any institutional reform project is undoubtedly difficult. This difficulty is compounded when projects are implemented without a basic understanding of local conditions. Thus, as well as some considerable achievements, Bank officials have encountered serious problems during the implementation stage. In some cases, judicial reform programmes have been launched even though a prudent assessment of prevailing political conditions would have counselled to proceed with utmost caution. In Ecuador, for example, despite the achievements mentioned above, the implementation of the project was seriously affected by persistent political instability (World Bank 2003b). During the life of the project there were seven Presidents of the Republic and as many Ministers of Justice, making it unlikely that any institutional improvement achieved by the project could be sustainable. It should be noted as well that after the completion of the project the whole of the Supreme Court was sacked and the country spent nearly a year without a Supreme Court. More recently, the World Bank's representative in Ecuador was expelled from the country, although the issue that prompted his expulsion had nothing to do with the Bank's legal or judicial reform project. In Russia, a legal reform project was rushed through by the Bank's internal approval process in order to support the speedy implementation of the privatization programme – generally known as the Big Bang policy – which was also promoted by the Bank (World Bank 2005d). As it turned out, however, neither the Big Bang economic policy nor the hastily assembled judicial reform project was successful (Hoff and Stiglitz 2004, United States General Accounting Office 2001). In Bolivia, the aims of the legal and judicial reform project were never clearly defined as some Bank officials wanted the project to concentrate on improving the efficiency of courts, so as to support market-based policies, while stakeholders within the judiciary favoured long-term structural reform (World Bank 2000a). In Georgia the Bank's project lost its initial impetus when the government failed to fulfil its commitment to provide the necessary financial resources (World Bank 2004b).

Problems associated with chronic political instability or faltering political commitment by the authorities in recipient countries are exacerbated by unrealistic and exaggerated expectations. In Kazakhstan, for example, one of the objectives of the project was to strengthen judicial independence. Yet those who designed the project failed to take into account that the political elites had no experience of constitutionalism and hence could not be easily persuaded to accept the notion of separation of powers (World Bank 2003a; see Kazakhstan Project website). Those who designed the reform project in Kazakhstan would have done well if they had taken into account the experience of many Latin American states which, after two centuries of experimenting with constitutions, are still unable to build political regimes that fully respect the principle of separation of powers. A better approach in the case of Kazakhstan would have been to set less ambitious, but achievable, intermediate goals. In Tanzania, the project had expected to introduce modern management information systems into some legal sector organisations such as the Office of the Registrar of

Companies, but the goal could not be achieved as the complex nature of such technological innovation was seriously underestimated by those who designed the project (World Bank 2001).

## Amartya Sen's Challenge

By the late 1990s, the Bank was fully aware that some of its legal projects were confronting serious difficulties. Critics from various quarters pointed out that the Bank's ambitious projects were not yielding the expected benefits (United States General Accounting Office 2001), that some of the project components were wasting valuable financial resources (Lawyers Committee for Human Rights 1995) and that in some cases the Bank's proposed participation in judicial-reform projects had the indirect effect of supporting unpalatable regimes (Lawyers Committee for Human Rights 2000). The Bank's Legal Department took these criticisms seriously and some of its publications stressed that the reform projects could not be imposed from outside, that local ownership was essential to ensure success of the project, that top-down approaches do not work, that participatory processes are more likely to be successful and that those who design projects should ensure that local officials and elites have the political will to carry them out. The Bank also accepted that the advice it had offered in the recent past had not always been sensitive to the importance of the local context, partly because of the excessive demand for technical assistance. Thus, 'one size does not fit all' became a frequently used phrase in the Bank's publications (World Bank 2000b). Despite the misgivings about the outcome, timing and suitability of some legal projects, the place of law in the Bank's development agenda was not under immediate threat. On the contrary, while the Bank's critics raised questions about the efficacy of legal-reform projects in the late 1990s, the Bank was developing the notion of a Comprehensive Development Framework (CDF), which implicitly guaranteed a place for law in the development enterprise.

The CDF, defined by the Bank as a process rather than a blueprint, characterizes development as a holistic process in which no single component – be it markets, education, gender equality or dams – has priority over any other. Thus, the social and political dimensions of development, such as achieving gender equality and empowering the poor, have the same, if not higher, priority as market-friendly policies (World Bank 1999). Indeed, the CDF suggests that the eradication of poverty and other social goals cannot be achieved without political action at the grass roots (Blake 2000). The implications of this shift in the Bank's rhetoric for law were naturally quite significant. Although the documents mentioned above do not explicitly refer to the rule of law, the rhetoric of empowerment and participation suggest that the Bank was beginning to move away from a conception of legal systems as passive receptacles of economic policies, towards a conception of law and legal institutions as essential instruments to further the interests of the poor and other disadvantaged groups.

Not surprisingly, the Legal Department began to consider ways of readjusting the Bank's legal strategy to fit with the new and more ambitious approach reflected in the CDF. It convened a massive international conference, held in Washington in November 2000, with the objective of setting an agenda for a just and equitable society in the twenty-first century (Van Puymbroeck 2001). At the conference, some 600 judges, government ministers, academics, members of NGOs and Bank officials exchanged views about their experience and their proposals to improve and expand the legal-reform agenda. The proceedings of the conference were published in 2001, but curiously did not include the keynote paper delivered by Amartya Sen. Instead, his paper was buried in the Bank's website and only published in 2006 by the World Bank Legal Review, together with the proceedings of another World Bank Conference (smaller in scale than the one held in 2000), at which Sen did not participate (Sen 2006).

I am sure that there is a perfectly good explanation for not including Sen's paper in the book of the first conference, which he attended, and for publishing his paper six years later, in the proceedings of a conference which he did not attend and to which he was perhaps not even invited. What I find odd about the delay in publishing this paper is that it addresses the central question that had prompted the Legal Department to convene the conference: what is the role of legal and judicial reform in the development process? Sen's answer to this question is worth recounting because his paper poses a major challenge, which the Bank chose to ignore.

Sen's answer to the question concerning the role of law in development is based on his well-known view that development is not only about economic growth, as measured by standard indices such as GDP per capita or capital accumulation (Sen 2000b). Development, in his view, is a broader process that should aim at enhancing people's capabilities. As such, development practitioners and scholars should take into account all the domains of social life – economic, social, political and legal – since they all have a bearing on the development process. Thus, from his perspective, the different spheres of social life cannot be considered independently of each other. Economic growth without social equity or economic redistribution without effective political participation could hardly be regarded as making a meaningful contribution to development. Conceptual integrity, according to Sen, requires that we regard all these different domains as part of a single process, since each plays an equally important role in enhancing people's capabilities. Thus, within Sen's conceptualization, even if it were established that law did not contribute one iota to economic growth, law's central role in the process of development would not be questioned (Sen 2006: 38).

As it happens, Sen believes that law does make an important contribution to both economic growth and other domains of social life. Yet he cautions that while law's contribution to economic growth is crucial, its role is not self-evident. Because social life is complex, it is necessary carefully to investigate the causal interconnections between the economic, social, political and legal domains in order to understand the role of law in development. He points out, for example, that it would be futile to extend rights to economically and socially deprived individuals without simultaneously overcoming the obstacles that prevent them from exercising these rights. Thus, Sen's advice is that if the Bank wishes to design an effective strategy for legal and judicial reform, it should investigate the interconnection between law and all the other spheres of social life. Focussing on the link between law and markets, though important, is insufficient (Sen 2006: 47–48).

Bank lawyers probably welcomed Sen's point that the role of law in the development process is important, even if it were established that it does not directly contribute to economic growth. Yet neither the lawyers from the Legal Department nor officials from any other department at the Bank followed up Sen's recommendation to carry out detailed research on the link between law and other social spheres. Instead, after considerable bickering over which department within the Bank should have overall control of legal and judicial reform, and some minor adjustments to the rhetoric of legal reform, the practice of legal and judicial reform remained virtually unchanged.

### Taming the governance agenda

Bank economists would probably regard Sen's approach to development as a costly diversion from the objectives of the Washington Consensus. Moreover, since his approach calls for Bank involvement in areas of social practice in which the tools of economic analysis cannot be easily deployed, his approach also poses an indirect threat to the economists' intellectual dominance within the Bank. While economists can easily develop econometric models to gauge the impact of trade liberalization on rates of economic growth or the impact of deregulation on levels of GDP, assessing the impact of access to justice policies or policies that seek to improve citizens' participation requires an entirely different methodology (Lerrick 2002, Messick 1999, Posner 1998). Yet, although Bank economists may have good reasons for disagreeing with Sen, they could not easily ignore the difficulties encountered by most countries in the implementation of Washington Consensus policies. Therefore, whether willingly or not, they had no choice but to expand their intellectual horizons and explore areas that hitherto development economists had largely ignored. It was thus that 'governance' and the slogan 'institutions matter' began to make their way into the Bank's agenda (Kaufmann et al. 1999).

Although initially the Bank's use of the concept of governance was somewhat vague – suggesting, perhaps, that it was merely used as a substitute for the political concepts of government and regime – today it is fully consistent with the economic policies promoted by the Bank. The process that has led to a clearer conceptualization of the notion of governance has reinforced the role of law in the development agenda, but its orientation and its content are firmly subordinated to the requirements of the Washington Consensus, as interpreted by

Bank economists. In this way, the outcome of this process entails a total rejection of Sen's often-quoted observation that 'even if legal development were not to contribute one iota to economic development … legal and judicial reform would be a critical part of the development process' (Sen 2000a:10).

The Bank's rationale for turning its attention to governance was simply that weak institutions in developing and transition countries were hindering the success of market-based policies introduced under the aegis of the Washington Consensus. The first step was to augment the Washington Consensus to include new components such as corporate governance, anti-corruption, financial codes and standards, flexible labour markets, the implementation of WTO Agreements, establishment of social safety nets and the development of targeted policies of poverty reduction (Rodrik 2002). Addressing each of these new components requires reforming or changing a wide range of institutions, and the governance agenda expanded at a rapid pace. There were 45 items in the new good governance agenda in 1997, by 1999 there were 66 items and by 2003 there were 116 (Grindle 2004: 528). The measures and policies of this new agenda included checks and balances in government, decentralization, efficient and independent judiciaries, sound regulatory systems, civil-service reform, transparent budgeting processes, land reform, community development, asset-creation strategies for the poor, environmental protection, empowering the poor and knowledge development (Grindle 2004: 528).

The rapid expansion of the governance agenda is hardly surprising. Institutional change is complex, especially in the public sector where institutions are closely interrelated so that any attempt to reform one institution often requires attention to several others that are directly or indirectly related to it.

The numerous reforms proposed by the governance agenda placed an unbearable stress on most targeted countries, especially on those that had the greatest need for change because of their weak institutional capacity. Moreover, countries required to implement such a lengthy agenda were not provided with any indication of the relative priority among the proposed reforms or their mutual interdependence. Thus, Merilee Grindle, a leading development expert, advised the Bank that instead of promoting an agenda that seeks to achieve an ideal state of good governance, it should focus on more modest goals, which she describes as 'good enough governance' (Grindle 2004: 530). According to Grindle, a good-enough governance agenda would carefully seek to identify the needs of individual countries and its recommendations would be appropriately calibrated to the needs of those particular countries. It would also provide clear guidance on how and when to implement specific policy recommendations.

The Bank took notice of at least one of Grindle's suggestions. It circumscribed the scope of its governance agenda. Yet it did not follow her advice to carry out a detailed country assessment of governance needs. Instead, the Bank's approach was to rein in the governance agenda and place it firmly within the framework of the Washington Consensus. It thus defined improvements in governance as improvements in the economic functions of the public sector. These improvements in turn comprise three dimensions: making and implementing economic policy; delivering social, legal and regulatory services; and securing accountability for the use of public resources and public regulatory powers. In order to address each of these three dimensions the Bank decided to focus its efforts on what it describes as core public institutions, which include the civil service, public-expenditure management, tax administration, public-enterprise reform and legal and judicial reform (World Bank 2000b).

As well as providing a more precise definition of the governance agenda, the Bank also acknowledged the shortcomings of most of its projects in the area of institutional reform. It acknowledged that, hitherto, its approach had been technocratic, focusing largely on government interlocutors, and largely insensitive to wider demands for change. It also recognized that its institutional-reform projects had been based on the incorrect assumption that one size fits all, whereas the correct approach would have been to focus on good fits. The Bank also acknowledged that its lending instruments were defective, as they did not allow enough time for the implementation of institutional-reform projects. It should be noted that the Bank's exercise in self-criticism applies especially to its portfolio of legal- and judicial-reform projects. Indeed, at the turn of the century, just before the publication of this assessment, legal- and judicial-reform projects were one of the top three areas of Bank expenditure in institutional reform. The other two were decentralization and financial management (World Bank 2000b: 3).

The Bank's decision to control the inordinate expansion of the governance agenda was undoubtedly correct, since not every failing in governance can be addressed at the same time. Its decision to focus more rigorously on the economic aspects of governance was also right, since the Bank does not have the expertise or the mandate to tackle every aspect of governance. Indeed, the Bank's emphasis on economic governance was simply a return to Shihata's original aspiration of securing institutional frameworks that are friendly to market-based policies. The Bank's assessment of the shortcomings of its work in the area of institutional reform is also correct, since institutional reform cannot be effective unless it is properly targeted, based on an adequate understanding of the needs of the local institutional environment, and unless the promoters of the reform process acknowledge that institutional change is slow and complex. Yet, although the Bank, along with the International Monetary Fund, was careful to ensure that the governance agenda did not deviate from the principles of the Washington Consensus, it did not move away from the 'one size fits all' approach repudiated in its self-criticism. Indeed, with the intellectual support of a small group of US-based economists, the Bank has embraced an approach to the link between institutions and economic growth that reaffirms the notion that one size fits all and implicitly rejects the notion that institutional change is a slow process (Botero et al. 2003, Glaeser et al. 2004, Hay et al. 1996, La Porta et al. 1999, López-de-Silanes 2002).

The Bank's confidence that institutional reform is both desirable and achievable in the short term is reflected in its recently adopted policy of publishing annual country rankings on the quality of governance and on the ease of doing business. These rankings award the highest points to countries that introduce reforms consistent with the institutional models advocated by the Bank.

The intellectual basis for the Bank's confidence that institutions provide an answer to the mystery of economic growth is drawn from a series of studies that relate cross-country data on GDP growth and levels of GDP per capita to several measures of institutional quality. Institutional quality is generally measured by three standards: the quality of governance (level of corruption, political rights, public-sector efficiency), the extent to which private property is protected, and institutional restraints placed on political leaders. In general, these studies confirm the intuition that in high-income countries the quality of institutions is high, while the opposite is the case in low-income countries. More specifically, these studies demonstrate that institutions have a statistically significant impact on levels of GDP per capita and on the level of growth generally. Indeed, according to an IMF study, variations in the quality of institutions explain three quarters of cross-country variations (IMF 2003: 98).

Although these studies do not purport to establish a causal connection between economic growth and institutions, but merely a correlation, the Bank, as well as the IMF, has relied on these findings to argue that improvements in the quality of institutions will inevitably bring about improvements in economic growth. Thus, for example, the IMF argues that if countries in sub-Saharan Africa were to improve the quality of their institutions to the mean of developing countries in Asia, their income per capita would increase by 80 per cent; that is, from $800 to over $1,400 (IMF 2003: 106). This claim is impressive, but misleading, as it suggests that there is a causal link between economic outcomes and the quality of institutions. Indeed, most of the studies that link institutions to economic outcomes are careful to note that they only identify statistically significant correlations, not causal links. The reason for this caution is that these studies have not yet resolved the thorny issue regarding the endogeneity of institutions; that is, whether institutions are the consequence of successful economies or whether they are external factors that bring about the desired economic outcomes. Moreover, the claim that improvements in the quality of institutions can bring about improvements in economic growth is far too general to be useful, as it does not tell us which institutions have to be changed in order to achieve the desired goals.

Aware that these studies, though intellectually stimulating, do not yet provide a reliable guide for policy recommendations, the Bank and the IMF have adopted an eclectic approach. While acknowledging that these studies do not establish an undisputed link between better institutions and improved rates of growth, they point out that causality is a two-way street: that institutions have an effect on economic outcomes as much as some economic outcomes and economic policies contribute to strengthen institutions' development. Policies that allegedly have a positive effect on institutions include trade openness, stronger competition and financial liberalization (IMF 2003: 101). Bank and IMF publications also place special emphasis on the impact that membership of international organizations, such as the EU, the WTO and regional trade agreements, has in promoting and setting the direction of national economic policies (IMF 2005: 144).

As well as adopting an eclectic approach to the link between institutions and growth, the Bank and the Fund have recently begun, albeit indirectly, to challenge the widely held view that institutional reform is a long-term process (IMF 2005: 132, IMF 2003: 112). They point out, for example, that the pace and direction of institutional change in countries in Central and Eastern Europe has been rapid and generally very positive. A similar argument is made in relation to post-conflict countries such as Kosovo, Afghanistan and Timor-Leste (IMF 2003: 112). Moreover, relying on statistics drawn from the International Country Risk Guide (ICRG), the IMF points out that most regions of the world made significant progress in the observance of the rule of law in the early 1990s. It should be noted that the concept of rule of law employed by ICRG is quite narrow (contract and property) and based largely on a small sample of business people's and lawyers' perceptions. In any event, the eclectic approach to the issue of causality and the argument that institutional change is not necessarily slow are handy since they enable the Bank and the IMF to reaffirm the validity of Washington Consensus policies, within the framework of governance and institutional reform.

## *Doing Business* and legal reform

The Bank's confidence that institutional change and positive economic outcomes are easily achievable through clever institutional design is reflected in its annual survey entitled *Doing Business* (World Bank 2004, 2007). This survey, which was launched in 2003 and is today the Bank's largest circulating publication, ranks countries in terms of their policies towards business. Those that achieve the highest ranking are those that do not over-regulate businesses or establish procedural obstacles that slow down market transactions. Annual surveys also contain detailed advice on how to reform or manage public policy in various areas relating to business. Among the favourite topics in these annual surveys are the well-known delays that businesses people experience when they register companies, enforce contracts or simply when they have to relate to government bureaucrats. The information on these topics updates and further develops the data presented some years ago by Hernando De Soto (1986) in his bestselling book *The Other Path*. These surveys do not tell us, however, why these problems persist, even though lawyers, politicians and development specialists have been aware of them for quite some time. Could it be that over-regulation in developing countries, which the editors of *Doing Business* identify as the cause of market inefficiency, is in fact a consequence of more complex problems that cannot be easily resolved by clever social engineering?

The editors of *Doing Business* are not, however, interested in the root cause of the problem of over-regulation. Instead, their objective is to provide a simple package of measures that supposedly can easily resolve the problem. Unsurprisingly, these measures are all based on the assumption that any form of regulation is suspect and the politicians' appetite for regulation should not be allowed to spoil the operation of the market (Berg and Cazes 2007, Davis 2007). While it is undisputed that over-regulation should, by definition, be avoided, the steps that countries should take to achieve this objective are not self-evident. The contributors to *Doing Business*, however, appear to assume that there is a single way of doing things right for business and that there is a single model of reforms that all states should follow if they wish to be friendly to business. This point is well demonstrated through the example of labour regulation.

## The 'right' way to regulate labour

For example, in the area of labour regulation the authors of *Doing Business* award low marks to countries that have laws that afford basic protection to workers consistent with international labour standards sanctioned by the ILO. So countries that set minimum wages above 25 per cent of GDP per capita, set a maximum working week below sixty-six hours, require advance notice for dismissal or provide specific procedures for job termination are awarded low marks in the *Doing Business* Index on Employing Workers, on the grounds that their labour laws are unfriendly to business (World Bank 2007). By contrast, the Index awards the highest points to countries such as Saudi Arabia which do not allow freedom of association, the right to organise or collective bargaining. Countries that introduce mechanisms to reduce the number of hours that count as overtime, that discard extra pay for overtime and that allow companies to sidestep unions when they make workers redundant are also singled out as good examples of friendliness towards business.

Prominent US politicians and representatives of the international trade-union movement have made strong representations to the World Bank over their recommendations in the area of labour law. Indeed, on 13 October 2006, six US Senators wrote a strongly worded letter to Paul Wolfowitz, the Bank's President, pointing out that the 2007 edition of *Doing Business* was recommending practices that discouraged countries from complying with established international labour standards (Engler 2006). They also pointed out that these recommendations were inconsistent with the labour standards that the US Government encourages developing countries to adopt through its programme of Generalized System of Preferences. They thus urged Wolfowitz to reaffirm the Bank's commitment to the protection of workers' rights and ensure that the Bank should coordinate with the ILO whenever it issues public statements on matters relating to labour. The unions have also made representations to the Bank. Peter Bakvis, from the International Confederation of Free Trade Unions, has pointed out that if countries in sub-Saharan Africa were to follow the Bank's recommendation and keep their minimum wage under 25 per cent of GDP per capita, the minimum wage in most countries would be less than one dollar a day – a figure that is difficult to reconcile with one of the Millenium

Development Goals of reducing the proportion of people living on less than a dollar a day by half (Bakvis 2006, 2007).

Bakvis also points out that the analysis and recommendations on labour law contained in *Doing Business* have a major impact on the policies that the Bank, as well as the IMF, requires states to adopt when they review their investment climate, assess country policies for the purposes of approving loans or carry out surveillance reviews under Article IV of the IMF Articles of Agreement.[1] Thus it appears that the editors of *Doing Business*, who are largely economists, have more influence in determining the nature and content of the process of legal reform than lawyers working for other departments of the Bank.

### Moving away from North

The editors of *Doing Business* have also definitely shifted the Bank's conception of governance away from Douglass North's historically rooted views about institutions, institutional change and governance (North 1990). Indeed, in the early 1990s Bank documents often quoted – approvingly – North's celebrated definition of institutions as humanly devised constraints that shape human interaction (North 1990:3). The Bank's approach to institutional reform, as reflected in *Doing Business* and in its practice, is not, however, fully consistent with North's conception of the link between institutional change and economic performance. First, while North points out that institutions comprise both formal and informal rules that govern social behaviour, the Bank approach to institutional reform all but ignores the role played by informal constraints, such as social conventions and codes of behaviour. Second, while North acknowledges that institutional change is slow and largely incremental, the Bank – committed as it is to annual country league tables – assumes that clever social engineering will instantly enable developing countries to establish institutions that took industrialised countries hundreds of years to achieve. Third, while North painstakingly points out that in order to construct a dynamic theory of change mainstream economics must take into account that institutional constraints vary radically through time and across different economies, the Bank, relying on a textbook notion of the way a market economy should work, identifies the ideal type of institutions that countries must establish in order to achieve a good place in international governance rankings. Thus, although the Bank often invokes North's work as authority for the proposition that institutions play a fundamental role in economic performance, its policy recommendations and operational policies do not fully take into account the complexity and depth of North's approach to the role of institutions in economic growth.

## Conclusion

Economic theories that postulate new interpretations about the relationship between institutions and economic growth have revived the Bank's and the

IMF's confidence that institutional reform is necessary and feasible. They have provided the basis for reaffirming the principles of the Washington Consensus. They have also been used to lend credibility to international rankings published in *Doing Business*, the Bank's influential annual survey. The new-found confidence in the possibility of rapidly achieving institutional reforms that will inexorably bring about improvements in economic outcomes contrasts sharply with the view of development experts, who continue to caution that institutional reform is a slow process (Sachs 2003), that there are no quick fixes for accelerating the transition to a market-based economy (Bardhan 2005) and that policy recommendations that assume that one size fits all do not generally succeed (Upham 2002).

The Bank's objective of ensuring that legal and judicial reform should be closely linked to a wider governance agenda is reasonable and desirable. Yet its determination to limit the scope of the reform process to that which serves the narrowly construed objectives of the Washington Consensus, in particular the goal of deregulation, is inconsistent with the ideal underlying the Bank's vision of development, as embodied in the Comprehensive Development Framework, according to which social and political objectives of development have the same, if not higher, priority as market-friendly policies. It is also inconsistent with the Bank's view that justice, equity and development are inseparable (World Bank 2005a).

Against this background, the revival of the one-size-fits-all approach, as reflected in the country rankings prepared by *Doing Business*, suggests that the Bank advocates and promotes, purposely or inadvertently, contradictory approaches to development. How else can one interpret the Bank's espousal of policies in the area of labour law that are inconsistent with basic international standards of human rights and which, if implemented, will inevitably hurt the same groups that the Bank claims it is seeking to protect and empower? The revival of the one-size-fits-all approach also entails a rejection of Amartya Sen's view that in order to develop an effective strategy for legal and judicial reform the Bank should carefully investigate the interconnections between law and other spheres of social life.

The Bank's decision to reaffirm the Washington Consensus and to quietly discard the alternative vision of development reflected in the Comprehensive Development Framework is regrettable. For under the current interpretation of the Washington Consensus, law continues to be seen as a negative device that protects citizens against power-hungry governments and provides a neutral mechanism for the development of market transactions. This view about the role of law is far too narrow as it neglects to take into account that law does not merely have an economic dimension, but is deeply embedded in all aspects of social life, including the all-important political process of democratization.

## Note

1 For an example of the impact of *Doing Business* indicators on national politics see Perry-Kessaris 2008: 126–27.

# References

Alford, W. P. (2000) 'Exporting the "pursuit of happiness"', *Harvard Law Review*, 113: 1677–1715.

Bakvis, P. (2006) *How the World Bank & IMF Use the Doing Business Report to Promote Labour Market Deregulation in Developing Countries*. Online: <http://www.gurn.info/en/topics/poverty-reduction-strategy-papers-prsps-and-international-financial-institutions-ifis/global-union-publications-statements-to-the-imf-and-world-bank/how-the-world-bank-and-imf-use-the-doing-business-report-to-promote-labour-market-deregulation-in-developing-countries-icftu-jun-06>

——(2007) 'Testimony of Peter Bakvis, Director Washington Office of the ITUC/Global Unions Before the Committee on Financial Services'. Online: <http://www.aflcio.org/mediacenter/prsptm/tm10032007.cfm>

Bardhan, P. (2005) 'Institutions matter, but which ones?' *Economics of Transition*, 13(3): 499–532.

Barron, G. (2005) *The World Bank and Rule of Law Reforms*, London School of Economics: Development Studies Institute, Working Paper Series No. 05–70. Online: <http://www.lse.ac.uk/collections/DESTIN/pdf/WP70.pdf>

Berg, J. and Cazes, S. (2007) *The Doing Business Indicators: measurement issues and political implications*, Geneva: ILO, Economic and Labour Market Paper 2007/6.

Blake, R. C. (2000) 'The World Bank's Draft Comprehensive Development Framework and the Micro Paradigm of Law and Development', *Yale Human Rights and Development Law Journal*, 3: 159–89.

Botero, J. C., La Porta, R., López-de-Silanes, F., Shleifer, A. and Volokh, A. (2003) 'Judicial Reform', *World Bank Research Observer*, 18(1): 61–88.

Carothers, T. (2003) *Promoting the Rule of Law Abroad – The Problem of Knowledge*, Washington: Carnegie Endowment for International Peace, Working Papers – Rule of Law Series – No. 34.

Chodosh, H. E. (2002) 'Reforming Judicial Reform Inspired by U.S. Models', *DePaul Law Review*, 52 (Winter): 351–81.

Davis, K. E. (2004) What can the rule of law variable tell us about rule of law reforms? *Michigan Journal of International Law*, 26: 141–61.

Davis, K. E. and Kruse, M. B. (2007) 'Taking the measure of law: the case of the *Doing Business* project', *Law & Social Inquiry*, 32(4): 1095–1119.

Davis, K. E. and Trebilcock, M. J. (2001) 'Legal reforms and development', *Third World Quarterly*, 22(1): 21–36.

De Soto, H. (1986) *El Otro Sendero*, Mexico: Editorial Diana.

Dezalay, Y. and Garth, B. G. (2002) 'Legitimating the new legal orthodoxy', in Dezalay, Y. and Garth, B. G. (eds) *Global Prescriptions: the production, exportation, and importation of a new legal orthodoxy*, Ann Arbor: University of Michigan Press, 306–34.

Engler, M. (2006) *Calling Bad Business Good*. Online: <http://www.tompaine.com/print/calling_bad_business_good.php>

Faundez, J. (2005) 'The rule of law enterprise: promoting a dialogue between practitioners and academics', *Democratization*, 12(4): 567–86.

——(2001) 'Legal reform in developing and transition countries – making haste slowly', in R. V. Van Puymbroeck (ed.) *Comprehensive Legal and Judicial Reform*, Washington DC: World Bank, 369–96.

——(1997) 'Legal technical assistance', in J. Faundez (ed.) *Good Government and Law*, London: Macmillan, 1–24.

Finnegan, D. L. (2006) 'Applied comparative law and judicial reform', *Thomas M. Cooley Journal of Practical and Clinical Law*, 8: 97–132.

Garth, B. G. (2002) 'Building strong and independent judiciaries through the new law and development: behind the paradox of consensus programs and perpetually disappointing results', *DePaul Law Review*, 52 (Winter): 383–400.

Glaeser, E. L., La Porta, R., López-de-Silanes, F. and Shleifer, A. (2004) 'Do Institutions cause growth?', *Journal of Economic Growth*, 9: 271–303.

Grindle, M. S. (2004) 'Good enough governance: poverty reduction and reform in developing countries', *Governance*, 17(4): 525–48.

Hammergren, L. (2003) 'International assistance to Latin American justice programs: towards and agenda for reforming the reformers', in E. G. Jensen and T. C. Heller (eds) *Beyond Common Knowledge*, Stanford: Stanford University Press, 290–335.

Hay, J. R., Shleifer, A. and Vishny, R. (1996) 'Towards a Theory of Legal Reform', *European Economic Review*, 40: 559–67.

Hoff, K. and Stiglitz, J. (2004) 'After the Big Bang? Obstacles to the emergence of the rule of law in Post-Communist societies', *American Economic Review*, 94(3): 753–63.

IMF (2003) *World Economic Outlook*, Washington DC: IMF.

——(2005) *World Economic Outlook*, Washington DC: IMF.

Jensen, E. G. (2003) 'The role of law and judicial reform: the political economy of diverse institutional patterns and reformers' response', in E. G. Jensen and T. C. Heller (eds) *Beyond Common Knowledge*, Stanford: Stanford University Press, 336–81.

Kaufmann, D., Kraay, A. and Zoido-Lobatón, P. (1999) *Governance Matters*, World Bank: Policy Research Working Paper 2/96.

La Porta, R., López-de-Silanes, F., Shleifer, A. and Vishny, R. (1999) 'The quality of government', *Journal of Law, Economics and Organization*, 15(1): 222–79.

Lawyers Committee for Human Rights (1995) *Halfway to Reform: the World Bank and the Venezuelan justice system*. Joint report by the Lawyers Committee for Human Rights and the Venezuelan Program for Human Rights Education and Action.

——(2000) *Building on Quicksand: the collapse of the juridical reform project in Perú*. Online: <http://www.humanrightsfirst.org/pubs/descriptions/perubuilding.htm>

Lerrick, A. (2002) 'Are World Bank claims of success credible?' *Carnegie Mellon Quarterly International Report*, March: 1–4.

López-de-Silanes, F. (2002) *The Politics of Legal Reform*, UNCTAD, G-24 Discussion Paper No. 17.

Messick, R. E. (1999) 'Judicial reform and economic development: a survey of the issues', *The World Bank Research Observer*, 14(1): 117–36.

Nader, L. (2006) 'Promise or plunder: a past and future look at law and development', *The World Bank Legal Review: law equity and development*, 2: 87–112.

Ngugi, J. M. (2006) 'The World Bank and the ideology of reform and development in international economic development discourse', *Cardozo Journal of International and Comparative Law*, 14: 313–45.

North, D. C. (1990) *Institutions, Institutional Change and Economic Performance*, Cambridge: Cambridge University Press.

Perry-Kessaris, A. (2008) *Global Business, Local Law: the Indian legal system as a communal resource in foreign investment relations*, Aldershot: Ashgate.

Posner, R. (1998) 'Creating a legal framework for economic development', *The World Bank Research Observer*, 13(1): 1–11.

Rodrik, D. (2002) After Neoliberalism, what? Online: <http://ksghome.harvard.edu/~drodrik/After%20Neoliberalism.pdf>

Sachs, Jefrey D. (2003) 'Institutions matter, but not for everything', *Finance and Development*, June: 38–41.

Santos, A. (2006) 'The World Bank's uses of the "rule of law" promise in economic development', in D. M. Trubek and A. Santos (eds) *The New Law and Economic Development* Cambridge: Cambridge University Press, 253–300.

Sen, A. (2006) 'What is the role of judicial reform in the development process?' *The World Bank Legal Review: law equity and development*, 2: 33–51.

——(2000a) 'What is the role of legal and judicial reform in the development process?' World Bank Legal Department Conference on the Role of Legal and Judicial Reform in Development, Washington, DC June 5, 2000. Online: <http://siteresources.worldbank.org/INTLAWJUSTINST/Resources/legalandjudicial.pdf>

——(2000b) *Development as Freedom*, Oxford: Oxford University Press.

Srinivasan, T. N. (2000) 'The Washington Consensus a decade later: ideology and the art of policy advice', *The World Bank Research Observer*, 15(2): 265–70.

Tshuma, L. (2000) 'The political economy of the World Bank's legal framework for economic development', in J. Faundez, M. E. Footer and J. J. Norton (eds) *Governance, Development and Globalization*, London: Blackstone Press, 7–27.

United States General Accounting Office (2001) *Former Soviet Union – U.S. Rule of Law Assistance Has Had Limited Impact and Sustainability* (GAO-01-740T).

Upham, F. (2002) *Mythmaking and the Rule of Law Orthodoxy*, Washington: Carnegie Endowment for International Peace, Working Papers – Rule of Law Series – No. 30.

Van Puymbroeck, R. V. (2001) *Comprehensive Legal and Judicial Reform*, Washington DC: World Bank.

Williamson, J. (1999) 'What should the Bank think about the Washington Consensus?' Online: <http://www.iie.com/publications/papers/paper.cfm?ResearchID=351>

World Bank (1995) *The World Bank and Legal Technical Assistance* – Initial Lessons, Washington DC: World Bank.

——(1999) *World Development Report 1999/2000 – Entering the 21st Century*, Washington DC: World Bank.

——(2000a) Implementation Completion Report on a Loan (SDR 7.6 million) on Regulatory and Judicial Reform (Bolivia), Washington DC: World Bank.

——(2000b) 'Reforming public institutions and strengthening governance: a World Bank strategy', Public Sector Group, Poverty Reduction and Economic Management Network, Washington DC: World Bank. Online: <http://www.worldbank.org/publicsector/Reforming.pdf>

——(2001) Implementation Completion Report on a Credit (SDR 14.6 million) for Financial and Legal Management Upgrading (Tanzania), Washington DC: World Bank.

——(2003a) Implementation Completion Report on a Loan (US$ 16.5 million) for a Legal Reform Project (Kazakhstan), Washington DC: World Bank.

——(2003b) Implementation Completion Report on a Loan (US$ 10.7 million) for a Judicial Reform Project (Ecuador), Washington DC: World Bank.

——(2004a) Implementation Completion Report on a Loan (US$ 5.3 million) for a Judicial Development Project (Morocco), Washington DC: World Bank.

——(2004b) Implementation Completion Report on a Loan (US$ 13.4 million) for a Judicial Reform Project (Georgia), Washington DC: World Bank.

——(2005a) *World Development Report – Equity and Development*, Washington DC: World Bank.

——(2005b) *Doing Business in 2005 – Removing Obstacles to Growth*, Washington DC: World Bank.

——(2005c) Project Appraisal Document on a proposed Credit to the Republic of Honduras for a Judicial Modernization Project, Report No. 32128-HN, Washington DC: World Bank.

——(2005d) 'Implementation Completion Report on a Loan (US$ 50 million) for Law and Justice and Public Administration (Russia)', Washington DC: World Bank.

——(2007) *Doing Business in 2007 – How to Reform*, Washington DC: World Bank.

——(2004) *Initiatives in Legal and Judicial Reform*, Washington DC: World Bank.

## Useful websites

Amartya Sen's Nobel Prize Biography
    <http://nobelprize.org/nobel_prizes/economics/laureates/1998/sen-autobio.html>
Doing Business (World Bank)
    <http://www.doingbusiness.org>
Honduras Project (World Bank)
    <http://web.worldbank.org/external/projects/main?menuPK=228424&theSitePK=409
    41&pagePK=64283627&piPK = 73230&Projectid=P081516>
Kazakhstan Project (World Bank)
    <http://web.worldbank.org/external/projects/main?Projectid=P046046&theSitePK=
    40941&pagePK=64283627&menuPK=228424&piPK=73230>
Tanzania Project (World Bank)
    <http://web.worldbank.org/external/projects/main?pagePK=64283627&piPK=73230
    &theSitePK=40941&menuPK=228424&Projectid=P002817>

# Chapter 12

# With friends like these: can multilateral development banks promote institutional development to strengthen the rule of law?

## Linn Hammergren

Although multilateral development banks (MDBs) entered late into judicial reform activities, they are frequently credited with initiating the movement and driving it toward a pro-business outlook. This chapter contests these arguments and goes on to question how effective the MDBs can be in leveraging the changes needed to improve the rule of law, however defined. The MDBs' business model (loans to governments, designed and managed at long distance) severely constrains their ability to produce institutional change, forces them into an emphasis on infrastructure, equipment and the occasional new law, and makes it nearly impossible for them to monitor results and introduce mid-course corrections. However, the apparent innocuousness of their contributions may also be overstated. Financing buildings, equipment and training for a politicized, incompetent and possibly corrupt court or other sector institution may eliminate the incentives for more fundamental improvements to their operations.

### Introduction

There is a notable tendency for academic and civil-society observers to blame or credit MDBs, and the World Bank in particular, for leading donor efforts to strengthen the rule of law. Those leaning toward blame often add a second claim: that the MDBs have pushed the movement toward a pro-business or thin rule-of-law model. Julio Faundez's chapter in this volume is one example, but it is hardly the only one. Some of the strongest expressions of this belief come from developing countries. For years, a group of Brazilian jurists has accused the World Bank of attempting to impose its globalizing model of judicial reform on their country, depicting its offers of assistance as a sort of Trojan Horse intended to strengthen the hand of multinational investors and undo local efforts at promoting social justice (Cavelcanti 2003, referring to Dakolias 1996).

In the present chapter I challenge both arguments. This is not out of a belief that the banks are above criticism, but rather because I would like to see the critics aiming at the right targets, and to ensure that their recommendations for change consider some further weaknesses which they too often overlook. As the subtitle indicates, I am less concerned about the banks' underlying goals (which

I also believe to be less homogenous than depicted) than about certain structural characteristics which make it difficult for them to promote any institutional change effectively. Before getting to that topic, this chapter first examines the initial critique, holding that claims of MDBs' leadership are dubious given their late entrance to the rule-of-law movement, that their influence on its contents is far less than supposed, and that their orientation is less uniform, and hardly driven only by economic concerns. That may be the part that pleases the banks. The rest of the chapter, perhaps less pleasing, examines the question of how successful they have been, or can be, in this area given the many obstacles imposed by their 'business model'. It suggests that even if they are single-mindedly devoted to making justice safe for, or pro-, business, their ability to do so is very much constrained.

I am basing these arguments on over 20 years' participation in the design and implementation of donor rule-of-law projects. My involvement presents certain problems of bias, but it also provides something the critics usually lack – an understanding of how donors do their work and what internal and external constraints affect them. Although my principal experience has been working in Latin America with the United States Agency for International Development (USAID) and the World Bank, the following also draws on interactions with other donors and with projects in a variety of regions.

## Validity of the 'MDBs as Leaders' thesis

The critics' thesis rests on three interrelated assumptions: that, because of the timing or the nature of their entry, the MDBs constituted a vanguard; that they have focused on the economic impacts of judicial reforms; and that their programmes are organized to promote the latter. The respective counter-arguments, expressed as questions, are reviewed below.

### How can MDBs be in the vanguard when they entered late and produced few innovations?

The donor community's now worldwide emphasis on judicial reform and rule of law first took shape in Central America in the 1980s, as a largely US Government response to the region's civil wars and political instability. However one interprets the sincerity of that interest, it did result in a substantial investment of money to strengthen judicial performance in El Salvador, Guatemala, Honduras, Costa Rica, Nicaragua and Panama. The President's Bipartisan Commission's Report (1984) on the state of the region, often called the Kissinger Report, famously referred to the judicial branch as the weak pillar of democratic governance, setting the tone for the programmes. Within a few years, USAID (and other US Government organizations with somewhat different agendas, largely combating drug trafficking) was joined by UN observer missions and other UN bodies, and then by numerous other members of the donor community. The initial emphasis was on criminal justice, the reduction of impunity and human-rights abuses, and the introduction of new criminal-justice proceedings as a means to achieving these goals (Hammergren 2007, Langer 2007). As crime rates rose in the region, combating crime was added to the list of objectives. Many donors, including USAID, continue in this criminal-justice vein, extending their operation throughout all of Latin America and beyond, often substituting or adding a component called 'citizen security' – the protection of citizens from crime and violence.

International Financial Institutions (IFIs) – the International Monetary Fund (IMF) and the MDBs – were later arrivals, entering in the early 1990s. They faced what appeared to be significant impediments in so far as their articles of agreement prohibited political activity and their lawyers tended to interpret any work with judicial systems as crossing that line. It is hard to imagine that 'reductions in force' in the civil service and the privatization of state enterprises are any less political acts than making courts more independent or ensuring that indigent defendants have counsel, but these are the points at which bank lawyers have drawn the line. Over time, a way around the prohibition was found. The Chief Counsel of the World Bank made a Solomonic decision that while criminal justice was political, working with non-criminal law was entirely consistent with the Bank's mandate of promoting economic development. Gradually, the bright line distinction has dimmed, and MDBs are venturing into areas first considered taboo.[1]

The entrance of MDBs into rule-of-law activities was facilitated by changes to their development paradigm in the late 1980s and early 1990s, which considerably enhanced the intellectual justification for working in that field. As chinks began to appear in the Washington Consensus, with its emphasis on one-off changes in macroeconomic and market-reform policies, the banks promoted a view that 'institutions matter' in advancing broadly based economic development, good governance, and poverty reduction (Burki and Perry 1998). Moreover, in line with neo-institutional economists such as Douglass North (1990), they portrayed courts and the rule of law as especially critical to economic growth. The MDBs' development of this argument doubtless affected other donors, but another historical event had greater influence: the collapse of the former Soviet Union and the resulting interest in promoting market-based development throughout the region. Whether the MDBs led in developing programmes here, I leave for experts in that region, but it appears that all donors entered nearly simultaneously.

The donor community's first efforts took an overly narrow cut on 'institutions', focusing on changing laws without paying much attention to organizational capacity for implementing them or to the various other institutional factors (informal norms, incentive systems, reigning mental models, the broader political environment) that would inevitably impede their impact. Once the problems were identified, the proposed solutions mirrored those already developed for criminal-justice programmes: restructuring of organizations; training; efforts to improve the quality of the bench and other sector personnel by depoliticizing appointments, increasing budgets and salaries and creating career systems; improvements to administrative services; and automation of processes.

The MDBs also provided more loans[2] to finance these inputs and others, such as infrastructure, which those working through grants generally avoided because of their high costs.

Aside from infrastructure and the roll-out of automation programmes first introduced by the bilateral donors, it is hard to identify innovations that can be specifically attributed to the MDBs. The banks have been able to finance larger diagnostic and other studies, many of which revealed interesting details on current operations and the obstacles to change. However, for reasons discussed below, that diagnostic work has had a limited impact on their programmes. The MDBs also financed econometric analyses to identify statistically relevant relationships between judicial and other types of development. The results provided justifications for programmes based not only on economic impacts but also on the quality of governance and poverty reduction. While many of these studies, and especially those by the World Bank Institute (see Kaufman et al. 2007 on governance indicators) and *Doing Business* (World Bank 2005), are criticized for their methodologies, atheoretical foundations and numerous heroic assumptions (Arndt and Oman 2006, Perry-Kessaris 2003), many programme designers (including the author) cite them to circumvent debates about the value of a proposed project. It is important to understand that such justifications do not limit the scope of a project, especially given the studies' usually vague definition of 'judicial' or 'justice' reform. They provide the entry pass after which, as others (Pásara 2004) have observed, project designers are relatively free to incorporate anything they choose to define as reform.

In conclusion, the MDBs' late entrance and tendency to adopt practices established by others substantially weaken the argument about their leadership, as does the fact that the rest of the donor community continued to pursue its additional lines of work, adding 'economic justice', but not to the exclusion of other objectives. The World Bank in particular did provide a strong intellectual argument for using rule-of-law reforms to advance economic growth, but did not accompany it with novel means of advancing these aims. The 'efficiency' emphasis (reduction of court congestion and delays) was already being pursued in criminal justice, and the lines of action here (automation, procedural simplification, reform of courtroom and system administration, judicial training, etc.) had been set. Moreover, as the MDBs entered the scene, other donors were already moving on to new areas. As early as 1994 (Blair and Hansen) donors such as USAID were questioning the emphasis on 'top-down', capacity-building reforms and insisting that access strategies take priority in their own programmes. This criticism was not lost on the MDBs and has in fact motivated them to focus on broadening access as well.

### Do MDBs focus exclusively on economic justice?

The impression that the development banks are exclusively interested in economic justice – that is to say judicial reforms that benefit predominately economic actors – deserves further exploration. Here it is important to distinguish between the initial justification for their entrance into judicial reform activities and the objectives they pursued once the blanket prohibition on such activities was removed, as well as between what they say they were doing and what they actually did. I leave the second topic for the next section and here concentrate on the first.

As several authors have noted (Hammergren 2007, Kleinfeld Belton 2005, Santos 2006, Tamanaha 2004) the concepts of rule of law, justice and judicial reform encompass a series of objectives, definitions and approaches. The banks may have justified their entrance into this field in economic terms, but their programmes included additional goals from the start. Furthermore, at least over the past decade, their justifications for their involvement in these activities, and the range of bank personnel involved in operationalizing it, have expanded considerably. First there was anti-corruption, then poverty reduction, improved governance and so on. Since the earliest days, various interest groups within each organization – the gender, indigenous peoples, environmental, and civil-society networks – have exercised their mandates to vet the contents of operations. Politically, it often is easiest to buy them off by adding a component representing their particular concerns.

The multiplicity of definitions, objectives and approaches is evident in the number of units or departments working on what could be considered rule-of-law topics. Within the World Bank, there is first the Private Sector Development Group and its 'Doing Business' project (now located in the International Finance Corporation, IFC), which does indeed focus on economic impacts, and especially on laws, procedural simplification in commercial justice and facilitating debt collection, contract enforcement and the like. The Private Sector Development Group has been instrumental in promoting the passage of bankruptcy, secured-collateral and related legislation, although these are relatively small operations and often financed through other loans. In recent years, in response to the renewed emphasis on poverty reduction, its members have argued that these same measures benefit micro- and small business as well as the economic elite.

Second, larger judicial reform loans are usually prepared by other units, such as the Legal Department or the Public Sector Group, which rarely pay more than lip service to the economic impacts. Relying on economic studies demonstrating the benefits of a 'well functioning justice system' for economic growth, they have put most emphasis on 'institutional strengthening' – training, automation, infrastructure and so on – largely for the judiciary. Within the last few years, the World Bank's renewed emphasis on poverty reduction has spurred more project components aimed at expanding access to the poor: public education campaigns, legal assistance, judicial sensitization to the needs of marginalized groups, construction of facilities in rural and peri-urban areas and mobile courthouses to take services to removed areas.

Within the Bank's Legal Department, the Legal and Judicial Reform Practice Group has coordinated bank-wide support to the UN Commission on Legal

Empowerment of the Poor (CLEP) and had previously developed its own access programme, called Justice for the Poor (J4P). Those working in these areas promote a focus on community and traditional justice, rather than restricting support to formal state structures, and they point to ongoing programmes in Indonesia and Cambodia and research being undertaken in Africa as possible models. In part because of the way community justice is organized, the programmes seem to place an equal emphasis on local governance and conflict-resolution structures. This may account for outsiders interested in justice reform being unaware of their existence.

The regional development banks (Asian Development Bank (ADB), Inter-American Development Bank (IDB) and so on) have followed similar paths – focusing first on strengthening formal state institutions, and more recently moving into parallel systems (alternative dispute resolution (ADR), community and traditional justice) to increase access for the poor. In conjunction with their efforts or independently, the banks' various social networks have also moved into operations, often providing grant funding to NGOs and civil-society organizations serving the poor and exploring means to work with traditional conflict-resolution systems. Within the World Bank, several stand-alone access projects are currently under preparation, some with little connection to formal judicial organizations.

Quantitatively, it is hard to compare these efforts, as any single project may contain several components. In general, institutional strengthening (infrastructure, equipment and training, with a little legal change) has probably received most funding. Projects focusing only on access are relatively small, although there are signs that this may be changing. While the Inter-American Development Bank finances even more infrastructure and equipment than the World Bank in Latin America, this is increasingly linked to objectives such as advancing alternative dispute resolution, community justice and citizen security. Although the results may benefit economic actors, the main justifications are social benefits, not economic growth.

In short, the argument that the World Bank and/or all development banks have been dedicated to legal and judicial reforms exclusively to promote economic growth seems overstated. Although economists rule the development banks,[3] they are not very interested in rule-of-law projects, whether economically oriented or not. Hence, these operations, which in MDB terms are relatively small and thus less important, are not closely scrutinized for their economic, or for that matter any other, content. They have privileged state institutions as opposed to traditional or informal justice – but not because the latter is undervalued. The problem is the lack of ideas for dealing with it. The final question then, as discussed below, is what the operations have actually done to further economic or other goals.

### Are MDB programmes organized to promote economic impacts?

Official goals are one thing; where the resources go is another.[4] It is true that the MDBs still pay considerable attention to 'modernizing legal frameworks' and making them compatible with market economies. However, most of this is done not through legal- and judicial-reform projects but rather as part of other sector operations. This is especially true of World Bank work in Africa as opposed to Eastern Europe, Latin America and Asia. In the latter regions, there are stand-alone justice projects that work directly with courts and other sector institutions. In Africa there is still no stand-alone loan project, and thus the sector in which the justice work is inserted often gives it a more economic focus. As the World Bank has moved into a poverty-reduction mode, this is also changing, and several new operations in Africa are, because of their insertion in a Poverty Reduction Strategy Paper, or a larger socially-oriented programme, focusing on access elements in particular.

It is important to remember that titles can be misleading. Bureaucrats are very good at disguising what they have always done with some cosmetic semantics. This phenomenon first became visible not in the MDBs' work, but in USAID. USAID's first strategic framework (Blair and Hansen 1994) took the Agency to task for too much 'capacity building' (training, equipment and technical assistance to reorganize work processes) and too little attention to creating constituencies for change and expanding access. Over the protests of many project managers, the framework was adopted as the official guide for future project design.[5] Obviously, the framework had little impact on projects already under implementation. It does not appear to have had much more effect on what the Agency has done since. Instead, project designers used the framework language to describe their conventional capacity-building programmes, only adding more civil-society participation, citizen education and services for the poor to the usual repertoire. Moreover, the peculiar organization of USAID's justice work (one half in the democracy bureau, the other in the economic development or private-sector bureau) allowed those projects with an economic focus (largely in Eastern Europe) to escape the framework's constraints.

As the World Bank still lacks a strategic framework, its operations have no need to fit into one. Nonetheless, designers of stand-alone projects are very good about adopting new terminology so as to please evolving internal constituencies. Consequently, while the objectives of the 'typical' project have expanded, its contents remain fairly constant – some legal change, training, automation and administrative reforms, and a good deal of construction. In line with the Bank's 'holistic' approach most stand-alone projects now feature at least three objectives: increasing access, efficiency and fairness or transparency. However, it is argued that the same inputs will advance them all simultaneously, with a little more emphasis on one or another depending on the objective pursued. Automation increases efficiency and fairness (as it makes proceedings more transparent). Training enhances all, but is particularly important for fairness or transparency (judges are trained in ethics codes) and access (they are sensitized to the needs of the poor or those of marginalized ethnic groups). Infrastructure, once presumed to augment efficiency, now has an access-enhancing purpose, *regardless of whether the buildings are located in areas with predominately poor inhabitants or where services were not previously provided.*

Until recently, most World Bank project evaluations only focused on input delivery. No-one asked whether the inputs were producing the desired impact on services. Now that this question is being posed, the answers are not very positive. Training clearly could play a role in advancing any of the objectives, but the type of training delivered often appears irrelevant to all of them. Moreover, when institutional practices are not redesigned to ensure training will be used, its impact is further lessened. Automation could increase efficiency by speeding up processes directly and by allowing supervisors to monitor what individuals are up to. Unfortunately, the second objective is rarely served, further diminishing the impact of the first. The various impacts associated with infrastructure have been questioned since the first World Bank project in Venezuela in the early 1990s. Following a critique by two non-governmental organizations (Lawyers Committee 1996), the project was redesigned to pass the substantial costs of building new courthouses to Venezuela. The courthouses were built, but subsequent developments in Venezuela (especially President Chavez's interference with the judiciary) make it impossible to assess their impact, however defined.

In Guatemala, both the IDB and the World Bank recently completed moderately-sized loan operations (US$ 25 million and US$ 33 million respectively) in which construction figured predominately. Subsequent evaluations of both projects raised questions as to their impact on 'access'.[6] Both noted that access is only partly a question of physical proximity and that, given the overwhelming lack of confidence in the courts, their ability to attract more business just because they were more conveniently located is doubtful. As many of the new facilities (including those for a pro-poor ADR programme) remain underutilized, the critics may well have a point (World Bank 2008a). As regards the World Bank project, the internal evaluation also questioned the impacts on other objectives – efficiency and transparency – noting that initial steps taken to advance both lacked the necessary follow-up and at best produced 'a potential' for future improvements were such a follow-up to be done. The evaluation further observed that the project lacked adequate indicators to track progress in any of its three goals, thereby taking the pressure off counterparts and Bank management to push for more change.

Thus, except for the emphasis on new, business-friendly laws, which for the most part are financed through non-judicial operations (and which also have had a very mixed, but generally disappointing impact), the MDBs' approach to advancing any objectives in the legal field seems to involve a series of measures to build capacity in a very general sense. However effectual or ineffectual, it would be hard to contend that these 'capacity' or 'institution'-building activities had a particularly pro-business impact. Unless one believes that working with formal state structures is inherently pro-business, what MDBs do, as opposed to what they say they are doing, would appear to be neutral in terms of the ultimate beneficiaries. The principal beneficiaries in fact appear to be judges, other judicial staff and lawyers. Unfortunately, measures to enhance their working conditions have not translated into better services for the final users, be they entrepreneurs, middle-class clients with ordinary civil or criminal complaints or poor citizens seeking to resolve conflicts or access rights. That issue is addressed in more detail below.

## Effectiveness in promoting rule-of-law reform

Having, I hope, dispensed with the critics' usual arguments – MDB or World Bank leadership, their emphasis on pro-business reforms and their tendency to organize their projects to advance that end – the rest of this chapter focuses on the more basic question: whether they can do much to promote the rule of law, however the latter is defined. My argument rests on the contention that rule-of-law reform is essentially about institutional change – getting organizations and those working within them to operate differently so as to produce different results. The challenge does not change with the ends pursued – whether making justice more business friendly or using it to improve the situation of the dispossessed or combat impunity. Somewhere in the 1990s, the MDBs recognized this principle, as indicated by their 'institutions matter' mantra. However, they are not very successful agents of change for a variety of reasons, and when they enter this arena they can also operate counterproductively. Interestingly, although various donors are now reviewing the efficacy of their rule-of-law work, the development banks have not been leaders in that regard.

Weak institutions certainly explain some of the shortcomings of the Washington Consensus reforms: corrupt privatizations, control agencies that controlled nothing and 'improved legal frameworks' that were ignored or circumvented. As the development banks move into areas such as rule of law and broaden their aims to include equitable (pro-poor) and sustainable (environmentally sound) growth, better governance and direct poverty reduction, institutional change becomes, if anything, more critical. Yet the same reservations apply. Can they encourage the development of institutions that will apply and enforce the law more fairly, expand benefits to marginalized groups and otherwise ensure that the usual operations, stuffed with new laws, equipment and buildings, will do more than reinforce the control exercised by the traditional elites and politicians? My suggestion is that the answer is largely negative, and that until they radically change their business model their contributions will remain marginal at best. The problem is thus not what they propose to do, but rather their ineffectiveness in carrying it out. The following reviews a series of problem areas all of which constrain their efficacy.

### Conceptual problems

Part of the problem is that, as organizations ruled by economists, the development banks simply lack the skills and perspectives required to engage effectively in this area. They may say they are building institutions, but their subsequent actions suggest a limited understanding of what this implies or requires.

## Inadequate understanding of what institutional development means

After a World Bank economist complained that institutional development was 'too expensive' because, for example, in education it required 'constructing all those schools', it struck me that many Bank employees are not well versed in the topic. There are also those who believe institutional development means pushing harder on the Washington Consensus formula, and still others who equate it with 'enacting and enforcing the right laws.' Despite acknowledging that institutions matter, the economists who rule the development banks seem to consider only formal laws and structures, ignoring North's emphasis on the role of informal rules, mental models and incentives in shaping systems of collective behaviour. In fact, a World Bank study on institutions affecting market development explicitly excluded informal ones 'because they were too difficult to work with' (World Bank 2002).[7]

The World Bank is not exclusively composed of economists. Most of those working with judicial-reform programmes are in fact lawyers. However, with apologies to many readers, it would be hard to think of a discipline less prepared to tackle the challenges of institutional reform. When faced with the problems of how to introduce change, lawyers seem to think in terms of laws. As the judicial-reform movement has amply demonstrated over the past 25 years, laws are fairly ineffectual in that regard. Alternatively, lawyers, and especially inexperienced ones (and unfortunately development banks are filled with that category – lawyers whose careers, long or short, are limited to working in an international bureaucracy), seem to see change as a product of litigation. So, in addition to those promoting law revision, most MDBs have another category of reformers, usually working with pro-poor projects, who want to litigate their way to change, using a counter-hegemonic rights strategy to force flawed institutions to provide what international or national laws may 'guarantee' to citizens. The jury is still out on how far one can get with that approach, but progress to date has been fairly sketchy.

## Inadequate grasp of how institutional development occurs

To be fair, promoting institutional development remains an underdeveloped art. We may know which rules, models and incentives need modification, but how one does that is another issue. Institutional-change techniques are not something one learns in school, but are a product of direct experience (and I would hazard a guess, a certain intuitive grasp of the basics). The inputs which donor programmes finance do not vary much – technical assistance, training and certain material support. The secret lies in the details of their contents, sequencing and interactions and in constant monitoring and frequent readjustments of the mix. Their successful application also requires direct and constant interaction with the targeted organizations, so having an in-country presence has an advantage here. Unfortunately, although the development banks have staff in country offices, their judicial-reform experts usually work from headquarters.

Furthermore, success does not depend solely on the donors. It hinges on local stakeholders and participants buying into the process and internalizing the goals being pursued. If they are not interested in the official outcomes, no amount of investment will change much of anything whatever the formal agreements may say.

Unfortunately, the MDBs appear to assume otherwise and to believe that financing a predefined series of activities is sufficient. It can be, but usually only where the cooperating country already knows what it wants, and is only seeking financing to achieve its goals more rapidly. Examples from Latin America include projects financed by USAID and the IDB with the Costa Rican Court, or Chile's self-financed criminal-justice reform. Criticisms of both programmes abound, but the larger point is that, when organizational leaders have a clear idea of what they want to do, it may be enough to provide them with the necessary financing (in Chile's case from the national government). For less advanced courts, prosecutorial or other agencies, the provision of financing for a series of predefined inputs has not been a recipe for success.[8] The World Bank project in Guatemala referred to above did lay out a very complete set of inputs, indeed it was criticized for doing so (only because it conflated inputs with impacts). Although the Court implemented most of them, it clearly viewed them as a compliance checklist, not as a means to improve performance. Moreover, where unreformed institutions select their own sources of external technical assistance, as is usually the case with loans, the only bank requirements involve compliance with the procurement rules, but this hardly guarantees that borrowers will choose wisely, whether from local or international sources. This results at best in a haphazard identification of providers, at worst in corruption.

To recap, development banks tend to pursue institutional change by relying on financing recipes that at best are incomplete. An iterative process, requiring constant testing and readjustment, is thereby reduced to so many dollars of training and so many of infrastructure. Where organizations want some of the inputs, but do not want to change, or cannot because of external political pressures, the results are sadly predictable. The critical elements – internalization of the goals and a dedication to readjusting inputs to achieve them – are missing, but the MDBs' formula neither recognizes nor pursues means to achieve them.

### Operational problems

Based on practices developed when they financed mainly infrastructure, the MDBs' business model seems especially ill-suited for working with themes where detailed knowledge of in-country practices is essential. Donors (those working with grants) face their own problems: the political agendas of their national governments, a demand for rapidly visible results (increasingly an MDB requirement) and reliance on staff members who may be inadequately prepared for the task. However, they usually have two advantages: an in-country presence (meaning they are in constant contact with operations) and, where they manage their own funds, greater flexibility in modifying plans (because they are not bound by the blueprint model of the banks' loan agreements). Grant funding also provides more control over content; a gift horse incurs less resistance from the recipient than one that comes with a price tag.

## Impact of loan formats (and its extension even to their grant programmes)

Here there are two problems: the traditional inflexibility of the loan format and the increasing availability of other sources of credit, making the banks' offerings less attractive to potential borrowers. A loan essentially starts with a legal agreement between the parties that so far as possible lays out objectives, principal activities and monitoring mechanisms. This scheme may be adequate for operations aimed at building X kilometres of roads or vaccinating Y children, but its relevance to reducing judicial corruption, providing court services to more citizens or even cutting delays is highly dubious.

This would be different if institutional change had as clear-cut a set of requirements as bridge-building, so that the amount and type of training needed to improve contract enforcement or deal with disadvantaged citizens, for example, could be specified to the same extent as the tons of concrete and steel needed to build a bridge. As this obviously is not the case, those designing loan agreements must choose between two equally inadequate alternatives: to attempt to lay out in great detail the inputs and sequencing needed to produce the desired results or to leave the agreement very open-ended, putting inputs into large categories and estimating overall costs. They nearly always opt for the second strategy, recognizing the impracticality of the first. Still, they probably could do a better job of prioritizing and sequencing some inputs. In the World Bank's Guatemala project mentioned above, one evaluation finding was that certain critical activities (especially key studies) were either done too late to have an impact or simply not done at all. Thus an inventory of court cases, needed to 1) identify the extent and causes of delays; 2) develop remedies; 3) determine where demand was going unmet; and 4) provide some baseline data for tracking improvements; only began in the sixth year of an eight-year project, and was never completed. A study on indigenous dispute resolution, critical to the development of a policy for its formal recognition, was not conducted. Another study meant to serve this purpose (which it did not) was done in the sixth year and likewise had no impact. A more common example is the installation of computer software and equipment to facilitate case processing before courtroom procedures are modified. The result is that the original, inefficient procedures are automated, probably making them more difficult to alter later.

The attractiveness of MDB loans has diminished considerably over the past decade, as has their consequent potential for leveraging fundamental change. The World Bank recently reduced its interest charges to attract more borrowers, but strictures of conditionality (as an effort to force fundamental change) and procurement regulations still make their offerings less attractive than those from other sources. An MDB, especially World Bank, loan may still provide a certain cachet (a stamp of approval) but why fuss with bank requirements when the Chinese or Citibank will provide credit without all the additional strings? Most recipient countries now recognize that the MDBs need the loans more than they do, and thus that their bargaining position as borrowers is greatly enhanced. Even if this is not official MDB policy, it certainly motivates the project managers, whose internal careers depend on their ability to make loans that disburse. If this is most easily done by financing redundant infrastructure and computers, then so be it. Unless the internal evaluation offices get far tougher, no-one is likely to notice.

### Limitations of long-distance management I: project identification and design

The development banks have in-country representatives, but most work on justice (and other institutional development) projects is done through periodic 'missions'. This system functions adequately for fine-tuning economic policies or designing and monitoring a road-building operation, but it is a poor means of identifying, promoting and monitoring institutional change. First, to identify a problem and its likely solutions, considerable knowledge of the in-country situation is required. This is unlikely to be achieved in the standard two-week identification mission usually devoted to consultations with government officials, the heads of the court system and a few local experts and stakeholders. Moreover, the banks' usual practice is to have those working on justice and other public-sector issues manage projects in several countries, making it still more difficult to develop in-depth knowledge of each one. As opposed to areas such as health, public works or education, the quantity and quality of statistical information on the justice system are usually abysmal, providing little basis for desk analysis. Information on communal or traditional systems, or on the needs and experience of groups unable to access state services, is often non-existent.

Local non-state experts, often recommended by outside observers (and by the experts themselves), do provide a different picture, but not necessarily one more accurate in identifying problems or their underlying causes. Nor is institutional analysis usually the forte of such experts, and while they can provide a more critical vision of the status quo, their explanations too often hinge on bad laws and bad actors. In a recent World Bank exercise asking several Latin American non-governmental organisations to analyze the vested interests obstructing, inter alia, criminal justice reforms, the explanation most often offered was 'the persistence of an inquisitorial mentality' (World Bank 2008b). This is not a terribly useful diagnosis on which to build a reform. Both government and opposition stakeholders in the justice sector also seem inordinately fond of magic bullets – the single solution that will unblock all the obstacles to success. Bank staff could conceivably provide more useful suggestions, but are either unprepared to do so or unwilling to enter into debates with potential clients.

An understanding of why organizations operate ineffectively requires a focus on the 'boring bits', ranging from how judges or prosecutors are really selected and promoted (and not just on the formal rules) to knowing how they spend their time and to what ends, as well as where new resources really go (to the agency heads or to the workers who need them) and what kind of monitoring is done. If bank staff do not have the time or means to investigate these details, and local informants are not attuned to them, a project is indeed likely to focus on less relevant elements. Local informants may well understand the intricacies of judicial selection processes, although their solutions may be no more successful. However, problems originating in inordinately complex internal procedures or ambiguous legal requirements may go unnoticed because there is no basis for comparison. Local observers are also unlikely to notice things like an extraordinarily high judicial budget, not that uncommon in Latin America, or very low productivity. For example, a recent World Bank (forthcoming) review of court, prosecutorial, defence and police productivity in Honduras revealed levels that were well below regional standards. This came as a surprise even to local critics who had never consulted comparative statistics. Nor had an ongoing Bank project registered this problem.

As the World Bank moves into new areas such as access enhancement, its lack of preparation is still more glaring. I know of no project, supported by any donor, that has been formulated on the basis of adequate studies of the juridical needs of the target populations. This type of research requires an investment of resources which no donor or lender appears willing to provide. Instead, the usual practice is to assume one can predict the needs and place physical installations, train staff and make any legal changes accordingly. The approach is not limited to assistance agencies. During the early 1990s, El Salvador was seeking external support for a new agricultural jurisdiction, based on models derived from mid-twentieth-century Spain and Italy, countries not sharing El Salvador's problem of too little land and too many people working it (Hammergren 2007: 144). The proposed Salvadoran law, thankfully not enacted, appeared to have the goal of keeping farm families on the land, rather than encouraging other forms of employment. In addition, Costa Rican observers noted that the Salvadoran proposal to place minimum lengths on all tenant contracts had been rejected by tenant farmers in Costa Rica – they wanted greater flexibility (Hammergren 2007: 230, note 21). Similarly, debates over the criminalization of domestic violence rarely benefit from extensive discussions with real or potential victims, revolving instead around academic experts' notions as to what would serve them best. And ongoing debates about the value of transitional justice (reconciliation tribunals or truth commissions) seem not to draw on the demands of 'beneficiary' populations, many of whom now question the large investments needed for their creation and subsequent operations. Finally, when the poor demand 'justice', they may well not be referring to the courts offered by the reformers, but rather to the direct provision of services offered by other agencies specialising, for example, in education, health or public security.

Although the problems discussed above affect lenders and donors alike, lenders tend to be more constrained because their in-country contacts tend to be high-ranking officials, who are consulted for their views on the most urgent needs. The answers usually translate into buildings, equipment and training, often with little mention of the problems they are intended to resolve. In contrast, donors with an in-country presence tend to have a more complete view of institutional operations, being more able to develop a network of informants, and thus a more balanced picture of the needs, as well as being better situated to hear complaints about the performance of their partner institutions, and to understand the political economy of the underlying situation. This is not to say that they always take advantage of their privileged position, only that it allows them to do what the banks find nearly impossible. It is thus no surprise that at the height of the Fujimori dictatorship in Peru (1992–2000) the World Bank manager for a proposed judicial project insisted that the project was being designed with the participation of a large number of judges. Subsequent conversations with the judges revealed that they had been called to meetings when the Bank staff were visiting, but with a firm understanding that they were to criticize nothing (author's interviews, Lima, May 2001).

### Constraints of long-distance management II: monitoring progress

Poorly designed projects might be improved by close monitoring of their advances. Here the development banks once again usually rely on periodic supervision missions rather than on in-country presence. In this context, the ability of staff to identify problems in implementation, or the fact that the agreed-upon plan is not producing the promised results, is extremely limited. This is true of many types of projects and not just those in the judicial sphere. Returning to the Peruvian example, once the Fujimori regime collapsed several World Bank staff members (those who visited periodically) found themselves wondering how they had not noticed the high levels of corruption in all areas. Likewise, IMF and World Bank staff seemed blind to the economic problems emerging in the last years of the Menem regime in Argentina – a Washington Consensus poster child until its economy collapsed in 2000–2001.

Again, supervision missions usually involve interviews with high-level counterparts and only limited, very controlled, visits to review project operations. Even when the control is imperfect, many staff members seem unprepared or unwilling to recognize discrepancies. In several World Bank projects in Central America new infrastructure is conspicuously underutilized. However, none of the supervision reports comments on that situation. For example, an IDB project building 'justice modules' (combined-service courthouses) in rural Peru was eventually cut back because of problems with constructions, but a more basic setback – the failure of participating agencies to staff the new units fully – went unrecorded. A skilled observer can recognize failings even in a short visit, as was demonstrated by the three-day visit of a European judge to the Guatemala project (World Bank 2008a: 33). However, his unanticipated criticisms are still contested by Bank staff.

It is hard to say whether lack of preparation or of motivation accounts for the frequently superficial results of supervision missions. In any case, even with skilled and motivated participants, the long-distance formula and infrequent visits work against an identification of problems and provide only limited means for dealing with them. One can hardly tell a Chief Justice that his new, multi-million dollar courthouse is underutilized and request that he do something about it. The initial observation will have to be verified, more diagnosis done, some alternative solutions developed and discussed, and even then no response may be forthcoming. It is thus no wonder that most supervision missions find everything 'satisfactory'.

### Doing needlepoint with an 800-lb gorilla

The multilateral development banks are also hampered by their tools for leveraging change in the vast majority of projects which are executed by recipients. Here banks must rely on disbursements of funds against 'conditionality' or the tracking of agreed-upon benchmarks and indicators. Designing conditionality is extremely difficult, given the uncertainty as to how institutional change occurs. For want of better alternatives, the emphasis is usually on enacting laws, creating new organizations or introducing improved practices, such as examinations for new staff. All that is fine but the real question is how these innovations are used – for example, did the examinations really affect appointments? Determining the answers to such questions requires much longer time frames than those required for project start up or a quick disbursement on a structural readjustment loan. Benchmarking or indicators of progress pose similar quandaries. First, the quality of data is usually poor, and even where projects propose to improve them, this often is accomplished late or not at all. Second, as with conditionality, benchmarks and indicators are hard to design and, as they are intrinsically sparse, they rarely get at more than one dimension of a complex change process – for example, what beyond examinations continues to determine appointments? Third, they can be easily manipulated.[9] Where the MDBs depend on the counterpart to do the counting, the latter has a high incentive to cook the numbers.

While donors such as USAID have been attempting to insert impact indicators in judicial projects for over a decade, the multilateral development banks were, once again, latecomers. Interestingly, USAID backed off a little once it realized that the aim of producing one set of indicators for all projects was unreasonable, and that even project-specific indicators were frequently inadequate: what can be counted is often not what counts most, but softer benchmark indicators introduce considerable subjectivity and thus more room for positive spin. Nonetheless the Millennium Challenge Corporation (MCC), an apparently new approach by the US Government to providing assistance, has reintroduced the notion of development by numbers, going so far as to adopt the highly contested World Bank governance indicators to allocate aid.[10] It will be another few years before the first round of results can be evaluated, but the MCC approach is already widely criticized, especially for its counter-intuitive rankings of countries.[11]

This is not to discount the importance of indicators, but only to suggest that adequate monitoring of progress also requires softer techniques to capture unanticipated problems and successes, identify new trends less susceptible to measurement and build working alliances with local staff and service users. This is the fine work (needlepoint) of institutional-change processes, and it is not well suited to being done through periodic missions and tracking of a short set of indicators of progress (the gorilla). This is not only because gathering this information takes time, but also because its collection and interpretation are best done jointly with a representative set of stakeholders who can then collectively identify problems and decide on a response.

## Political constraints

For all their claims to a non-political nature, the multilateral development banks are victims of politics and this places further limitations on what they can do in judicial reform, not to mention many other areas. The focus here is on external politics, but it should be noted that the internal politics facing any large bureaucracy – lack of a broad consensus on objectives and means of reaching them, constant infighting among internal groups over who will control resources and policies – also pose constraints within the banks.[12]

### MDBs are membership organizations – what members do not approve of will not be done

When Paul Wolfowitz introduced his Governance and Anti-Corruption initiative (the infelicitously titled GAC) during his short tenure as President of the World Bank, there was immediate resistance from member countries over the emphasis on corruption and the idea that civil-society organizations should be enlisted to fight it. Again, it is important that, whereas in the heyday of the Washington Consensus the development banks operated in a seller's market, today their pronouncements are increasingly challenged from without and within, and countries can turn to other sources of finance.[13] Governance themes, including but hardly limited to judicial reforms, are, as Wolfowitz's experience indicates, particularly prone to awaken the sensitivities of members.

This may partly explain why the World Bank still lacks a strategic framework for its rule-of-law programmes. To adopt one would require taking positions on issues such as judicial independence, the power of judiciary over other branches of governance and, if a thick rule-of-law model is adopted, its substantive contents – that is, which values will be enforced. In an era where 'universal' human rights standards and the once widely accepted 'Western' model of court operations and organization are increasingly questioned, forging a framework acceptable to all appears less and less possible. The once-presumed connection between judicial reform and economic growth has also been challenged, ideologically and theoretically, and efforts to reinstate it as the sole justification for such reform activities probably would not work. Consequently, any legal reform strategy ought to remain at a vague and glorious level, and would be ill-advised to get down to the operational basics. So, judicial independence or efficiency can remain as goals, but efforts to specify some essential conditions or structural characteristics enhancing either would likely meet opposition. Similarly, no-one will officially oppose 'legal empowerment of the poor', or greater access, but their translation into more specific conditions at the global or country level may well meet resistance.

This may also explain why development-bank projects have focused so extensively on rather innocuous inputs – buildings, equipment and training – and have not pushed for them to be targeted against performance failings. Staff may or may not understand the difference, but if they do understand it there is still the uphill battle of making the changes count. This is true even of the economic goals, where there has been a notable failure to push for, or even track, such obvious improvements as shortening time to resolution of key cases, introducing measures to ensure enforcement and insisting on effective anti-corruption mechanisms (and not just training in ethics codes). There are some clear exceptions, but for the most part the larger operations seem to work off the field-of-dreams approach to justice – build a courthouse and it will come. This is the path of least resistance, but is also the one least likely to advance economic or any of the other promised impacts. It will, nonetheless, keep the loans coming and disbursing and so meet the first criteria for the success, or at least survival, of the multilateral development banks.

*They work with sovereign governments and are prohibited from political involvement*

Unless development banks find like-minded, powerful allies within their partner countries, their chances of getting more than symbolic acceptance of their recommendations are slight. During the heyday of the Washington Consensus this was easy because so many ministers of finance and so many of their staff shared the economic ideologies of the banks. The rebellion against the Washington Consensus raised doubts about the apolitical or universally beneficial consequences of its macroeconomic remedies.

Institutional reforms, whether for macroeconomic health or for good governance, are inherently political, always posing a threat to the status quo and to the existing power structure. Judicial reformers have rarely enjoyed ideological support from government officials, and have faced the further problem of needing allies both in the ministries of finance/economy, who must approve loans,[14] and in the judiciary. Political alliances on the justice side have most often been based on material benefits or increases in agency power, and these are now being resisted by the losers in the process.

Solutions to the emerging dilemmas promise not to be easy, but a first step is for the MDBs to recognize that whatever direction they take they will be engaging in a political debate. Matters are now complicated by the pro-poor emphasis which, if taken seriously, those in power will hardly view as anything other than the effort to advance redistributive justice that it is.

In short, like it or not, the MDBs have stumbled into a highly political arena where only their substantial ineffectiveness has protected them from more serious attacks. They could, as they appear to be doing in the economic arena, take a step back, emphasizing their technical skills in helping their clients (governments) resolve problems which the clients define. However, in the justice sector they will be impeded by their shallower skill endowment and more substantial internal disagreements as to the ends they are pursuing. Two positive, if largely unintended, consequences of their presence, along with that of other donors, have been to expand expectations, thereby fomenting debates about the direction reform should take, and to build up technical and analytic skills among the local groups they have hired to do some of their footwork. While most of those skills are held by individuals working outside the public sector, in independent research institutes, NGOs and public and private universities, they should still enrich the discussions to follow. With luck their contributions should move reform beyond the provisions of buildings and equipment and into real changes in performance and in the institutional base.

## Conclusions

Ever since the MDBs began their justice operations, outside observers have tended to credit them both with creating the movement and with pushing it in the direction of reforms with a pro-business content. As I hope to have demonstrated, their influence on the donor community and even their own single-minded dedication to economically relevant justice are very much overstated. Moreover, their own projects have a questionable ability to advance this or any of the many other goals they purport to pursue. Justice or rule-of-law reforms require institutional change, and the traditional operating procedures of development banks are not well suited to that purpose. Their long-distance management, reliance on loans, use of the loan logic even for smaller grant programmes, and the requirement that they work with governments do not permit the inherently subversive logic required to alter how organizations operate. At best, as was argued for the Bank's Guatemala project (World Bank, 2008a), their usual inputs can prepare a base for future change, but until they escape their other impediments they are unlikely to accomplish more.

A further, more disturbing, question is whether these same operations are undermining the potential for real improvements by providing public-sector organizations with the things they most want and at the same time giving them a sort of seal of approval. Following the latter logic, Peru's Fujimori administration pushed very hard for a medium-sized (US$ 22.5 million) World Bank project, not because it needed the money (it was investing 5 times that much of its own and IDB funds in the sector), but because the Bank's presence was important to it. The loan was never put into operation, but the Bank's role in halting it was debated internally and is still not openly admitted.[15] In short, the effects of the banks' projects may be less innocuous than they seem, and this should give them pause for thought. Providing a corrupt, inefficient and inaccessible court system with goods and a seal of approval hardly seems like an incentive for that system to change. Whatever the MDBs' objectives in the sector, they are arguably not being met and, despite their protests to the contrary, this may have perverse consequences. To the extent that this is true, their alternatives, aside from more of the same, with the risks that increasingly entails, are pretty stark: get out of the business entirely or radically change how they conduct it.

## Notes

1 Some regional MDBs, like the Inter-American Development Bank, were aided by the inclusion of 'social' goals in their articles of agreement, thus widening the areas in which they could work.
2 As opposed to grants. For more on the distinction between the two see below and Decker in this volume.
3 For evidence of how economics trumps other disciplines in the World Bank see Safarty (2008).
4 See Jensen (2003: 349) on 'following the money'.
5 It has only recently been replaced. See USAID (2008).
6 In the interests of transparency, I should note that I was the principal author of the World Bank report, but that the published version, cited here, was approved by the Bank following an internal review and certain modifications (including the emphasis on the creation of a 'base for future change').
7 The comment was made to the author when she inquired why only formal institutions were being considered.
8 The same applies to institutional reforms in other sectors – health, education and even finance.
9 Development banks have found such manipulation even in respect of 'harder' economic data.
10 The creators of the governance indicators have themselves deplored their use in determining flows of aid: see Kauffman et al. (2002).
11 For example, although regional experts would find the distinctions nonsensical, Nicaragua and Honduras score higher than Paraguay, and all three higher than the Dominican Republic, on the basic quality of governance.
12 See, for example, Santos (2006) on the internal divisions affecting legal reform within the World Bank.
13 They look elsewhere for loans, and can increasingly rely on large grant operations from entities such as the European Union.
14 Possibly buying into the economic growth arguments or, in the case of Eastern Europe, lured by the carrot of accession to the European Union, many ministries of finance initially endorsed the judicial-reform programmes.
15 The official view is that the Peruvian government cancelled the project. This is technically correct, but omits that it refused to meet Bank conditionality.

# References

Arndt, C. and Oman, C. (2006) *Uses and Abuses of Governance Indicators*, Paris: Centre for Development Studies, OECD.

Blair, H. and Hansen, G. (1994) *Weighing in on the Scales of Justice*, Washington, DC: USAID.

Burki, S. J. and Perry, G. (1998) *Beyond the Washington Consensus: institutions matter*, Washington, DC, The World Bank.

Calvalcanti Melo Filho, H. (2003) ' A reforma do poder judiciário Brasileiro: motivações, quadro actual e perspectivas', *Revista CEJ*, 21: 79–86.

Dakolias, M. (1996) 'The judicial sector in Latin America and the Caribbean: elements of reform', World Bank Technical Paper Number 319.

Hammergren, L. (2007) *Envisioning Reform: improving judicial performance in Latin America*, University Park: Penn State Press.

Jensen, E. (2003) 'The rule of law and judicial reform: the political economy of diverse institutional patterns and reformers' responses', in E. Jensen and T. Heller (eds) *Beyond Common Knowledge: empirical approaches to the rule of law*, Stanford: Stanford University Press, 336–81.

Kaufman, D., Kraay, A. and Mastruzzi, M. (2007) *Governance Matters VI: governance indicators for 1996–2006*, World Bank Policy Research Working Paper No. 4280. Online: <http://ssrn.com/abstract=999979>

Kleinfeld Belton, R. (2005) *Competing Definitions of the Rule of Law: implications for practitioners*, Washington, DC: Carnegie Endowment for International Peace, Carnegie Papers, Rule of Law Series, No. 55.

Langer, M. (2007) 'Revolution in Latin American criminal procedures: diffusion of legal ideas from the periphery', *The American Journal of Comparative Law*, 55: 617–76.

Lawyers Committee for Human Rights and the Venezuelan Program for Human Rights Education and Action (1996) *Halfway to Reform: the World Bank and the Venezuelan justice system*, New York.

North, D. (1990) *Institutions, Institutional Change and Economic Performance*, Cambridge: Cambridge University Press.

Pásara, L. (2004) 'Lecciones ¿aprendidas o por aprender?', in L. Pásara (org) *En busca de una justicia distinta: experiencias de reforma en América Latina*, Lima, Peru: Consorcio Justicia Viva: 515–70.

Perry-Kessaris, A. (2003) 'Finding and facing facts about legal systems and direct foreign investment in South Asia', *Legal Studies*, 23(4): 649–89.

President's Bipartisan National Commission on Central America (1984) *Report*, New York: Wiley.

Santos, A. (2006) 'The World Bank's uses of the 'rule of law' promise in economic development', in D. Trubek and A. Santos (eds) *The New Law and Economic Development: a critical appraisal*, Cambridge: Cambridge University Press, 253–300.

Sarfaty, G. A. (2008) 'Doing good business or just doing good: competing human rights frameworks at the World Bank', in B. Morgan (ed.) *The Intersection of Rights and Regulation: new directions in socio-legal scholarship*, Ashgate Press.

Tamanaha, B. Z. (2004) *On the Rule of Law: history, politics, theory*, Cambridge: Cambridge University Press.

USAID (2008) *Guide to Rule of Law Country Analysis: the rule of law strategic framework*, Washington DC, August.

World Bank (2004) *Making Justice Count: measuring and improving judicial performance in Brazil*, Washington, DC: The World Bank, Report No. 32789-BR.

——(2005) *Doing Business in 2005: removing obstacles to growth*, Washington DC: The World Bank, the International Finance Corporation, and Oxford University Press.

——(2008a). *Implementation Completion and Results Report (IBRD 44010) on a Loan in the amount of US$ 33.0 million Equivalent to the Republic of Guatemala for a Judicial Reform Project*, Report No: ICR0000623, Washington DC: The World Bank, March 31.

——(2008b) *Vested Interests in Legal and Judicial Reform*, Washington DC: The World Bank, May.

——. (forthcoming) *Honduras Institutional and Governance Review* (working title), Washington DC: The World Bank.

## Useful websites

(ADB) Asian Development Bank
    <http://www.adb.org>
(CLEP) UN Commission on Legal Empowerment of the Poor
    <http://www.undp.org/legalempowerment/>
(IDB) Inter-American Development Bank
    <http://www.iadb.org>
Justice for the Poor (J4P) (World Bank Legal Department)
    <http://go.worldbank.org/SMIKY7M6O0>
(MCC) Millennium Challenge Corporation
    <http://mca.gov.org>
USAID
    <http://www.usaid.gov/>
World Bank
    <http://www.worldbank.org>

# World Bank rule-of-law assistance in fragile states: developments and perspectives

## Klaus Decker*

'Our dream is a world free of poverty'. This bold sentence, emblazoned at the entrance to the World Bank's main building in Washington D.C., seems to summarize the institution's broad mandate of poverty alleviation through economic growth and social equity.

The first loans from the International Bank for Reconstruction and Development (IBRD) were made to support the reconstruction of Western European countries ravaged by the Second World War. Established in 1944 to facilitate post-war reconstruction, the World Bank has had to constantly adjust, sometimes even reinvent, both its structure[1] and its agenda. The first loan of US$ 250 million was made to France on 9 May 1947, followed some time later by loans to the Netherlands, Denmark and Luxembourg. Soon after, the Marshall Fund took over the support to reconstruction in Europe and the IBRD turned its focus away from the 'R' and towards the 'D' in its name.

As the world's premier development organization, the Bank typically provided assistance only once a country had completed the transition from humanitarian emergency to a phase of reconstruction with more long-term development issues (World Bank 2004b: 3). The problem of ensuring the transition from emergency aid to post-crisis development aid (International Development Association 2007: 8) was left to others in the international community.

It would take the World Bank until the early 1990s to put the 'R' back fully on the agenda (see further World Bank 2004b). In 1994 it was asked to administer the multi-donor Trust Fund for the West Bank and Gaza; in 1995 it was approached to assume the leadership role with the European Commission for the coordination and planning of international assistance in post-conflict Bosnia and Herzegovina.[2] These two events caused the World Bank to begin attempting to fill the gap between emergency aid and the start of reconstruction and development assistance. The World Bank has recently identified activities in so-called 'fragile states' as one of the six strategic priorities of its work (see World Bank Strategic Themes website).

Some of the most important, and complex, issues facing fragile states relate to the rule of law. It is commonly accepted that disorder, insecurity and injustice do enormous damage (OECD 2007: 8). As the experience with rule of law in recent post-conflict environments such as Afghanistan and Iraq has shown, failure to address these challenges can substantially undermine development efforts in other sectors, as well as the overall credibility of the state and international development organizations. Rule of law[3] is a key issue in fragile states. However, as World Bank President Robert B. Zoellick has recently highlighted,

> the international security and development communities have let the task of building of justice and law enforcement systems fall between the cracks. It is not clear to me where the international capacity exists to help establish basic courts and tribunals to resolve disputes, train judges and advocates, and build prisons and police forces, all of which need to recognize local cultural and legal traditions.
>
> (Zoellick 2008)

This chapter examines the Bank's work on rule-of-law issues and its work in fragile states. It sets out the current and potential inter-connectedness of these two fields of operation, analyzes their remaining disconnects, and suggests ways for the World Bank to overcome them where necessary.

## Two evolving fields

This section gives a general overview of the Bank's activities in (a) fragile states and (b) rule-of-law projects. The following section covers projects dealing with rule-of-law issues in fragile states.

### Fragile states

The World Bank defines fragile states as (a) 'low-income' countries which (b) score 3.2 or below using the Bank's Country Policy and Institutional Assessment (CPIA) methodology.

The CPIA assesses the different policy and institutional dimensions of an effective poverty reduction and growth strategy. It rates countries against a set of 16 criteria grouped in four clusters: (a) economic management; (b) structural policies; (c) policies for social inclusion and equity; and (d) public sector management and institutions (see World Bank 2007d). It is used as input for the performance-based allocation system (PBA) of the International Development Association (IDA) of the World Bank. Depending on the definition, the category of 'fragile states' currently comprises between 35 and 50 low-income countries 'which lack either the capacity and/or the willingness to deliver on their core functions' (OECD 2007: 10; see World Bank Fragile States website). Many fragile states are post-conflict countries, but others are in prolonged crisis situations, are experiencing deteriorating governance, or are gradually improving while remaining fragile.

*Policy*

The Bank's involvement in Bosnia opened the door to its future involvement in post-conflict countries and fragile states (World Bank 2004b: 8). It provided the blueprint for Operational Policy/Bank Procedures 2.30 (hereinafter 'Policy 2.30'), *Development Cooperation and Conflict* in 2001. The Policy clearly shifts the focus from infrastructure to economic and social stability.[4] It also explicitly acknowledges the link between development cooperation and conflict, noting that:

> economic and social stability and human security are pre-conditions for sustainable development. Violent conflict … results in loss of life and destruction of assets, contributes to social and economic disintegration, and reverses the gains of development, thereby adversely affecting the Bank's core mission of poverty reduction (Policy 2.30 section 1).

The Policy sets out the parameters for World Bank engagement in conflict-affected countries, depending on the conflict situation in the state in question (see World Bank 2004b: 9). In countries vulnerable to conflict, the Bank will use its 'usual instruments … to promote economic growth and poverty reduction through development assistance that minimizes potential causes of conflict' (Policy 2.30 section 2 (a)). In countries that are actually in conflict, the Bank will decide to continue its assistance in accordance with the Country Assistance Strategy (CAS), to initiate an Interim Strategy Note, or to discontinue assistance while initiating a watching brief (Policy 2.30 sections 1 and 2). Finally, in countries in transition from conflict, the Bank will provide support 'through investment and development policy advice, with particular attention to the needs of war-affected groups who are especially vulnerable by reasons of gender, age, or disability' (Policy 2.30 section 2 (c)).

Policy 2.30 also emphasizes the limits of World Bank involvement in conflict affected states, noting that 'it is not a world government' and that 'in view of its mandate [it] does not engage in peacemaking or peacekeeping, … [nor] provide direct support for disarming combatants … [nor] provide humanitarian relief' (Section 3(a); see further below).

Mirroring trends in the Bank's overall operations, there has been a significant shift in emphasis in fragile states from the 'bricks and mortar' issues of rebuilding infrastructure to a more holistic approach comprising support to economic recovery, the evaluation of social needs, institutional capacity building, revitalization of local communities and restoration of social capital. This holistic approach also comprises specific efforts to support de-mining, demobilization and reintegration of ex-combatants, and the reintegration of displaced people and groups. Over time, the World Bank has also mainstreamed measures to prevent the onset, exacerbation or resurgence of violent conflict (see World Bank Fragile and Conflict-Affected Countries website and IDA 2007). In a nutshell, what has evolved is a rather sophisticated and differentiated approach to the quite heterogeneous category of fragile states and the bridging of the humanitarian-development continuum.

## Financial instruments

The World Bank is able to provide two main forms of financial assistance to developing countries: lending, in which the sum provided is repaid by the developing country to the Bank; and grants, in which the sum is not repaid.

Fragile states, like all 'low income' countries, are eligible for 'soft lending' from IDA.[5] IDA divides fragile states into four groups: the first group comprises some fragile states that receive IDA funding through the ordinary PBA system, which tends to favour non-fragile states since these score better with the CPIA. The second category is post-conflict countries, for which IDA makes exceptional allocations to meet their special needs if there is a serious likelihood of peace. The third group encompasses countries re-engaging with IDA after a longer period of inactivity. The fourth category is countries unable to access IDA resources as they are in non-accrual status (International Development Association 2007: 21–36). Lending for projects in fragile states has increased dramatically since the 1980s. Between 1980 and 1998, lending to post-conflict countries increased by 800 per cent (World Bank 2007b). More recent figures suggest that World Bank assistance to post-conflict countries amounts to some 25 per cent of total lending (World Bank 2007b: 4).

Although a significant portion of the World Bank's development assistance is now made available through trust funds, development projects involving lending have traditionally represented a core part of the World Bank's work. However, fragile states have increasingly had access to IDA grants, as opposed to credits.[6] Grants are either made by the Bank from its own administrative funds, or are administered as trust funds by the Bank on behalf of other donors.

In 2008, the World Bank consolidated two pre-existing special purpose funds to establish the State and Peace-Building Fund (SPF) with US$ 100 million for fiscal year 2009–11, to be supplemented by donor contributions (World Bank 2008; see World Bank State and Peace-Building Fund website). Its objective is to consolidate the Bank's approach to conflict and fragility by addressing the needs of state, local governance and peace building in fragile, conflict-prone and conflict-affected states.[7]

In recent years, various trust funds have complemented IDA lending in fragile states, particularly in post-conflict settings where their flexibility can be an advantage. From 2002 to 2006, contributions by trust funds to fragile states increased more than sixfold from US$ 136 million to US$ 821 million. The bulk of these funds are provided by multi-donor trust funds (MDTFs),[8] for example for Afghanistan,[9] Iraq,[10] Sudan,[11] and West Bank and Gaza[12] (International Development Association 2007: 37).

## Rule of law

The term 'rule of law' can mean different things in different contexts. In the field of development cooperation, rule-of-law assistance refers to a field of work generally aimed at improving the functioning of the justice system. Its contours are somewhat ambiguous and changeable, depending on the context in which the label is used and by whom.[13] As Thomas Carothers (2006) has noted, this diversity is due to the fact that this field has roots in at least four types of activity, namely: politically motivated democracy promotion;[14] top-down governance projects often focusing on economic growth and investment climate;[15] bottom-up human-rights and social-justice promotion, predominantly by non-governmental organisations (NGOs); and international law enforcement projects with strong criminal law undertones such as the 'war on drugs' and the 'war on terror'. It is only recently that these four variants have begun to interact and blend with each other.

Although absent from the list of the World Bank's six strategic priorities mentioned above, rule-of-law reform is very much a part of current Bank activities in developing and transition countries. However, the term 'legal and judicial reform' has long been preferred in the Bank. Over time, it became evident that the term 'legal reform' was too broad, since projects in nearly every sector of development cooperation involve some kind of change in laws.[16] At the same time, the term 'judicial reform' turned out to be too narrow as it refers solely to court reform. Today, the preferred language within the Bank is 'justice reform', which can be understood as being roughly equivalent to the core of rule-of-law assistance as it is understood by other development agencies.[17]

### Historical development

Prior to the end of the Cold War, the notion of the 'rule of law' was simply not part of the World Bank discourse (Santos 2006). This changed in the late 1980s and early 1990s as the World Bank began to develop its 'good governance' agenda. The conventionally recognized starting point for the World Bank's governance agenda is the 1989 study on sub-Saharan Africa published under World Bank President Barber B. Conable. Under the heading 'Governance for Development' it identified a 'crisis of governance' underlying the entire range of development problems in Africa (World Bank 1989: 60–61). Although it deals with various facets of the rule of law, this 200-page text only twice refers explicitly to the term. The first reference appears in the context of the need to 'improv[e] the business environment' by defining 'contract and property rights clearly' and providing 'an equitable forum for settling disputes' (World Bank 1989: 143). The improvement of the business environment remains a key entry point and justification for justice reform to this day. The second explicit mention of the rule of law appears towards the end of the study where a 'strategic agenda for the 1990s' is laid out (World Bank 1989: 189–92). Once again, the starting point is the investment climate and the 'lack of a reliable legal framework to enforce contracts'. However, the text then opens up an entire rule-of-law field in terms that, for some, continue to resonate within the institution to this day:

> The rule of law needs to be established. In many instances this implies rehabilitation of the judicial system, independence for the judiciary, scrupulous respect for the law and human rights at every level of government, transparent accounting of public monies, and independent public auditors responsible to a representative legislature, not to an executive. Independent institutions are necessary to ensure public accountability. The widespread perception in many countries is that the appropriation of the machinery of government by the elite to serve their own interests is at the root of this crisis of governance.
>
> (World Bank 1989: 192)

The first project in the rule-of-law field seems to have been a 1990 adjustment loan that required Bangladesh to establish special debt-collection courts. It was not obvious whether the World Bank's mandate, which prohibits the institution from interfering in member countries' political affairs, allowed this kind of intervention.

To clarify the limits of the mandate at a time when the institution was developing its governance agenda, the World Bank's General Counsel Ibrahim Shihata issued a legal opinion in 1991 on the extent to which the World Bank is allowed to address governance challenges in member countries (Shihata 2000). This was an important milestone as it opened the door for World Bank assistance with aspects of governance that are within the World Bank's mandate of poverty alleviation. These do encompass aspects directly linked to economic considerations even when they have political causes or origins (Shihata 2000: 271). However, as Julio Faundez notes in his contribution to this volume, this legal opinion also reiterated the prohibition on the institution taking 'political considerations' into account, unless they have a direct and preponderant economic effect that can be established in a clear and unequivocal manner. According to Shihata, 'the linkage between economic considerations and political factors cannot be presumed, but has to be clearly established in each case where it is alleged to exist' (Shihata 2000: 271). In his legal opinion, Shihata himself admits the difficulty of making such a distinction between economic and political factors, a difficulty that World Bank staff continue to struggle with until today, as we will see.

In any event, the World Bank subsequently got more involved in rule-of-law assistance, both as a component of broader projects and in the form of 'standalone' rule-of-law projects. For example, in 1992 funds were provided to train judges, upgrade legal libraries and publish court decisions in Tanzania as one component of a project to improve the business environment. In the same year, the World Bank also approved a US$ 30 million loan for Venezuela solely for judicial reform, the first of a series of more than 30 so-called stand-alone justice-reform projects to date.

Another milestone for the World Bank's rule-of-law involvement was the speech by World Bank President James D. Wolfensohn in 1996, where he identified the 'cancer of corruption' as the single biggest obstacle to development. Before that date, the issue of corruption was considered to be too political to be addressed by the World Bank. For example, Wolfensohn recounts a telling encounter with then General Counsel Shihata in July 1995, briefly after he became President:

> When I came to the Bank we were not allowed to mention the word 'corruption'. It was called the 'C' word. I was told by the General Counsel within days of my getting to the institution, and in great secrecy, 'Don't mention the 'C' word. So I asked, 'What's the 'C' word' He replied, 'Corruption'.
>
> (Wolfensohn 2005: 22)

The World Bank's focus on the fight against corruption has increased ever since and the institution's portfolio of public-sector reform has grown accordingly. In fiscal year 2008, the theme of public-sector governance represented 19 per cent of the entire IBRD and IDA lending portfolio (World Bank 2008b).[18] This growth also strengthened the rationale for World Bank involvement with justice reform.

The picture would be incomplete without mentioning the World Bank's Comprehensive Development Framework (CDF), launched in 1999 under President James D. Wolfensohn. It encompasses a set of principles to guide development and poverty reduction, stressing the interdependence of all aspects of development, including not only economic growth but also social equity (Wolfensohn 1999). It is especially significant that it emphasizes not only the instrumental importance of the rule of law for a good business environment (see Faundez in this volume), but also that without 'the protection of human and property rights, and a comprehensive framework of laws, no equitable development is possible' (Wolfensohn 1999: 11).[19] The CDF thus complements the economic focus with considerations of social equity.

Today, justice reform at the Bank is a cross-cutting issue addressed by justice-reform practitioners across the Bank with a legal, public-sector-reform, private-sector-development or social-development background.[20] In 2004, World Bank General Counsel Roberto Dañino launched a Legal Modernization Initiative (LMI) to identify strengths and to improve delivery of service[21,] but there is no Bank-wide strategy for justice yet.[22]

## Practice

The evolution of the rule-of-law agenda has caused, and been shaped by, concrete World Bank activities and projects in the rule-of-law field. These take many different forms, including loans, credits, grants, technical assistance and analytical services (World Bank 2004).

Since 1992, there have been more than 30 stand-alone[23] World Bank justice-reform projects in all regions of the developing world, totalling more than US$ 800 million in lending (loans or credits), predominantly in Europe and Central Asia, and Latin America and the Caribbean.[24] Roughly half of them are closed, and a dozen or so additional projects are currently under preparation. The amounts of current and closed projects range from US$ 2.5 million to US$ 138.22 million.

In addition to these stand-alone projects, there are numerous projects in other sectors that have one or more justice-reform components. Since 1992, there have also been more than 90 justice-reform grants, many of them in Africa, totalling almost US$ 50 million. The World Bank has also undertaken 'justice sector assessments' in around 30 countries, usually in preparation of a justice-reform activity (see World Bank Law and Justice Assessments website).

## Trends

Despite the geographical diversity and variety of development objectives of the Bank's rule-of-law field activities, it is possible to identify some general trends (for further details see World Bank 2004). First, in addition to focusing on improving the business environment, justice reform is now also addressed as a subset of broader public-sector reform. Second, projects are increasingly complementing activities on the supply side (training, equipment, construction, rehabilitation, etc.) with support on the demand side – that is, to civil society, NGOs, and users such as citizens and businesses. Third, there is an increasing emphasis on tailoring projects to local needs. Fourth, there have been improvements to the empirical basis of projects through research and surveys to generate baseline data and input for monitoring and evaluation throughout the project cycle, for example through the World Bank's Justice for the Poor Program (J4P; see World Bank Justice for the Poor website).

With variations in focus and balance, there are three broad themes generally covered by World Bank justice-reform projects: court management and performance; access to justice; and legal information and education. Under the first theme, projects tend to address issues such as court delay and corruption in the courts by improving judicial services and their efficiency through enhanced work processes, increased transparency, sound strategic planning, financial management, data collection approaches and efficient ICT-based case-management systems. Under the access-to-justice theme, one can often find activities to improve legal services and legal aid, for example through community-based alternative dispute-resolution (ADR) mechanisms and community paralegals, but also activities ranging from the establishment of mobile courts to the strengthening of ombudsman offices. The third theme of legal information and education often comprises the training of judges and court staff, the establishment of judicial academies, support to law schools and civic education, targeting especially the poor and marginalized, to enhance rights awareness.

In addition to project work in the justice sector, the World Bank is involved in a number of international partnerships and initiatives in this area. To give just two examples, the World Bank was one of many institutions that acted as an advisor to the Commission on Legal Empowerment of the Poor, which released its report on *Making the Law Work for Everyone* in June 2008, and works together with the European Commission for the Efficiency of Justice (CEPEJ) established by the Council of Europe, which aims at improving the functioning of the justice systems across its 47 member countries (see CEPEJ website).

## Rule-of-law activities in fragile states

So what of the intersection of these two fields of development cooperation that have emerged separately within the World Bank since the early 1990s? What does the World Bank rule-of-law assistance in fragile states look like? Below are some concrete examples of each of the instruments that it has available: loans and credits, grants and analytical and advisory services.

### Loans and credits

### Stand-alone projects

At present, there are no examples of World Bank lending for stand-alone justice-reform projects in states currently regarded as 'fragile'. Before the concept of fragile states was used by the World Bank and other development partners, three justice projects were developed in countries that at that time exhibited features of the institution's current definition of fragility.[25]

First, a Judicial Reform Project in Guatemala, approved in 1998, dedicated US\$ 33 million to creating a more effective, accessible and credible judicial system. To strengthen the institutional capacity of the judicial branch, it improved court administration and human-resource management, strengthened the judicial career and improved the general operation of the courts. To support the fight against corruption, it designed ethical standards and training programmes, established a judicial-sector anti-corruption commission and enhanced administrative and disciplinary procedures. To improve access to justice, the project introduced and expanded ADR mechanisms, such as justice-of-the-peace courts, mediation centres and mobile courts, improved service delivery to court users and developed a civil-society participation programme (World Bank 2004: 59). The project closed in 2007.

Second, a US\$ 22.5 million Judicial Reform Project was approved for Peru in 1997 at the tail end of the regime of President Alberto Fujimori, a time when some saw Peru exhibiting all the features of a fragile state. The loan was intended, among other things, to modernize judicial administration, implement judicial and community-training programmes, refine laws and regulations, promote ADR and develop the Public Defender's Office. But it was cancelled before disbursement in 1998.[26]

It is interesting to note that for both Peru and Guatemala, project documents relied upon instrumentalist justifications for their design: they emphasize the projects' contributions to private-sector development and economic growth and focus on the supply side of reform (provision and improvement of laws and institutions).[27] But in practice the projects contain many demand-side elements that go beyond the investment-climate-oriented instrumentalist brief of the project documents.

Third, a US$ 18.2 million Legal and Judicial Reform Project was approved for Sri Lanka in 2000. Once again, it adopted an instrumentalist, private-sector and supply-side-oriented approach. Its objectives were to improve efficiency, transparency and responsiveness to the needs of the public at large, and the private sector in particular, by modernizing aspects of the legislative framework that impacted private-sector activity; improve the Company Registry; and to build capacity of the judiciary and other dispute-resolution institutions.[28]

It is also significant that the outcome evaluations of such projects can be less than satisfactory.[29] For example, the Implementation and Completion Report for the Guatemala project mentioned above evaluates its outcomes as moderately unsatisfactory. It states explicitly that 'some lessons learned included: Although so obvious as to hardly bear mention, without counterpart buy-in, a judicial or institutional reform effort will not get far.' It specifies that 'buy-in' means not just accepting the donor contributions, but rather internalizing and actively pursuing the change goals behind them' (World Bank 2008c).[30] Similarly, when the Sri Lanka project closed in 2007, its outcomes were evaluated as 'moderately unsatisfactory' in its Implementation and Completion Report. The report noted that 'in rushing to fulfill conditions agreed with International Financial Institutions' government bodies 'can be prone to over-commit themselves … [not] realizing the technical and managerial capacity as well as the political capital that is required to deliver' on their promises. Projects must be 'realistic and simple to ensure effective implementation'. However, the project had faced special difficulties caused by Sri Lanka's highly volatile political economy, with four successive governments in the last five years of the project, each of which had to become familiar with the project's activities (World Bank 2007c).[31] A rule-of-law project in a fragile state was undermined by that very fragility. On that note it is significant that these projects in fragile states appear to have been similar to justice-reform projects undertaken in the same period in non-fragile countries.

## Components of larger projects

It is more common to find justice reform undertaken as a component in a larger project. Three examples of such projects will serve to demonstrate that these reforms tend to be conceived as instruments for the achievement of objectives such as private-sector development or public-sector reform.

One example is Angola. In 1992, an IDA credit was approved for US$ 15.5 million under the Public Sector and Legal Institutions Development Project, one month after the signing of the General Peace Agreement. One of the project's objectives was to strengthen legal institutions and professional capabilities. Activities under this US$ 7.2 million component included strengthening the legal profession and the judiciary, training for lawyers and the judiciary, designing automated legal information systems, supporting law libraries and providing support to the legal reform process (World Bank 2009). The project closed in 2000.

Second, in the Gambia, the US$ 15 million Capacity Building for Economic Management Project approved in 2001 supports the strengthening of macro-economic analysis and policy formulation through the provision of technical advice to the Department of State for Finance and Economic Affairs, the strengthening of public-resource management and the facilitation of private-sector development, by building capacity, primarily on the legal, financial and regulatory sectors (World Bank 2001). The latter component comprises justice-reform activities such as training of judges, magistrates, court registrars and court officials; preparation of a judicial information strategy and establishment of a Court Case Administration System for the High Court; establishing a pilot dispute-resolution system; restructuring of the Registrar General, Curator of Interstate Estates and the Registrar of Companies and attachments to appropriate institutions in small commonwealth countries; and refinement of the legal and judicial sector strategy (World Bank 2009).

Third, in Guinea-Bissau, the armed conflicts of the late 1990s had critically affected the social and economic fabric of the already deeply impoverished country. The purpose of the US$ 26 million Private Sector Rehabilitation and Development Project, approved in 2002, is to support efforts to stimulate increased investment, competitiveness and participation in the private sector. The project has three main components: building partnerships and private participation through reforms aimed at the telecommunications, air transport, port, water and energy sector; improving the investment climate by modernizing business laws and making access to fair and equitable justice readily available for individuals and private enterprises; and supporting implementation and capacity building (World Bank 2009).

By contrast, a later grant-funded project approved in 2003, the Mozambique Public Sector Reform Project, includes a legal-sector capacity-building component (around US$ 6 million) strengthening the supply side through training, capacity building and institutional development in court administration, but also supports the demand side, for example through legal-awareness campaigns.

### Grants

Current World Bank rule-of-law assistance in fragile states seems to be predominantly in the form of justice-reform grants. It is useful to distinguish projects funded under multi-donor trust funds in post-conflict countries, which tend to be relatively large and complex, from grant-funded justice-reform activities in fragile states in general, which tend to be smaller, to focus more on demand-side activities and non-state actors and to be used to test innovative ideas and develop new approaches.

### Multi-donor trust funds in post-conflict countries

In two countries where the World Bank administers multi-donor trust funds for post-conflict reconstruction and development, the institution is involved in rule-of-law projects: Afghanistan and Sudan.

In Sudan, the World Bank administers two multi-donor trust funds established after the end of the civil war, one for Northern Sudan (MDTF-N) and the other one for Southern Sudan (MDTF-S). Under the MDTF-N, the World Bank has worked with UNDP and the judiciary to develop a Capacity Building for the National Judiciary Project. The World Bank supervises the implementation of this US$ 18 million project by UNDP. US$ 13 million is provided by the MDTF-N and US$ 5 million is national contribution. It was approved in 2006 and closes in 2009. The project's objective is to strengthen the capacity of the judiciary to effectively and fairly apply the law and deliver justice. The project's four components include support to the National Judicial Service Commission to build capacity for managing the judicial system, judicial training at the central and state levels, the establishment of a National Legal Training and Resource Centre and the rehabilitation of an existing training facility and court facilities in selected areas. This project focuses on the supply side at central and state level (World Bank 2009).

Under the Afghanistan Reconstruction Trust Fund (ARTF), the US$ 27.5 million Judicial Sector Reform Project was approved in 2008. It is the first phase of a two-phase engagement and will close at the end of 2009. Its objective is to enhance the capacity of the justice-sector institutions to deliver legal services through activities under three components. The first component, enhancement of the capacity of legal institutions, includes activities to improve strategic management of human capital and physical infrastructure, to increase the skills of justice-sector professions, and to provide rapid information, communications and technology enhancements. The second component, empowerment of the people, will improve legal awareness, as well as the capacity to provide legal aid throughout the country. The third component will provide support to Afghan justice-sector institutions to implement the National Justice Sector Strategy and Program (World Bank 2009).

The World Bank team developing this project chose a flexible and strategic approach. During the first phase, there is a focus on quick and tangible results. The second phase (five years) will aim at sustaining these results and addressing more complex justice-sector challenges in the country in a comprehensive manner. The team also made the deliberate choice to focus primarily on the state justice system.

As World Bank President Robert B. Zoellick mentions in his speech on the development, governance and security nexus, building a police force and improving prisons are important activities to secure development in post-conflict environments. It is therefore not surprising that in Afghanistan as well as in Sudan the World Bank was approached to fund projects and activities aimed at exactly these activities. This situation had already been anticipated at the time when the World Bank was approached to administer these multi-donor trust funds.

Ever since the World Bank's General Counsel Ibrahim Shihata issued his 1991 legal opinion on the extent to which the World Bank is legally allowed to address governance challenges in member countries (Shihata 2000: 268) it has been understood that criminal justice, police and prisons remained off-limits for the institution.

Because of this interpretation of the World Bank's Articles of Agreement, the World Bank did not get involved in the design of the rule-of-law activities in these post-conflict environments. It also meant that the institution refrained from building its own capacity and expertise in this area. As a consequence, UN agencies received more than US$ 20 million in Afghanistan from the World Bank-administered multi-donor trust fund for police salaries, non-lethal equipment, rehabilitation of facilities, training and institutional development without further involvement of the World Bank in the design of the activities.

In 2006, a similar issue arose in the context of Southern Sudan under the MDTF-S. After the signing of the Comprehensive Peace Agreement, the Government of Southern Sudan is facing the challenge of literally rebuilding the entire police and prison service. Demobilized soldiers from the Sudan People's Liberation Army (SPLA) kept joining the police service, composed of the unified police forces of Sudan in the then government-controlled areas and Sudan People's Liberation Movement (SPLM) police. The need for training and infrastructure was immense so the basic rule of law could be maintained and built upon for further capacity building.

Again, because of this interpretation of the World Bank's mandate, the institution did not participate in the design of these rule-of-law activities. The MDTF-S administered by the World Bank funded a US$ 45 million Police and Prison Support Project under a fiscal agent arrangement. The project was ultimately designed and implemented by UNDP (World Bank 2009).

## World Bank grants in fragile states

The World Bank administers a variety of grants, such as the Japanese Social Development Fund (JSDF), the Institutional Development Fund (IDF) and the Post-Conflict Fund (PCF) and Low Income Countries Under Street (LICUS) Trust Fund. These fund a further collection of justice-reform activities, whether stand-alone or as part of larger projects.

One common focus of these grants is capacity building in state institutions. For example, in East Timor a US$ 300,000 IDF grant ('Institutional Development of the Ombudsman'), approved in 2003 and closed in 2006, supported the creation and institutional development of the Ombudsman's Office. Similarly, the US$ 486,000 IDF grant ('Judicial Statistics') in Kosovo, approved in 2007, supports the Kosovo Judicial Council in increasing the efficiency of the court system by establishing a system allowing for differentiated case-management (World Bank 2009). In Liberia, the US$ 2.3 million Senior Executive Service Project, approved in 2007, enables the government to recruit a cadre of technical and managerial public servants to meet immediate high-level capacity needs and to help transform the civil service, including the Ministry of Justice, into a more professional, effective and accountable institution.

Another common focus of such grants is legal education. In Nigeria, for example, a US$ 500,000 IDF grant ('Legal Education Capacity Building Project'), approved in 2007, supports efforts to enhance the country's legal environment by strengthening the training programme for legal professionals at the Nigerian Law School (World Bank 2009).

Third, World Bank grants are particularly useful for funding those activities for which states, fragile and non-fragile alike, tend to be reluctant to borrow. These include activities that are more 'bottom-up' or which deal with gender. In Burundi, for example, a US$ 458,000 IDF grant ('Capacity Building to Sustain Gender-Responsive Legal Reform Initiatives'), approved in 2003 and closed in 2006, aimed at eradicating gender bias in legislation, improving legal literacy and access to legal-aid services, as well as bridging the gap between formal and informal systems (World Bank 2009). Another example is a US$ 470,700 IDF grant in Cambodia ('Rule of Law Development: Labour Law Education of Women'), approved in 1998 and closed in 2001. It funded labour-law training for various stakeholders, including judges, women's groups and employers, a pilot programme for dispute resolution between women workers and their employers, and forums for the empowerment and promotion of labour rights for women and children (World Bank 2009). Yet another example is Mauritania, where a US$ 286,000 IDF grant ('Application of the Law and the Advancement of Legal Status of Women'), approved in 1999 and closed in 2002, supported efforts by both the government and civil society to promote greater women's participation in the legal- and judicial-reform process (World Bank 2009). In Rwanda, a US$ 400,000 IDF grant ('Institutional Strengthening Initiative for the Legal Advancement of Women') was approved in 2001 and closed in 2005 (World Bank 2009).

A recurrent theme of such bottom-up grants is legal aid, especially the provision of legal-aid services by civil-society organizations. In Mauritania, for example, a US$ 863,520 JSDF grant approved in 2005 ('Legal Aid Services to the Poor') aims at institutional strengthening and capacity building of civil-society organizations to promote access to justice for the poor and socially vulnerable (World Bank 2009). In Nigeria, a US$ 400,000 IDF grant ('Legal Reform and Legal Aid for the Advancement of Women'), approved in 2002 and closed in 2006, included activities to develop a more comprehensive approach to legal aid, in addition to support that it provided to the National Centre for Women's Development and to the Legal Affairs Division of the Federal Ministry of Women Affairs and Your Development (World Bank 2009).

When justice-reform issues are dealt with as part of a larger grant-funded project, the main focus of the project may be private-sector development, as was the case in early World Bank rule-of-law assistance. In Kosovo, for example, a US$ 3 million Private Sector Development Technical Assistance Grant was approved in 2001 and closed in 2004. It supported the establishment of a company registry; strengthening the capacity of the Commercial and Supreme Courts and improving the quality of legal services; and assisting in the development of basic accounting standards and training for local accountants. Its justice component provided training for commercial judges and legal practitioners, drafting commentaries for the new package of commercial regulations, assisting the judges of the Commercial Court, establishing a law library in the Commercial Court and developing a pilot legal-aid programme focused on small businesses (World Bank 2004: 79–80). The project's Implementation and Completion Report evaluated the outcome as satisfactory and noted that 'locally-based' World Bank support plays a crucial role in ensuring good project design, effective supervision, and good policy dialogue with relevant stakeholders, including donors' (World Bank 2004c).

Finally, it is important to understand that grants are also key to funding World Bank empirical research for rule-of-law reform, in fragile states and elsewhere. Relying on a variety of different grant-funding sources, the World Bank's J4P programme, for example, undertakes justice-related empirical research in Cambodia, Sierra Leone and Vanuatu that directly feeds into ongoing or planned projects in various sectors (see J4P website). J4P is planning to expand its programme in East Asia and the Pacific, for example to fragile states such as the Solomon Islands and Papua New Guinea, with Australian trust-fund money.

A major concern in fragile states seems to be achieving visible results in early stages. In Liberia, for example, a US$ 750,000 LICUS grant ('Capacity Building for Justice Services'), approved in 2008 and closing in 2010, aims at accomplishing practical projects that are visible and have a tangible impact in the short and medium term (World Bank 2009). It supports training of judges, clerks and other judicial officers from the lower courts. In addition, the grant provides funding for a clinic programme carried out in cooperation with the Bar and Law School.

## Trends

The focus of World Bank-funded justice-reform activities in fragile states has developed from 'top-down' to a mix of activities that increasingly takes into consideration 'bottom-up' issues. Also, many of the activities reflect multi-disciplinary and cross-sector approaches. Although there are examples of lending activities for justice-reform in fragile states, the bulk of the World Bank's portfolio consists of grants. The ones funded under multi-donor trust funds look more like lending projects with a supply-side focus. The other grant-funded activities tend to focus on 'bottom-up' approaches, for which countries are probably reluctant to borrow. Increasingly, there is also more involvement of non-state actors. The institution is also making an effort to have a better empirical basis for justice-reform activities. Compared to earlier legal and judicial sector assessments, which tended to reflect the structure and issues 'on the books', the current empirical research focuses more on the reality on the ground and takes more of a user perspective.

## Complications

One series of challenges to enhancing justice and security services in fragile states results from the fact that they are delivered by a large variety of actors including both state and non-state organizations and systems (OECD 2007: 18–29). These actors often have different levels and sources of legitimacy vis-à-vis different groups, and may conflict with each other within a deteriorated social fabric. As a consequence, successful development cooperation in these contexts is very complex and highly context-specific. The Bank is increasingly engaging with non-state actors, and has an increasing field presence of roughly 3,000 staff in more than 100 country offices worldwide. However, more than two thirds (around 7,000) of its staff continue to be based in Washington and, like most development organizations, it mainly deals with governments.

A second series of challenges relates to the fact that the state and non-state providers of security and justice in fragile states are actually sources of insecurity and injustice (OECD 2007: 17–18). The relationship between these service providers and different segments of the population, especially the poor and marginalized, can be based on a long and dreadful history of exploitation, bias and rent-seeking (OECD 2007: 17). Navigating this minefield of political economy and deeply entrenched conflicting interests to achieve pro-poor development and improvement of the rule of law for all is a daunting challenge.

A third series of challenges relate to the context-specific complexities of sequencing issues and conflicting objectives (OECD 2007: 18–29). For example, strengthening the capacity of the state to deliver justice and security may appear to be the best solution in the short term, but it may serve to enhance the capacity to continue existing abuses. Where there are no state delivery structures in place, building this capacity may be a worthy long-term goal, but will leave a vacuum in the short-term. In cases where an existing system must be reformed, altering incentive structures and training in order to change attitudes and entrenched practices requires mid- and long-term horizons. State building at the central level may conflict with equally important local needs. Engaging with non-state actors is equally challenging and much, again, is context-specific. These heterogeneous actors are often loosely organised and tend to have a local focus, which makes donor engagement challenging. Yet engagement may be required in the absence of any state capacity to deliver justice and security services. At the same time, it is important that such engagement does not undermine state legitimacy, which should ultimately enable the state to become what some refer to as 'the hub of a network of justice and security providers' (OECD 2007: 28).

It is not surprising, then, that the international community finds it hard to deliver the multilayered and flexible approach required to enhance the rule of law in fragile states (OECD 2007: 29–41, Samuels 2006).[32]

## Limitations

Like any organization, the World Bank approaches fragile states through its own institutional lens, focusing on those things that it regards as being appropriate for its focus on poverty reduction and within its legal remit. The challenge is to deliver on what Robert Zoellick has identified as 'the toughest development challenge of our era', namely development cooperation in fragile states, within the scope of the Bank's Articles of Agreement.

### Human rights

It is not unusual for fragile states, especially those which are conflict-affected, to suffer a legacy of massive human-rights abuses, which can constitute a serious obstacle to achieving development outcomes.

The international human-rights agenda and the development agenda have only recently begun to merge (Decker et al. 2005). Philip Alston (2005) has compared them to 'ships passing in the night', held apart by the Cold War until 1990 and subsequently by the barriers of discipline. He finds that, in spite of obvious interlinkages and more recent interdisciplinary efforts, development practitioners could do better at mainstreaming human rights into development efforts, while human-rights lawyers could engage more fully with the development agenda.

The Bank is clearly rooted in the international development agenda and few people inside and outside the institution would seriously think of it as a human-rights organization. Also, the World Bank has 184 member states representing the international diversity in government attitudes when it comes to human rights.[33] Explicit human-rights language or considerations therefore remain rare in World Bank project documents. Some of its development partners though do approach development work by using human-rights based approaches.

In a legal opinion on 'The Prohibition of Political Activities in the Bank's Work', issued in 1995, General Counsel Ibrahim Shihata made the following conclusion with respect to human rights:

> In fact, the Bank's work has promoted a broad array of economic, social and cultural human rights. Its proclaimed overriding objective at present is to enable its borrowing countries to enjoy freedom from poverty, a basic freedom which many find to be required for the full enjoyment of human rights. The Bank increasingly contributes to the borrowing countries' efforts to develop their human resources, through its lending for education, health and nutrition, and to strengthen their systems of governance, through its lending for legal, regulatory, judicial and civil service reform … Clearly, these activities have a direct effect on the amelioration of non-political

human rights. They may even pave the way for greater awareness and protection of political rights in the borrowing countries.

(Shihata 1995: 233–34)

Some years later, General Counsel Roberto Dañino (2005: 513) identified three legal limitations to the World Bank's activities.

First, there has to be a reasonable rationale for World Bank involvement of any kind, whether it is about improving human rights or building roads (Dañino 2005: 513). The rationale requires that the activity undertaken by the Bank furthers the purposes for which the Bank was established. At present this purpose is very broadly defined as poverty alleviation through economic growth and social equity based on the Comprehensive Development Framework launched by President James D. Wolfensohn in 1999 (Wolfensohn 1999). Many welcomed the fact that this framework addressed the criticism of the Bank as a 'one-eyed giant' by acknowledging that development is a multi-faceted concept requiring a comprehensive approach linking all strands of the development process (Marshall 2008: 142). Others considered this framework as an example of the World Bank's 'mission creep' (Marshall 2008: 142).

In any event, the contemporary theory and practice of international development cooperation increasingly provide evidence of the interrelatedness of the development and human-rights agendas (Decker et al. 2005). Some development agencies go as far as to use a human-rights-based approach to their development cooperation across all sectors.[34] Most have by now incorporated human-rights dimensions into their development agenda.[35]

Second, the Articles of Agreement provide that only 'considerations of economy and efficiency and without regard to political or other non-economic influences or considerations' shall be relevant to the decisions of the Bank and its officers (Article III Section 5). It is obvious that there are some political considerations that have more of an economic impact than others. Dañino explains that those political aspects with an impact on considerations of economy and efficiency have to be incorporated by the World Bank, and that this is also consistent with current World Bank practice (Dañino 2005: 516). He highlights, for example, that when taking into consideration a country's business climate, political issues of governance such as 'internal political instability or uncertainty' have already been identified by Shihata (2000) as consistent with the World Bank's mandate. Dañino suggests going even further by incorporating social, political and any other relevant factors which may have an impact on the Bank's economic decisions. Based on scientific research, he explicitly includes 'violations of political and civil rights' in case these have an economic impact (2005: 516–17).

Third, the Articles of Agreement contain two explicit political prohibitions in Article IV Section 10:

The Bank and its officers shall not interfere in the political affairs of any member; nor shall they be influenced in their decisions by the political character of the member or members concerned. Only economic considerations shall be relevant to their decisions, and these considerations shall be weighed impartially in order to achieve the purposes stated in Article I.

The prohibition on interfering in the political affairs of any member applies to partisan politics, both domestic and foreign (Shihata 2000: 219). The ban on basing decisions on the political character of a member state is interpreted as preventing 'the Bank from endorsing or mandating a particular form of government, political bloc, or political ideology' (Dañino 2005: 517). Dañino made it clear, though, that neither of these prohibitions prevents the Bank 'from considering political issues that have economic consequence or implications – so long as this is done in a non-partisan, non-ideological, and neutral manner' (Dañino 2005: 518).

According to Roberto Dañino[36] 'concerns and uncertainties about the '"constitutional" restrictions under the Articles of Agreement of the Bank have somewhat inhibited a more proactive and explicit consideration of human rights' as part of the World Bank's work'.

As Dañino himself states, Article IX of the Articles of Agreement 'vest[s] the role of interpretation in the Executive Directors'. By contrast, the 'General Counsel of an international organization does not decide on the questions addressed to him; he only provides advice based on thorough legal analysis' (2005: 513, note 14).

In a 2006 article published in the World Bank Development Outreach, then-General Counsel, Ana Palacio, observes that interpretations of the Articles of Agreement must change with the times, and she indicates that she thinks their interpretation is rightly 'founded on a mainstream interpretation of the concepts of legitimate global concerns', including the understanding that in the field of human rights, the notion of sovereignty cannot provide absolute protection to states from interference. She suggests that human rights must be recognized:

> as legal principles which may inform a broad range of activities, and which may enrich the quality and rationale of development interventions, and provide a normative baseline against which to assess development policies and programming (Palacio 2006: 36).

Palacio resigned in May 2008, and the power of interpretation remains with the World Bank's Board.

The World Bank indeed intends to further its understanding of human rights and to develop a 'learning by doing' approach (World Bank Human Rights FAQ website). The establishment of a Justice and Human Rights Trust Fund is indeed a significant milestone on that path (see World Bank Human Rights FAQ website).

### Crime, violence and security

Crime, violence and lack of security are challenges faced by most developing countries, but are often a primary concern in fragile states and conflict-affected countries, where they threaten fundamentally to undermine development efforts across most other sectors. The international community has learned this lesson over and over, most recently in Afghanistan and Iraq (Call 2007). Dañino said in a speech in Manila that:

the Bank is at the brink of taking its comprehensive approach to justice reform to the next level, through the recognition of the significance of criminal justice ... ] The Bank has recognized that security and safety are the biggest concern of the poor and therefore functioning criminal justice is critical for development (Dañino 2005b).

The development impact of crime, violence and lack of security has long been acknowledged (Call 2007). Beyond anecdotal evidence of shop owners struggling to rebuild their businesses after armed robberies, for example in Nigeria (Narayan et al. 2002: 99), and villagers in Ghana and Malawi seeing their lives spiralling downward after the theft of their cattle (Narayan et al. 2002: 24, 70), development practitioners have proof of the negative effect on development of a lack of human security, basic order and property rights. Indeed, the World Bank's own recent research concludes that '[c]rime and violence are a development issue' since they affect 'human welfare in the short-run' and 'economic growth and social development' in the long-run. Indeed, it may be that 'were Jamaica and Haiti to reduce their rates of homicide to the level of Costa Rica, each country would see an increase in its growth rate of 5.4 per cent annually' (World Bank and UNODC 2007: i).

The evidence shows the negative impact of crime and violence in three ways. First, crime and violence negatively affect human capital. Injuries or illnesses can be life-threatening in developing countries, and in the absence of social safety nets, the loss or disablement of a breadwinner can have devastating consequences for relatives (UNODC 2005: 68). The poor are disproportionately affected since they are unable to afford private security guards, who may outnumber police officers, for example by a factor of three in South Africa (UNODC 2005: 79). Also, some studies demonstrate that fear of crime and violence limits the education opportunities of younger people and their economic prospects, for example in Jamaica (Moser et al. 1997), South Africa (Human Rights Watch 2001) and Zambia (UNODC 2005: 72).

Crime and violence also have a negative impact on the economy. Those who fear for their lives tend to reduce their mobility and engage less in economic activities (Picciotto 2006). Some of the positive impact of Hernando De Soto's land-titling projects in Peru, for example, was due to the fact that people who had benefited from the programs have seen their de facto property legally recognized and protected (De Soto 1989: 19–33). As a consequence, children can go to school and adults to work instead of staying at home to protect their 'property' against other illegal occupants taking it over. Theft of cattle, a liquid asset on which families rely during bad seasons (UNODC 2005: 71), can reach a scale with disastrous effects for households, for example in Malawi (World Bank

2002b). Also, developing countries with high levels of crime and violence suffer brain drain and low levels of foreign direct investment, despite potentially high rates of return. The potential for development of tourism is also considerably reduced (UNODC 2005:74, 77 and 85–86).

Crime and violence also undermine trust in the state and destroy social capital, especially if the state tends to provide safety to some social groups, but not to others. The socially excluded may take their safety into their own hands by organizing vigilante groups, which can lead to conflicts between different organized groups (UNODC 2005: 87–88). The state is thereby weakened and unable to facilitate development.

Other multilateral development banks such as the Inter-American Development Bank (IDB) and the Asian Development Bank (ADB) have criminal-justice programmes, and so do many other donors such as the UNDP, UNODC, DFID and USAID. They all acknowledge the importance of development assistance in the criminal-justice sector.

### Existing criminal-justice involvement

There are World Bank initiatives related to the criminal justice system that have received attention inside and outside the institution. Ever since former World Bank President James D. Wolfensohn identified 'the cancer of corruption' as the single most important obstacle to development, in a now famous 1996 speech, the World Bank has turned it into a high-profile priority. Among other things, it supports anti-corruption agencies, accountability institutions and the like (see World Bank Anticorruption website).

The Bank is involved in fighting crime in the area of money laundering and financing of terrorism, in light of the 'devastating effects of these criminal activities on the integrity and functioning of financial systems, good governance, financial stability and development'. The Bank therefore undertakes assessments to determine what improvements are needed, supports capacity building and provides technical assistance to guide improvements, and undertakes research and policy development to address these specific criminal-justice challenges (see World Bank Financial Market Integrity Group website).

Another recent addition to the World Bank's anti-corruption agenda is the Stolen Asset Recovery (StAR) Initiative launched in 2007 (see World Bank Star website). World Bank President Robert B. Zoellick highlighted the development rationale of this criminal-justice initiative when he commented that:

> helping developing countries recover what is rightfully theirs is not only a matter of justice. It is a fundamental development issue. Recovered funds can be used to fund social programs. The very certainty the kleptocrats will no longer be allowed to enjoy the proceeds of their crimes can significantly boost the economic prospects of countries suffering from endemic corruption (Zoellick 2007).

Drawing on parallels with other multilateral development banks and their experience with similar mandates (Biebesheimer 2005), the limitations seem to be less legal than practical in nature. Interestingly, the Inter-American Development Bank, placed in a similar dilemma, has decided that this is not a question of legal limits, but of risk management (Biebesheimer 2005: 287).

A practical justification for limited involvement of the institution in the area of criminal justice, namely limited capacity and lack of specific expertise, is provided by a 2003 World Bank publication (World Bank 2003: 71).

## Opportunities

The World Bank is just one institution among numerous multilateral, bilateral, governmental and non-governmental institutions involved in rule-of-law reform in developing and transition countries. Its involvement in this area has grown and matured since the early 1990s, but remains focused for the most part on aspects of civil and commercial justice. Robert B. Zoellick has made fragile states one of the priority themes of the World Bank and observed that 'the international security and development communities have let the task of building of justice and law enforcement systems fall between the cracks'. But the institution's answer to Zoellick's question about 'where the international capacity exists' to address rule-of-law challenges in fragile states could be that it exists to a certain extent in his own organization, that it could be utilized, and that it could be nurtured.

It is worthwhile noting that other institutions have faced very similar situations. For example, the Charter of the Inter-American Development Bank (IDB), another Washington-based multilateral development bank (see IDB website), includes limitations very similar to those in the World Bank's Articles of Agreement. Like the World Bank, the IDB must ensure that its activities 'contribute to the acceleration of the process of economic and social development of the regional developing member countries, individually and collectively' (Article 1(i), Agreement Establishing the Inter-American Development Bank 1959). There is also a prohibition against political interference very similar to the one in the World Bank's Articles of Agreement.[37]

Yet the IDB has developed projects to promote the rule of law in Latin America and the Caribbean since the early 1990s. After initially limiting its justice-reform support to civil-court administration and case management (Biebesheimer 2005: 276), the IDB's rule-of-law programme now includes criminal-justice reform, human-rights training and many more activities to support not only judges but also prosecutors, police and prison officials (see IDB website). The IDB overcame the apparent limitations in its Charter in the following way. In 1994, the Governors of the IDB set out the strategic directions for the organization in the Eighth Replenishment Report. This report not only acknowledges that 'democracy and respect for human rights have helped create appropriate conditions for development', but also provides a mandate for public-sector reform by stating that 'effective and efficient government will require institutional strengthening of the executive, legislative, and judicial branches, and other public entities' (IDB 1994). The IDB's 2003 strategy on 'Modernization of the State' clearly states that promoting human rights as well as fighting crime, violence and insecurity is fully part of the institution's rule-of-law agenda (IDB 2003: 15–17).

The World Bank's Governance and Anti-Corruption Strategy emphasizes the role of courts as oversight and accountability institutions and recommends scaling up judicial reform (World Bank 2007). At the same time, the World Bank and the IMF claim they are the main providers worldwide of technical assistance to law-enforcement agencies in the area of money laundering (World Bank 2009: 66).

There is clearly a demand from member states for assistance in the area of criminal justice, and there are many situations in fragile states where it is increasingly difficult to communicate to client countries that the World Bank can build highways but not guard posts to maintain security; that it can renovate courts but not rehabilitate the one prison cell in the court building. However, there is also a nexus between criminal justice and human rights, and the institution may be ill-advised to work on the criminal-justice and security aspects without looking at the human-rights implications. Building legitimacy is key in fragile states. Strengthening the capacity of institutions that are not committed to the safeguard of human-rights standards may do more harm than good for the country's development.

The World Bank could build on existing experience with justice reform and give itself the means and capacity to address effectively the challenges posed by the nexus between economics, governance and security. Indeed, if the institution continues to let 'the task of building of justice and law enforcement systems fall between the cracks' (Zoellick 2008), the institution does it at its own, and our, peril.

## Notes

* The views and opinions reflected in this paper are those of the author and do not represent those of the World Bank, its Executive Directors, nor the countries they represent. The quality of the text has greatly benefited from editing by Amanda Perry-Kessaris, for which the author expresses his profound gratitude.
1 For example, the institution initially had a rather homogeneous staff of engineers and financial analysts, all based at the Washington D.C. headquarters. Today, there is a multidisciplinary staff of 10,000 employees comprising economists, public policy experts, lawyers, sector experts, social scientists, and many more. Around 30 per cent of them are now based in country offices.
2 A trust fund was created upstream of lending operations, followed by flexible emergency lending.
3 Instead, we find 'poorest countries', 'middle-income countries', 'Global Public Goods', 'The Arab World', as well as 'Knowledge and Learning' in addition to 'Fragile States'.
4 This goes beyond the 1995 OP/BP 8.50 on Emergency Recovery Assistance, which focused on infrastructure.

5 Low-income countries are so-called 'IDA countries', i.e. the currently 78 countries eligible for assistance by the World Bank's 'soft-lending arm', the International Development Association (IDA). Eligibility for IDA support depends on a country's relative poverty, defined as gross national income per capita below an established threshold and updated annually. In general, the assistance provided to IDA countries can take various forms: credits, grants and analytical and advisory services. IDA credits have no interest charge and repayments are stretched over 35 to 40 years, including a 10-year grace period (see IDA website).

6 During IDA 13 (fiscal year 2003–5), about 30 per cent of resources committed in fragile states were grants, compared to 15 per cent in non-fragile states. During IDA 14 (fiscal year 2005–8), this number increased to almost 60 per cent in fragile states, and decreased to 8.5 per cent in non-fragile states.

7 It replaces the Post-Conflict Fund (PCF; US$ 46 million between 2002 and 2006) and the Low-Income Countries Under Stress Trust Fund (LICUS TF; US$ 51 million between 2004 and 2006), which were two separate special-purpose trust funds (International Development Association 2007: 38–40).

8 For a more detailed analysis see World Bank, Norwegian Ministry of Foreign Affairs and Norwegian Agency for Development 2007.

9 Afghanistan Reconstruction Trust Fund with US$ 1,363 million between 2002 and 2006.

10 Iraq Reconstruction Trust Fund with US$ 325 million between 2004 and 2006.

11 Multi-Donor Trust Fund for Government of South Sudan with US$ 167 million and Multi-Donor Trust Fund for North Sudan with US$ 73 million in 2006.

12 Non-IBRD funded US$ 414 million between 2002 and 2006, IBRD funded 93 million in 2003 and 2004.

13 The World Bank follows none of Carothers' definitions. A working definition occurring in several publications defines rule of law as a governance system where the government itself is bound by the law, where every person in society is treated equally under the law, where the human dignity of each individual is recognized and protected by law; and where justice is accessible to all (World Bank 2003: 1).

14 This work focuses on the independence and efficiency of the justice system and has been undertaken, for example, by the United States Agency for International Development (USAID).

15 This work is conducted through international development cooperation between developing countries and bilateral and multilateral donors such as the World Bank. For a review of legal aspects of the World Bank's work on investment climate see Perry-Kessaris (2008: Chapters 1 and 2).

16 Indeed, by 2004 the Legal Department was able to claim that the Bank had supported more than 600 activities related to legal and judicial reform (World Bank 2004: 3). Many of these projects also belonged in other well-established sector-specific categories with strong traditional organizational owners, such as energy, infrastructure, health and education.

17 Both terms are used in this chapter: 'rule of law reform' in relation to perspectives external to the Bank and 'justice reform' for internal perspectives.

18 This percentage can only give a rough idea of the lending volume for public-sector governance. Note that there is an additional rule-of-law theme as well as the public-sector governance theme in the annual report. The lending under this category only represents around one per cent of the total lending portfolio.

19 According to the CDF, a

government must ensure that it has an effective system of property, contract, labor, bankruptcy, commercial codes, personal rights laws and other elements of a comprehensive legal system that is effectively, impartially and cleanly administered by a well-functioning, impartial and honest judicial and legal system (Wolfensohn 1999: 11).

20 Santos 2006: 278-81 provides an attempt to 'disaggregate the World Bank' to identify the range of World Bank approaches with respect to legal and judicial justice reform projects.

21 Dañino 2004.

22 Publications by the World Bank's Legal Vice Presidency (2002 and 2003) on strategic directions for legal and judicial reform are not a Bank strategy in the proper sense.

23 These are projects focusing entirely on justice reform, as opposed to projects in other sectors that may include one or more justice-reform components.

24 Albania, Argentina, Armenia, Azerbaijan, Bangladesh, Bolivia, China, Colombia, Croatia, Ecuador, El Salvador, Georgia, Guatemala, Honduras, Kazakhstan, Macedonia, Mexico, Mongolia, Morocco, Peru, the Philippines, Romania, Russia, Sri Lanka, Tanzania, Sudan, Venezuela, West Bank and Gaza, Yemen. In some of these countries, there has been more than one World Bank justice-reform project.

25 For project documents see World Bank Project and Operations website. An authoritative list of fragile states for different years in the past does not exist. There may be discussion about whether or not these countries belonged in the category of fragile states at the time of their respective projects.

26 It is noteworthy that, after cancellation of this lending activity, there was a US$ 500,000 grant ('Ombudsman Office Institutional Development'), approved in 1999, to enhance access to the services of the Ombudsman's Office, and to improve the efficiency of the internal processing of complaints against other state agencies. At a time when other state institutions were under authoritarian rule, this grant supported the independence of the Ombudsman's Office (World Bank 2004: 62–63). Furthermore, the World Bank approved the US$ 12 million Justice Services Improvement Project in 2004, after the end of the Fujimori regime. This project, closing in 2009, aims at setting the foundation for a long-term, participatory and sustainable reform process for Peru's justice sector. More specifically, it strengthens the institutional capacity to lead the reform process; establishes human-resource management systems that ensure independence, transparency and integrity; and enhances access to justice services, particularly for the poor, through support for the establishment of legal aid, improvement to ADR mechanisms, community justice and public outreach and dissemination activities (World Bank forthcoming).

27 It is important to understand that the emphasis on supply-side reforms may well be driven by borrowing states who may wish to avoid demand-side reforms even though they tend to cost less.

28 For a critique of this project in relation to its anticipated and actual effect on stimulating inward foreign direct investment see Perry (2001).

29 In another rehabilitated fragile state, Albania, a US$ 9 million Legal and Judicial Reform Project was approved in 2000 and closed in 2005. Its broad objectives were to improve legal education, strengthen the justice system, enhance ADR and improve the dissemination of legal information. The project's implementation and completion results report evaluates the project's outcome as unsatisfactory. It states that promoting judicial independence is a challenge for the World Bank because of the political ramifications of this issue. Also, in an environment in which the World Bank is not the only donor-organization involved, there is a need for better donor coordination. Importantly, the report also highlights that reforming existing institutions is a mid- and long-term challenge. The report recommends that 'leadership should be made aware that reform is the real goal, not computerization' (World Bank 2006a).

30 It is noteworthy that, in parallel to this lending activity, there was a US$ 130,000 grant ('Strengthening the Ombudsman Office'), approved in 2003, to provide support to the Ombudsman Office for Indigenous Women in Guatemala in order to improve access to justice for indigenous women and to create new laws to protect their rights (World Bank 2004: 59–60).

31 It is worth mentioning that, in parallel to this lending activity, there was a US$ 282,000 grant ('Legal Aid Services to Poor Women'), approved in 2001, to local NGOs to provide legal services to poor women. The grant's objective was to improve access to justice for women in Sri Lanka (World Bank 2009).

32 The World Bank faces its own organizational challenges, but the same is true for other organizations. For example, the United Nations Department for Peacekeeping Operations (UNDPKO) is also struggling with integrating rule-of-law programming into complex multi-dimensional peacekeeping operations (Carlson 2006).

33 Palacio 2006: 36.

34 For example Sweden (Picciotto 2006).

35 For example the United Nations Development Programme (UNDP).

36 Dañino 2005: 511.

37 'Article VIII(5)(f): The Bank, its officers and employees shall not interfere in the political affairs of any member, nor shall they be influenced in their decisions by the political character of the member or members concerned. Only economic considerations shall be relevant to their decisions, and these considerations shall be weighed impartially in order to achieve the purpose and functions stated in Article I.'

# References

Agreement Establishing the Inter-American Development Bank (1959). Online: <http://idbdocs.iadb.org/wsdocs/getdocument.aspx?docnum=781584>

Alston, P. (2005) 'Ships passing in the night: the current state of the human rights and development debate seen through the lens of the millennium development goals', *Human Rights Quarterly* 27: 755–829.

Biebesheimer, C. (2005) 'The Inter-American Development Bank', in P. Alston and M. Robinson (eds) *Human Rights and Development: towards mutual reinforcement*, Oxford: University Press, pp. 269–96.

Call, C. T. (2007) 'What we know and don't know about post-conflict justice and security reform', in C. T. Call (ed.) *Constructing Justice and Security After War*, Washington DC: United States Institute of Peace Press, pp. 3–26.

Carlson, S. N. (2006) *Legal and Judicial Rule of Law Work in Multi-Dimensional Peacekeeping Operations: lessons-learned study*, New York: United Nations Department of Peacekeeping Operations. Online: <http://www.reliefweb.int/rw/lib.nsf/db900SID/HMYT-6QRKBF?OpenDocument>

Carothers, T. (2006) *Promoting the Rule of Law Abroad: in search of knowledge*. Washington DC: Carnegie Endowment for International Peace.

Dañino, R. (2004) Speech delivered in Turkey in December 2004. Online: <http://siteresources.worldbank.org/INTLAWJUSTICE/214576-1139604306966/20818396/JudicialReformforImprovingGovernanceinTurkey120804.pdf>

——(2005) 'Legal aspects of the World Bank's work on human rights', in P. Alston and M. Robinson (eds) *Human Rights and Development: towards mutual reinforcement*, Oxford: Oxford University Press, pp. 509–524.

——(2005b) Speech delivered in Manila, Philippines in November 2005.

Decker, K., McInerney-Lankford, S. and Sage, C. (2005) *Human Rights and Equitable Development: 'ideals', issues and implications*, Washington DC: World Bank. Online: <http://siteresources worldbank.org/INTWDR2006/Resources/477383–1118673432908/Human_Rights_and _Equitable_Development_Ideals_Issues_and_Implications.pdf>

De Soto, H. (1989) *The Other Path: the economic answer to terrorism*, New York: Harper & Row.

Human Rights Watch (2001) *Scared at School: sexual violence against girls at South African schools*, New York: Human Rights Watch.

Inter-American Development Bank (IDB) (1994) *Report on the Eighth General Increase in the Resources of the Inter-American Development Bank*, A-1704, 12 August 1994, Washington DC: Inter-American Development Bank.

——(IDB) (2003) *Modernization of the State: strategy document*, Washington, DC: Inter-American Development Bank. Online: <http://www.iadb.org/sds/doc/SGC-GN-2235-1-e.pdf>

International Development Association (2007) *Operational Approaches and Financing in Fragile States*, Washington DC: International Development Association. Online: <http:// go.worldbank.org/RPX3HTLF40>

Marshall, K. (2008) *The World Bank: from reconstruction to development to equity*, New York: Routledge.

Moser, C. and Holland, J. (1997) *Urban Poverty and Violence in Jamaica*, Washington, DC: World Bank.

Narayan, D. and Petesch, P. (eds) (2002) *Voices of the Poor: from many lands*, Oxford: University Press.

OECD (2007) *Enhancing the Delivery of Justice and Security: governance, peace and security*, Paris: OECD. Online: <http://www.oecd.org/dataoecd/27/13/38434642.pdf>

Palacio, A. (2006) 'The way forward: human rights and the World Bank', in *World Bank Development Outreach*, Washington DC: World Bank October 2006. Online: <http:// web.worldbank.org/WBSITE/EXTERNAL/TOPICS/EXTLAWJUSTICE/0,content MDK:21106614~menuPK:445673~pagePK:64020865~piPK:149114~theSi-tePK:445634,00.html>

Perry, A. (2001) *Legal Systems as a Determinant of FDI: lessons from Sri Lanka*, London: Kluwer.

Perry-Kessaris, A. (2008) *Global Business, Local Law: the Indian legal system as a communal resource in foreign investment relations*, Aldershot: Ashgate.

Picciotto, R. (2006) *What is Human Security*, conference paper. Online: <http://www. gdnet.ws/pdf2/gdn_library/annual_conferences/seventh_annual_conference/ Picciotto_parallel_3_6.pdf>

Samuels, K. (2006) *Rule of Law Reform in Post-Conflict Countries: operational initiatives and lessons learnt*, Washington, DC: World Bank. Online: <http://siteresources.worldbank.org/ INTCPR/Resources/WP37_web.pdf>

Santos, A. (2006) 'The World Bank's Uses of the 'Rule of Law' Promise', in D. M. Trubek and A. Santos (eds.) *The New Law and Economic Development*, Cambridge: University Press, pp. 253–300.

Shihata, I. (1995) 'The Prohibition of Political Activities in the Bank's Work', in *World Bank Legal Papers*, The Hague: Martinus Nijhoff, 2000: 219 at 233.

——(2000) 'Issues of 'Governance' in borrowing members – the extent of their relevance under the Bank's Articles of Agreement', in The World Bank Legal Papers 245 (2000), 268.

United Nations Office on Drugs and Crime (UNODC) (2005) *Crime and Development in Africa*, New York: UNODC. Online: <http://www.unodc.org/pdf/African_report.pdf>

Wolfensohn, J. D. (1999) *A Proposal for a comprehensive development framework.* Online: <http://siteresources.worldbank.org/CDF/Resources/cdf.pdf>

——(2005) 'Some reflections on human rights and development', in P. Alston and M. Robinson (eds) *Human Rights and Development: towards mutual reinforcement*, Oxford: Oxford University Press, pp. 19–24.

World Bank (1989) *Sub-Saharan Africa: from crisis to sustainable growth. A long term perspective study*, Washington, DC: World Bank.

——(1998) *Development and Human Rights: the role of the World Bank*, Washington DC: World Bank.

——(2001) *Project Appraisal Document for a Capacity Building for Economic Management Project in the Gambia*, Washington, DC: World Bank. Online: <http://www-wds.worldbank.org/external/default/WDSContentServer/WDSP/IB/2001/07/31/000094946_01071404015070/Rendered/PDF/multi0page.pdf>

——(2002) Legal and judicial reform: observations, experiences, and approach of the Legal Vice Presidency (Washington, DC: World Bank). Online: <http://go.worldbank.org/DG534WOHK0>

——(2002b) *Malawi: poverty reduction strategy paper*, Washington, DC: World Bank.

——(2003) *Legal and Judicial Reform: strategic directions*, Washington, DC: World Bank. Online: <http://go.worldbank.org/ZONFO1H6C0>

——(2004) *Initiatives in Legal and Judicial Reform*, Washington DC: World Bank.

——(2004b) *The Role of the World Bank in Conflict and Development: an evolving agenda*, Washington DC: World Bank. Online: <http://siteresources.worldbank.org/INTCPR/214578–1112884026494/20482669/ConflictAgenda2004.pdf>

——(2004c) *Implementation Completion Report (TF-27806) on a Grant in the Amount of US$3.0 Million to Kosovo, Serbia and Montenegro for a Private Sector Development Technical Assistance Grant.* Online: <http://www-wds.worldbank.org/external/default/WDSContentServer/WDSP/IB/2004/12/14/000090341_20041214090552/Rendered/PDF/29844.pdf>

——(2006a) *Implementation Completion and Results Report (IDA-33270) on a Credit in the Amount of SDR 6.6 Million (US$ 9.0 Million Equivalent) to Albania for a Legal and Judicial Reform Project*, Washington DC: World Bank. Online: <http://www-wds.worldbank.org/external/default/WDSContentServer/WDSP/IB/2006/07/25/000090341_20060725100911/Rendered/PDF/35351.pdf >

——(2007) *Governance and Anti-Corruption Strategy*. Online: <http://go.worldbank.org/NUDME22A40>

——(2007b) *Independent Evaluation of the Post-Conflict Fund (FY 03-FY06)*, Washington DC: World Bank. Online: <http://siteresources.worldbank.org/INTLICUS/Resources/PCF_Evaluation_FY03–06.pdf>

——(2007c) *Implementation Completion and Results Report (Cr. 3384-CE) on a Credit in the Amount of SDR 13.6 Million US$ 18.2 Million Equivalent to Democratic Socialist Republic of Sri Lanka for a Legal and Judicial Reform Project*, Washington DC: World Bank Online: <http://www-wds.worldbank.org/external/default/WDSContentServer/WDSP/IB/2008/07/04/000333037_20080704000151/Rendered/PDF/395380ICR0P0441isclosed0July0202008.pdf>

——(2007d) 'Country Policy and Institutional Assessment Questionnaire'. Online: <http://siteresources.worldbank.org/IDA/Resources/CPIA2007Questionnaire.pdf>

——(2008) *Establishment of a State- and Peace-Building Fund*, Washington DC: World Bank. Online: <http://www-wds.worldbank.org/external/default/

WDSContentServer/WDSP/IB/2008/04/01/000334955_20080401075958/
Rendered/PDF/431490BR0NO0PR1580and0IDAR200810056.pdf>

——(2008b) *Annual Report 2008*, Washington DC: World Bank. Online: <http://go. worldbank.org/VLWFADE5O0>

——(2008c) *Implementation Completion and Results Report (IBRD-33010) on a Loan in the Amount of US$33.00 Million Equivalent to the Republic of Guatemala for a Judicial Reform Project.* Abstract. Online: <http://www.wds.worldbank.org/external/default/WDSContent-Server/WDSP/IB/2008/08/28/000333038_20080828034304/Rendered/PDF/ICR6230Box03341IC010disclosed081261.pdf>

——(2009) *Initiatives in Justice* , Washington, DC: World Bank.

World Bank, Norwegian Ministry of Foreign Affairs & Norwegian Agency for Development (2007) *Review of Post-Crisis Multi-Donor Trust Funds.* Online: <http://siteresources. worldbank.org/INTLICUS/Resources/388758–1094226297907/MDTF_FinalReport.pdf>

World Bank and UNODC (2007) *Crime, Violence, and Development: trends, costs, and policy options in the Caribbean*, Washington DC: World Bank. Online: <http://go.worldbank. org/HDBCAXW850>

Zoellick, R. B. (2007) Speech delivered on 17 September 2007. Online: <http://go. worldbank.org/U2ZCWCDKR0>

——(2008) *Fragile States: securing development*. Speech delivered on 12 September 2008 at the International Institute for Strategic Studies in Geneva, Switzerland. Online: <http:// go.worldbank.org/EE1KBSJV60>

## Useful websites

Anti-Corruption (World Bank)
   <http://go.worldbank.org/QYRWVXVH40>
(CEPEJ) European Commission for the Efficiency of Justice
   <http://www.coe.int/cepej>
(CLEP) Commission for the Legal Empowerment of the Poor
   <http://www.undp.org/legalempowerment>
Financial Market Integrity Group (World Bank)
   <http://go.worldbank.org/ZVIJSUC6J0>
Fragile and Conflict-Affected Countries (World Bank)
   <http://go.worldbank.org/JHPKRCXS40>
Fragile States (World Bank)
   <http://go.worldbank.org/TV8VJ1PRB0>
Human Rights FAQ (World Bank)
   <http://go.worldbank.org/72L95K8TN0>
(IDB) Inter-American Development Bank
   <http://www.iadb.org>
(IDA) International Development Association
   <http://go.worldbank.org/55TJCXJ4D0>
Justice for the Poor (J4P) (World Bank)
   <http://go.worldbank.org/SMIKY7M6O0>
Law and Justice Assessments (World Bank)
   <http://go.worldbank.org/CHGBS43QV0>

Law and Justice Institutions (World Bank)
    <http://www.worldbank.org/lji>
Projects (World Bank)
    <http://go.worldbank.org/M7ARDFNB60>
Project and Operations (World Bank)
    <http://go.worldbank.org/0FRO32VEI0>
Stolen Asset Recovery (StAR) Initiative (World Bank)
    <http://go.worldbank.org/1G0IH8RSK0>
State and Peace Building Fund (World Bank)
    <http://go.worldbank.org/J13I66CRO0>
Strategic Themes (World Bank)
    <http://go.worldbank.org/56O9ZVPO70>

# Chapter 14

# Assessing the sociocultural viability of rule-of-law policies in post-conflict societies: culture clash

*Dzenan Sahovic*

## Introduction

As Klaus Decker notes in his contribution to this volume, the fate of post-conflict states, and the role of law in determining that fate, have become the focus of increasing international attention in recent years. The absence of the rule of law is perceived as the cause of all failures, and rule-of-law promotion the panacea to all experienced difficulties, in the reconstruction of war-torn societies. So the promotion of rule of law has become the cornerstone of each and every internationally assisted post-conflict peace-building policy. Although the principles underlying rule-of-law reforms are usually presented as universal, non-political, objective and globally agreed upon, in fact they are guided by socially constructed notions of what a good society is.[1] As such, rule-of-law policies are part of a larger process of political and social engineering.[2] To the great surprise of policymakers, who perceive their own policies as rational and universally accepted, almost commonsensical, rule-of-law reforms in post-conflict societies are being contested, resisted and even derailed by local political and social actors.

This chapter demonstrates how Cultural Theory[3] can help us to assess critically the implementation of rule-of-law policies by international peace-building missions in post-conflict societies. The Cultural Theory framework, which is based on the work of anthropologist Mary Douglas (1970), allows us to map actors' cultural biases, social relations and strategic behaviours. By focussing our attention on how people choose to define a problem, how they choose to organize themselves and where they look for solutions to that problem, this framework allows us to identify and assess different socially constructed approaches to policymaking and policy implementation.

The argument set out in this chapter is that the attitudes, behaviours and strategies adopted by peace-building missions can be classified into four ideal sociocultural types (individualism, egalitarianism, hierarchy and fatalism). More often than not, the sociocultural type of the post-conflict mission does not correspond to the sociocultural setting of the war-torn society in question. The potential for such culture clashes goes some way to explaining the misunderstandings, conflicts and failures of internationally driven rule-of-law policies in war-torn societies.

## Cultural Theory framework

The Cultural Theory framework rests on the 'grid-group' model, the roots of which are to be found in Emile Durkheim's observations on how society shapes the thinking of individuals. According to Durkheim (1915: 456), individual action is based on an individual's values and beliefs, which are in turn defined by his or her preferred form of organizing with others. In addition, Durkheim defined two dimensions of social organization: 'social regulation', the extent to which social life is governed by role, rule and social facts; and 'social integration', the extent to which individuals are held accountable to larger collectives (Durkheim and Wilson 1973: 288). These ideas provided the epistemological and ontological foundations for the understanding of a 'social solidarity', the institutionalized form of social organization (Durkheim 1964: 439).

British anthropologist Mary Douglas (1970) drew on these concepts to develop her 'group-grid model' of cultures: a two-by-two matrix of, to use Douglas' term, 'ways of life' (Figure 14.1). The grid dimension refers to the extent to which individuals accept external prescriptions as legitimate. The group dimension refers to the extent to which individuals are bound in groups.[4] The resulting matrix produces a four-field typology of ways of life or cultures.

This typology is perceived by most cultural theorists as the 'taxonomy of social context and their supporting cosmologies' (Douglas 1982: 247). As we shall see, scholars in different fields of social sciences have used it to explain how and why individuals in different cultural settings can have quite differing views on everything from basic human nature and environmental concerns to views about risk, technology, consumption and so on.[5]

### Individualism

The individualist way of life is characterized by low group membership (low group) and few external constraints (low grid). Individuals are bound by neither group incorporation nor clearly prescribed roles. The ideal type is a self-made

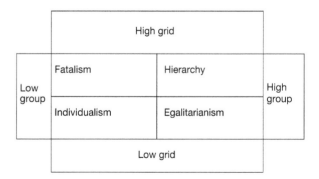

*Figure 14.1* Grid-group Cultural Theory model

manufacturer. Aggregated to entire societies[6] and exaggerated for the purpose of argument, the domination of the individualist way of life would lead to an American Dream-style capitalistic society, where everyone is expected to pursue their own interests and their own happiness, described in materialistic terms, with a minimum of prescriptions from the outside.

Individualists tend to engage in 'network'-type social relations: they are not bound in strong groups (low group) and external prescriptions are few and weak (low grid) (Douglas 1978). Individualists maintain and use networks – temporary utility-based relations – in their search for material gain and respect based on merit and competence. The result is that egocentric networks are the primary form of social organization in individualist societies (Dixon et al. 2003: 43).[7]

Individualists are pragmatic materialists who consider themselves to be masters of their destinies. Because they see nature as able to absorb whatever we throw at it, they are content for managing institutions to act in a laissez-faire manner. Because they view human beings as perpetually self-serving, they embrace the use of incentives to channel human behaviour (Thompson et al. 1990: 7–8,26–37). Risk is perceived as an opportunity for gain (Schwarz and Thompson 1990) and when things go wrong, individualists blame personal incompetence (Wildavsky 1987). Economic growth is regarded as possible and desirable, resources as unlimited (Thompson et al. 1990: 39–51). This means of socializing is also referred to as 'equal individualization' (Mamadouh 1999a: 345–50).

### Egalitarianism

The egalitarian way of life[8] is characterized by high group membership (high group) and few external constraints (low grid). Individuals are bound by incorporation into groups, yet their behaviour is not constrained by prescribed roles. An example is a member in a Western commune in which the individual members have strong bonds to their group (the commune), yet their lives are not controlled by external prescriptions (sense of freedom is experienced as high). Domination of the egalitarian way of life would lead to a welfare-state-type society, where people are perceived as equal, expected to trust each other and expected collectively to pursue common interests.

Egalitarians tend to engage in 'enclave' social relations: they are bound in strong groups (high group) but external prescriptions are few and weak (low grid). The enclaves are created and maintained by egalitarians who seek out people with similar values and beliefs and organize in tight groups. Respect is awarded by virtue of membership. Power relations within the enclave are flat and all members have equal value. This manner of socializing is also referred to as 'collectivized equality'.

In contrast to individualists, egalitarians believe they influence their own lives indirectly, through participation in collective decision-making. Because they view nature as unforgiving, the least jolt threatening to cause total collapse, they expect managing institutions to treat the ecosystem with great care. Human beings are viewed as born good, but corrupted by power and evil institutions, in both the market and the public sphere. Because they reject authority, egalitarians blame the system when things go wrong. Economic growth is regarded as unimportant, or at least as less important than equality. Natural resources are thought to be limited and over-exploited by the system. Egalitarians are not risk takers; they view nature as unforgiving.

### Hierarchism

The hierarchical way of life is characterized by high group membership (high group) and many external constraints (high grid). One example is a high-caste Hindu who has strong bonds to his/her group (family, caste) while his/her life is highly regulated by the social context (strong traditions).

Hierarchists tend to engage in 'pyramid' (or 'positional') social relations: they are bound in strong groups (high group) and their lives are controlled by strong and numerous external prescriptions (high grid).[9] Hierarchists create and maintain these pyramid-type relations in order to improve stability. Respect is awarded to the loyal, rule-obeying members.

Hierarchists regard human beings as bad (born evil), incapable and in need of guidance from rules and regulations, strong institutions and knowledgeable elites.[10] When things go wrong, hierarchists either blame no-one[11] or they blame deviants. They view nature as forgiving, but vulnerable to extreme interruptions. Managing institutions should, therefore, regulate and minimize unusual occurrences. Economic growth is, as in the case of the individualists, considered possible and desirable, but hierarchists see increases in wealth as a result of group sacrifice rather than individual competence. Resources are, as in the case of the egalitarians, considered to be limited, but the hierarchists are ready to trust the experts within the system to decide about use of resources. Risks are of concern, but they are manageable, and once again the experts within the system are to be trusted.

### Fatalism

The fatalistic way of life is characterized by low group membership (low group) and many external constraints (high grid). One example is non-unionized weavers who, although not strongly bound to groups, are subject to external prescriptions which guide their everyday life. A caricature of the fatalist society would be a troubled society where most of the people keep their heads down, isolate themselves and focus on their own survival, without any hope that improvements could come from their own engagement in any collective endeavours or own capability. The clearest example of such an environment in the contemporary world is the example of a failed or collapsed war-torn society.[12]

Fatalists tend to engage in 'isolate' social relations: they are not bound in strong groups (low group) and external prescriptions are many and strong (high grid).[13] The isolates are excluded, voluntarily or involuntarily, from group activities, yet their lives are controlled by factors outside their control. They view social cooperation as problematic; they neither give nor receive respect. The possibility of having any kind of influence is perceived as low. Fatalists view nature as a part of a random world and human beings are viewed as unpredictable and, therefore, not to be trusted. When things go wrong, the fatalists blame fate and bad luck. Managing institutions are not expected to manage or learn, only to cope with erratic events. Economic growth is regarded as generally desirable, but unlikely to be profitable, except by chance or luck. Risk taking is viewed as unnecessary, to be avoided, since it can never lead to gains.

## Peace-building interventions

In this section, we explore the potential impact of the sociocultural background (individualist, hierarchist, egalitarian, fatalist) of those responsible for international peace-building interventions, including rule-of-law assistance, upon the design and implementation of those interventions. The full range of findings revealed by the application of the Cultural Theory framework to this field are set out in Table 14.2. Some key highlights of those findings are discussed in the following subsections.

### ... by individualists

The individualist definition of peace is closely connected with individual freedoms. Rational people would not choose war, since war reduces resources for all. Consequently, if people were allowed to make free choices, there would be no wars. Furthermore, people are perceived as self-seeking. Therefore, the sum of their individual choices must lead to cooperation, since cooperation increases wealth and well-being for all. Wars and conflicts exist due to failures of the market, as rules of the game are unfair, unclear or non-existent. The path to peace, according to individualist cultural bias, is through market mechanisms that allow rational individuals to make free choices with as few market failures as possible. Free and fair elections, freedom of movement, organization and trade and freedom of information are seen as ultimately leading to problem solving. The peace-building process is defined as a short-term process[14] in which the international community has only a limited role, providing temporary assistance. International involvement can, temporarily, provide security, as well as technical expertise to support commerce, justice delivery, elections and the building of bridges between the parties.

The adherents of individualist social solidarity define people as good, capable and needing nothing more than opportunities.[15] They see market mechanisms as a solution to all that is private and public. They envision a non-intrusive and small government, which allows for individual preferences to sum up to a collective definition of public interest, as a solution to all problems in the public arena.

Table 14.2 Typology of peace-building approaches

| | Individualism | Egalitarianism | Hierarchy | Fatalism |
|---|---|---|---|---|
| Human nature | Good, self-seeking | Good, corrupted by evil institutions | Born sinful, redeemed by good institutions | Not to be trusted |
| Paths to peace | Democracy Interdependence and free trade | Reconciliation and forgiveness | Security and stability | Absence of war Lasting peace unreachable |
| The goals of the process | Economic integration Political freedom | Social integration | Order | Survival |
| The role of the international community | Technical assistants | Teachers | Guardians | Undefined (possibly survivors) |
| Basis of authority of intervention | Competence and skills | Moral ground | Legal grounds – Peace agreement and int. law | No legitimate basis of authority |
| Time span of intervention | Short | Indefinite | Medium long | Unpredictable |
| Scope of intervention | Narrow | All-encompassing | Medium-size | - |
| Democracy style | Procedural | Participatory | Guardian | Unimportant |
| Management Mode | Choice-ism | Group-ism | Boss-ism | Chance-ism |
| Policy based on: | Interests | Values | Structure | Survival |
| Governance challenge | To enable markets to function | To facilitate promotion of public interests | To enable domination of elites and experts | Does not expect and require participation |
| Perception of politics | 'I decide what I want to do' | 'We decide what we want to do' | 'We decide what they must do' | 'They decide what I must do' |
| Social organization | Egocentric networks | Enclaves | Positional | Isolates |
| Relations | Many and loose | Many and tight | Few and tight | Few and loose |
| Invited to the table | All who want to participate | All | All who have power | None |
| Strategic Behaviour | Individualist | Egalitarian | Hierarchical | Fatalist |
| Policy style | Top-down and Bottom-up, through the market | Bottom-up through civil society | Top-down through the apparatus of the state | Top-down |
| Policy implementation tools | Pricing, economic incentives | Training and information | Regulation and legislation | None–(garbage can) |

Individualists find arguments about the causes of problems based on group differences and the inherent malignance of human beings inaccurate and offensive. Individuals might be incapable, but such generalization about groups of people is unacceptable in their frame of reference. Thus, they find intrusive intervention to be counterproductive, since the results do not express the will of the people, through either markets or the electoral process. Any interference that sets aside market mechanisms and democratic procedures is not productive. It can be tolerated only when it is indisputably aimed at correcting the behaviour of the incompetent elites who stand in the way and represent obstacles to the proper functioning of market mechanisms. The individualists also reject the egalitarian cultural bias, particularly because it focuses on what individualists perceive as the private sphere, thus limiting individual freedom.

The adherents of individualist social solidarity, when in charge of a peace-building process, would create egocentric networks. From among their contacts with the representatives of other agencies working in the field and with the local authorities, they would 'invite to the table' those who shared the same interests and were willing to help. Eternally optimistic about the possibility of achieving their goals, the individualists would seek out, without regard for their position or their right to participate, those perceived to be capable and able to contribute, and would avoid others. This would result in their dealing with both top-level and low-level officials, in both civil society and in public office, in both business (private) and politics (public) and from both (or all) groups in the conflict, regardless of their past atrocities. The effect of this would be many loose relationships among a variety of actors, organized in egocentric temporary networks.

Concerning the preferred strategic behaviour, the adherents of individualist social solidarity would attempt to influence the behaviour of others through negotiations based on rational arguments. They would gladly engage in competition between opinions, confident in the rationality and logic of their own meta-narrative, expecting others to be rational and accept their arguments. When faced with the prospect of failure, they would use their 'hammer', their all-purpose tool – economic incentives. Supporters of individualist social solidarity believe that society is governable and social contexts can be influenced through economic incentives that change the calculations of rational actors and thus enable them to make the right choices.

### ... by egalitarians

The egalitarian definition of peace is closely connected with notions of equality, but not with equality of opportunity as is the case with individualist cultural bias, but with their specific definition of true equality – equality of outcome. The peace-building process after an inter-communal conflict is therefore all about civil-society solutions that enable participation and that lead to integration, reconciliation, forgiveness, justice and equality between groups in conflict. The path to peace is not found in negotiating compromises between elites or in good rules that regulate behaviour, but is based on a higher moral stance – notions of inherent goodness and equality between human beings, regardless of their group membership. The peace-building process is therefore defined as a broad, long-term, almost indefinite process.[16]

Egalitarians see people as good, capable and primarily in need of access to decision-making.[17] Accordingly, they would claim that active participation is the solution to all problems in the public arena. Given that they have an inherently collectivist view of social life, their definition of public interest is wide, encompassing almost all aspects of society.[18]

Egalitarians involved in a peace-building process will see themselves as teachers. Standing on a higher moral ground, they seek to educate the people and make them understand their collective interest, which is defined by the egalitarians as peace and cooperation through collective action and through participation in the public arena. They perceive international interventions in a war-torn society as a moral obligation of the international community to get involved and teach good values, human rights, equality and justice – all the basic principles behind rule of law.

Egalitarians find arguments about causes of the problems based on group differences and inherent malignance of human beings to be inaccurate, even offensive. Thus, they judge that the approach of the hierarchists, which includes intrusive intervention involving the international community forcing solutions on the local society, to be counterproductive because the result is not based on the will of the people. Furthermore, they are reluctant to accept the ideas of an individualistically biased intervention since they see it as utterly inefficient, possibly even counterproductive. There can be no lasting peace based on the rules of the market, which might possibly increase competition and thus increase inequalities. Lasting solutions to all problems, they assert, are to be found in cooperation, a deeper understanding between the parties in conflict and through a commitment to collective action, driven from the bottom up, by civil society.

If in charge of a peace-building process, egalitarians would seek out a wide range of actors with a similar moral stance. In their contacts with other representatives of the international community and in contacts with the local political elites, their inclination would be that those willing to participate would be invited to the table. Egalitarians would deal with lower-level officials and even directly with the population, through NGOs and civil society. In contact with other organizations and agencies working in the same process, they would try to create many tight relationships between a variety of actors who would all be perceived as being equally important.

Concerning the preferred strategic behaviour, adherents of egalitarian social solidarity would attempt to influence the behaviour of others through information and education. They would engage in consensus-seeking negotiations, confident in the moral superiority of their own point of view, expecting others to learn and accept their will and their values. When faced with the prospect of failure, they would use their 'hammer', their all-purpose tool: education. In the view of the adherents of egalitarian social solidarity, society is governable and its social context can be influenced by the people, if they act collectively and if their action is based on higher moral values, i.e. if they seek justice and equality.

### ... by hierarchists

For hierarchists, peace is about stability and order, and it is achievable by ensuring the existence of strong institutions to which people will be submissive. They therefore adopt conflict-management mechanisms which revolve around maintaining a balance of power and strengthening the institutions that regulate the behaviour of various groups in conflict.[19] Lasting and sustainable peace is therefore found in institution building, strong government, good elites and institutional checks and balances. In practical terms, all of the above translates into an acknowledgement of group differences, of a consociational democratic system where minority participation is ensured through institutional mechanisms, principally the right of veto[20] and development of other institutional control mechanisms.

Hierarchist peace-builders would see themselves as guardians, charged with controlling the local society and building the institutions necessary to establish and maintain peace.[21] International involvement is thought to have the potential to correct the 'bad behaviour' of elites, to replace the authority of the state (where it has been rejected by different groups) and, ultimately, to build a strong and stable system – social, legal, administrative and political.

Those coming from a hierarchical perspective find narratives about the inherent goodness of man to be incorrect and naïve. Accordingly, they do not accept the individualist narrative that has democratic procedures as a universal solution. On the contrary, they might view a democratization process as risky, likely to destabilize the society. Nor do they accept the egalitarian narrative which has an active and developed civil society, characterized by vertical participation and horizontal consensus seeking, removing the risk of renewed fighting. They find that approach unrealistically extensive, almost indefinite. In that sense, the adherents of hierarchical social solidarity are pragmatists, believing that a lasting peace is best built through mechanisms that will ensure a well-functioning, balanced and stable system of government.

Hierarchists organize peace-building processes into pyramid-like structures. In their interactions with representatives of other field agencies and with local authorities, they attempt to organize a command-and-control-oriented structure building few relationships with top-level officials. On the other hand, if faced with the prospect of failure, they would use to the fullest extent the power given to them by virtue of their position. For example, if the local governmental elites are thought not to be up to the task – that is, they do not respect the legal-rational authority and the knowledge of the experts – then hierarchists would seek to establish a higher position in the pyramid, to gain more power with which to force others into obedience.

With respect to strategy – the choice of method to reach set goals – hierarchists would attempt to influence the behaviours of others through command and control, constructing legal and administrative practices to guide the behaviour of local elites, and basing their authority on the legal framework (mandate) guiding the process. In case of failure, they use their 'hammer,'[22] their all-purpose tool: straightforward and top-down regulation.

## ... by fatalists

Fatalists define people as untrustworthy, incapable and in need of luck in order to succeed.[23] They see the public sphere as threatening, an arena where people get hurt. The path to peace, according to fatalist cultural bias, is predetermined by higher powers, luck or chance. It follows then, they contend, that little or nothing can be done to build a lasting peace – managing institutions (representatives of the international community) can only pretend to do something and only time will tell if peace becomes stable or if armed conflict explodes again. The peace-building process is, therefore, not defined in terms of time limits.[24] Fatalistic peace builders see themselves as drops of water in a sea, unable to influence events. They try to survive: they create policies that will enable them to raise funds and stay longer, hoping that things outside their control will provide the desired result, namely, a lasting peace. International involvement cannot build peace and it cannot influence the local society, the fatalists claim. It can only fool the people (in the local society as well as in the international community) that something is being done in the name of peace.

Fatalist cultural bias rejects the narratives of the other social solidarities. The causes of war are neither institutional nor structural; likewise they are not caused by bad elites. It is bad luck, bad history, bad neighbours and other things that cannot be controlled that are to blame. They also reject the other solidarities' notions of peace and their ideas about how it can be achieved. The ideas that democratization, reconciliation through dialogue and participation in the civil society might lead to a lasting peace are considered naïve. The regulation of behaviour through institutional arrangements is the only accepted narrative. Yet even here, the fatalists wonder who will regulate it and conclude that those people, whether they are the old elites, new elites or the international peacebuilders and experts, have evil intentions and cannot be trusted. Thus, they reject the idea that someone could regulate and prevent bad things from happening. While not endorsing it, they could possibly tolerate a hierarchical approach since it neither requires nor expects active participation.

If placed in charge of a peace-building process fatalists would isolate themselves from the risks they see arising from participation. In their contacts both with other international agencies active in the process and with the local authorities, fatalists would not attempt to organize in a meaningful manner. Eternally pessimistic concerning the possibilities of achieving their goals, the fatalists would go with the flow and hold on to the status quo, with no grand ideas about achieving dramatic changes. Accordingly, they would create as few and as loose relationships as possible.

The preferred strategic behaviour of fatalists is to avoid attention, keep their heads down and avoid taking unnecessary risks. They would engage in a competition of meta-narratives with the adherents of other social solidarities, acting as prophets of doom. When faced with the prospect of failure, i.e. the prospect of a disaster due to their inactivity, they would use their 'hammer', their all-purpose tool – isolation and avoidance of the problem. Supporters of fatalist social solidarity believe that society is not governable and social contexts cannot be influenced.

## The sociocultural viability dilemma

An important theme arising from the above section is that members of each sociocultural type reject the narratives of other sociocultural types. The potential for culture clashes during peace-building activities is, therefore, high. Picture a caricature of a US lawyer, working as a consultant in Afghanistan throwing money at any encountered problem, attempting to create some kind of basic structure that will enable the most basic financial transactions and the upholding of contracts – all in order to open up for some kind of economic development with the ultimate goal of creating a sustainable peace. Imagine the surprise such a lawyer experiences when local strongmen proclaim 'We do not care about your dollars' – for how can someone deny food to the hungry, for the sake of some political or religious idea? Consider also a caricature of a north-European NGO activist, training lawyers in basic human rights, appealing for their sense of justice in the midst of a discussion of which ethnic group 'deserves' access to justice in Bosnia. Imagine their surprise when this activist experiences racist debates, for how can the society be rebuilt on a principle of justice, when not even the intellectuals and elites can appreciate the basic moral arguments of equality of all people, regardless of colour, ethnicity or religion? Finally, think of a UN-employed expert on judicial systems attempting to force the provisional parliaments and transitional administrations in, say, Timor-Leste to reform the judicial system entirely, from above, in order to once and for all create a functioning and stable judiciary. Imagine their surprise when politicians argue back and say 'new laws will not solve anything' – for how can one change anything if not even parliaments believe they have any power?

These caricatures of individualist, egalitarian and hierarchical field workers, exaggerated and prejudicial as they might be, are probably recognizable to most people working in difficult post-conflict environments and they are quite useful in the search for understanding policy failures in post-conflict environments.

In addition to illuminating these cultural types, the Culture Theory framework also has a role to play in helping us to reduce the incidence and severity of cultural clashes. Apart from being a tool for the mapping of cultural biases, social relations and strategic behaviours, grid-group cultural theory also identifies what are 'good policies' and/or 'good governance modes' in a given social setting, through the notion of sociocultural viability. A policy will succeed if it is viable – that is, if it contains elements that are appropriate to its sociocultural context. Similarly, a governance institution will be perceived and accepted as legitimate if it is socioculturally viable – that is, if it contains elements that are in line with its sociocultural context. Thus, even in the case of international peace-building and rule-of-law promotion in war-torn societies, policies and institutions will succeed if they are socioculturally pluralistic to the extent that at least some of their elements align with the sociocultural context (the dominant shared values and beliefs and the preferred mode of social relations existing in the war-torn society).

When representatives of the international community arrive, introduce policies and engage in the process of governance of the war-torn society, they do so based on their own cultural biases, their preferred social relations and their preferred behavioural strategies. The local society, on the other hand, represents a sociocultural context that is presumably different, especially given that a war-torn society constitutes a collapsed state, a non-functioning social system. Thus, there is an inherent conflict between international policies and the local context; a conflict that will most likely cause difficulties and lead to misunderstandings. In the case of rule-of-law promotion policies, such conflicts arise despite the fact that rule-of-law principles are usually perceived as universal.

Logically, there can be only two ways of attempting to attack this problem. First, the representatives of the international community can attempt to introduce policies and engage in governance in a manner that is consistent with their own values and beliefs, social relations and strategic behaviours, and force the local society to adapt. While the possible and intended benefit is a change in the political culture of the local society as it learns new ways of governance, there is a risk of misunderstandings, conflict and policy failures.

The second option is for representatives of the international community to adapt to the local sociocultural context, introduce policies and engage in governance in a manner similar to that preferred by the local authorities and local social elites in order to achieve sociocultural viability, policy success and governance legitimacy. The possible benefit is short-term policy success. The possible risk is failure to achieve major changes in the local society in the long run, since the socioculturally viable policies reinforce the already dominant values and beliefs. In this case, it is the representatives of the international community who are learning and changing, rather than the local authorities and the local society in general.

In this way the Cultural Theory framework reveals a basic problem in international peace building that has the goal of promoting political and social change; a problem that can be labelled a 'sociocultural viability dilemma'. On the one hand, representatives of the international community can attempt to teach the locals and thus risk failure. On the other, the representatives of the international community can attempt to learn from the locals and thus risk reinforcing the social solidarities already dominant in the society, consequently failing to achieve significant social and political change. The same dilemma arises in relation to rule-of-law assistance in the unforgiving post-conflict socio-cultural contexts. Should one attempt to teach (legal-system transplantation) or to learn (technical assistance to locals in their search for their own solutions)? The question for empirical researchers is to define which of the two is occurring in a specific case and with what effects.

## Conclusion

The first contribution of the Cultural Theory framework to the conceptual understanding of international peace building consists of a classification of approaches to peace building into four coherent, distinct and conflicting ideal types.[25] This process leads to the second contribution of Cultural Theory: the revelation that cultural clashes are likely to arise in the course of international peace building, and to have serious consequences. Finally, we are confronted with a sociocultural viability dilemma: having identified the potential for culture clashes in peace building, how do we determine which of the cultures ought to prevail?

## Notes

1  For more on the concept of rule of law, see discussion on rule of law as a means and rule of law as an end in Bergling 2006: 14–19.
2  For more on broadening of peace building, see Sahovic 2007: 7–9.
3  For more on use of the term Cultural Theory, see Mamadouh 1997: 345–409. The theory is also known as 'grid-group analysis', grid-group theory or 'sociocultural via-bility'. See Dake and Thompson 1999: 417–24.
4  The 'legitimacy of external prescriptions' refers to the varying ease with which people accept judgments of others as valid for, and binding on, them. For a career-enlisted person in military service, for instance, this legitimacy is apt to be high because he or she will have chosen a life that routinely involves accepting the instructions of officers, with no questions asked. See Lockhart 1999: 862–92.
5  For an excellent overview of cultural biases with regard to a variety of different con-cepts, see Dixon et al. 2003.
6  For more on aggregation of individual ways of life to political cultures of societies, see Thompson et al. 1990: 87–88. See also Mamadouh 1999b:138–53 and 1997:17–25.
7  This means of socializing is also referred to as 'equal individualization' (Mamadouh 1999a: 345–50).
8  Also referred to as 'sectarian'.
9  This way of socializing is also referred to as 'collectivized inequality'.
10  Myths of human nature corresponding to the four social solidarities are discussed in Thompson et al. 1990: 33–37.

11  This is known as 'blame shedding'.
12  For more on the sociocultural context of failed and collapsed states, see for example Rotberg 2003.
13  This way of socializing is also referred to as 'unequal individualization'.
14  Once again, time perspective of adherents of different social solidarities is outlined in Schwarz and Thompson 1999: 67.
15  Myths of human nature corresponding to the four social solidarities are discussed in Thompson et al. 1990: 33–37.
16  The time perspective for adherents of different social solidarities is outlined in Schwarz and Thompson 1999: 67.
17  Myths of human nature corresponding to the four social solidarities are discussed in Thompson et al. 1990: 33–37.
18  On the definition of public and private, see the introductory chapter in Thomas et al. 1999.
19  This translates into state-building and institution-building agendas in peace building. For an elaborate discussion on the necessity of building strong institutions, see Paris 2004: 151–212.
20  For more on consociational democratic systems see, for example, Lijphart 1969: 207–25.
21  The guardian model of democracy is the preferred model of democracy according to the hierarchical cultural bias. See further Hendriks and Stavros 1999: 25.
22  As in the saying 'when all you have is a hammer everything looks like a nail'.
23  Once again, the myths of human nature corresponding to the four social solidarities are discussed in Thompson et al. 1990: 33–37.
24  Once again, the time perspective of adherents of different social solidarities is outlined in Schwarz and Thompson 1999: 67.
25  See Table 14.2, adapted from Sahovic 2007.

# References

Bergling, P. (2006) *Rule of Law on the International Agenda*, Antwerpen: Intersentia.
Dake, K. and Thompson, M. (1999) 'Making ends meet, in the household and on the planet', *GeoJournal*, 47(3): 417–24.
Dixon, J., Goodwin, D. and Wing, J. (2003) *Responses to Governance: governing corporations, societies and the world*, Westport, Connecticut: Praeger.
Douglas, M. (1970) *Natural Symbols: explorations in cosmology*, London: Barrie & Rockliff.
——(1978) 'Cultural bias', Royal Anthropological Institute Occasional Paper, 35.
——(1982) *In the Active Voice* London: Routledge and Kegan Paul.
Durkheim, E. (1915) *The Elementary Forms of the Religious Life* 6 impr. edn, London: Allen & Unwin.
——(1964) *The Division of Labor in Society*, 6 pr. edn, New York: Free Press.
Durkheim, E. and Wilson, E. K. (1973) *Moral Education: a study in the theory and application of the sociology of education*, New York: Free Press.
Hendriks, F. and Stavros, Z. (1999) 'Cultural biases and new media for the public domain', in M. Thompson, G. Grendstad, and P. Selle (eds), *Cultural Theory as Political Science*, London: Routledge, 121–38.
Lijphart, A. (1969) 'Consociational democracy', *World Politics*, 21(2): 207–25.
Lockhart, C. (1999) 'Cultural contributions to explaining institutional form, political change and rational decisions', *Comparative Political Studies*, 32: 862–93.
Mamadouh, V. (1997) 'Political culture: a typology grounded on culture theory', *GeoJournal*, 43: 17–25.

——(1999a), 'Grid-Group cultural theory: an introduction', *GeoJournal*, 47(3): 345–409.

——(1999b) 'National political cultures in the European Union', in M. Thompson, G Grendstad, and P. Selle (eds), *Cultural Theory as Political Science*, London: Routledge 138–53.

Paris, R. (2004) *At War's End: building peace after civil conflict* Cambridge University Press.

Rotberg, R. I. (2003) *State Failure and State Weakness in a Time of Terror*, Washington, DC World Peace Foundation; Brookings Institution.

Sahovic, D. (2007) *Socio-Cultural Viability of International Intervention in War-Torn Societies: a case study of Bosnia Herzegovina*, Umeå: Print & Media.

Schwarz, M. and Thompson, M. (1990) *Divided We Stand: redefining politics, technology and social choice*, Philadelphia: University of Pennsylvania Press.

Thompson, M., Ellis, R. and Wildavsky, A. B. (1990) *Cultural Theory* Boulder, Colorado: Westview Press.

Wildavsky, A. (1987) 'A cultural theory of responsibility', in Jan-Erik Lane (ed.) *Bureaucracy and Public Choice*, Sage modern politics series; London: Sage, 305.

## Useful websites

Fourcultures.com
    <http:www.fourcultures.com>

# Chapter 15

# Land and power in Afghanistan: in pursuit of law and justice?

*Patrick McAuslan*[*]

## Introduction

It is becoming increasingly clear to virtually everyone involved, or taking an intelligent interest, in Afghanistan, except, it would seem, the British Government, that the war in Afghanistan is unwinnable;[1] that the Government in Afghanistan is corrupt, ineffective, composed of warlords and drug barons, is pandering to Islamic obscurantism, and overall has very little support amongst the citizenry. This chapter, based on my experiences working in Afghanistan in 2005 and 2007, discusses one important area of public policy and management – that of land – to see what light this area can throw on how and why, more than seven years on from the invasion of November 2001, the Government, despite the substantial sums expended by its Western backers on the country, is still in the category of a 'failed state'.

Somewhat belatedly, the international community have come to realize that in virtually all failed states, conflicts over land have been at least a part of the cause of the wider conflicts within or between the countries concerned. Moreover, they have come to realize that even where conflicts over land have not been a particularly significant cause of the outbreak of a conflict, such conflicts are likely to break out during attempts to bring about and consolidate peace and internal stability, as those who fled the original conflicts return to find that their land has been appropriated by others; or that those who have 'won' seize the land of those who have 'lost' a civil war; or – a very common occurrence – documentary records of land administration have been deliberately destroyed during the conflict so that conflicts over who owns what land are almost bound to occur.

Reacting to this phenomenon, there has been an outpouring of official literature on what to do about land administration in post-conflict societies. In summary, the principal reports analysing the problems suggest that the reforms to land policy and practice must:

- be taken seriously as a major contribution to restoring peace;
- be based at the local level;
- build on local systems and institutions;

- place effective and fair dispute settlement at their heart;
- prefer 'soft' to 'hard' systems of land administration, for example by preferring deeds to title registration, allowing oral and hearsay, as well as documentary, evidence of title and using the private sector in land administration;
- make land restitution central to restoring trust in land administration;
- provide land to people rather than reassert government ownership of land; and
- involve donors whose approaches are co-ordinated, and who do not impose *their* own systems.

This last point may be emphasized. Reports have criticized donors for not being sufficiently aware of the role of land in contributing to violence and of the importance of seeing the need to tackle land conflicts as a key element in re-establishing peace within a post-conflict society. Finally, concern has also been expressed at the lack of coordination between donors on land matters. In some cases, there are too many donors involved in land issues, each imposing their own systems for their own purposes, and getting in each other's way.

## Afghan land policy and law

How does Afghanistan rate against these key indicators? To make an assessment, we must turn to consider in some detail the state of affairs relating to land.

### National Land Policy

The most important development in land administration since the Bonn Agreement (2001)[2] has been the development of the National Land Policy (NLP) between 2005 and 2007.[3] The policy is short and confines itself to broad, general principles. However, the extent of the gap between the proposed policies and reality may be judged by the introductory rationale for the Policy:

> Land management in Afghanistan is governed by an ineffectual and inadequate legal framework. The strict application of existing laws is limited both administratively and judicially. In many respects the situation of land management and use is characterized by informality. While many provisions embodied in existing laws are useful, many other provisions have not been sufficiently adjusted to address the post conflict reality. ... The legal drafting and enactment of any new or amended land laws should be guided by a cogent, clearly established policy.
>
> (Quoted in CPHD 2007: 64)

Although couched in more general and diplomatic language, this more or less sums up the thrust of my 2005 report on the matter to UN-Habitat.[4] To get some idea of the real world of land relations in the country, we must turn to the existing land law and its administration. There are a plethora of post-2001 reports and books on the land law of Afghanistan and this overview is based on the excellent work that has been published, quoting from it to set out the main elements of the law.

'[T]he ownership of real property (land and fixed assets like buildings and houses)' is, Liz Alden Wily notes, 'regulated by a complex of customary, religious and statutory law.' State-based law 'is derived as often through dictatorial decree and edict as through parliamentary enactments'. The latter include 'the civil code, land subject laws and the overriding supreme law, the national Constitution' (Wily 2004: 28).

The Constitution of Afghanistan (2004) contains some important statements about the general approach to governance and the specific approach to land management. These include that 'no law' in Afghanistan 'shall contravene the tenets and provisions of the holy religion of Islam' (Article 3); that the state is obliged 'to create a prosperous and progressive society based on social justice ... ' (Article 6); and that property shall not be confiscated except as set out in law and on the 'decision of an authorized court' (Article 40). These precepts must be borne in mind as we review current land laws and practices.

The practical effect of these provisions, notes Colin Foley, is that Afghans 'are permitted to acquire and make use of property within the limits of the law and are protected from arbitrary or unlawful interference with their privacy and home'. The State is 'obliged' not only to 'protect individuals against the arbitrary deprivation of their property' by non-state actors, but also to ensure that property is restored to its rightful owner, or that they are compensated for their loss. Finally, the State may only 'deprive individuals of their property, or control its use' where such 'interference' is 'lawful' and where 'a "fair balance" is struck between the interest of the general community and the right of the individual property owner' (Foley 2005: 11–12).

As McEwan and Whitty explain, '[i]dentifying the current law is a challenge' since 'land law has been one of the main vehicles for interventionist government policy' in recent years.

> The Gazettes are littered with statutes enacting mutually contradictory, overlapping and piecemeal legislation from successive regimes ... The present legislation, therefore, comprises an unfortunate mosaic of inconsistent provisions ...
> (McEwan and Whitty 2006: 2)

## Customary rights

McEwan and Whitty, who conducted fieldwork amongst several villages in three provinces, set out a typology of *non-urban* land as either 'pasture' or 'wilderness', both of which are defined in Decree 57 of 2000. Pasture is described 'very broadly' as 'all types of land, including hills, deserts, mountains, river beds, forests that have places where grass grows and supports animals'. Wilderness (*mawaat*) is defined as 'unused lands', which extends to 'desert, mountains, rivers, virgin land, barren lands and forests' (McEwan and Whitty 2006: 2).

They then set out a six-fold typology of major forms of (urban and rural) land ownership. 'Private' ownership affords the private individual 'exclusive rights to the property'. 'Government' ownership provides those same exclusive rights to the government. Third, some state land (including *mawaat*) is subject to 'public' ownership by the government, but for a 'public purpose'. Interestingly, the present Government has a policy of claiming as much land as possible for the state, and is said to hold, by 'government' or 'public' ownership, 86 per cent of land in Afghanistan (Foley 2003: Chapter 3, 13–14 quoting Wily). Fourth, 'communities might claim rights to public or government-owned pasture land which might be either exclusive or non-exclusive based on customary usage or a deed' (McEwan and Whitty 2006: 43). The fifth form of ownership is 'common', most notably of *maraha* land or 'commonly-owned village pasture'. Here grazing rights 'arise' out of the ownership of a house in a 'neighbouring community'. Sixth, there is *waqf* ownership. Here, a private individual may 'offer land as a gift as long as it is used for religious or charitable purposes ... Once gifted its status is fixed ... it can no longer be transferred' (McEwan and Whitty 2006: 3–4).[5]

Finally, McEwan and Whitty identify a further three lesser or derivative rights to land:

> ... *heker* has a term of up to 50 years and pertains to land leased for construction or plantation purposes ... [S]econd ... is a hybrid contract with both real and contractual consequences [lasting up to three years]. While it is described as a contract which does not bind third parties to whom the property is transferred, it does survive the death of the lessor ... [Third is sharecropping which is classified under the Civil Code] as a form of lease ... The Code ... elaborates the duties binding both sharecropper and landlord ... It is interesting to note that sharecropping has effect against third party inheritors of the sharecropped property, at least until harvest. Such contracts therefore have real implications.
>
> (McEwan and Whitty 2006: 3–4)

The 'legal landscape' over public and common land is much more confused than that over private land. Many villagers they encountered during their fieldwork were not clear as to what land they were claiming. The state's vision of the legal status of much land was different to that of many villagers.[6] It was also the case that '[n]o landowner interviewed held a formal title; a few were in possession of an informal [customary] title' (McEwan and Whitty 2006: 47). Thus, many could rely only on community recognition of ownership or oral tradition; often one and the same thing. This is problematic because government officials are usually unwilling to accept customary deeds or local community recognition as evidence of ownership, so disputes arise as to who has what rights to what land and so who is entitled to what compensation.

Customary law also applies to land in urban areas, where it is especially important in relation to proof of title in informal and unplanned settlements. As the authors of a 2003 UN-Habitat report on urban land tenure in Afghanistan note:

> Any political and administrative decision related to land ownership and its distribution must take into consideration Islamic principles and traditional practices which are the basis of Civil Law [and] are engraved in the collective mind of Afghan civil society and differing provincial and regional practices.
>
> (d'Hellencourt et al. 2003: 1)

## Statutory law

Current statutory law applicable to urban land is for the most part law promulgated by the Taliban, principally the Law on Land Management Affairs (2000), overlaid with various decrees promulgated by President Karzai since his assumption of office in 2002.[7] In order 'to counter what was perceived as widespread distribution of public lands to undeserving beneficiaries', the Government 'froze distributions of public land countrywide' under a decree issued in April 2002. The 'ban remains in effect', but has been 'placed ... under great strain' by the needs of the flood of refugees and displaced persons who have returned to the country in recent years, and who need 'access to land, either for shelter or livelihood', if they are to reintegrate successfully into Afghan society. Some local authorities responded in 2003 and 2004 by making ad hoc distributions of state land without the approval of the Central Government. Accusations abounded of favouritism on the grounds of 'family, tribal and political links to local authorities', and of corruption, with 'powerful commanders' allegedly claiming land and selling it on for vast profit to 'ordinary Afghans' (Foley 2003: Chapter 2, 14–15).

Today the stated policy of the Government is, in the words of Foley, to:

> enforce the rule of law with regard to land and property rights; to restore ownership to those who have suffered arbitrary deprivations; to encourage private investment in land and property; to increase the efficiency with which it is used and to realise its potential equity for investment and tax-raising purposes ...
>
> (Foley 2003: Chapter 3, 1–3)

With those objectives in mind, the Government has issued a number of decrees intended to stop the illegal occupation of land and requiring the return of such land to the Government. These decrees, worthy though their intentions may have been, have been widely ignored by those to whom they were addressed and no attempt has been made to enforce them. This casts some doubt on the commitment of the Government to taking its own policies seriously.

## Key problems in Afghan land relations

It is not possible to provide an overview of the existing land laws without at the least adverting to some of the problems inherent in the laws and their implementation or, more often, non-implementation. The following section addresses more centrally the principal problems of land in Afghanistan.

### Tenure in unplanned and unauthorized settlements

All major cities in Afghanistan have outgrown their Master Plans. Settlements have been developed in unplanned areas; that is areas that had not been allocated for residential, or in some cases for any, development in Master Plans prepared in the 1970s and 1980s. Many of these settlements have been developed on government land, and the terms on which the current users of the land are occupying it are in most cases of dubious legality. Few of the houses constructed have received any kind of building or planning permission from municipalities. Nor do they in fact conform to any building regulations or any other regulatory regime that in theory applies to urban development.[8]

Informal settlement has taken place because the legal system of land allocation and planning has failed to provide for the needs of the occupiers over the last three decades. Many 'illegal' occupiers paid for their plots; the original illegal acquirers of the land are warlords or commanders whom no-one can or is willing to touch.

Behind the arguments for the reassertion of law and planning is the desire to clear the poor from what has now become very desirable and valuable real estate. It would not be the first time that law and planning have been used in cities to penalize the poor, who are the innocent victims of illegality, and benefit the rich and powerful, who are the instigators of illegality. Such practice was highlighted in the report of the UN Special Rapporteur who visited Afghanistan from August to September 2003,[9] a report which would seem to suggest that such a perspective is uppermost in the minds of the governing elite.

### Land grabbing

Since the collapse of the communist regime in 1992, warlords and commanders have taken the object of fighting for the capture of territory quite literally, and have helped themselves to large amounts of real estate in the areas over which they now exercise de facto power. These practices have not markedly changed since 2001, although the manner of the exercise of land grabbing has changed or expanded. In particular, land grabbing through the use of illegal and forged deeds is more prevalent than open, public invasion of land.

It is immaterial whether land subject to such takings is occupied or unoccupied, planned or unplanned, with or without (formal or customary) title. Commanders have quite often created or caused unofficial markets for the land they have acquired. Land is allocated to followers or sold to developers, and followers either sell the land on or build and then rent out or sell on. When undeveloped land is sold on, it may be bought by a developer who then sells the houses and other buildings to users. Title deeds are faked and officials who decline to sanction these totally illegal transactions are either bypassed or beaten up and then bypassed. Officials who assist in the acquisition of land or sanction the transactions are rewarded.

The original illegality, backed up by the use of force, cannot in any way be condoned. Unfortunately the government actors have, too often, done just that, being unable or unwilling to do anything about it, or even actively participating in the grabbing. Once the grabbed land has been cut up, allocated to followers, developed, lived on and/or sold off, it is effectively too late to do anything about it.

## The opium economy

The opium economy is conspicuous by its absence in any discussions of land markets and land administration, but it cannot be ignored, however impolitic it may be to take account of it. The influence of the opium economy can be seen, albeit without precision, both directly in the value of land used for the growing of poppies, and indirectly in the effect it has on prices for other land (Mansfield 2001, Koehler and Zuercher 2007: 62–74).

'[O]ne needs to recognize that the socio-economic and political structures that create and maintain poverty in Afghanistan also encouraged the cultivation of opium poppy.' Poppies are not always 'a profitable crop' in Afghanistan. Cultivation is concentrated 'in areas where landholdings are small, access to both irrigation water and markets more difficult'. Indeed, the production of opium is driven not so much by expected profitability (and crop substitution calculations) as by 'the livelihood strategies of the poor', because poppy cultivation offers access to land, credit, and a vital source of off-farm income necessary for household survival (Herold 2006: Part 1, citing Mansfield 2001). This important explanation and analysis of the economy of poppy growing seems to escape the attention of those within the donor community attempting to eliminate this particular type of agricultural production.

## Deficient formal land transfer and land registration system

There is no fully comprehensive system of land registration operative in Afghanistan. An attempt was made in the 1970s to create such a system but it does not cover very much land. Quite apart from the lack of a comprehensive system, there are many other problems connected to the formal land transfer and registration system. Gebremedhin (2005), who worked on upgrading and reforming the formal registration system for almost three years, concluded that 'the corrupt and inefficient nature' of the formal property-titling system ensures that it 'does not provide a suitable mechanism to accommodate the potential demand for real estate transactions'. Potential participants in the formal land market are put off by 'lawful and unlawful exorbitant transaction costs' and delays associated with judicial and administrative procedures which are caused by inappropriate rules and corruption. Furthermore, the 'collapse of government institutions, corruption, illegal land sales to multiple individuals, multiple allocations of a plot of land and fraud' have all contributed to ensuring that 'multiple claimants' have frequently been 'able to support their claims over the same property with formal deeds, which *prima facie* carry equal validity' (Gebremedhin 2005: 8–9).

### Lack of a coherent and efficient land administration system

The Draft Land Policy summed up as well as any report the present situation when it observed that 'Afghanistan's land administration system lacks coordination and efficiency.' Specifically, it noted 'confusion among competing agencies which often vie for pre-eminence due to ill-defined or overlapping roles and differing agendas.' The result is 'inefficient and uncoordinated land administration' as well as 'conflicts.' Because '[t]here is no formal method of resolution of such conflicts' administrators are unable 'to tackle urgent problems as they arise' (Draft Land Policy 2007: Paragraph 3.1.2).

Alongside this lack of coordination and efficiency is the lack of capacity and professional expertise. An interim report on capacity building for land policy and administration with respect to rural land puts this aspect of the matter thus:[10]

> It can be fairly stated that the Afghan land administration system does not have the capability at the level needed to resolve land tenure problems, let alone to implement and agree on shared working rules about the following critical questions:
>
> 1. How to know who 'owns' land and attached constructions;
> 2. How and on what basis to tax the holders of land;
> 3. How land holders should use the land;
> 4. How individuals can get the rights to use land;
> 5. What people in conflict over uses or ownership of the land should do to resolve their conflicts.
>
> (ADB/DFID 2006)

### Dispute settlement

The number and type of disputes about land and the manner, form and content of their settlement is a barometer both of sociopolitical tensions within society and of the ability of post-conflict administrations to restore social order. The current system of dispute settlement has been the subject of two reports, one looking at land and property disputes in Eastern Afghanistan (Flyktningerådet Norwegian Refugee Council 2004) and one looking at urban land-dispute settlement in Kabul (Wily 2005).[11] This section draws on their findings.

### Special Property Disputes Resolution Court

Within the formal court system, a Special Property Disputes Resolution Court (hereinafter the Special Court) was created by Presidential Decree 89, in 2003, to deal with property disputes concerning returnees.

The Special Court is tasked with 'looking after returned refugees in Afghanistan and addressing their complaints, so as to hasten the process of resolving property disputes' (Article 1). Property or real estate is defined as including: 'land, residential areas, apartments, shops, *mendavi* (market) and other immovable properties' (Article 5). Property disputes covered under the Decree include and are limited to those which took place in the absence of the owners from the date 7th Saur 1357 (27 April 1978) (Article 6). Cases may be brought either directly by the parties to a dispute or through a referral by 'relevant governmental authorities' (Article 10). Cases involving the Government may not be heard before the Special Court and must be 'reviewed in accordance with relevant laws and with the authority of the relevant court … ' (Article 11).

It should be noted that the Special Court does not have exclusive jurisdiction over land and property cases involving refugees and returnees. Its creation does not prevent other courts at the district and provincial levels from continuing to deal with such cases, if the returnees are willing to submit them. It also does not prevent the settlement of such disputes through Afghan customary law (Foley 2005: Chapter 1, 14–16).

Many of Kabul's property disputes relate to 'high value properties owned by wealthier persons or public figures.' Although property disputes do occur in relation to the 'much larger sector of privately-owned middle income and small homes and premises' their 'resolution is broadly contained within the household and related informal social domain (neighbourhood)' (Wily 2004: 2).Wily considers the potential for significant contestation over property in Kabul is very high in relation to the ever-expanding informal sector: '*de facto* home-owners number at least one million.' They engage in formal or informal disputes over their property rights 'but live in a state of suspended tenure insecurity' (Wily 2004: 3). Wily identifies five potential sources of conflict involving these informal ownership rights: genuinely unjust evictions (the Shirpur case is a good example); disputes between old and new members of neighbourhoods (new members coming in via 'wilful invasions'); regularisation ('the de facto policy of the Administration'); unbridled rent-seeking ('illegal and/or dubiously ethical property dealing'); and mismanaged and corrupt allocations (sums paid to the Municipality for building plots on land the Municipality does not yet own and which may be occupied).

Of most concern is her finding that a significant proportion of disputes have their origins in post-Bonn malfeasance, outright corruption, collusion or at the very least a failure of due vigilance on the part of government employees. This ranges from alleged corrupt or nepotistic allocation of building plots or apartments since 2001, providing (or turning a blind eye to) fake documentation, to being bribed to ignore construction on government land – a widespread occurrence in the so-called informal property sector. '[P]olice, ministry officials, municipality officials and judges are all deeply implicated' (Wily 2004: 36).

Wily's report is concerned principally with the Special Court, and she is critical of its overall performance. It is failing to deal with claims swiftly or effectively. Few cases go to court direct; most pass through other agencies first. When they get to court, progress is slower still. Enforcement is a problem; judges estimate only a minority of their rulings are acted upon. Bribery of police by defendants means that cases are not heard because the defendant is not brought to court. Some claimants allege corruption by the court itself. There is no systematic method of collecting and evaluating evidence. The judges are insufficiently trained in the law that they have to apply.

'For reasons of fear, futility, or lack of means' many decide to resolve disputes in the community and to avoid the formal court. 'The poor and very poor' avoid the courts because 'they do not possess the status, financial means, documents, or knowledge to pursue the matter successfully.' Others are put off by the likelihood of 'ethnic favouritism', delays associated with 'continuous challenge and upward appeal to the Supreme Court' and the fact 'that even if they win the case, the court and police are likely to be impotent to enforce the decision'. Cases involving 'Government land (or land claimed by the government)' are also kept out of the formal courts since they 'must be submitted to the Ministry of Justice's *Hoquq* Department' (Wily 2004: 41).

### Community-based procedures

Community-based procedures may be seen as the urban equivalent of reliance on and use of customary law procedures in rural areas.[12] Here there are three dispute-resolution mechanisms which may be used to resolve property disputes:

> firstly the decisions arrived at with the help of neighbours and elders; secondly in those arrived at with the help of the Mosque Council (generally representatives of each Mosque in the neighbourhood) and thirdly those arrived at with the help or endorsement of the *Wakil-e-Gozar* ...
>
> An important feature of these mechanisms is that actors are not always the same and none of those ... assisting in resolving the dispute are paid ... No permanently standing council for dispute resolution exists ... This informal status makes them less vulnerable to bribe-taking.
>
> (Wily 2005: 30)

On balance, those interviewed by Wily preferred community resolution of disputes on grounds of time, cost, trust, enforceability and the ability to avoid scrutiny by the formal courts of their informal tenure, especially where 'the State or its agencies are the defendants or where the land base belongs to Government' (Wily 2005: 30).

However, community dispute settlement requires a community to bring social coercion to bear for the decision to be acted upon. This may not be apparent in wealthy and developed suburbs, or in the 'rapidly developed' informal settlements which 'have no particular ethnic or other community-driven cohesion.' There is also the risk that 'the *Wakil-e-Gozar* may refuse to assist disputants where they consider both parties are acting illegally … [i.e.] where settlements have recently been established on Government Land.' Finally, such community mechanisms may be ineffective in the face of a powerful defendant such as 'a commander or other notable' (Wily 2005: 31).

It is clear that formal and informal dispute resolution on land and real property issues within cities and especially Kabul are not working at all satisfactorily.

## Regularisation

Wily draws two conclusions that are of considerable interest in relation to the question of regularisation or formalisation of land rights. First, insecurity of tenure and conflicts over land need to be treated separately. Regularisation needs to be considered as a solution to insecure tenure, but it may well trigger more disputes between developers and house owners that will need their own management.

Second, lack of formal documentation of title, as compared to informal titling, is not a cause of disputes. So, formal titling will not on its own resolve or eliminate property disputes.

> The promised sanctity of [formal] title deeds has broadly not been upheld. There are few grounds at this point for claiming that issue of legal title deeds is indispensable to security. There are however grounds for claiming that security of title is primarily premised on local cohesion and social stability (Wily 2005: 35).

A later study of the handling of conflicts over land in rural areas supports the conclusions of Wily's work:

> [There] is a clear indication of a tendency in rural Afghanistan to 'solve' conflicts by means of bribes, patronage and raw power. It not only points to a situation where the rule of law appears to have little weight in rural areas. It also implies that conflicts are not processed in an orderly fashion and thereby resolved, but … they may break out again as soon as power relations change … Of relevance is also the fact that most respondents thought

that money was by far the most important asset for influencing the outcome of conflict ...

(Koehler and Zuercher 2007: 67)

The authors concluded that the state's capacity for dealing with conflicts appeared low.

## An effective, efficient and just system of post-conflict land administration?

Standing back from this very broad overview of the law and land issues, what conclusions can be drawn, in particular about the decrees promulgated since 2001?

First, it is clear that a determined effort is being made to acquire, or re-acquire, as much land as possible for the state, and little attention is being paid to due process in pursuit of this effort. Second, no attention whatsoever is being paid to the realities of life for the overwhelming majority of urban dwellers: the lack of secure tenure and the lack of any legal means to improve their security. Third, a totally unrealistic assumption is being made that current Master Plans can and should be enforced and/or replaced by more of the same. Fourth, little real effort is being made to tackle the problem of land grabbing, and an air of unreality affects attempts to get land back from land grabbers with no recognition of what has taken place on the land since the original grab. Fifth, the Special Court apart, the land-dispute settlement problems are being largely ignored. Finally, very minor efforts are being made to address the problems of rural land.

This pattern of legislation and non-action fails virtually every principle of equity and social justice. This is significant in legal terms because the Constitution mandates the State to adopt principles of social justice in its approach to governing and 'to adopt necessary measures for housing and distribution of public estates to deserving citizens in accordance with financial resources and the law' (Article 14). Current land laws do not do that.

Perhaps more important is that the whole *raison d'être* of the Government's being and the constant refrain of its numerous national statements of development ideals is to introduce into Afghanistan those very principles of equity and social justice which, along with democracy, have been in short supply over the past 30-odd years. There is no place where it is more important for Afghanistan's political and social stability, the advancement of respect for the law, and economic development that applied policies and laws in the country match the rhetoric of international conferences than with respect to the people's rights of access to land, to security of tenure and to efficient, effective and honest ways and means of settling their disputes about land.

The Government of Afghanistan has created, or rather has continued and enhanced, a land legal system which combines the worst of all possible worlds: it is not based on the fundamental principles of *Sharī'a*. It does not cater for the majority of citizens. It neither facilitates the market nor regulates it. It ignores the major law-breakers and encourages action against the victims of the system. The planning system it maintains contradicts the market system it claims to be furthering. Worst of all, it has stumbled into this position because it has adopted a reactive approach to law making: instead of thinking through the problems, possible solutions and preferred options and then legislating, it uses legislation as a substitute for policy. Furthermore, the promulgated decrees themselves are for the most part inadequate; they are too short; they lack process; they have an air of unreality about them. The only saving grace is that for the most part they are ignored.

So, how does Afghanistan rate against the keys to creating an effective, efficient and just system of post-conflict land administration? Of the nine keys outlined above relevant to national policy and action, Afghanistan is deficient in every single one, and of the one applicable to donors, the donors fail on that. National land policy has never been seen as central to restoring peace. Local systems of land administration exist because there is nothing else in many places, not because of any policy to develop them. The judicial system both generally and in relation to land disputes is woefully inadequate. Hard systems are preferred to soft ones in land titling and in evidential matters in relation to land. There is no clear policy on using the private sector in land administration. Land restitution in relation to returnees is slow and opaque; in relation to land grabbers, non-existent. The Government's preference is to acquire or reacquire ownership of land at the expense of providing citizens with the opportunity to own land. Donors do not coordinate policies or programmes on land.

## Why the inaction over land?

There remains then the issue of 'why'? If the international community is now so aware of the importance of a just system of land administration as a major contribution to stabilizing a post-conflict society, then, given its overwhelming role in policymaking and prioritising governmental actions in Afghanistan, why has it not made more effort to push grappling with land up the Government's agenda and why has it not put more resources into the sector? Why so many reports on the problems and so little follow-up action? There are two possible approaches to answering this question which are in no way mutually exclusive.

### A space to be kept empty

According to Marc Herold (2006), the US and its allies have an interest in ensuring that this strategically significant 'space ... in a volatile region of geopolitical import' is 'kept vacant from all hostile forces'. Afghanistan thus 'represents merely a space that is to be kept empty':

> Western powers have no interest in either buying from or selling to the blighted nation ... The only populated centers of any real concern are a few

islands of grotesque capitalist imaginary reality – foremost Kabul – needed to project the image of an existing central government ... [Here a] sufficient density of foreign ex-pats, a bloated NGO-community, carpetbaggers and hangers-on of all stripes ... warrants the presence of Western businesses. The 'other', the real economy – is a vast informal one in which the Afghan masses creatively eke out a daily existence. They are utterly irrelevant to the *neo-colonist interested in running an empty space at the least cost* ...

(Herold 2006: Part 1; emphasis original)[13]

### Incoherence and squabbling among donors

The other answer is more prosaic but, given Herold's thesis, may be connected to it. This is the sheer muddle, confusion, competition and non-cooperation that exists between and amongst agencies operating in Afghanistan. Too much of their energy is devoted to inter- and intra-bureaucratic squabbling, so that the objectives which they are allegedly there to pursue get set aside or forgotten about. I have worked for two agencies – UN-Habitat and the World Bank – on three projects – urban land and municipal government for UN-Habitat and land acquisition for the World Bank. But even with that limited involvement I observed and found myself caught up in rivalries between agencies and projects.

I observed the tension between the United Nations Assistance Mission to Afghanistan (UNAMA), headed by a person who was styled the Secretary-General's Special Representative in Afghanistan, and the United Nations Development Programme (UNDP), headed by the Resident Representative, a UN official with the status of an ambassador. Both agencies provided technical assistance to the Government. I found that there was no linkage between UNAMA's programme of developing municipal law and UN-Habitat's. The two programmes were proceeding in ignorance of each other and on very different principles – UNAMA's on principles derived from French local-government law where their consultants were drawn from, UN-Habitat's on basically English principles but with a stress on utilizing the Afghan Municipal Law of 1957, which was more English/Indian inspired than from any other system. UNDP too had a programme of local-government reform proceeding without regard to other programmes.

There was, too, rivalry between the Ministry of Urban Development and the Ministry of the Interior as to who should take the lead on local-government reform. The Minister of Urban Development wanted UN-Habitat to continue its assistance to his ministry but then found that he had been, as it were, trumped by the Ministry of the Interior which obtained assistance from UNDP for its programme of local-government reform. There was then likely to be a situation of rival draft laws from different ministries being put to the Draftsman's Office. This has happened with other projects and it resulted in both or all the rival laws being put to one side by the office.

The situation was no better in relation to land. There was distrust between the UN-Habitat office and the US Agency for International Development/ Emerging Markets Group (USAID/EMG) with respect to their land programmes. UN-Habitat was concentrating on sorting out the land issues connected with the urban poor, most of whom had no clear titles to their land. The USAID project was focusing on formal land titling, which was thought to be irrelevant, if not counterproductive, by UN-Habitat. Information, though constantly promised, was not divulged from either side to the other.

Here too it was not clear which ministry was in charge – Justice, Urban Development or Agriculture. Different donors related to different ministries and included overlapping projects within their overall programmes. Italy was the lead agency on justice.[14] UN-Habitat had good contacts with the Italian special ambassador responsible for the justice programme and persuaded the ambassador to include funding for land-law reform in the justice budget. A UNDP official was unhappy at that development since they thought it might allow UN-Habitat to get on the inside track to land-law reform in the Ministry of Justice in preference to their preferred option of supporting the USAID/EMG initiative. I was present at a tense meeting between the Italian ambassador, the UNDP official and the UN-Habitat consultant who had set up the Habitat land programme where it was made clear that unless the UNDP was prepared to accept the Italian money for land-law reform, there might be a lot less Italian money for justice reform. The UNDP official gave way.

The World Bank was strangely ambivalent about getting involved in land. It has funded several studies but the project on land acquisition was the first one where there was to be a specific output – a draft law – for a specific purpose – to enable Bank funds for infrastructure involving land acquisition to be made available to the Government. Perhaps the Bank had noted the morass of land policy and the tensions between various donors and ministries and decided, wisely, to stay out of becoming involved. But it must also be noted that lurking in the background was a study, prepared by a consultancy hired by the US Trade Development Agency and funded by the World Bank Group, on a pipeline to carry natural gas through Afghanistan, a pipeline which would need land acquisition in order to be realized (Hill International Inc 2004).

The failure of the donors to push land issues up the Government's agenda must not be allowed to absolve the Government from its failures of responsibility. The Government's failure is the greater precisely because it is the Government. Its ineffectual efforts via presidential decrees and orders to address the problems of land indicate that it is aware of the need to, at least, show some willingness to demonstrate concern. The fact, however, that there was no land policy in place until late 2007, and that there has been no concerted effort to take any *actions*, is a good indication that there is little willingness in government or ruling circles generally to do anything that might disturb their own land acquisitions.

## Conclusion

The collective failure of the governing authorities – ministers, administrators, legislators, mayors – to address the injustices of the land-tenure system and the collective unwillingness of the donor community to confront these same authorities on this issue lends credence to Herold's analysis, but more importantly shows the irrelevance of many of the aid programmes aiming to bring development and stability to Afghanistan when the Government of Afghanistan lacks the will to tackle the one matter that could transform the lives of its citizens: a just and lawful system of land management. No wonder, as Foley noted on his return in 2008: 'Time and time again I was told that "things were going backwards" and that the international community had "got the template wrong" for the country' (2008: 11).

The lesson that land issues must be taken seriously in a post-conflict society is clearly being completely ignored by the donors, and the penalty for this is being paid by ordinary people in Afghanistan and the NATO countries whose young men and women are being sent to fight and die in an unwinnable war to support an unsupportable government.

## Notes

* This paper is based on two reports written for respectively UN-Habitat in 2005 on the state of urban land law and possible reforms thereto and for the World Bank in 2007 on land acquisition law. Neither agency must be taken to agree with any views expressed either in those reports or in this paper.

1 The latest comment to that effect is Foley (2008) Chapter 4, especially 115–19. Foley worked long and hard in Afghanistan in 2004–5 on land and access-to-justice issues.

2 The Bonn Agreement (2001) set out a plan agreed between the donors and the interim government of Afghanistan for the redevelopment of Afghanistan.

3 The Draft Land Policy (DLP) was completed by the Land Working Group of the Ministry of Urban Development in January 2007. That Policy was approved by the Cabinet in September 2007 (Annex 1) and became the National Land Policy.

4 This analysis was also echoed by the Minister of Urban Development in his introductory speech to a workshop held to review the World Bank land acquisition law report in June 2007.

5 The classification follows the usual *Sharī'a* classification of land tenure.

6 The Land Management Department of the Ministry of Agriculture, Animal Husbandry and Food (Amlak) is the responsible state authority.

7 Until a legislature was elected, laws were made by presidential decree, which had to be ratified by the legislature once it came into being.

8 This is not to suggest that these buildings are ramshackle. Many 'illegal' developments consist of solid well-built houses and represent a considerable investment on the part of the owner/developer.

9 Kothari (2004). At about the time the UN Commissioner visited Afghanistan, a particularly egregious example of land grabbing had taken place in the district of Shirpur in Kabul where many poor people had been unceremoniously chased away from some land and the land carved up amongst land grabbers and their allies. Kothari produced a highly critical report on the incident and the failure of the government to do anything about it. Strong exception was taken to his report by the principal

occupying power in Afghanistan and Kothari was unceremoniously chased away from Afghanistan by the UN – virtually declared *persona non grata*, just as the poor had been from the land they were occupying in Kabul.

10 This was the interim report for Asian Development Bank Project 38221: Capacity Building for Land Reform conducted jointly with the Department for International Development of the United Kingdom (DFID) between 2007 and 2009. The final report and other project documents can be found on the project website.

11 A summary of some of the themes of that report (Wily 2005, unpublished) appears in Wily (2004).

12 Foley (2005: Chapter 7) provides a good general overview of customary-dispute-settlement procedures. Wily (2004: Chapter 3) contains useful information in relation to pastures and disputes.

13 A good deal of Herold's information and analysis come from a more soberly written but equally gloomy report: Rubin, Hamidzada and Stoddard (2005). Herold goes on to note that: 'Much of the reconstruction aid has been devoted to high visibility projects of questionable value to average Afghans ... [T]erribly little of the $3 billion in reconstruction aid has trickled-down ... whereas a significant portion has ... trickled-up[.]'

14 On efforts to reform the justice system, see Tondini (2007), which reports much the same approach to this area as I found in the areas of local government and land.

# References

ADB/DFID (2006) *Capacity Building for Land Policy and Administration Reform*, Kabul, Interim Report.

(Bonn Agreement) (2001) 'Agreement on provisional arrangements in Afghanistan pending the re-establishment of permanent government institutions', done in Bonn on December 5 2001. Online: <http://www.un.org/News/dh/latest/afghan/afghan-agree.htm>

(CPHD) Centre for Policy and Human Development (2007) *Afghanistan Human Development Report 2007: bridging modernity and tradition, rule of law and the search for justice*. Islamabad: UNDP-Kabul University. Online: <http://www.undp.org.af/Publications/KeyDocuments/nhdr07_complete.pdf>

Constitution of the Islamic Republic of Afghanistan (2004). Online: <http://www.president.gov.af/sroot_eng.aspx?id=68>

d'Hellencourt, N. Y, Rajabov, S., Stanikzai, N. and Salam, A. (2003) *Preliminary Study of Land Tenure Related Issues in Urban Afghanistan with Special Reference to Kabul City*, Nairobi: UN-Habitat.

(DLP) Draft Land Policy by the Land Working Group, Ministry of Urban Development/ Islamic Republic of Afghanistan, January, 2007. Version 4 (text identical to National Land Policy). Online: <http://www.ltera.org/index.php?option=com_docman&task=doc_download&gid = 80&Itemid = 162&lang = en>

Flyktningerådet Norwegian Refugee Council (2004) *Land and Property Disputes in Eastern Afghanistan*, Kabul.

Foley, C. (2003) *Afghanistan, the search for peace*, Kabul: Minority Rights Group. Online: <http://www.minorityrights.org/download.php?id=45>

——*A Guide to Property Law in Afghanistan*, Flytninghjelpen (Norwegian Refugee Council) and Kabul: UNHCRl.

——(2008) *The Thin Blue Line: how humanitarianism went to war*, London: Verso.

Gebremedhin, Y. (2005) *Legal Issues in Afghanistan Land Titling and Registration*, Kabul: Emerging Markets Group (LTERA). Online: <http://www.terrainstitute.org/pdf/ USAID_LTERA_2006%20LEGAL_ISSUES_AFGHANISTAN.pdf>

Herold, M. W. (2006) 'Afghanistan as an empty space'. Online: <http://cursor.org/ stories/emptyspace.html>

Hill International Inc. (2004) 'Evaluation of Investment Options for the Development of Oil and Gas Infrastructure in Afghanistan'. Project No. PAG238/R BORHAN/ REV.3. 9 October 2004. Task 4: Kabul – Sheberghan Gas Pipeline. Online: <http:// siteresources.worldbank.org/AFGHANISTANEXTN/Resources/ 305984-1173474957611/Task1B.pdf>

Koehler, J. and Zuercher, C. (2007) 'Statebuilding, conflict and narcotics in Afghanistan: The view from below', *International Peacekeeping*, 14: 62–74. Online: <http://www. polwiss.fu-berlin.de/people/zuercher/paper/cz/statebuildingconflictnarcotic.pdf>

Kothari, M. (2004) *Adequate housing as a component of the right to an adequate standard of living*, Geneva: Commission on Human Rights.

Law on Pasture and Maraa (2000) Decree 57 Official Gazette No. 795.

Law on Land Management Affairs (2000) Official Gazette No. 795. Online: <http:// www.ltera.org/index.php?option=com_docman&task=doc_download&gid=145&Itemid= 63&lang=en>

Mansfield, D. (2001) *The Economic Superiority of Illicit Drug Production: myth and reality of opium poppy cultivation in Afghanistan*, Munich: Paper prepared for the International Conference on The Role of Alternative Development in Drug Control and Development Cooperation, January 2002. Online: <http://www.davidmansfield.org/field_work.php>

McEwan, A. and Whitty, B. (2006) *Land Tenure, Case Study Series; Water Management, Livestock and the Opium Economy*, Kabul: Afghanistan Research and Evaluation Unit (AREU).

National Development Strategy 1387–1391 (2008–2013) Kabul: Government of Afghanistan. Online: <http://www.ands.gov.af/ands/final_ands/src/final/Afghanistan %20National%20Development%20Strategy_eng.pdf>

National Land Policy (see Draft Land Policy).

Rubin, B. R., Hamidzada, H. and Stoddard, A. (2005) *Afghanistan 2005 and Beyond: prospects for improved stability reference document*, The Hague: Netherlands Institute of International Relations 'Clingendael' Conflict Research Unit.

Tondini, M. (2007) 'Rebuilding the system of justice in Afghanistan: A preliminary assessment', *Journal of Intervention and State Building*, 1: 333–54

Wily, L. A. (2005) *Resolution of Property Rights Disputes in Urban Areas: rethinking the orthodoxies* Kabul: World Bank, unpublished.

——(2004) *Looking for Peace on the Pastures: rural land relations in Afghanistan*, Kabul: Afghanistan Research and Evaluation Unit. Online: <http://www.areu.org.af/index.php ?option=com_docman&task=doc_download&gid=352&Itemid=26>

## Useful websites

(ANDS) Afghanistan National Development Strategy
   <http://www.ands.gov.af>
(AREU) Afghanistan Research and Evaluation Unit
   <http://www.areu.org.af>
Capacity Building for Land Reform (ADB Project 38221)
   <http://www.adb.org/Projects/project.asp?id=38221>

(CPHD) Centre for Policy Research and Human Development (Kabul University)
&lt;http://www.cphd.af&gt;
Office of the President (Afghanistan)
&lt;http://www.president.gov.af/&gt;
(LTERA) Land Titling and Economic Restructuring Activity (USDAID)
&lt;http://ltera.org/&gt;
(UNAMA) United Nations Assistance Mission in Afghanistan
&lt;http://unama.unmissions.org&gt;
(UN-HABITAT) United Nations Human Settlements Programme
&lt;http://www.unhabitat.org&gt;

# Index

For Product Safety Concerns and Information please contact our EU
representative GPSR@taylorandfrancis.com
Taylor & Francis Verlag GmbH, Kaufingerstraße 24, 80331 München, Germany